ALFRED HITCHCOCK'S LONDON

A REFERENCE GUIDE TO LOCATIONS

ALFRED HITCH-COCK'S LONDON

A REFERENCE GUIDE TO LOCATIONS

by Gary Giblin

Interior and Cover Design: Susan Svehla

Copyright © 2006, Gary Giblin

Without limiting the rights under copyright reserved above, no part of this publication may be reproduced, stored in or introduced into a retrieval system, or transmitted, in any form, or by any means (electronic, mechanical, photocopying, recording or otherwise), without the prior written permission of the copyright owners or the publishers of the book.

ISBN 1-887664-67-X
Library of Congress Catalog Card Number 2006928703
Manufactured in the United States of America
First Printing by Midnight Marquee Press, Inc., July 2006

Acknowledgments: Linda J. Walter

On the top of the three steps which led up to the door, there stood the long, lanky
figure of a man, clad in an Inverness cape and an old-fashioned top hat....
"Is it not a fact that you let lodgings?" he asked, and there was something shrill,
unbalanced, hesitating, in his voice.
—Marie Belloc Lowndes, *The Lodger*

She sat down on the bed, rehearsing dully, as a beginner might,
the first lines of that colloquy. "What's happened?" "Murder!"
—Clemence Dane and Helen Simpson, *Enter Sir John*

The bare bones of the tale were all that was in the book—these,
and one queer phrase which occurred half a dozen times inside brackets.
"(Thirty-nine steps)" was the phrase.... I could make nothing of that.
—John Buchan, *The Thirty-nine Steps*

There was nothing he need fear in a search, but the impression
that it had been made confirmed his suspicion that he had been
denounced to the authorities as a secret agent.
—W. Somerset Maugham, *Ashenden, or The British Agent*

"A bomb outrage to have any influence on public opinion now must go beyond the
intention of vengeance or terrorism. It must be purely destructive. It must be that,
and only that, beyond the faintest suspicion of any other object."
—Joseph Conrad, *The Secret Agent*

In slight confusion she looked away quickly to the opposite seat.
To her surprise, Miss Froy's place was empty.
—Ethel Lina White, *The Wheel Spins*

Suspicion is a tenuous thing, so impalpable that the exact moment of its birth is not
easy to determine. But looking back...[e]ven her very first meeting with Johnnie...
seemed a red triangle of danger whose warning she had deliberately ignored.
—Francis Iles, *Before the Fact*

He seemed to see the Paradine Case rise up before him like
a huge black shape drawing him on into its devouring darkness.
—Robert Hichens, *The Paradine Case*

No man living knew better [than Bulldog Drummond]
that strange things took place daily in London, things which would
tax the credulity of the most hardened reader of sensational fiction.
—Sapper, *The Third Round*

We don't have pages to fill, or pages from a typewriter to fill.
We have a rectangular screen in a movie house.
—Alfred Hitchcock on "The Art of the Cinema" (1973)

Table of Contents

8 Introduction
16 Acknowledgments
17 Organization & Key

CENTRAL LONDON

19 1. Bayswater
23 2. Belgravia
27 3. Bloomsbury
35 4. Chelsea
42 5. The City
55 6. Covent Garden
70 7. Fitzrovia
72 8. Holborn
78 9. Hyde Park
82 10. Kensington
84 11. Knightsbridge
87 12. Lambeth
93 13. Maida Vale
96 14. Marylebone/Regent's Park
109 15. Mayfair
131 16. Pimlico
132 17. St. James's
144 18. St. Pancras
147 19. Smithfield
148 20. Soho
171 21. South Bank
173 22. South Kensington
181 23. Strand
192 24. Victoria
194 25. Westminster

OUTER LONDON

224 26. Battersea
226 27. Brixton
229 28. Camberwell
230 29. Camden Town
232 30. Earl's Court
232 31. Fulham
233 32. Greenwich
236 33. Hammersmith
237 34. Hampstead
238 35. Highbury
239 36. Highgate
240 37. Holloway
244 38. Hounslow
245 39. Hoxton
247 40. Islington

248	41. Kennington	276	61. Berkshire
249	42. Kensal Green	277	62. Buckinghamshire
250	43. Leytonstone		
251	44. Limehouse	280	63. Cambridgeshire
251	45. Lower Holloway		
		281	64. Cornwall
253	46. New Cross	284	65. Cumbria
253	47. North Kensington	287	66. Devon
		288	67. Hampshire
255	48. Notting Hill	290	68. Hertfordshire
257	49. Roehampton		
258	50. St. John's Wood	295	69. Kent
		297	70. Oxfordshire
258	51. Shepherd's Bush	298	71. Suffolk
		299	72. Surrey
264	52. Spitalfields	301	73. West Sussex
265	53. Stamford Hill	302	Mr. Memory Answers
267	54. Stepney	304	Bibliography
271	55. Stratford	310	Appendix I English Literary Sources
271	56. Upper Sydenham		
272	57. Waddon		
272	58. Whitechapel	320	Appendix II The Schüfftan Pro-
274	59. Wimbledon		
275	60. Wood Green		
	OUTSIDE LONDON		

INTRODUCTION

Today, Alfred Hitchcock is celebrated largely for the thrillers and psychological dramas he directed *after* his move from London to Hollywood in 1939, classics such as *Notorious, Strangers on a Train, Rear Window, Vertigo, North By Northwest, Psycho* and *The Birds*. Yet from 1926 until his departure, Hitchcock directed no less than 21 feature films in the U.K., principally at the Islington (Gainsborough), BIP (Elstree) and Lime Grove (Shepherd's Bush) Studios in and around London. During his Hollywood years, he actually returned to London to shoot four additional features: *Under Capricorn, Stage Fright, The Man Who Knew Too Much* (56) and *Frenzy*. Further, of his American films, four—*Rebecca, Foreign Correspondent, Suspicion* and *Dial M for Murder*—have notable English settings, while five others—*Rope, The Trouble with Harry, The Birds, Marnie* and *Family Plot*—were adapted from English literary sources. Clearly, England, and especially, London, played a formidable role in the life and work of Alfred Hitchcock. He was, of course, born in London, on August 13, 1899. He was also educated here, first at Roman Catholic schools, later at the University of London. He entered the film business here, in 1920, married his one and only wife here in December 1926 and became a father for the first and only time here, in July 1928. He also developed his fascination with crime, detection, sensational trials (and the tabloid-style coverage of these) here in London, not to mention his love of the theatre and his penchant for the gourmet foods and wines proffered by London's finest restaurants and hotels. And, of course, it was here in London that Hitchcock discovered and developed the motifs, themes and techniques for all those classic films to come, on both sides of the Atlantic: the innocent man wrongly accused; fear of and fascination with the police and their methods; construction of the heterosexual couple; the transfer of guilt; flight and pursuit; love vs. duty (private vs. public responsibility); moral propriety; espionage; murder; attractive villains; sullied heroes; icy blondes; episodic plots; visual storytelling (the true "motion picture"); rapid pacing; montage; climaxes at incongruous public settings; and, of course, the famous MacGuffin, "the thing," to quote Hitchcock himself, "that the spies are after, but the audience don't care."

In speaking of his trademark cinematic motifs, reference is frequently made to Hitchcock's so-called "Victorian legacy." He was, of course, born of "Victorian-age" parents in 1899, less than two years before the death of the British monarch whose name conjures up images of sexual repression and excessive propriety. However, many of Hitchcock's motifs—international intrigue and espionage, the status of women, violence, class, criminality and the rule of law—more directly reflect the concerns of England's Edwardian Age (1901-1915), a period of immense economic, social and political change which, of course, coincided with Hitchcock's own formative years. Thus, it can scarcely surprise us that three of his most important British films should derive from three of the most important crime novels of that era: *The Lodger, The Thirty-nine Steps* and *The Secret Agent* (whence *Sabotage*). Nor, given the Edwardian fascination for crime and detective fiction (including works by Belloc Lowndes, Buchan, Chesterton, Conan Doyle, Conrad, Hornung, Mason and Wallace), can it surprise us that Hitchcock should be drawn and redrawn to tales in which an agent—professional or otherwise—of the law and established order strives against the forces of chaos and anarchy to maintain or restore that order. The director himself acknowledged his Edwardian affinity in the

1964 CBC program *Telescope*, in which he described *Marnie*'s Mark Rutland as "a real sort of Late Victorian, Edwardian type of hero....Very strong, very meaty."

Yet, for all that his hometown and its culture gave to him (and he to it), Hitchcock would evolve and sustain what can best be described as a "mixed" attitude toward the place of his birth. The patriotic Hitchcock of 1927, who championed *English* films depicting *English* ways of life, would, within a decade, become the rather more skeptical Hitchcock who bemoaned his country's snobbery and class consciousness, its superficial humor, its stifling political censorship and its impoverished film industry's

One of the London homes of Alfred Hitchcock

woeful lack of resources. America, a country that had long fascinated him, was a different story. Hollywood offered the best of everything he wanted and needed (money, equipment, talent), with the added bonus of warm, sunny weather. And so, on March 1, 1939, Hitchcock, his wife, Alma and their 10-year-old daughter, Patricia, set sail for the United States—perhaps to return to England after one or two pictures, perhaps to remain in Hollywood. Hitchcock played it cagey.

Not long after the outbreak of the Second World War (September 1939), Hitchcock was castigated by some of his fellow countrymen (including former boss Michael Balcon) for abandoning Britain in its time of need. Nothing, of course, could have been further from the truth. Hitchcock had signed his contract with American producer David O. Selznick in July 1938 and was duly bound to honor it. Moreover, the 40-year-old director was actually better able to serve his country's wartime needs in Hollywood, making pro-British pictures, than in England, where the government had drastically curtailed film production. Later in the war, he actually returned to London to make two short propaganda films for the Ministry of Information, *Bon Voyage* and *Aventure Malgache*, both intended as morale boosters for the French Resistance. Yet, Alma was apparently so stung by the unjust criticism that she vowed to make America her permanent home. And that's precisely what she and her husband did.

Of course, there were still many trips back to England—to scout for locations, to work on scripts and even to shoot an occasional film. But once he had a taste of life and working conditions in America, there was never any question of a permanent return. "He really wasn't too fond of making pictures in England after making pictures here," Pat Hitchcock told me, "because of all the different tea breaks and everything that goes on while they're making a picture over there. If they have to work late then they have to have a meeting about working late. There was an awful lot of time that he felt was wasted." And so, on April 20, 1955, Hitchcock took the practical and symbolic step of becoming a U.S. citizen, five years after Alma herself had done so. "They believed," Pat explained, "that the country where you earned the money was where you should pay the taxes. They abhorred people who kept their money in Swiss bank accounts so as to avoid paying taxes." The Hitchcocks now had their feet planted squarely on the western side of the Atlantic. Or did they? A quarter of a century later, Her Majesty's Government offered to bestow an honorary knighthood upon the East London greengrocer's son and he dutifully accepted. The director was now "Sir" Alfred Hitchcock (an unofficial title, given his U.S. citizenship), born and raised in England, honed to perfection in America: a true Anglo-American hybrid whose best British films betrayed his debt to American cinematic techniques and whose best American films betrayed his debt to his English, and specifically, London roots.

The purpose of this book, then, is to identify and describe important London locales from the life and work of Alfred Hitchcock; and to celebrate the culture, heritage and legacy of the land of his birth. In fact, Hitchcock's work itself is a virtual celebration of London life, from bobbies on the beat and barristers at the Old Bailey, to fruit-sellers in Covent Garden and punters at the local pub; from double-decker buses and overcrowded Tube trains to traditional black cabs and even the occasional horse-drawn cart. As the London tour guide par excellence, Hitchcock escorts us to some of the most famous attractions in London (and the world), including the Houses of Parliament, St. Paul's Cathedral, Trafalgar Square, Piccadilly Circus, Tower Bridge, the British Museum, the Law Courts and both incarnations of New Scotland Yard. He treats us to lunch at the Savoy and Simpson's, to performances at the Palladium, the Scala and the Royal Albert Hall, then has us around to gatherings at some of the poshest digs in Mayfair and Belgravia. For green enthusiasts he includes stops in Hampstead, Hyde Park and the London Zoo; for railway buffs, he calls in at Euston, King's Cross, Victoria and Waterloo Stations. He also escorts us to a number of London's less glamorous districts—to the alleys and back streets of Docklands as it once was, to a seedy cinema in Camberwell, to a deserted house in Amhurst Park and, of course, to Her Majesty's infamous prisons at Holloway and Wormwood Scrubs. Truly, as the *Daily Mail* once said of *Blackmail* (although the sentiment certainly applies more generally), "London is [Hitchcock's] leading lady."

An additional purpose of this book is to help refute the myth (brilliantly exposed as such in Bill Krohn's *Hitchcock at Work*) that Hitchcock had already shot and edited his films in his mind before he ever stepped onto the set, that the actual production and postproduction merely executed that which had been meticulously planned and storyboarded weeks or even months before. In fact, examples of rethinking, improvising, experimenting, adding and deleting abound in Hitchcock's films. To take but one example, from *Frenzy*, we need look no further than the opening shot of Tower Bridge, which appears under the main titles. This shot, made from a helicopter, begins downriver and slowly tracks in to—and eventually "under"—the bridge. There is then a dissolve to another helicopter shot, above County Hall, where a politician is speaking about a pollution eradication scheme. The myth would have it that Hitchcock had planned these two shots during preproduction and merely executed them on location. The reality is that the tracking shot that *ended* at the bridge (the one we see in the film) was an improvisation—a last-minute replacement for a helicopter shot that had *begun* at Tower Bridge and *ended* at County Hall. (For the reason behind the switch, see the entries for **Tower Bridge** and **County Hall**.) Far from impugning Hitchcock's reputation as an artist, revelations of such ad hoc creativity merely serve to enhance it.

Another facet of Hitchcock's approach to filmmaking elucidated here is that of his concern—and occasional lack thereof—for verisimilitude. How long would a corpse take to develop rigor mortis in the late summer? What is the youngest possible age for a Scotland Yard Chief Inspector? How many scratches are there on the tables at the Old Bailey? What kind of wig does a Divorce Court judge wear? What kind of cars would be parked outside the Albert Hall? How would the patrons of a Mayfair pub differ from those of any other pub? What kind of clothes do schoolchildren in Bodega Bay, California wear? Memos and other production documents, as well as interview comments from the director himself indicate that Hitchcock frequently preoccupied himself with such details. However, the documents also reveal that there were limits to that preoccupation. Thus, in a conversation with *Stage Fright* production supervisor Fred Ahern, Hitchcock explained that he wanted to have a Scotland Yard man assigned to the picture because, "I don't want to do a lot of things that are wrong." On the other hand, he quickly added, "I don't want Scotland Yard to tell me, well, you can't do this and you can't do that." In other words, accuracy should never get in the way of a good story—or expedient filmmaking, a balancing act scarcely unique to Hitchcock. Which is why in *Blackmail*, for example, a car heading north in one London street, suddenly finds itself making a U-turn in another; why in *Sabotage*, a boy crossing the river from South to North London actually enters the bridge on the *northern* side; and why in *The Paradine Case*, a train approaching one railway station in an extreme long shot, actually arrives at another station in the following closer shot. Again, though, the point is not to asperse Hitchcock, but merely to document his methods, including the mildly audacious confidence with which he frequently fooled us.

The reader will also note that in addition to dozens of actual filming sites, I have included a number of locations from Hitchcock's English literary sources, e.g., Belloc Lowndes' *The Lodger*, Conrad's *The Secret Agent* (whence *Sabotage*), Iles' *Before the Fact* (*Suspicion*), Armstrong's "The Case of Mr. Pelham," du Maurier's "The Birds" and Canning's *The Rainbird Pattern* (*Family Plot*). In the rush to "auteurize" Hitchcock, it is easy to overlook the fact that the vast majority of his films began as someone else's novel or play. (Maurice Yacowar, in his 1977 study *Hitchcock's British Films*, and, coming up to the present, Ken Mogg, in *The Alfred Hitchcock Story*, and Charles Barr in *English Hitchcock*, are notable exceptions.) Many of these books and plays are quite good (*Easy Virtue* and *Rebecca* spring immediately to mind) and a few have actually been ennobled as "Literature" with a capital "L"

(Conrad's *The Secret Agent*, for example). Some have inspired remarkably faithful adaptations (*Rebecca, Dial M for Murder, The Trouble with Harry*), while others are scarcely recognizable (*Jamaica Inn, The House of Dr. Edwardes* [*Spellbound*]). The reasons for the latter—the "unusually bold adaptations," as Brian McFarlane calls them—apparently reflect Hitchcock's belief that great works of literature do not necessarily yield great works of film. By avoiding these and concentrating on "lesser" works, Hitchcock could, as McFarlane notes, "simply...take what he want[ed] from source material" and thus avoid the wrath of literary purists. Contrast this view with that of one of Hitchcock's most famous collaborators, producer David O. Selznick, who wrote (in a memo to Hitchcock himself): "I don't hold at all with the theory that the difference in medium necessitates a difference in storytelling....In my opinion, the only...omissions from a successful work that are justified are omissions necessitated by length, censorship, or other practical considerations. Readers of a dearly loved book will forgive omissions if there is an obvious reason for them; but very properly, they will not forgive substitutions." One wonders what Selznick thought about, say, *The 39 Steps* or *Sabotage*.

Yet, Hitchcock could even avoid the book itself, if he chose, for, as he told Truffaut, "I'm content just to take that basic idea, never look at it again, and now make a picture."[1] Conversely, if Hitchcock really liked a book, he could return to it over and over again. The most obvious example is John Buchan's *The Thirty-nine Steps*, the first and foremost of the so-called "chase novels," which blended elements of the traditional thriller and manhunt genres. Hitchcock had already dramatized stories of innocent men unjustly accused in *The Lodger* and *Downhill*, but in Buchan's Richard Hannay the director found his archetypal hero: an ordinary man, wrongly accused, on the run, forced to rely upon his wits (and his fists) to evade both the law and the bad guys. The most obvious examples occur in *The 39 Steps*, *Saboteur* and *North By Northwest*, but the hero who is both pursued and pursuer meanders through everything from *Young and Innocent* to *Frenzy*. In fact, the Buchan influence actually predates *The 39 Steps*, as the director himself reminded Truffaut. "[A] very important thing to remember: John Buchan is a strong influence *before The Man Who Knew Too Much*...a long time before." Thus, Bob and Jill Lawrence of *The Man Who Knew Too Much*—theoretically inspired by Sapper's Hugh and Phyllis Drummond—also evoke Buchan's Richard and Mary Hannay in *The Three Hostages*. The ending of *The Lodger*, quite different from that of the source novel (in which the title character is actually guilty), may also owe something to Buchan. So while accepting Hitchcock's distinction between "filling pages" in a book and filling a "rectangular screen in a movie house," we can still acknowledge that much of what we see on the cinema screen—characters, settings, actions and motifs—originated on the printed page. (For a more comprehensive examination of the ways in which Hitchcock adapted his sources, see Appendix I.)

In terms of fidelity, Hitchcock's adaptations may also be divided into those which retain the original British setting and those transposed to America. The former, and by far the larger, category requires little comment, except to note where and, if possible, why the director chose to alter locations described in the originals. In *The 39 Steps*, for example, St. Pancras Station becomes King's Cross Station because Hitchcock and scenarist Charles Bennett changed Hannay's Scottish destination from Galloway to Edinburgh, while in *Frenzy*, Piccadilly Circus becomes Covent Garden because of Hitchcock's nostalgia for the famous produce market. The second category, though, raises the question of why Hitchcock sought out English source material, only to transpose that material to America. English film writer Philip French surmised that the director "had to imagine the work, to seize its essence, in a European context before he could realise it in an American one." The fact is, that after 1939, Hitchcock lived and worked (primarily) in America and created films largely for an American audience. Yet, his subject matter, the themes and motifs that appealed to him, continued to reflect his English roots and, thus, to derive from English sources. Production designer Robert Boyle (who designed two of the "transposed" films, *The Birds* and *Marnie*) recalled that Hitchcock generally tried to find American locales that suggested England, such as the California coast that replaced the Cornish one in Daphne du Maurier's short story "The Birds."

Foreign poster for *The Lodger*

Hitchcock also tried to retain much of the typically English action and dialogue of the transposed works, e.g., the fox hunt in *Marnie* and Miss Gravely's deadpan response to the captain and the corpse in *The Trouble with Harry*. Indeed, the set-up of the latter film, as well as its source novel—the little boy's discovery of a corpse—evokes (and may well spoof) a rather bizarre Edwardian motif that originated in, of all places, the Boy Scout handbook. The original *Scouting for Boys: A Handbook for Instruction in Good Citizenship* was written by Sir Robert Baden-Powell, the British military hero who founded the Boy Scout organization in England in 1907. A devotee of Sherlock Holmes and his methods (as well as an important influence on John Buchan), Baden-Powell believed that solving murder mysteries—real or fictional—was a good way for boys to imprint such "masculine" behaviors and virtues as observation, logic, deduction and character assessment. Thus, in his immensely popular and highly influential *Handbook*, Baden-Powell admonished his young charges: "It may happen to some of you that one day you will be the first to find the dead body of a man, in which case you will remember that it is your duty to examine and note down the smallest signs that are to be seen on and near the body before it is moved." Poor little Arnie (*Abie* in the original): He would gladly do his "duty"—if only he could read and write.

Finally, and perhaps most obviously, Hitchcock reminds us of the English roots of these works in the casting: Leo G. Carroll in *Spellbound*; Sir Cedric Hardwicke and Constance Collier in *Rope*, Edmund Gwenn in *The Trouble with Harry*, Jessica Tandy and Ethel Griffies in *The Birds*, Alan Napier (and, to a lesser extent, Sean Connery) in *Marnie*, and Cathleen Nesbitt in *Family Plot*. In an effort, then, to reinforce the English roots of these so-called "American" films I have thus included a number of the original "pre-transposition" locales in this book.

For further reference, I recommend Ken Mogg's *The Alfred Hitchcock Story*, Charles Barr's *English Hitchcock*, Bill Krohn's *Hitchcock at Work*, and Tom Ryall's *Alfred Hitchcock & the British Cinema*. My research has been based on these and other books (see Bibliography), as well as a careful (I hope) scrutiny of the films and literary sources themselves. I also reviewed relevant materials at the Academy of Motion Picture Arts and Sciences' Margaret Herrick Library (hereafter, the Academy Library) and the Warner Bros. Archives at the University of Southern California, both in Los Angeles; and the British Film Institute and the City of Westminster Archive Centre, both in London. In addition, I interviewed a number of people who worked with Alfred Hitchcock (see below) and their reminiscences proved invaluable, to say the least. One "interviewee," director Ronald Neame, prompts a special comment. Nearing 90 when I spoke to him, Mr. Neame knew from the instant I uttered the words "Alfred Hitchcock's London" why I had rung him. He had served as an assistant cameraman on *Blackmail* and, thus, might provide valuable information on that landmark production. Unfortunately, Mr. Neame had, over the years, been nearly "Hitchcocked" to death. Everyone and his brother (and sister) had sought him out for comments and interviews on Hitchcock, whom he did not know well in London, and, frankly, he was rather tired of it all. Moreover, Mr. Neame was working on an autobiography and, as he rightly pointed out, whatever he still might wish to say about Hitchcock should be saved for his own book. I certainly couldn't argue with that. Yet, as we spoke, briefly, about his own films as a director (*The Card, The Prime of Miss Jean Brodie, The Poseidon Adventure, Hopscotch*, all of which I admire) and those of other directors, he seemed genuinely sorry that he had taken a vow of silence with respect to interviewers, for, as he told me, "I simply love to talk about film." But there it was, and Mr. Neame politely, but firmly reiterated his refusal to answer any questions. He concluded our chat by wishing me the best of luck with *Alfred Hitchcock's London* and then added that if I would drop him a line upon the book's publication, he would go out and buy a copy! His promise surprised me and, quite frankly, touched me deeply. The unanswered questions that lay before me now seemed far less important than they had just a few minutes before.

ACKNOWLEDGMENTS

The following people have helped me immensely during the course of my research and to them I extend my sincere gratitude: the staff of the Royal Albert Hall, London, and especially Marketing Manager Claire Ashby, Director of Building Development Ian Blackburn, Photographer Chris Christodoulou, and Senior Chef de Pâté Tim Elphick; The Savoy Group, London, and especially Charlotte Palmer, Press Office Coordinator and Susan Scott, Archivist; Kate Boyd, Telecommunications Reception Manager, Society of Motor Manufacturers and Traders, London; Danny Maher, Director, Eurospan, Ltd., London; BBC Written Archives Centre, London; Major David W. Clark, Social Historian, Salvation Army International Heritage Centre, London; Gerald Duckworth & Co., London; Bernard Brown, Metropolitan Police Historian, Chiselhurst, Kent; Michael Garner, General Manager, Thorney Court; Les Gilpin; Richard Griffin; PC Nigel Griffiths, New Scotland Yard, London; Andrew Lane, Assistant Diocesan Secretary for the Diocese of Southwark, London; Fran Mullins, Petersfield Library, Hampshire; John Oxlade; Martin Ward, Building Design Partnership, London; Tania Watkins, Photographic Officer, British Museum, London; Barbara Hall, Research Archivist, Faye Thompson, Special Collections Coordinator, and the staff of the Margaret Herrick Library of the Academy of Motion Picture Arts and Sciences, Los Angeles; Noelle Carter, Acting Director, and the staff of the USC Warner Bros. Archives, Los Angeles; Janet Moat, Anna Bramall and the staff of the British Film Institute; Paul Welsh, MBE, Historical Consultant, Elstree Film and Television Studios, Borehamwood, Herts.; the staff of the City of Westminster Archive Centre; and the Loh Family, Langley Court, Liss, Hampshire. I would also like to extend a special thanks to Hitchcock collaborators Robert Boyle, Production Designer of *North By Northwest*, *The Birds*, *Marnie* and *The Short Night*; Henry Bumstead, Art Director of *The Man Who Knew Too Much* (56); Syd Cain, Production Designer of *Frenzy* (not to mention three James Bond films, Kubrick's *Lolita* and Truffaut's *Fahrenheit 451*); Doc Erickson, production manager of *The Man Who Knew Too Much* (56); director Val Guest, an Elstree and Gainsborough colleague of Hitchcock's; Bill Hill, associate producer of *Frenzy*; Bob Laing, art director of *Frenzy*; Simon Wakefield, set decorator of *Frenzy*; Desmond Tester, star of *Sabotage*; and to Mr. Hitchcock's daughter, Patricia O'Connell, who graciously answered my questions about her family's London life. Finally, I must acknowledge the warm help and support of Hitchcock historians and researchers Nándor Bokor, Martin Grams, Jr., Bill Krohn, Patrick McGilligan, and, especially, Ken Mogg; of James Bond production designer Peter Lamont, who graciously escorted me around Pinewood Studios and its environs; and of my research assistant, proofreader, best friend and supreme inspiration, my wife, Lisa.

ORGANIZATION & KEY

This book is arranged by *location*, rather than by, say, event, topic, or film. London districts, e.g., Bayswater, Chelsea, Soho, are listed alphabetically, while location entries within each district are grouped to form convenient walking tours. Letters placed after the name of the location indicate the *type* of location, i.e., **H** for a location from Hitchcock's life, **F** for a filming location, **L** for a literary location and **C** for a real-life crime location (see below). Each entry concludes with directions to the site from the nearest Underground station. London itself is divided into two parts, **Central** and **Outer**. The last section, for day trips **Outside London,** contains a number of English locations outside the capital, including the Langdale Chase Hotel in Cumbria ("Hindley Hall" in *The Paradine Case*); Menabilly, the Cornwall estate that inspired the "Manderley" of *Rebecca*; and the Hitchcocks' former country home in Surrey. These locations are arranged by county, e.g., Buckinghamshire, Cambridgeshire, Cornwall, etc.

H = Alfred Hitchcock Locale: a location such as a home, office, restaurant, or hotel associated with the Master of Suspense

F = Film Locale: a location depicted in one or more of the films or television episodes directed by Alfred Hitchcock. This includes actual filming locations, e.g., the British Museum in *Blackmail*, Barrie House in *The Paradine House*, and Covent Garden in *Frenzy*; as well as locations recreated at the studio or elsewhere, e.g., the Royal Courts of Justice in *Sabotage* and the BBC in *Foreign Correspondent*. The bracketed symbol (**F**) indicates that a location was filmed (or had been intended for filming) but was ultimately dropped, e.g., St. Martin's Theatre in *The Paradine Case*; that a location is referred to but not depicted in a film, e.g., Charing Cross Station in *Dial M for Murder*; or that a location is associated with a production in some other way, e.g., the judicial costumier Ede and Ravenscroft on *The Paradine Case*. Quotation marks around the title of an entry indicate that the address is fictional, e.g., "Edgar Brodie's Home" at 84 Curzon Street in *Secret Agent* (there is no such number in Curzon Street).

L = Literary Locale: a location depicted in one or more of the Hitchcock source novels, stories, or plays (see Appendix I), e.g., Liverpool Street Station in *Goodbye Piccadilly, Farewell Leicester Square* (whence the film *Frenzy*). The bracketed symbol (**L**) indicates a location that is referred to in one of the literary sources or is otherwise associated with a work or its author, e.g., Selfridges in *The Wheel Spins* (whence the film *The Lady Vanishes*) and Menabilly, the inspiration for Daphne du Maurier's fictional "Manderley." Quotation marks around the title of an entry indicate that the address is fictional, e.g., "Ordinary Smith's Flat" at Sloane Avenue House in *Man Running* (whence *Stage Fright*).

C = Scene of the Crime Locale: a location depicted in or otherwise connected to a film associated with the real-life world of crime, espionage or police work, such as Scotland Yard and the house of the killer Crippen.

P = "Police Do Not Cross" Locale: a private home or other site that is off limits to visitors, such as Pinewood Studios or Winter's Grace.

ex = appears before the name of a location to indicate "former site of" or, if the building itself is gone, "site of the former"

Sprinkled throughout the text you will also find a number of "MacGuffins," trivial facts and anecdotes pertaining to the location under which they are placed. You will also be able to test your knowledge of Hitchcock arcana through the 53 "Ask Mr. Memory" questions (one for each of Hitchcock's 53 feature films) that appear throughout the book. The answers—and scoring—will be found at the end of the book, before the Appendices.

DIRECTIONS

N = North
S = South
E = East
W = West
R = Right
L = Left

UNDERGROUND LINES

BA = Bakerloo
CE = Central
CI = Circle
DI = District
EL = East London
HC = Hammersmith & City
JU = Jubilee
ME = Metropolitan
NO = Northern
PI = Piccadilly
VI = Victoria
WC = Waterloo & City
DL = Docklands Light Railway
NR = National Rail Service

Place names printed in **boldface** type within the text, e.g. **Forbes House**, have entries of their own. Consult the *Location List* on page 322 for the entry number of each location.

CENTRAL LONDON

1. BAYSWATER

1:1
ex **Coburg Hotel (*now* the Hilton Hyde Park) F**
129 Bayswater Rd, W2

It is to this Edwardian landmark that Babs and Dick Blaney retreat for a night of illicit fun in Hitchcock's penultimate film, *Frenzy*. In the source novel the couple stayed in the fictitious Lakes of Killarney Hotel, also in Bayswater Road, while the shooting script sequesters them in the "Pembroke Hotel," a name still in use during the shoot here at the Coburg. Several other hotels were also considered, including the Sandringham Hotel, the Commodore Hotel, Whites Hotel and the Dominions Hotel, all in nearby Lancaster Gate (see also the next entry). The script originally called for the couple to check in under the names of "Mr. and Mrs. John Smith," but actor Jon Finch objected that this was an old, unfunny gag (apparently unmindful of its evocation of Hitchcock's 1941 comedy *Mr. and Mrs. Smith*). He suggested substituting either "Bernard Shaw" or "Oscar Wilde"; Hitchcock chose the latter, which was thematically relevant in that, like Wilde, Blaney would eventually be held at the **Bow Street Police Station**. (For another of Finch's line changes, see **Victoria Station**.) The hotel's exterior hasn't changed much in 35 years, although the lobby, also shown in the film, has since been remodeled. A replica of the reception area was built at **Pinewood Studios** for closer shots of Dick registering and for the later sequence when Bertie and Glad discuss the Necktie Murderer. As art director Bob Laing pointed out, "It would have been difficult to do those dialogue scenes in a crowded hotel lobby." The "Cupid Room" and upstairs

The Coburg Hotel

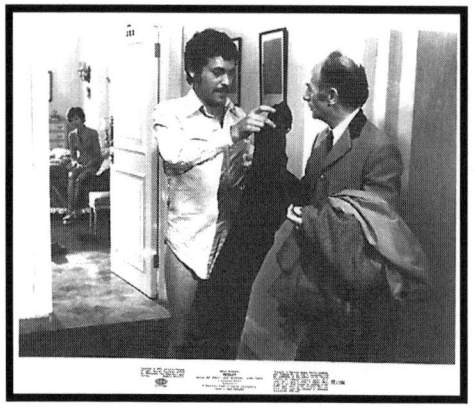

interiors were built on D Stage at **Pinewood Studios**; the corridor, swinging doors and lift were, in fact, modeled on their real-life counterparts, which, as a visitor to the hotel will readily note, comprise far too confined a setting to permit filming. The policeman's POV out of the Cupid Room window (following Dick and Babs' escape) was shot on location by assistant director Colin Brewer; the view is from the window of the fifth floor landing, overlooking the fire escape. (On the same day, October 15, 1971, Brewer also shot the establishing shots of **New Scotland Yard** and **Oxford Street**.) Interestingly, Hitchcock had originally intended to use the back of a building in Piccadilly for the rear of the hotel. To find out more about *that* building, see **Brenda Blaney's Club**.

Station: Queensway (CE) Exit into Bayswater and turn R; the hotel is just ahead on the R.

Ask Mr. Memory 1: What is the number of the suite to which Babs and Dick retire?

1:2
Sir Simon Flaquer's Home F
Barrie House
Lancaster Gate, W2

This prestigious, portered apartment building was home to Sir Simon Flaquer, the title character's avuncular solicitor in *The Paradine Case*. (In the novel, Sir Simon, his wife and two daughters live in Hyde Park Gardens, which, we are reminded, is "just round the corner [from] Lancaster Gate.") Hitchcock's second unit photographed the distinctive red brick building from across Bayswater Road, with the now-defunct Christ Church providing an appropriate touch of Victorian class in the background. Indeed, Christ Church was so prosperous during its heyday that it came to be known as the "thousand pound church," that being the usual amount collected in a Sunday morning service. The church—minus its tall spire—was torn down in 1978

Sir Simon Flaquer's home in *The Paradine Case*

and replaced with an apartment complex supposedly designed to look like a continuation of the original structure. (You be the judge.) Barrie House and the rest of the tiny square look much as they did some 60 years ago. And just in case you were wondering, a 4-bedroom, 2,000 square foot apartment in Sir Simon's building goes for a cool £1 million ($1.8 million).

Station: Lancaster Gate (CE) Exit R into Bayswater Road; the building is ahead on the R.

1:3
Horfield Home L
Sussex Square, SW1

According to Chapter 21 of *The Paradine Case*, Lord and Lady Horfield live in a large house in Sussex Square, a pleasant, Hyde Park-area setting once home to Winston Churchill. Hitchcock's adaptation includes scenes set in the Horfields' Dining Room, but does not mention the location of the house itself. Neither the shooting script nor the director's instructions to the second unit (for location footage) mention an exterior establishing shot of the house, so apparently none was ever considered.

Station: Lancaster Gate (CE) Exit L into Bayswater Road, veer L into Stanhope Terrace, which leads to the square. Sadly, much of the area has been redeveloped since the Horfields' day, although the buildings adjacent to Hyde Park Gardens give some idea of the older setting.

1:4
"Sir Edwin Proud's Home" L (F)
9 Cleveland Place, W1

The title character of both the novel and the unproduced film *No Bail for the Judge* lives with his daughter, Elizabeth, at 9 Cleveland Place, W, "not far from Whiteleys" (Chapter 2). There never was a Cleveland *Place* in W1 or W2, but there certainly was a Whiteleys, Britain's first department store, which opened in 1885, closed in 1981 and reopened as a shopping mall in 1989. And, just a few streets over from Whiteleys' massive Queensway complex, is none other than Cleveland Square, as well as Cleveland Gardens and Cleveland Terrace. This profusion of adjoining Clevelands apparently inspired author Henry Cecil's choice of names for a clever dodge that is precisely replicated in the screenplay. Briefly, Elizabeth Proud (*Prout* in the novel) returns home to find a locksmith attempting to break into her father's safe, the coveted booty—we later learn—being Justice Proud's extremely valuable stamp collection. Miss Proud promptly confronts the brains behind the burglary, a charming rogue named Anthony Low (Ambrose Low in the novel), who "just happens" to live in 9 *Clevedon* Place. In fact, Low had taken a lease on the Clevedon Place property precisely because of its name and location, replaced his own lock and key with ones identical to those of the nearby Proud home and dispatched the duplicate key to his locksmith confederate. The latter, in turn, then entered the judge's home—instead of Low's—in order to open the safe for which Low, according to the scheme, had supposedly lost the key. In this way, if the locksmith were caught before he could make off with the stamps (as indeed he was), he could simply claim to have confused one house for the other. Clearly intrigued by a man who could dream up such a scheme, Elizabeth decides not to turn in Low if he will help her find the real killer of the Mayfair prostitute, which will clear her father of the murder charge. Near the end of the story Elizabeth is returned here by the real murderer and his mother (!), who have given the young woman an overdose of sleeping pills to keep her from exposing their prostitution racket. To the rescue comes Anthony Low, who has no way to get into the locked house—until he remembers that duplicate key....It is also possible that in selecting the name and number of the judge's street, Cecil—actually County Court Judge Henry Cecil Leon—a nod was intended to the famous "Cleveland Street Scandal" of 1899, in which some of London's most prominent citizens were caught patronizing a male brothel at 19 Cleveland Street, Marylebone. For more *No Bail* locations, see **Old Bailey**, **Shepherd Market** and **HM Prison Brixton**.

Station: Bayswater (CI; DI) Exit L into Queensway and continue to Porchester Gardens, where you will turn R. (Whiteleys is just ahead on the L.) Turn L in Porchester Terrace and immediately R into Leinster Place. At Leinster Gardens turn R then L into Cleveland Square.

1:5
"Ambrose Chapel" F
17 Ambrose Street, W2

This is the address of the church that Ben and Jo McKenna visit in an attempt to find their kidnapped son in *The Man Who Knew Too Much* (56). (It is shown in the telephone directory and repeated in the dialogue.) In fact, there is no Ambrose Street in Bayswater and never has been, although there is a small street by that name off Southwark Park Road in Bermondsey (south of the Thames). It must be stressed that Hitchcock and the film's first scenarist, Angus MacPhail, had no interest in any real street. What they needed was an ambiguous name that could signify both a person and a place, like the "A. Hall" of the original film, or the "Barmaid Collins" of MacPhail's February 17, 1955 notes. (The latter would have been misunderstood to refer to a barmaid whose name was Collins, when in fact it referred to a barmaid *at* Collins Music Hall, Islington Green.) The choice also had to be obscure enough that no one by that name or profession might turn up and sue Paramount Pictures (the film's production company) for libel. Paramount's London office was finally able to clear both "Ambrose Chappell" and "Ambrose Chapel," there being no such person, church or taxidermist by those names anywhere in London. For the same reason, Dr. Ben *McKenzie* became Dr. Ben *McKenna*—there really was a physician by the name of Ben McKenzie and he wouldn't give permission for his name to be used. Similarly, Abbott, the villain of the original, became first Addison and eventually Drayton, Hitchcock's third choice after Middleton and Harwood. (The name Drayton actually pops up on more than one occasion in the Bulldog Drummond stories, the original inspiration for the story [see Appendix I].) The Bayswater setting arose because, as Dan Auiler points out in *Hitchcock's Notebooks*, MacPhail was concerned about the "anomalous" presence of an American couple in Wapping, the East End setting of the original film (see **Geo Barbor, Dentist**). MacPhail felt that the parents would "scarcely journey to Wapping, lion's-denwards, unless they had some effective form of disguise." Instead, he favored Notting Hill, where "the presence of Americans would scarcely be remarked" and neighboring Bayswater because it is "spotted with odd religions." Associate producer Herb Coleman and unit manager Doc Erickson actually visited Notting Hill in a vain search for a suitable location, then turned to Waterloo Road in an attempt to fulfill Hitchcock's desire that the chapel be located near **Royal Festival Hall**, where the climax was originally supposed to take place. In the end, they found their location in Brixton, at the **St. Saviour's Church Hall**.

2. BELGRAVIA

2:1
Paradine Home (*ex* Cuban Embassy) F P
33 Wilton Crescent, SW1

Constructed in 1827 as a grand entrance to Belgrave Square, the elegant Wilton Crescent quickly attracted its share of rich and powerful residents, including a number of MPs. It's no surprise, then, that the late millionaire Richard Paradine maintained a London home in such an exclusive enclave. In fact, the first shot of *The Paradine Case*, following the titles, begins on the northeastern side of the crescent, then pans across the street to No. 33 (just above Belgrave Mews North). Hitchcock and unit manager Fred Ahern discovered the locale—which turned out to be the Cuban Embassy—on a recce to London in April 1946. The Havana government took nearly three weeks to give permission for filming both inside and out. For the Paradines' country home, Hindley Hall, in Cumberland (now Cumbria), the two men chose the posh **Langdale Chase Hotel** overlooking Lake Windermere.

The former Cuban Embassy, which was used in *The Paradine Case.*

A REFERENCE GUIDE TO LOCATIONS

Station: Hyde Park Corner (PI) Take Exit 3 R into Grosvenor Place; turn R at Grosvenor Crescent. Follow this to Belgrave Square and look for Wilton Crescent to the R, at the NE corner of the square. Veer R into the crescent and look for No. 33 ahead on the L. Stand at the corner of Wilton Crescent and Wilton Row (to the R) for the view from the film. And in case you were considering a move, private homes in the neighborhood were going for as high as £10 million in 2005. The literary characters occupied a furnished house a little farther south, in Eaton Square.

Ask Mr. Memory 2: A portrait of the late Colonel Paradine hangs above the piano in his home. When, according to his widow, was the painting finished?

2:2
Forbes House F
Halkin Street, SW1

Doubles as: Unnamed Embassy in *The Man Who Knew Too Much* (56)

In the early months of 1955, *The Man Who Knew Too Much* production crew (art director Henry Bumstead, associate producer Herb Coleman and production manager Doc Erickson) scoured London's toniest districts for a suitable building to double as the unnamed foreign embassy in which the climax of the film would take place. (The building was originally intended to represent the Russian Embassy in Kensington Palace Gardens, with the assassinated leader the Czechoslovakian prime minister. In the end, Hitchcock decided to eliminate all specific political and international references.) Among the buildings considered were Crewe House, Curzon Street (near **Charlotte Inwood's Home [1]**); the Spanish Embassy, 24 Belgrave Square (near the **Paradine Home**); and Kenwood House, Hampstead Lane (not far from the **Gill Home**). By April, Hitchcock had decided that one building would not be enough. Rather, he would require at least

Forbes House

four separate locations: one for the entrance foyer and stairway (respectively, where Ben and Jo arrive for the reception and down which Ben will ultimately bring Hank); one for the ballroom (where Jo performs for the prime minister and his guests); one for the kitchen and corridor (where the embassy staff cools their heels while the Draytons escort Hank inside); and yet another for the front and rear exteriors of the building. In May Hitchcock found his ballroom here in Forbes House, a fine, late Georgian home originally built for Edward Hartley, the 5th Earl of Oxford and Mortimer. The majority of the ballroom sequence was shot here on location, although Doris Day's close-ups at the piano were subsequently filmed in Hollywood. On June 19, Hitchcock came back to Forbes House to shoot: (a) the scene in which the wounded prime minister takes the call from the McKennas and (b) six close-ups of stuffed animal heads (a moose, ibex, alligator, tiger, lion and rhino) that were supposed to "watch" Ben's fight in the taxidermy shop of **Edward Gerrard & Sons**. (Hitchcock subsequently dropped this idea, including only a single shot of a lion's head to conclude the taxidermy shop sequence.) In addition, Hitchcock had planned to shoot the scene in which the Draytons receive a dressing down from the ambassador here in Forbes House, but ultimately staged this sequence in Hollywood on July 19. He had also intended to film the scenes set in the McKennas' **Savoy** hotel suite here at Forbes House, primarily because shooting in The Savoy itself was out of the question and he wanted to use English actors to portray the couple's friends. In the end, he found his actors in Hollywood and shot the hotel scenes at Paramount. (For more on the Savoy scenes, see the **London Palladium**.) For the Embassy foyer and staircase, Hitchcock chose **Park Lane House**, which means that when the McKennas enter the embassy, they cross from a foyer in Mayfair to a ballroom in Belgravia! (Watch the scenes closely—note that you never see *into* the ballroom from the foyer or stairs and that you never see *out into* the foyer *from* the ballroom.) The embassy kitchen scenes were filmed at the **Royal Albert Hall** and the rear entrance at nearby **Thorney Court**.

Station: Hyde Park Corner (PI) Take Exit 3 R into Grosvenor Place and follow this to Halkin Street, where you will turn R. Look for the house ahead to the R. Forbes House is today the headquarters of the Society of Motor Manufacturers and Traders, which acquired the building in 1959. The ballroom, located on the first (U.S.: second) floor, now serves as the Council Room, while the ground floor ambassador's study serves as the Committee Room. Both are located on the L side of the building, as you face the front.

Ask Mr. Memory 3: Who, according to the ambassador, will be "the death of us all"?

2:3
"Jonathan Cooper's Flat" F P
13 Eaton Mews North, SW1

Novelist Selwyn Jepson located him at "21 Cary Mews" (really Cranley Mews; see entry 22:6), South Kensington. Alfred Hitchcock imagined him in Mayfair, near **Charlotte Inwood's Home (1)**. But the villain of *Stage Fright* actually ended up above

Jonathan Cooper's escape route used in *Stage Fright*.

a garage in tony Eaton Mews North, just a stone's throw from the most exclusive real estate in London. Exteriors were actually filmed by a second unit, with doubles for actor Richard Todd and the policemen; a small portion of the building and street were constructed at **Elstree Studios** for the closer shots, including rear-projection footage. The two-story interior—built as two separate, ground level sets—was also filmed in the studio.

Station: Hyde Park Corner (Pl) Take Exit 3 R into Grosvenor Place; turn R at Grosvenor Crescent. At Belgrave Square veer R along the top of the square, then L along the western side. Continue straight ahead into Belgrave Place and then turn R into Eaton Place. Take the first turn to the L and cross under the archway that Jonathan passes beneath while beating his hasty retreat. His flat is around the corner to the R, at No. 13.

2:4
ex **Russian Embassy L**
Chesham House
30-31 Chesham Place, SW1

For much of the 19th century (and a bit of the 20th), the Russian Empire maintained an embassy here in fashionable Belgravia, still the province of many a foreign dignitary. It was here that Adolf Verloc came for his odious instructions from Mr. Vladimir in *The Secret Agent*, a scene which Hitchcock transposed to the **London Zoo** in the film adaptation *Sabotage*. Actually, author Joseph Conrad does not name the embassy that employs Verloc, but he does name its location—Chesham Square. There is not now, nor was there in the late 19th century (when the novel is set), a Chesham *Square* in Belgravia. Nor was there a Porthill Street into which the embassy entrance was said to have faced. But there was—and remains—a Chesham *Place*, and it is reached by

The former Russian Embassy

walking west from Hyde Park Corner along Knightsbridge, then turning left, as Verloc does in the novel. And, as in the novel, there is "an imposing carriage gate in a high, clean wall between two houses," one of which is located in Chesham Place and one of which is located in an entirely different street (Lyall, not Porthill), as Conrad humorously notes. Speculation that Verloc's instructions came from the German Embassy, not the Russian, seems unwarranted given the geographical references in the novel, not to mention the fact that in the late 19th century, Kaiser Wilhelm's representative was located in 9 Carlton House Terrace, St. James's.

Station: Hyde Park Corner (Pl) Take Exit 3 R into Grosvenor Place; turn R at Grosvenor Crescent. At Belgrave Square veer R along the top of the square, then L along the western side. At the SW corner of the square, turn R into Chesham Place and follow this to the end, where you will turn L. Chesham House—Nos. 30-31 Chesham Place—is just ahead to the L, accessed via Lyall Street.

3. BLOOMSBURY

**3:1
University of London H
Malet Street, WC1**

Established in a rather complicated series of stages throughout the 19th century, the University of London is in fact a federation of some 50 institutions of higher education, boasting some 44,000 internal students. From its original headquarters in Somerset House, the university moved to Burlington House in 1858 and to its present, purpose-built home, in the 1930s. It is renowned for pioneering the teaching of such subjects as laboratory science, engineering and modern languages, as well as for its long liberal

The University of London

tradition. Indeed, it was the first to appoint a woman professor, in 1912. It was also the first and only university attended by Alfred Hitchcock, who, as a teenager working at **Henley's**, began taking evening classes at a branch in New Cross (see **Goldsmith's College**). Nearly 30 years later, Hitchcock came to Malet Street itself, where the university's massive new headquarters, Senate House, had been taken over by the government's wartime Ministry of Information. (George Orwell would base his towering "Ministry of Truth" upon Senate House and its wartime occupant in the novel *1984*.) The Ministry's films division was run by Hitchcock's old Film Society friend Sidney Bernstein (see **New Gallery Cinema**) and Bernstein now required the services of the great director. Specifically, he wanted Hitchcock to write and direct two propaganda films about the French Resistance, which were to be shown in France after its liberation from the Germans. Speaking of Bernstein's offer many years later to Truffaut, Hitchcock explained that "This was very important for me because I wanted to get into the atmosphere of the war. I wanted to [make] whatever little contribution I could make." So, on December 3, 1943, Hitchcock flew to London, checked into **Claridge's** and immediately began work with Angus MacPhail on the scripts for *Bon Voyage* and *Aventure Malgache* (*Malagasy Adventure*). Both films were shot at the **Welwyn Studios** in Hertfordshire, to which Hitchcock commuted each day. (See the entry on Welwyn for more on these films and their exhibition.) The following June, Bernstein, now in charge of the cinema section of the Psychological Warfare Department of SHAEF (Supreme Headquarters Allied Expeditionary Force), again enlisted Hitchcock's services. This time the director was to assist in assembling a joint Anglo-American documentary film of German war atrocities, compiled from service and newsreel footage taken of the liberated concentration camps. The film, then known only as "F 3080," was to be shown to German audiences in order to "shake and humiliate" them and to prove beyond any doubt that not only did such atrocities occur but that they were the responsibility of the German people themselves. Hitchcock's role actually began after the first three reels of the film had been assembled. "I wanted somebody to compile it together," Bernstein, by this time Lord Bernstein, recalled in a 1983 interview. "There was a very good man called [Peter] Tanner, and a number of good editors, but I wanted the imaginative touch that somebody like Hitchcock could give. He came over to edit it and give it some kind of extra thing besides straight documentary." Among other things, Hitchcock suggested that the film should begin with the camp at Dachau, "emphasising," in the words of Peter Tanner, one of the film's principal editors, "the large number of persons here"; that it include long continuous shots, to ensure that audiences would not think that anything had been "faked" (one of these was of the reactions of a Catholic priest, a rabbi and two Protestant clergymen as they inspected a camp); and of maps, with circles drawn around the concentration camps, to graphically demonstrate the proximity of the camps to villages and towns and thus preclude the defense that ordinary people were unaware of the atrocities. The Americans (who had originally suggested director Billy Wilder for the job assumed by Hitchcock) withdrew from the project on July 9 and went on to assemble and screen their own version of the footage. The Ministry of Information then assumed sole responsibility for F 3080, with Hitchcock continuing to work on the film until the end of the month, when he returned to America. By this time, Bernstein had already left the Ministry, but continued to work on F 3080 until the Government shelved the project that September. Apparently, the **Foreign Office** had decided to take a more conciliatory approach to Germany and believed that such a demoralizing film would hinder the Allies' efforts to rehabilitate the country. Moreover, since the concentration camp footage was already turning up in other films, the need for and impact of F 3080 was somewhat diminished. In 1952, the film was turned over to London's Imperial War Museum, where it was titled *Memory of the Camps*; it finally saw the light of day on American television in 1985, when the PBS series *Frontline* presented the five surviving reels (the sixth having apparently been lost in Russia) with a narration by Trevor Howard. As for Bernstein and Hitchcock, the two old friends went on to form a production company called **Transatlantic Pictures** in 1946 and it is to that entry that you should turn for the rest of their story.

Station: Goodge Street (NO) Cross Tottenham Court Road into Chenies Street and follow this to Gower Street, where you will turn R. Just ahead, to the L, is Keppel Street; turn here to see the University's imposing Senate House, where Bernstein had his offices.

3:2
Gordon Square (L)
WC1

Begun by architect Thomas Cubitt in the 1820s (and completed by his executors in the 1860s), Gordon Square today retains few of its original houses and, in fact, has been largely absorbed by the University of London. But its fame has nothing to do with the stature of its buildings, but rather of those who lived in them. For as the commemorative plaque at No. 50 states, Gordon Square was the home of the celebrated "Bloomsbury Group" of writers, artists and intellectuals who lived, loved and worked here in the early decades of the 20th century. The group actually evolved out of the weekly art discussions held at No. 46 Gordon Square, the home of Thoby, Adrian, Vanessa and Virginia

Gordon Square

Stephen (the latter being better known by her married name, Virginia Woolf). Virginia and Adrian moved to Fitzrovia in 1907 (Thoby, the founder of the discussions, had died at the age of 26 the year before), but returned for the regular Friday gatherings of the "Bloomsbury Group," as it had come to be known by 1910. Apart from Woolf and her husband Leonard, the Group included novelists Vita Sackville-West (Virginia's lover) and E. M. Forster, biographer Lytton Strachey, economist John Maynard Keynes, art critic Roger Fry and painter Vanessa Bell (Virginia's sister). American journalist and author James Vincent ("Jimmy") Sheean, whose best-selling, highly acclaimed 1935 memoir, *Personal History*, formed the basis for *Foreign Correspondent*, lived in and around Gordon Square throughout the 1920s. According to Sheean, the Bloomsbury Group "accepted nothing as true until it had been proved to be true" and "attempted to form their own view of the world upon a basis of reason." This "habit of mind" came to exercise a "moderating impulse" over the young American, who described his nature as "given to too much emotion, too much violence and too little thought." Indeed, during his years as a foreign correspondent (first for the European Edition of the Chicago *Tribune* in Paris, later for the North American Newspaper Alliance), Sheean threw himself body and soul into a number of harrowing international assignments, thoughtfully (and subjectively) covering everything from anti-colonial insurgencies in Morocco to the Arab-Israeli conflict in Palestine (his sympathies always seemed to lie with the underdog). Ironically, it was two of the less dramatic incidents in *Personal History*—covering the Lausanne Peace Conference of 1923, and falling in love with an idealistic American radical, Rayna Prohme, in 1927—that eventually found their way into the Hitchcock film. The screenplay had, in fact, been evolving under producer Walter Wanger's guidance for several years before Hitchcock was signed as director. For example, the John Howard Lawson/Budd Schulberg script of June 21, 1938 concerns American journalism major Joe Sheridan's efforts to help Jewish refugees escape from German-occupied Austria. Hitchcock and Joan Harrison's first crack at the story, dated

November 20, 1939, is far closer to the finished film (and even farther from Sheean's original), though, notably, the MacGuffin is not a secret clause in a treaty, but rather the formula for a "death ray" the villain plans to sell to Germany. Interestingly, a number of incidents from Sheean's Moroccan adventures seem to have found their way into the second version of *The Man Who Knew Too Much*, for which see Appendix I. As for Sheean's beloved Bloomsbury, the closest the film's foreign correspondent, Johnny Jones, comes to Gordon Square is nearby Charlotte Street, where the baddies torture Mr. Van Meer above the fictional **Maison Rouge** restaurant. Following *Personal History*, Sheean went on to cover the events leading up to World War II, including the Nazi occupation of Czechoslovakia, which he recalled in a second memoir, *Not Peace but a Sword* (1939). (Whether Hitchcock read *Not Peace but a Sword* during the preparation of *Foreign Correspondent* is not known, but, interestingly, the book contains a description of Sheean's trip on a Number 13 London bus from the Haymarket, past the **National Gallery** and **Trafalgar Square** and thence to the Strand and **The Savoy**—the precise route Jones and Van Meer take in the film.) Sheean served as a captain and lieutenant colonel in the U.S. Army Air Force during the war itself, after which he returned to writing. In addition to another volume of memoirs (and a plea for peace), *This House against This House* (1946), Sheean also published a number of novels and short stories, as well as biographies of Mohandas Gandhi, Jawarhalal Nehru (both of whom he interviewed), Sinclair Lewis, Oscar Hammerstein I and Giuseppe Verdi. He died of lung cancer on March 15, 1975. After his death, the New York University journalism department selected *Personal History* as one of the "Top 100 Works of Journalism in the United States in the 20th Century," along with Woodward and Bernstein's Watergate investigations for *The Washington Post*; John Hersey's book *Hiroshima*; H. L. Mencken's coverage of the Scopes trial for *The Baltimore Sun*; and Truman Capote's *In Cold Blood*.

Station: Goodge Street (NO) Cross Tottenham Court Road into Chenies Street, follow this to Gower Street and turn L. From Gower Street, turn R into Byng Place and follow this to Gordon Square, which will be on the L.

Ask Mr. Memory 4: For what newspaper does Jones work in *Foreign Correspondent*?

3:3
Royal Academy of Dramatic Art (RADA) F
62-64 Gower Street, WC1

Actor-producer Herbert Beerbohm Tree (later Sir Herbert), manager of **Her Majesty's Theatre** in the Haymarket, founded England's first drama school in 1904. The following year, Tree moved his Academy of Dramatic Art from the Haymarket to its present home—a rather nondescript Georgian building—in Gower Street. In 1920, the

Royal Academy of Dramatic Art

RADA as shown in *Stage Fright*

school received a royal charter of incorporation from George V, hence the name *Royal* Academy of Dramatic Art. Hitchcock paid a tribute of sorts to Tree in his 1930 whodunit *Murder!* (for which you should see the entry on Her Majesty's Theatre) and perhaps an even greater tribute in early 1948, when he enrolled his daughter Patricia, already an experienced actress, at RADA. (She would hone her craft here for the next two years.) Hitchcock himself came to RADA in the summer of 1949 to film both exteriors and interiors for *Stage Fright*, a production based at his old **Elstree Studios** home. He secured permission from RADA principal Sir Kenneth Barnes (who retired in 1955 after 46 years as the head of the school) to use the academy's Rehearsal Theatre for two scenes, only one of which would make it to the finished film. The first was the scene in which Jonathan interrupts Eve's rehearsal near the beginning of the film (and in which the drama coach, Miss Ashton says, "I shall certainly report your behavior to Sir Kenneth"). The second, intended as the final scene of the film, takes place during a dress rehearsal of the same play. This time, Eve really throws herself into the kissing scene, prompting Miss Ashton to exclaim: "I don't know what you've done to yourself but you've improved enormously." (Nudge, nudge.) Also watching the performance is Ordinary Smith, who, Eve notices, is looking a bit glum. Feigning illness, she asks Miss Ashton for a break, then meets Smith in the corridor outside the theatre. As a stand-in carries on inside, the camera (according to the shooting script) "caresses" Eve and Smith, who "fall into each other's arms" for the fade-out. (See the **Scala Theatre** for the present ending of the film.) All of the interior shooting apparently went fairly smoothly. Exterior filming, though, was a different matter. For one thing, Sir Kenneth Barnes kept putting his head up to the window and spoiling the shots; he was eventually asked to come outside and stand next to Hitchcock. Then the police demanded to know if the camera crane operator had a driving license, since he was in fact driving a self-propelled vehicle in a London street—and at a speed of two miles per hour! The crane operator, Jack Haste, did not have a London driving license (very serious, this), so calls were made to **Scotland Yard**, where the mess was eventually sorted out. Finally, with traffic having been stopped at both ends of Gower Street, a gentleman living on the other side of the street asked if a delivery motorcycle might be allowed to pass through the barricade. It seems that the man was on his way to an important engagement and, well, he simply couldn't get dressed until the laundry delivered his boiled shirt. Add to this the hassle of paid extras, autograph-seekers, nervous novices (the girl coming up the steps when the police arrive) and dozens (hundreds?) of men, women and children gawping from windows, balconies, rooftops and the street and you wonder how Hitchcock ever managed to get anything in the can, let alone retain that famous aplomb.

Station: Goodge Street (NO) Cross Tottenham Court Road to Chenies Street and follow this to Gower Street. Turn L at Gower and look for the school across the street.

Hitchcock and Dietrich on the set of *Stage Fright*

The MacGuffin: RADA students who went on to appear in Hitchcock films and teleplays include Anthony Dawson, John Gielgud, Cedric Hardwicke, Laurence Harvey, Margaret Lockwood, Alec McCowen, Laurence Olivier, Alan Napier, Torin Thatcher and Charles Laughton, who won the school's gold medal. Claude Rains, one of Tree's protegés, actually taught classes here in the 1920s. Jane Wyman did not attend RADA, but she did earn its undying gratitude in 1949 when she donated the proceeds of her London Drama Critics Award (for her work in *Johnny Belinda*) to help rebuild the school after bomb damage suffered during the War.

3:4
British Museum F
Great Russell Street, WC1

Founded on this site in 1755, the British Museum today occupies a neoclassical structure designed by Sir Robert Smirke and built in four stages between 1823 and 1848. The famous dome, surmounting the round Reading Room, was completed in 1857. The museum itself houses unrivaled collections of Egyptian antiquities (including the famous Rosetta Stone), Western Asiatic antiquities, Greek and Roman antiquities, Oriental antiquities and rare coins and medals. In this, according to Harwood and Saint, the British Museum embodies "the all-powerful romantic ideal of Culture—the belief that a nation's history, destiny and vigor were reflected in the art and antiqui-

The water fountain at the British Museum that appeared in *Blackmail*.

The British Museum "Old Mummy Room" seen in *Blackmail*

ties it could boast." And it was presumably to poke a bit of fun at such pretension (or at the very least to serve the cause of irony) that Alfred Hitchcock chose to stage the climactic chase of *Blackmail* inside and outside this imposing bastion of "British" culture. (There is no precedent for the scene in Charles Bennett's play.) The sequence follows the second *Blackmail* **Chase** and begins with a series of actual exterior shots in which Tracy the blackmailer (and wrongly suspected murderer) evades the police and slips through the museum's entrance gates. After a quick stop at one of the water fountains (still extant), Tracy enters the museum and the chase continues by means of the famous "Schüfftan process" (see Appendix II), in which photo transparencies of actual museum interiors were combined "in camera" with footage of the actors on the **Elstree** soundstage. Such subterfuge was necessary because of the difficulties in lighting the interiors of the museum itself. The sequence climaxes with the *relatively* innocent man falling to his death through the Reading Room dome, which, again, utilized a transparency of the actual dome combined with a ladder built at the studio. None of the contemporary reviewers seem to have noticed the tricks, although one did comment on Hitchcock's "mistake" in allowing Tracy to walk into the Reading Room without a reader's ticket. (You can certainly do so today.) The venerable institution is also mentioned near the beginning of *The 39 Steps*, when we learn that the stage performer "Mr. Memory" is leaving his brain to the British Museum. This prompts the raucous music hall audience to burst into applause and shout "Hooray, hooray!" Interestingly, Mr. Memory was based on a real-life music hall performer, Datas, the Memory Man, who had indeed willed his brain to science.

Stations: Russell Square (Pl) The museum is located on the opposite side of Russell Square from the station; or from **Tottenham Court Road (CE; NO)** take Exit 3 and go R into Tottenham Court Road and then R into Great Russell Street. The museum is ahead on the L. Tracy's view, looking west (toward Bloomsbury Street), is from opposite Coptic Street; the reverse angle is farther along, near the eastern end of the gate. The entrance hall, recently restored, appears much as it does in the film, as do the Egyptian Sculpture Gallery (ground floor, to the L) and the old Mummy Room (No. 61, above the Sculpture Gallery). Some of the exhibits in the Sculpture Gallery have been moved—Ramses II's Head, for example, is to the left of the frame in the film, but is now toward the rear of the gallery, in the center. The massive head that appears in the Schüfftan shot of Tracy climbing down the rope was not a "model," as some have claimed, but a full-sized cast of one of the heads—again, that of Ramses II—of the Abu Simbel Colossi in Egypt. These casts, originally displayed in the Sculpture Gallery, have since been removed to the Museum's storage facility and are no longer available for public viewing. The Reading Room (whose original book collection was transferred to the British Library in Euston Road) now constitutes the heart of the Queen Elizabeth II Great Court, which was opened on December 7, 2000 and represents the largest covered public square in Europe. **Hours:** Mon-Sat 10 am.-5 pm; Sun noon-6 pm.

The MacGuffin: There is, of course, no precedent for the giant head in the original play since the entire British Museum sequence was added for the film. One wonders, then, if Hitchcock was thinking of the passage from G.K. Chesterton's 1908 satire *The Man Who Was Thursday*, in which the hero, Mr. Syme, dreads his first encounter with the head of the anarchists' group for fear that the man's face may be too big. "He remembered that as a child he would not look at the mask of Memnon in the British Museum, because it was a face, and so large."

Ask Mr. Memory 5: How many new facts *does* Mr. Memory commit to memory every day?

4. CHELSEA

4:1
Royal Court Theatre (L)
Sloane Square, SW1

Opened in 1888, the Royal Court Theatre has introduced some of the most important plays of the 20th century, including works by Shaw, Ibsen, Yeats, Galsworthy, Osborne and Wesker. It is also notable for its association with the West Country novelist, poet and playwright Eden Phillpotts. Though the author of more than 250 works, Phillpotts is today remembered primarily for his quotability, the most often-repeated aphorism (from *A Shadow Passes*) being: "The universe

Royal Court Theatre

is full of magical things, patiently waiting for our wits to grow sharper." (My personal favorite [quoted in *Simple Truths* (1990)] is: "The people sensible enough to give good advice are usually sensible enough to give none.") For a three-year period in the 1920s, however, Phillpotts was one of the hottest properties in the London theatre world. His 1916 play *The Farmer's Wife* (adapted from his own novel of a few years earlier, *Wydecombe Fair*) opened here on March 11, 1924 and ran for an astonishing 1,329 performances. Among the cast was Birmingham Repertory player Cedric Hardwicke as handyman Churdles Ash. Hardwicke would be absent from the cast of Hitchcock's adaptation of *The Farmer's Wife*, although he would go on to appear in the director's American films *Suspicion* and *Rope*, both, perhaps not surprisingly, adapted from English sources (see Appendix I). (Interestingly, Charles Coburn, who would later appear in *The Paradine Case*, starred as Farmer Samuel Sweetland in the 1924 Broadway production of the play.) The cinematic Churdles was played by comic actor Gordon Harker, who had just made his film debut in *The Ring* (see **Wyndham's Theatre** for Hitchcock's discovery of Harker) and would go on to appear in *Champagne* and Hitchcock's segments of *Elstree Calling*. Cast members Maud Gill (as Thirza Tapper) and Olga Slade (as Mary Hearn) reprised their stage roles in the film, which was released in early 1928. Four years later, the theatre where the *Farmer's* phenomenon began was converted to a cinema, talking pictures having (temporarily) undone yet another of London's live performance venues (see the **London Palladium** for a further example). Bombed during the Blitz and rebuilt as a theatre in the 1950s, the Royal Court underwent a major—and mandatory—overhaul in the late 1990s. (Long famous for its creaky seats, frequent flooding and precarious structure, the theatre had failed 83 individual safety checks.) Reopened with great fanfare in February 2000, the new Royal Court now comprises the Jerwood Theatre Downstairs and the smaller, more intimate Jerwood Theatre Upstairs, both named after one of the benefactors of the restoration project.

Station: Sloane Square (CI: DI) Exit for the theatre, which is above the station.

4:2
Chelsea Police Station (L)
2 Lucan Place, SW3

According to Chapter 9 of *Man Running* (whence *Stage Fright*), Inspector Ordinary Smith works in the Chelsea Police Station and lives in nearby Sloane Avenue House. (In Hitchcock's adaptation, Smith is assigned to the **West End Central Police Station** in Savile Row and the location of his home is not disclosed.) Later in the novel, after his arrest at **Liverpool Street Station**, Jonathan Penrose (Cooper in the film) is held here for 24 hours before being shipped off to **Pentonville Prison**. *Blackmail* detective Harold Webber (Frank Webber in the film adaptation) also worked at the Chelsea Police Station, but at that time—the 1920s—the station was located at 385 King's Road, much closer to the primary settings of the play.

Station: South Kensington (CI; DI; PI) Take the Thurloe Street exit, turn L into Pelham Street and follow this to Fulham Road, where you will turn R then immediately L into Lucan Place. The station is at the end of the street, on the L.

Chelsea Police Station

4:3
"Ordinary Smith's Flat" L
Sloane Avenue House
Sloane Avenue, SW3

According to Chapter 7 of *Man Running*, Ordinary Smith lives in a "vast apartment block" called Sloane Avenue House, near the top of—what else?—Sloane Avenue. Eve Gill has followed Smith here from **Charlotte Inwood's Home** (see entries 15:13 and 22:6) and, as in the film adaptation *Stage Fright*, will eventually intercept the policeman in a neighborhood pub, the fictional "Four Feathers" (the actual local is the Blenheim in nearby Cale Street; for the cinematic setting, see **Shepherd's Tavern**). There is no evidence that Hitchcock ever intended to show Smith's flat, which in any case would have presumably been closer to his cinematic HQ in Savile Row (see **West End Central Police Station**). Nor is there any evidence that there was ever a Sloane Avenue House near the top of Sloane Avenue, although there certainly were and are two massive apartment blocks in the street—Chelsea Cloisters (built in the 1930s and famous for the call girls who serviced American GIs here during World War II) to the north and Cranmer Court to the south. Interestingly, policemen assigned to **Chelsea Police Station**, as Smith is in the novel, once called Lucan Place itself home, there being then a large apartment block set up especially for London's finest just across from the station.

Station: South Kensington (CI; DI; PI) Take the Thurloe Street exit, turn L into Pelham Street and follow this across Fulham Road into Sloane Avenue. Both apartment blocks are on the R.

A REFERENCE GUIDE TO LOCATIONS

4:4
Chelsea Old Town Hall (L)
King's Road, SW3

Famous for its fairs, festivals, functions and other public events, Chelsea Old Town Hall—the former headquarters of the borough council (local governing body)—was the setting for an important meeting prior to the events depicted in the play *Blackmail*. Here, at a dance, artist Peter Hewitt picked up young Alice Jarvis and escorted her back to his studio (see entry 4:6) just down the road. In Act I, he explains that he had first spotted Alice here, at another Town Hall affair, the previous October, then saw her again "at the Polytechnic fancy dress dance in March," and most recently at the Kensington Town Hall. In the film, the artist-stalker (now called Crewe) would meet his conquest in the **Lyons Corner House** between **Piccadilly Circus** and **Leicester Square**. The pick-up was based on a real-life event, which playwright Charles Bennett recalled had taken place here at the Chelsea Arts Ball.

Chelsea Old Town Hall

Station: South Kensington (CI; DI; PI) Take the Thurloe Street exit, cross (L) into Onslow Square and follow this (through Sydney Place) to Fulham Road, where you will turn R. Cross to the other side of the street and look for Sydney Street on the L; follow this to the end and turn L. The Old Town Hall will be just across the street.

4:5
"G. White Newsagents" F
227 King's Road, SW3

In the play *Blackmail*, the principal characters live, work and play in London's artsy Chelsea district. Hitchcock retained this setting for the homes of both Alice White and the artist, shifting her policeman boyfriend from **Chelsea Police Station** to the more glamorous **Scotland Yard** and the scene of their public row from **Chelsea Town Hall** to the **Lyon's Corner House** near **Piccadilly Circus**. (The

227 King's Road, the setting of the White family's news and tobacco shop in *Blackmail*.

latter change, of course, gives Alice a dramatically longer walk to the artist's flat than in the play.) In the play, the family's shop is "round the corner" from the King's Road (Act III), while the artist's studio is in the King's Road itself, opposite Carlyle Square (see the next entry). In the film, the family's news and tobacco shop is located at 227 King's Road (replicated on the **Elstree Studios** backlot), while the artist is now located "just round the corner" (see entry 4:7). In fact, there was no such shop at 227 in 1929 (the year of the film), nor was there even a 227. At 229 King's Road, however, there was Henry Kent Tobacconist, while next door to him, at 231, was the John Middleton Picture Frame Company. In fact, the block still contains a newsagent's, at No. 237.

Station: South Kensington (CI; DI; PI) Take the Thurloe Street exit, cross (L) into Onslow Square and follow this (through Sydney Place) to Fulham Road, where you will turn R. Cross to the other side of the street and look for Sydney Street on the L; follow this to the end and turn R. The 220 block is ahead on the L, between Glebe Place and Bramerton Street.

Ask Mr. Memory 6: What was located next to White's in the film?

4:6
"Peter Hewitt's Studio" L
King's Road, SW3 (opposite Carlyle Square)

According to the play *Blackmail*, artist Peter Hewitt lives on the first floor of a King's Road building overlooking Carlyle Square. Here he paints, occasionally entertains young ladies and, at the climax of the first act, actually dies from a knife wound inflicted by heroine Alice Jarvis (or so it first appears). In the film, Hitchcock relocated Alice herself (now surnamed White) to King's Road (see photo pg. 38) and the would-be rapist, now called Crewe, to what is apparently Sydney Street (see pg. 40). He also eliminated playwright Charles Bennett's cop-out revelation that the artist died of a heart attack, not the superficial wound Alice inflicted, and made the young woman the true killer.

Above is the location of Peter Hewitt's studio in *Blackmail* where he is killed by Alice (Anny Ondra), shown below.

Station: South Kensington (CI; DI; PI) Take the Thurloe Street exit, cross (L) into Onslow Square and follow this (through Sydney Place) to Fulham Road, where you will turn R. Cross to the other side of the street and look for Sydney Street on the L; follow this to the end and turn R. Carlyle Square is ahead on the R and the artist's studio would have been across the street, in the 240s or 250s. Carlyle Square itself was home to Dame Sybil Thorndike (*Stage Fright*) from 1921 to 1932, as an English Heritage Blue Plaque at No. 6 reminds us.

Crewe's Studio

4:7
"Crewe's Studio" F
31 Sydney Street, SW3

A fairly strong case can be made for locating the studio of *Blackmail* artist and attempted rapist Crewe here in Sydney Street. Recall that as they are en route to Alice's home (at 227 King's Road [see entry 4:5]), Crewe stops in front of a house and tells Alice that he lives there. She says that he needn't carry on, then, as she lives just round the corner. Now, assuming the pair have walked from the West End (see **Lyons Corner House**), the most direct route to Chelsea (avoiding the King's Road itself, which they have manifestly done) is down Piccadilly to **Hyde Park Corner**, then via Knightsbridge Road into Brompton Road. (You may want to pull out a London atlas at this point.) The latter road becomes Fulham Road in Chelsea itself and the first (and last) major turning to the King's Road *before* 227 (remember they are *en route* to her home) is Sydney Street. Following this down to the King's Road would have put them literally round the corner from 227. Note that streets such as Oakley or Old Church, which approach the King's Road on either side of 227 from the *south* (i.e., from Cheyne Walk, along the **Thames**), are excluded as possibilities if for no other reason than that after the artist's death, Alice walks back in the direction from which they had come—and this leads to the West End and Piccadilly, not to the Thames.

Station: South Kensington (CI; DI; PI) Take the Thurloe Street exit, cross (L) into Onslow Square and follow this (through Sydney Place) to Fulham Road, where you will turn R. Cross to the other side of the street and look for Sydney Street on the L. No. 31 is ahead on the R.

Ask Mr. Memory 7: What is the name of Mr. Crewe's landlady?

Carlyle Mansions, site of C.A. Swann's flat in *Dial M for Murder*

4:8
"C.A. Swann's Flat" (L) (F)
127 Carlyle Mansions
Cheyne Walk, SW3

Actually, according to the play *Dial M for Murder*, this was the flat of a Mrs. Moretti, whose late husband had left her "two hotels and a block of flats, furnished." As of the most recent July, August and September, however, the wealthy widow has been sharing her tony Chelsea flat with a certain Mr. Wilson, a.k.a. Lesgate, Adams and, oh yes, Swann. (Although the character is officially billed as "Lesgate" in both the play and film, I have referred to him as "Swann" throughout this book, which better accords with the actual dialogue.) The exchange in which we learn of Swann's latest conquest occurs almost word for word in the film, except that the widow is now Mrs. Van Dorn and the apartment building has been altered to "Carlyle Court." In fact, playwright Frederick Knott himself did a bit of altering—or perhaps he simply erred—for he actually spells the name "*Carlisle* Mansions," not *Carlyle*, in the original British version of the play. There can be no mistake, however, that it was Carlyle Mansions, overlooking Chelsea Embankment and the **Thames**, that Knott had in mind. The building was well known for its famous and well-to-do residents, including James Bond creator Ian Fleming, who lived here, on the top floor, from 1950 to 1953, the year after the play's London debut.

Station: Sloane Square (CI; VI) Cross Sloane Square, walk down the King's Road and turn L into Oakley Street. Follow this toward Albert Bridge, just before which, you will turn R into Cheyne Walk. The building is ahead on the R.

The MacGuffin: There are, in fact, two versions of the play *Dial M for Murder*, a British and an American, which differ slightly in the names of characters, places and other minor details. The film accords more closely with the American version, but in this book, all references, unless otherwise noted, are to the British version. The title of the play/film also exists in different forms. American versions of the play tend to render the title *Dial "M" for Murder*, while the British version omits the quotes around the *M* and capitalizes *for*. Studio documents and pressbooks also generally omit the quotation marks, but are inconsistent in the capitalization of *for*. Knott's final draft screenplay retains the quotes, but is no help with *for* since the entire title is typed in caps. The film itself abjures quotes and appears to capitalize *For* (as in the British version of the play). I have followed conventional usage among Hitchcock scholars and used *Dial M for Murder* throughout, for both the play and the film.

Hitchcock on the set of *Dial M for Murder*

5. THE CITY

5:1
ex **W.T. Henley Telegraph Works Co., Ltd. H**
14 Blomfield Street, EC2

Britain's premier manufacturer of electric cables and wiring accessories was founded by William T. Henley in 1837. Henley pioneered in the development of submarine telegraph cable, which was manufactured at the massive North Woolwich factory, along the Thames. Fifteen-year-old Alfred Hitchcock came to work in the firm's headquarters, just off London Wall, in 1915. He initially worked as an estimating clerk, but was subsequently transferred to the firm's advertising department. His artistic ambitions found an additional outlet through the firm's in-house publication, *The Henley*, for which Hitchcock

1935 photo of W.T. Henley Telegraph Works Co., Ltd.

contributed both designs and short stories, including the oft-reproduced "Gas." As secure as his job may have been (Henley had greatly prospered during the recent war), Hitchcock the artist obviously wanted an even greater outlet. So in the spring of 1920 he began working part-time as a title-card designer at **Islington Studios** in Hoxton. Within a year, the studio offered him full-time employment and 21-year-old Alfred Hitchcock quit his job at Henley for a career in show business. Henley itself moved to new premises at 11 Holborn Viaduct shortly after Hitchcock's departure; its former home was replaced by the present stone-faced building in 1928. In 1958, Henley's was acquired by Associated Electrical Industries (AEI)—now part of Marconi plc—which continues to operate the AEI Henley works in Gravesend, Kent.

Station: Liverpool Street (CE; CI; HC; ME) Exit into Old Broad Street, turn L, then turn R into New Broad Street and continue to Blomfield Street. Henley's was to the R, at the corner of Blomfield and New Broad Street.

5:2
Tower Bridge F
E1, SE1

London's most famous—and distinctive—bridge is surprisingly new (for London), having been completed in 1894. Yet this flamboyant Victorian Gothic marvel has become, along with **St. Paul's Cathedral**, **Trafalgar Square** and the **Houses of Parliament**, one of the most internationally recognizable symbols of the British capital. In *The Man Who Knew Too Much* (34), Hitchcock employed a dark, foreboding shot of the bridge from Wapping Pier to indicate the passage of the heroes from central London

Tower Bridge as seen in *The Man Who Knew Too Much.*

The Tower Bridge shot from the opening of *Frenzy*

to the wilds of Docklands. According to an early draft of the *Secret Agent* screenplay, Hitchcock intended to stage Brodie's meeting with "R" aboard a steamer that has just passed beneath Tower Bridge, en route to the Continent. In the end, the director staged their meeting in the **War Office** in Whitehall. Thirty-five years later Hitchcock would devote the entire opening title sequence of *Frenzy* to a continuous helicopter shot of the eastern approach to Tower Bridge, ending just as the camera zooms in under the lower span, which has been opened as if for a passing ship. Associate producer Bill Hill recalled that Hitchcock originally intended the helicopter shot to *begin* at Tower Bridge and continue upriver, over seven more bridges, until it reached **County Hall**, where the political speech would already be in progress. *That* shot was rehearsed on July 25, 1971 and photographed (in five takes) by aerial cameraman Peter Allworth on August 2, 1971. Unfortunately, owing to the distance between Tower Bridge and County Hall, the shot ran some nine minutes—three times as long as the intended title sequence. "Well, I know what we'll do," Hill recalls Hitchcock saying. "We'll come in from the east side, on to Tower Bridge and end on a tugboat belching out a cloud of black smoke." And on August 8 that is precisely what he did, with the tug provided by Grazeley & Knight, Isle of Dogs, and the black smoke effect (à la *Shadow of a Doubt*) provided by special effects director Derek Meddings. (Note that, because it is illegal to fly under the bridge, Allworth had to simulate the movement by zooming in on the boat.) Hitchcock, however, was still not satisfied and so on August 26 he restaged the *original* helicopter shot *from* Tower Bridge to County Hall, where he himself stood leaning against the parapet. Yet, for precisely the reason Hill mentioned (its length), the bulk of this shot was ultimately scrapped. *Frenzy* now opens with the August 8 *approach* to the bridge (ending on the cloud of smoke), from which there is a dissolve to the *end* of the August 26 helicopter shot, above County Hall, where Hitchcock makes the first of his *three* cameo appearances in the film. (See the entry on the County Hall for more about the cameos.) There is one final difference from the script to screen versions of this scene: Originally, a close shot of a London map, filmed on October 15, was to have preceded the title sequence. In the end, Hitchcock simply superimposed a City of London seal over the August 8 helicopter shot.

Station: Tower Hill (CI; DI) Follow the signs to the bridge, which is adjacent to the SE corner of the Tower of London. The towers, upper walkway and Bridge museum are open daily from 10 am to 6:30 pm (until 4:45 pm Nov-Mar).

The MacGuffin: Hitchcock did not fly in the helicopter for that August 8 shot, but he was definitely on the scene. In fact, he was *in the scene*: he and the crew were actually on the upper level of Tower Bridge itself, monitoring the helicopter's approach.

5:3
St. Paul's Cathedral F
Ludgate Hill, EC4

Built on the site of an ancient Roman temple, the first St. Paul's cathedral was dedicated by King Ethelbert of Kent in 604. A second St. Paul's was constructed in the 680s and yet another, a massive Norman structure, was begun in 1087. The latter, now known as Old St. Paul's, was due for extensive renovation when the Great Fire of 1666 completely destroyed it. Its replacement was designed by the Baroque genius Sir Christopher Wren, who saw the monumental undertaking through from the planning stages in 1671 to its completion in 1711. Its massive Renaissance dome has become one the most famous symbols of London, along with **Tower Bridge** and the **Houses of Parliament**, all three of which Hitchcock photographed on more than one occasion. Indeed, in *Foreign Correspondent* Hitchcock has Rowley mention the cathedral as one of the famous London sights that Johnny Jones should see from the top of **Westminster Cathedral**. Four years earlier, the director spotlighted St. Paul's, or at least a back-lit photographic cut-out of it, near the beginning of *Secret Agent*, immediately

St. Paul's Cathedral

before Brodie's meeting with "R" at the **War Office**. Searchlights on either side of the cathedral, as well as the sound of exploding bombs, indicate that an air raid is in progress. Although set in WWI and filmed in 1936, this shot ominously foreshadows the famous 1941 images of St. Paul's, defiant and unbowed, against the fiery backdrop of the London Blitz. Hitchcock actually exploited that very defiance in the two wartime shorts *Bon Voyage* and *Aventure Malgache*, both of which begin with a shot of St. Paul's Cathedral, the logo of the production company, Phoenix Films. The director confined St. Paul's to the background in two shots of the **Old Bailey** in *The Paradine Case*, but more fully showcased the cathedral three years later in *Stage Fright*. The latter opens with a theatre safety curtain slowly rising to reveal a magnificent high-angle shot of St. Paul's, surrounded by the bomb-blasted ruins of buildings destroyed during the Blitz. A car speeds toward us, along Watling Street, away from the cathedral; a subsequent two-shot (aided by a rear-projected image of the cathedral) introduces us to the film's heroine, Eve Gill, and to the film's villain, Jonathan Cooper. The stage is now set—literally—for that infamous flashback.

Station: St. Paul's (CE) Take the St. Paul's exit, turn to the L and walk back past the station entrance to the cathedral. Veer around to the R and out into Ludgate Hill for an approximation of the view in *Bon Voyage* and *Aventure Malgache*. For the *Stage Fright* view, go R out of the station into New Change, turn L into Watling Street and continue to Watling Court, just past Bread Street; turn around and voilà! The view will, of course, differ rather dramatically from that of the film since the war-era rubble has been replaced with the massive Bank of England Extension (to the R) and other buildings. **Open for sightseeing:** Mon-Sat 8:30 am-4 pm (admission charge).

Ask Mr. Memory 8: Which *Stage Fright* cast member doubled for Jane Wyman in the driving scenes here at St. Paul's?

5:4
ex **London Chief Post Office (F)**
King Edward Building
King Edward Street, EC1

London's Chief Post Office moved from nearby St. Martin's-le-Grande to the purpose-built King Edward Building in 1911, remaining here until the 1990s. It was here, in the Post Office Sorting Room, that Alfred Hitchcock envisioned a sequence for what proved to be his final film project, the unrealized *The Short Night*. What the director wanted to show was the route of a parcel being sent from the London flat of escaped traitor Gavin Brand (see entry 30:1) to his anxious family in Helsinki, Finland. In the published script, agent Joe Bailey, Brand's pursuer, spots the parcel and its "General Delivery" address in the flat of Brand's landlady, then, later, watches and waits to see who collects it from the Main Post Office in Helsinki. According to screenwriter David Freeman's published account, he and Hitchcock discussed showing "the parcel go through the British postal system—bouncing along a conveyor belt, having its stamps canceled, being put on an airplane, and ... [a]s the parcel moved along, it would get more beat [*sic*] up." Indeed, in May 1978, months before Freeman's involvement with the project, production designer Bob Boyle and long-time Hitchcock associate Hilton Green conducted a recce of the King Edward Building, as well as a number of other possible London locations. "As with all of Hitchcock's films," Boyle recalled, "we were going to do a minimum of location work [at the Post Office] to establish where we were and then the rest of it would be done in the studio." Freeman himself disparaged the post office idea because it would have slowed down the story, for which reason, presumably, it never made it to his final draft of the screenplay. Yet, properly executed, one could imagine a suspenseful, documentary-like montage, not unlike the news transmission sequence of *The Lodger* (see the **Evening Standard**), with Bailey and the audience wondering when and if the parcel will arrive, who will come to claim it, will they lead the hero to Brand….

Station: St. Paul's (CE) Take the St. Paul's exit and turn R into Newgate Street. Cross to King Edward Street, where you will see the Post Office to the L.

5:5
Central Criminal Court (The Old Bailey) F L
Old Bailey, EC4

Familiar from its countless appearances in films and television series, the Central Criminal Court occupies an imposing granite structure erected on the site of Newgate Prison in 1900-1907. (The first "Old Bailey Sessions House" had been built beside the prison in 1539.) As Britain's leading criminal court, the "Old Bailey" (so called from the street on which it stands; cf. **Scotland Yard**) serves not only Greater London but also portions of the neighboring counties of Essex, Kent and Surrey. It also served Alfred Hitchcock on many notable occasions, both personally and professionally. As a young man, Hitchcock followed many of the sensational trials here, even attending sessions as time permitted. (As an adult he once claimed that if he hadn't become a filmmaker he would have liked to be "a hanging judge.") Among the trials during this period were those of **Dr. Hawley Crippen**; **George Joseph Smith**, the "Brides in the Bath" killer (1915); and Thompson and Bywaters (1922). The latter is noteworthy because it inspired Selwyn Jepson's novel *Man Running*, as well as Hitchcock's adaptation,

The Old Bailey

A REFERENCE GUIDE TO LOCATIONS 47

Hitchcock returned to Court No. 1 for *Frenzy*.

Stage Fright. The principals were 29-year-old Edith Thompson, her 20-year-old lover, Freddy Bywaters, and her 32-year-old husband, Percy. Thompson was stabbed to death on the night of October 3, 1922. Edith and Freddy were arrested, tried for the murder at the **Old Bailey**, convicted and hanged—she at **Holloway Prison**, he at **Pentonville**. The case remains a cause celebre among death penalty opponents, who claim that the evidence against both was scant and that Edith was condemned more for her morals than murder. Jepson was apparently not among those who felt the woman was innocent—he gives her not one but two lovers and has her conspire with one lover (Freddy) to kill the husband and make it look like the other lover (Jonathan) actually did it. Hitchcock retained both lovers and the set-up of the younger man, but, truer to life, has the younger man kill the husband. Hitchcock once claimed (in a 1937 *Sight and Sound* essay) to have wanted to film the true story, presumably including its sensational trial, but obviously never got the chance. (Hitchcock actually knew the family of Edith Thompson, née Graydon, although, as biographer Patrick McGilligan notes, whether he knew Edith herself is unknown.)

Nevertheless, as a filmmaker, he did stage a number of important trials at the Old Bailey, beginning with *The Paradine Case* in 1947. That film actually opens with a shot of the famous Sword of Justice (presumably a replica) being hung on the wall of the courtroom. The sword dates from the 16th century and always hangs in Court No. 1, or in whichever court the senior judge is presiding. Contrary to popular myth, it is not made of gold or jewels and thus has no great monetary value. Hitchcock also includes several magnificent establishing shots of the building, its dome and figure of Justice, highlighting in two of them the bomb damage that had occurred on the night of May 10-11, 1941. The interior of Central Criminal Court No. 1, the setting for the trial in Robert Hichens' novel, was faithfully replicated on the Selznick Studios stages in Hollywood, at a cost of some $80,000. Described as "Hollywood's most authentic set," the faux Old Bailey took 85 days to construct, occupied 2,600 square feet and was accurate right down to the moldings on the walls and the scratches on the tables. (Hitchcock himself had actually attended a trial here in May 1946, making sketches that he would later pass along to the film's art director.) The only departure from the original came in the ceilings, where 250 yards of tightly stretched Chinese silk were used in place of glass panels, a concession undertaken to prevent reflected glare from studio lights. The elaborate recreation was actually vetted by the Keeper of the Old Bailey, Mr. Alfred William Burt, the first Corporation of London official to ever act as a film adviser. In addition to the costly replication, the Old Bailey sequence is also notable for the fact that Hitchcock employed four separate cameras to simultaneously record the examination and cross-examination of Latour, a fact duly commented upon at the time. For the first set-up, the cameras were trained on Keane, Latour, Horfield and Farrell (the prosecutor); for the second, when Keane grills Latour, Hitchcock repositioned the fourth camera to cover the reactions of Mrs. Paradine. Coverage of the attorneys was made easier by the fact that, as Hitchcock's July 8, 1946 research notes showed, during a trial British barristers never leave their seats, merely rising to their feet to address the jury and the witnesses. Unfortunately, this very fact also made for a somewhat "static" sequence, which Hitchcock attempted to compensate for through a montage style of cutting, but which producer David Selznick ultimately gutted in any case. (Hitchcock's rough cut ran nearly three hours; the final version runs two. For some of the missing bits, see **Lincoln's Inn** and **Bond Street**.)

A little over a decade later, Hitchcock planned a return to the Old Bailey, where he would film portions of Henry Cecil's 1952 novel *No Bail for the Judge*, which again included dramatic scenes set in Court No. 1. (See Appendix III for a synopsis of the story.) The year was 1959 and the stars were to be John Williams (*Dial M for Murder*, *To Catch a Thief*) as an esteemed judge accused of murdering a prostitute; Audrey Hepburn as his barrister daughter, determined to prove him innocent; and Laurence Harvey as the gentleman crook who comes to her aid. In the end, as related elsewhere, the project was abandoned and Hitchcock was denied his day in court. (He did, however, take another stab at Cecil when he directed "I Saw the Whole Thing," an adaptation of the writer's radio play—and subsequent novel—*Independent Witness*. In that story, set in England, defendant Michael Barnes is actually tried here at the Old Bailey, a setting switched to an unidentified courtroom in the Americanized TV adaptation.) Hitchcock finally returned to London—and to Criminal Court No. 1—in the summer of 1971, this time for *Frenzy*. Prior to researching this book, I had assumed that, as with *The Paradine Case*, Hitchcock's crew had replicated the interior on a studio soundstage. But as art director Bob Laing explained, "Oh, no, that was the whole point, you see, that we were shooting in the *actual* court room." Indeed, associate producer Bill Hill recalled that Hitchcock was one of the last directors—perhaps *the* last—actually allowed to film inside the famous criminal court. "It was quite incredible, really. The night we went along for the first recce we met the Keeper of the Old Bailey [Jack Gamble]. And when we went downstairs to look around, Hitchcock said, 'You've changed all this!' And the next morning the Keeper rang me up and said, 'He was absolutely right. I've got the plans right here.' You see, Hitchcock had remembered [the layout] from that earlier film." For the *Frenzy* shoot, Hitchcock rehearsed his cast and crew here on Saturday, August 7, 1971, then shot the sequence the following day, both inside and outside Court No. 1. The doors of the court were rigged with wires so that the special effects crew could control the speed with which they closed. The shot of Chief Inspector Oxford, seated at the table, recalling Blaney's outburst, was filmed at **Pinewood Studios**, as was the overhead shot of Blaney being locked in his cell and almost literally bouncing off the walls. In fact, the first take of the latter scene was spoiled when actor Jon Finch leaned against one of the walls and it wobbled. (Notice that the actor hits the rear wall rather delicately in the film itself.) The entire sequence lasts little more than a couple of minutes, far shorter than its counterpart in the La Bern novel, which also takes place in Court No. 1.

Hitchcock also invokes the criminal court in two of his 1950s films: directly, in *Stage Fright*, where the Commodore warns Eve that for helping Cooper she'll probably be tried at the Old Bailey and end up in **Holloway Prison**; and, indirectly, in *Dial M for Murder*, where, in a brief montage, Margot is tried and sentenced before a plain red background. (The play [Act 3, scene 1] explicitly states that this is the Old Bailey.) The court is also mentioned in another source play, Patrick Hamilton's *Rope*, the setting of which Hitchcock transposed from Mayfair to Manhattan. In Act II, the conversation has turned to the subject of murder and Leila (renamed Janet in the film) makes a comment about bringing assassins to justice by having them arrested. Rupert retorts that assassins may be brought to the Old Bailey, but they are seldom brought to justice. "Why, what's wrong with the Old Bailey?" Leila asks. "[I]ts blemish is single but ineradicable," Rupert explains. "It is human. Justice is not." A trace of this exchange occurs in the film when Janet asks Rupert if Brandon's description did her justice and Rupert retorts: "Do you deserve justice?"

Station: St. Paul's (CE) Take the St. Paul's exit, go L at the top of the stairs into Newgate Street and look for the Old Bailey ahead on the L. **Hours:** Mon-Fri, when Courts are in session, from 10:30 am-1 pm and 2 pm-4:30 pm

The MacGuffin: It is perhaps a shame that while everyone was vetting the Old Bailey sets for *The Paradine Case*, no one vetted the film's Defense Counsel. As Paul Bergman and Michael Asimow point out in *Reel Justice*, Sir Anthony Keane makes a number of critical blunders in the film, including ignoring his client's instructions, putting her on the stand (his cross-examination of Latour was sufficient to raise doubt in the jury's mind) and assuring her that they would win the case. In fairness to Hitchcock, all of the above originated in Robert Hichens' novel, for more on which, see Appendix I.

5:6
Blackfriars Bridge F
EC4

The present Blackfriars Bridge was constructed in the 1860s as a replacement for the original span of a century earlier. Queen Victoria, accompanied by her Scottish servant John Brown, officially opened the bridge in 1869; she was then so unpopular that some of the crowd actually hissed as she rode through the Strand. The bridge was widened—without incident—in 1907-10 and committed, ever so briefly, to film in 1936. Here, Hitchcock staged a brief shot of Stevie crossing the bridge during his suspenseful trip to **Piccadilly Circus Underground Station** in *Sabotage*. The westernmost of the two Blackfriars Railway Bridges is visible to Stevie's left, which means of course that he is heading *south*, away from Central London. For more on this circuitous route, see **Stevie's Final Journey**.

Station: Blackfriars (CI; DI) Take Exit 3 for Blackfriars Bridge (East side).

Blackfriars Bridge as seen in *Sabotage*

5:7
ex **Evening Standard F**
47 Shoe Lane, EC4

London's only surviving evening newspaper was established in 1827 and originally based here in Shoe Lane, just off world-famous Fleet Street. In 1926, Alfred Hitchcock incorporated shots of the Shoe Lane presses and delivery trucks for a montage sequence near the beginning of *The Lodger*. The sequence begins with the discovery of yet another "Avenger" victim—the seventh—on the **Embankment**, then continues as the event is literally transformed into news, from the wire service reporter who first phones in the story to the delivery of the "wet from the press" latest edition of the *Evening Standard*. (A major concern of the novel was the power of the press, both as it affected the work of the police and the everyday workings of the family.) Sandwiched in amongst the location footage (which included a ride down Shoe Lane itself) and the studio shots was none other than Hitchcock himself, who appears on the telephone, with his back to the camera. Thus was born the tradition of the Hitchcock cameo, although these would be sporadic throughout his English years. The *Evening Standard* is today based at Northcliffe House, 2 Derry Street, W8.

Station: Blackfriars (CI; DI) Exit into New Bridge Street and continue N to Fleet Street, where you will turn L. The site is today occupied by the Deco-style *Daily Express* building, which was built in 1932.

Ask Mr. Memory 9: Hitchcock never forgot an old friend—or firm. In which film(s) does a character buy a copy of the *Evening Standard*?

5:8
London Bridge F
EC4

London Bridge

The first and most famous name in London bridges was already ancient when King Ethelred burnt it down in 1014 to divide the Danish forces. Subsequent wooden structures were also burnt down or swept away, so a stone structure was finally constructed toward the close of the 12th century. The stone bridge was soon overrun with wooden houses—some as high as seven stories—which explains why the fire that engulfed the bridge in 1212 claimed some 3,000 lives. Apart from fires and famous crossings (e.g., Charles II's return to London at the Restoration of 1660), London Bridge was also famous for its displays of traitors' heads on the portico above the gatehouse, a tradition that began with the display of William (Braveheart) Wallace's detached dome in 1305. The heads were removed in 1661, the houses a century later and the bridge itself in 1831. A new London Bridge was built just upstream between 1823 and 1831 and it was this five-span stone structure that Hitchcock photographed (in a marvelous panning shot) to mark Roddy's return to the "civilized" world in *Downhill*. The present London Bridge, a three-span pre-stressed concrete structure, was begun in 1967 and officially opened in 1973. Hitchcock's London Bridge (really architect Sir John Rennie's) now stands, in of all places, Lake Havasu City, Arizona.

Station: Monument (CI; DI) Exit for King William Street (South) and London Bridge; the bridge is just below the station. The shot appears to have been taken from just over halfway across the (old) bridge.

5:9
"Lake, Pelham & Co." L
Cornhill, EC3

According to the opening of Anthony Armstrong's story "The Case of Mr. Pelham," the title character works in an office "halfway along Cornhill," presumably in the vicinity of Birchin Lane. Here, he is accosted by a friend who claims to have seen him at the **London Hippodrome** the night before, when, in fact, Mr. Pelham was at home in his Maida Vale flat (see 13:4). In the Americanized television adaptation, the name of the company is changed to "Albert Pelham Investments," and while the meeting itself is mentioned, the name of the street is not. Also mentioned in the short story is nearby Lombard Street, the City's traditional banking center, where Pelham is alleged to have snubbed another acquaintance, James Mason (renamed Tom Mason in the episode). The TV version of the snubbing itself is said to have occurred "right out here at the corner," near the gentlemen's club.

Station: Bank (CE; CI; DI; NO; WC; DL) Exit for Cornhill.

5:10
Lloyd's of London (F) (L)
1 Lime Street, EC3

The most famous "insurance company" in the world originated in Edward Lloyd's Tower Street coffeehouse in 1688. In fact, Lloyd's is not an insurance company in the traditional sense, but rather an insurance *market*—a group of some 150 companies and wealthy individuals (known as the "Names") who accept risks for personal profit or loss, being liable to the full extent of their individual assets. Early on, the society specialized in the provision of marine insurance, as well as providing reliable shipping news to ship owners, ship's captains, and merchants. Thus, in *Jamaica Inn*, it is Lloyd's who alert the **Home Office** to the suspicious wrecks along the Cornwall coast, thereby prompting the government to dispatch James Trehearne to investigate; and in the novel *Rebecca*, it is a Lloyd's agent who comes to investigate the ship that ran aground near the cove where the title character was killed. It is also Lloyd's (specifically, R. Bellason & Co. [Foreign] Limited, Park House, Wardour Street, W1) who dispatch Hughson to the French Riviera to watch over all those precious jewels in *To Catch a Thief*. (In the novel, the Hughson character is called Paige and the "large London insurance company" is never named.) Finally, in *The Short Night*, Joe Bailey poses as an insurance agent during his visit to Gavin Brand's London flat (see 30:1), telling the **Scotland Yard** inspector that his American company "has an arrangement with Lloyd's." For much of the 18th and 19th centuries, Lloyd's was based in the Royal Exchange (across from the Bank of England), a building it would have occupied during the time of *Jamaica Inn* (see "The MacGuffin," below). In 1928, a purpose-built headquarters was completed on the present site, the only vestige of which is the old entrance in Leadenhall Street. The next move, in 1958, was to an even larger building next door, although by 1977 this, too, was deemed inadequate. The present high-tech HQ, which officially opened in 1986, was designed by Richard Rogers and Partners.

Lloyd's of London

Station: Bank (CE; CI; DI; NO; WC; DL) Follow Cornhill past Gracechurch Street and into Leadenhall Street. Turn R into Lime Street and look for the biggest thing around.

The MacGuffin: Early in the film *Jamaica Inn*, Sir Humphrey refers to "His brand new Majesty George IV," which would make the year 1820. Later, one of the wreckers at the inn says that it's been four years since he was with Annie in Penzance, which, according to his tattoo, was 1815. This discrepancy—1819 vs. 1820—may be resolved if we take Joss at his word about his "poor lads": they really "can't read nor reckon"!

5:11

**Leadenhall Market F
Gracechurch Street, EC2**

Poulterers have been selling their wares in Leadenhall Market since at least 1377. The venue then was the grounds of a mansion with a lead roof (the "leaden hall"); later, permanent market buildings were erected and provision was made to sell meat, vegetable, fish and dairy products as well. From the 17th to the 19th centuries, the market centered upon three large courtyards, which Dickens alludes to in *Nicholas Nickleby*. In 1881, the present buildings were constructed, and it would have been to these that a certain Major Cooke-Finch journeyed in October 1903. You may recall that in "Banquo's Chair," Mr. Stone comments on the "beautiful birds" that the major's dinner guests are about to devour. Major Cooke-Finch explains: "I was lucky last week. I bagged a brace of partridge and two pheasant—at Leadenhall Market!"

Station: Bank (CE; CI; DI; NO; WC; DL) Follow Cornhill to Gracechurch Street, where you will turn R; the Market is ahead to the L.

Leadenhall Market

5:12

**Liverpool Street Station L
Liverpool Street and Bishopsgate, EC2**

Opened in 1874 (and beneficiary of a £150 million refurbishment in the 1990s), Liverpool Street remains one of London's busiest railway stations, handling some 72 million passengers a year. It was here, according to Chapter 19 of *Man Running*, that Jonathan Penrose was arrested in connection with the murder of Charlotte Inwood's husband, Joseph. In fact, his friend Eve Gill had told the police when and where to apprehend Jonathan in hopes of saving him

Liverpool Street Station

from Charlotte and Freddy Williams, the real murderer. (In Hitchcock's adaptation, *Stage Fright*, Eve's friend, now surnamed Cooper, *really is* Inwood's murderer.) It was also here, according to Chapter 4 of *Goodbye Piccadilly, Farewell Leicester Square*, that Richard Blamey [*sic*] came for a bath and a shave after spending the night in the **Salvation Army Hostel**. The time is just after 5:00 a.m. and apart from the newspaper vendor setting up outside the station, "Bishopsgate was almost deserted." Blamey is relieved to find that the men's room is actually open at that hour, "most public authorities being of the opinion that recourse to such conveniences should not be necessary before eight or nine o'clock in the morning or after eleven at night." Once inside, Blamey is cynically amused by the "Beware of Pickpockets" sign therein: an RAF friend once told him that such signs prompt people to immediately feel for their wallets, thus tipping off the lurking thieves as to precisely which pockets to pick. Hitchcock apparently liked the scene, for his *Frenzy* location list of January 4, 1971, mentions Liverpool Street Station as one of the film's exteriors. At that point, *Frenzy* the film would have differed little from the La Bern novel. By spring, however, Hitchcock and screenwriter Anthony Shaffer had undertaken a number of important changes, notably, the switch from the original **Leicester Square** setting to Covent Garden, which plays a less prominent role in the novel, and the change in Blamey's age from pushing 50 to barely 30. In fact, Hitchcock had considered even younger actors for the role: Michael York, then 29, and Timothy Dalton, then 25. Finch himself was originally interviewed for the part of Bob Rusk. For other "lost" *Frenzy* locations see **Charing Cross Station**, **HM Prison Brixton** and the **RAF Club**.

Station: Liverpool Street (CE; CI; HC; ME) Exit into Liverpool Street; the Railway Station is across the street.

Ask Mr. Memory 10: A London railway station *is* mentioned in the film *Frenzy*. Which one?

6. COVENT GARDEN

6:1

Bow Street Magistrates' Court and *ex* Police Station   C F L
28 Bow Street, WC2

The original Bow Street magistrates' court was established on the western side of Bow Street, at No. 4, in 1740. The Chief Magistrate, or Justice of the Peace, was a lay official who earned money from the fines he imposed—a system all too easily abused. In 1848, novelist Henry Fielding (of *Tom Jones* fame) was appointed Westminster Chief Magistrate and he vowed to clean up the corruption. Among his reforms was the creation of a band of paid, professional "Thief-takers," who patrolled the streets by day and night in search of a notorious gang of local robbers. The Thief-takers were popularly known as "Robin Redbreasts," from their scarlet waistcoats (vests), but today London's first true policemen are more famous as the "Bow Street Runners." For the better part of a century, these two disparate judicial functions—apprehending *and* trying crimi-

Bow Street Magistrates' Court/Police Station

nals—were combined under a single roof here in London's principal magistrates' office. Then in 1829, Parliament created the Metropolitan Police Force (a.k.a. **Scotland Yard**), which, in turn, absorbed the Bow Street patrol into its own nearby Divisional Station, the original F Division (Covent Garden), in 1839. (Interestingly, the Met did not absorb the City of London Police Force, which to this day remains a separate organization.) Stripped of its policing duties, the Bow Street Office became an ordinary stipendiary magistrates' court (i.e., one with a paid, professional magistrate), covering a district of its own like any other. In 1881, the magistrates' court was reunited geographically, if not judicially, with the police station as both took up residence in a new, purpose-built headquarters on the eastern side of the street, opposite the Royal Opera. The new facility maintained its reputation as the premier magistrates' court in London and is today perhaps best remembered as the site where Oscar Wilde was charged and imprisoned in 1895. (Gay rights advocates commemorate it for this reason.) During preproduction of *The Paradine Case*, in April 1946, Alfred Hitchcock conducted a recce of the famous police station, whose charge room his art department would ultimately reproduce at the Selznick Studio in Hollywood. Here, in accordance with Robert Hichens' novel, the title character would be officially charged in the presence of her avuncular solicitor, Sir Simon Flaquer. In the finished film, there is also a shot of the building's exterior, which was filmed on location by the second unit. (A portion of the façade was also built in the studio for closer shots.) Interestingly, Hitchcock's schedule for the second unit (dated May 18, 1946) also specified a shot of the station exterior that included a crowd of extras and doubles for actors Gregory Peck and Charles Coburn. Apparently at that point, Keane himself was to have visited Bow Street, although nothing in the shooting script nor the film itself suggests such a scene.

In 1959, Hitchcock planned an even more elaborate sequence here in Bow Street, for a pivotal sequence in *No Bail for the Judge*. On trial for receiving funds from prostitutes is hero Anthony Low, whose elaborate scheme to prove the title character innocent has backfired rather dramatically (see Appendix III). The establishing shot was to have been from the top of the street shooting down toward the Strand, with the court itself on the left and the **Royal Opera House** on the right. Later, after Low has managed to get the charges dropped (in what would have been a wonderfully comic scene of confused witnesses, angry pimps and frustrated legal types), he joins the judge's daughter, Elizabeth, in the nearby Covent Garden **Central Market**, where she has overheard a conversation between the real killer and one of his prostitutes. Her route from the court, down Bow Street and into the market, precisely anticipates that eventually taken by *Frenzy* hero Dick Blaney from the **Globe**, down **Russell Street** to Bob Rusk's stall. (See **Shepherd Market** for another *No Bail* bit that would eventually find a home in *Frenzy*.) Sadly, Hitchcock's plans to film in and around Bow Street were thwarted when star Audrey Hepburn dropped out and the production was cancelled. Still, he managed a return of sorts in 1972, when Dick Blaney was brought to the CID room of the Bow Street police station (which was closed in 1992) after his arrest in **Bob Rusk's Flat**. Although not mentioned in the film itself, the station is specifically named in the Arthur La Bern novel, the shooting script and production documents. The brief scene was shot at **Pinewood Studios** and involved no location work.

Second unit shot from *The Paradine Case*

Station: Covent Garden (Pl) Exit for the Royal Opera House in Bow Street; the court is on the eastern side of the street, directly opposite Floral Street. The original court/station, at No. 4, was demolished in 1887 and replaced by a warehouse.

6:2
Royal Opera House H F
Bow Street, WC2

London's world famous opera house was built in 1858—the third on this site—and greatly expanded in the 1980s and '90s (see **Russell Street**). Given its location, the opera house is popularly, if confusingly, known as Covent Garden. This confusion is exploited in *Elstree Calling*, the 1930 "cine-radio revue" to which Hitchcock contributed "sketches and other interpolated items." Overall direction of the film is credited

Royal Opera House

A REFERENCE GUIDE TO LOCATIONS

onscreen to Adrian Brunel, so precisely which bits are Hitchcock's has long been debated. (The director himself generally refused to elaborate upon his involvement, as, for example, when he responded to Truffaut's statement that "you did one or two sequences in a musical picture," with a scarcely audible: "Not much.") *English Hitchcock* author Charles Barr attributes to Hitchcock those sequences and running gags that feature members of the director's informal Elstree "company" (John Longden, Donald Calthrop, Jameson Thomas, Hannah Jones and Gordon Harker). I would go further and include the comedy sequences featuring radio star Tommy Handley as the show's compère. Not only are his bits of a piece with other running gags, but they also contain references to several London locations with Hitchcock associations. Thus, Handley uses a weather report fresh from the **Air Ministry** as a set-up for a gag ("There is a deep depression traveling from the North, and my mother-in-law arrives here tonight"), foreshadowing a similar use of the ministry's report in *Rich and Strange*. He then segues to the following: "I understand that Mr. Jack Hurlbert of the **Adelphi Theatre** is of the opinion that we ought to have a little opera in this revue....And he has collected three friends from Covent Garden. He doesn't say whether it's the opera or the market." The latter, of course, was a familiar landmark from Hitchcock's childhood and would provide an important setting for *Frenzy* some 40 years later (see the **Central Market**, below). As for the Royal Opera, Hitchcock not only attended performances here, but also planned to incorporate its exterior in the proposed 1959 film *No Bail for the Judge* (see Appendix III). First, the opera house would have appeared in an establishing shot of Bow Street looking down toward the Strand (see **Bow Street Magistrates' Court**, above), then as the backdrop for heroine Elizabeth Proud's walk from the court to the Central Market itself. Unfortunately, the only time the director was able to work this magnificent building into a film was when Dick Blaney bought a copy of the *Evening Standard* near the beginning of *Frenzy*.

Station: Covent Garden (PI) Exit for the Royal Opera House.

6:3
The Globe F
37 Bow Street, WC2

Exteriors of the principal *Frenzy* pub (where Babs, Dick and Forsythe work—or worked, in Blaney's case) were filmed here at No. 37 Bow Street, a site occupied by public houses since at least the 17th century. The pub's interiors, as with **Nell of Old**

The Globe pub was used as a location in *Frenzy*.

Anna Massey as Babs and Jon Finch as Richard Blaney, after Richard has been fired from the pub in *Frenzy*.

Drury, were filmed on D Stage at **Pinewood Studios**. Interestingly, production notes continued to refer to this pub as "The Spotted Wonder" (its name in the Arthur La Bern novel) until shortly before the start of principal photography in July 1971, when the name was finally changed to reflect that of the actual location.

Station: Covent Garden (PI) Exit for the Royal Opera House (visible in the film) and look for the Globe catty-cornered across Bow Street.

Ask Mr. Memory 11: Who owns the Globe?

Russell Street

6:4
Russell Street F
WC2

    Near the beginning of *Frenzy*, a newly sacked Dick Blaney exits **The Globe** into Bow Street and then stops to buy an ***Evening Standard*** at the northeast corner of Bow and Russell Streets. (Note the majestic **Royal Opera House** in the background.) As he walks out of the frame, we cut to a high-angle shot that pans Blaney across Bow Street, down Russell Street and into the Covent Garden Piazza. This extreme long shot, taken from the roof of the building at 49 Wellington Street (on the southwest corner of the intersection), was the very first set-up of the first day of principal photography, Monday, July 26, 1971. (Hitchcock had actually suffered a fall and minor back injury on the previous Friday, but after a weekend of bed rest at **Claridge's** was able to assume his directorial duties first thing Monday morning.) Associate producer Bill Hill recalls that first day in Covent Garden: "I was driving into London very early [to be on the set by 7:00 a.m.] and on the radio I heard someone saying, 'If you are in London or going to London today will you please avoid Covent Garden because Alfred Hitchcock is starting his new movie there today.' So, naturally, when we got there, we couldn't move! And Mr. Hitchcock was sitting in his car [a Rolls Silver Shadow], waiting for me, and I remember walking up to him and saying, 'Mr. Hitchcock, until you get out of your car and walk across to the camera and everybody shouts and screams and takes a photograph, we're not going to [be able to] start the film.' And so he did it. Then I said [to the crowd], 'There you are, that's it.' And once they'd seen him, and taken their 'happy snaps,' they all walked away and we got on with making the film. And that was the very first morning!" Simultaneous with the high-angle shot from Russell Street, Hitchcock had a second roof-top camera (on the Jubilee Market Hall) covering Blaney as he crosses Russell Street, enters the Piazza and continues around past the lorries. This movement is in fact missing from the finished film, which cuts directly from the first high-angle shot to a ground-level shot of Blaney approaching Rusk's shop in the **Central Market Building**. Sadly, the north side of Russell Street (the side visible in the film) looks completely different today, the 18th-century coffee houses having been demolished to make way for the **Royal Opera**'s expanded—and controversial—Floral Hall complex.

Station: Covent Garden (PI) Exit for the Royal Opera House, walk down Bow Street and turn R into Russell Street. Look for the tower at the SW corner of the intersection.

Central Market Building

6:5
Central Market Building F
Covent Garden Piazza, WC2

"This is the famous London wholesale fruit and vegetable market, Covent Garden. Here you may buy the fruits of evil and the horrors of vegetables..." So begins Alfred Hitchcock's personal introduction to the market in the trailer for *Frenzy*, the first film he had shot in London in over 15 years. Hitchcock, of course, knew Covent Garden well (his father had been a greengrocer), so it's no surprise that he chose to shift the focus of Arthur La Bern's novel *Goodbye Piccadilly, Farewell Leicester Square* to this traditional London setting. Thus, whereas La Bern's Bob Rusk is a professional gambler who lives in Endell Street, Covent Garden, but works and socializes in the novel's title locations, Hitchcock's serial killer is a wholesale fruiterer who both lives and works in Covent Garden. Rusk's shop—Hartlett's (in real life managed by a Mr. Donovan)—was located in the southern colonnade of the distinctive Central Market Building, to which thousands of tons of fresh produce were delivered daily and from which that same produce was then distributed to retailers and other suppliers throughout southeastern England. Our first view of the bustling market occurs as Dick Blaney strolls down Russell Street and through the throng of tradesmen, many of whom were actual Covent Garden porters, employed by the wholesalers to transport and load the produce onto waiting trucks. Associate producer Bill Hill explained that "The porters work in a very exacting way, pushing trolleys, lifting heavy sacks of potatoes and vegetables and God knows what. They are masters at the way they handle everything....Our crowd [the extras] couldn't do what the porters do without days of training," which is why Hitchcock struck a deal with the porters' union to include a number of its members in the film. Hill also confirmed that Hitchcock was indeed as happy as he appears in photos taken during the Covent Garden shoot. "There's no question about it. Everything went very, very smoothly. Everybody had a great respect for him and he was very pleasant, with a *great* sense of humor. Everybody in front of and behind the camera was very relaxed, but doing their jobs, doing exactly what he said. We all learned very early that you don't change anything he says. If that's what he wants, that's what he's going to get." One of the things the director wanted was a portion of Hartlett's stall replicated at the studio, for the scene in which Rusk and Forsythe discuss Babs' body, and for the scene immediately following this, in which Blaney, now on the lam after Babs' murder, seeks Rusk's help in hiding from the police. (Prior to researching this book, I had always assumed that the Rusk-Forsythe exchange was filmed on location. However, if you compare the look, especially the lighting, of this scene—shot in the studio—with the subsequent shot of Rusk carrying Dick's bag out of the shop—shot on location—you'll notice the difference.) Another of the things Hitchcock wanted was a high-angle night shot of the market building as Rusk wheels Babs' body across Henrietta Street (see entry 6:7) and over to one of the potato trucks. This was actually done as a matte shot (more specifically, as a "glass shot") at the studio. The reason for this, as Hitchcock explained to Peter Bogdanovich, was that "to light that area would have been impossible." Thus, at the bottom of the frame, a double

Hitchcock at the Covent Garden location

for actor Barry Foster pushes a cart across a parking lot at the studio, while the top half of the frame comprises a matte painting by artist Albert Whitlock. The beauty of such shots, as Hitchcock told Bogdanovich, "is that you can become God." (There is one other glass shot in *Frenzy*, for which, see **Wormwood Scrubs**). Sadly, Covent Garden is today a shell of its former self: the entire market moved to a much larger facility in Nine Elms Lane, Battersea, in November 1974; the buildings on the northeast side of the Piazza have been demolished to make way for the expanded Floral Hall (see also **Russell Street**); and the Flower Market has been converted into London's Transport Museum. The Central Market Building is now a—ho, hum—shopping and entertainment complex, but the good news is: the southeastern lodge, where Hartlett's was based, and the southwestern lodge, near which Rusk deposited Babs' body, are still intact.

Station: Covent Garden (Pl) Exit to the R into James Street and walk into the Piazza, where you will see the old Market Building. Turn L, then follow the building around to the R. Hartlett's—Rusk's stall—was located in the southeast corner of the building, opposite the Jubilee Hall. It is now Mullin's of Covent Garden.

Ask Mr. Memory 12: When Rusk gives Blaney the box of grapes near the beginning of *Frenzy*, he relates an apposite quote of his mother's. What is it?

6:6
St. Paul, Covent Garden F
Covent Garden, WC2

Built in the 1630s for Francis Russell, 4th Earl of Bedford, St. Paul's Church is popularly known as the Inigo Jones Church, after its famous architect. According to Horace Walpole, the cost-conscious Earl told Jones, "I would not have it much better than a barn," to which Jones famously replied, "Well then, you shall have the handsomest barn in England." The handsome barn's Tuscan portico, facing east onto the Piazza, looks like the main entrance, but isn't. Though originally intended as just that, with the altar located on the western side, a last-minute switch was mandated by the Bishop of London. It seems that altars must always be on the eastern side, entrances on the western. Main entrance or not, the portico has had its uses: Shaw set the opening scene of *Pygmalion* here, when the locals take shelter from the rain and Eliza Doolittle makes an important acquaintance (a scene replicated in the film version, *My Fair Lady*). For *Frenzy*, Alfred Hitchcock determined to incorporate St. Paul's into the Covent Garden scenes, and this he did on two occasions. The church first appears, frame left, in an establishing shot preceding the scene in which Rusk and

St. Paul, Covent Garden

Forsythe discuss the identification of Babs' body (see 6:5). Its second appearance follows the scene in which Blaney is arrested in **Rusk's Flat (1)** and driven off in a police car. Here, on that famous portico, Hitchcock staged the brief exchange in which the police sergeant thanks Rusk for his help in apprehending Blaney. "Anything to oblige, Sarge," says Rusk. "No reward, I'm afraid," adds the policeman. "Well, you know what they say, Sarge. Virtue is its own reward." Rusk is about to speak again when he glances across the street (to his unseen flat), seems to recall something unpleasant, and abruptly takes leave of the sergeant. The church thus provides a suggestive contrast to the murder scene a few yards away, not to mention an ironic setting for the revelation of a friend's betrayal.

Station: Covent Garden (PI) Exit to the R into James Street and walk into the Piazza, where you will turn R; the church is ahead, past the **Central Market Building**. Among the many theatrical personalities commemorated here is none other than Ivor Novello, the matinee idol who appeared in two of Hitchcock's silent films.

6:7
"Bob Rusk's Flat" (1) F
3 Henrietta Street, WC2

Located above the publishers Duckworth & Company, Ltd., the flat occupied by *Frenzy* serial killer Bob Rusk appears in one of the most famous shots in Hitchcock's oeuvre: a slow reverse tracking movement from the door of Rusk's flat (where Babs is about to become the strangler's latest victim), back down the quiet stairs, through the entrance of the building and out into the noisy, bustling street. We know what's going to happen—we've seen it before, and not just in *Frenzy*, but as far back as *The Lodger*. And we are helpless to do anything about it, helpless to resist the inexorable (and inevitable) withdrawal into the ordinary, everyday world outside. Interestingly, the inspiration for this movement from private to public space may be found in Arthur La Bern's novel *Goodbye Piccadilly, Farewell Leicester Square*, although not in connection with Babs' murder, which otherwise proceeds much as in the film. Rather,

Bob Rusk's flat in *Frenzy*

when Rusk—still only identified as "the man"—threatens Brenda in her **Leicester Square** office, the author takes great pains to link the chamber of horrors inside with the ordinary, everyday world outside. He reminds us that the music on Brenda's radio was so loud that it "obliterat[ed] even the traffic sounds from Leicester Square" and that Brenda "knew that the sound of her voice could not have penetrated through the outer office." Then, as Rusk begins his assault she thinks that "[i]t can't happen to me. It can't happen in the centre of London in the middle of the day." Later, when Brenda begins her prayer, La Bern informs us that "[i]n Leicester Square, the linkman outside the Odeon was calling: 'Seats in all parts'" and, later still, that "an ice-cream salesman was attracting customers to his van by playing on a miniature xylophone." (For the cinematic version of this scene, see **Blaney Bureau**.) Finally, having raped, killed and robbed Brenda, the man "went down the stairs, closing the front door behind him and strolling casually towards a small cinema where ice-cream licking adults were queueing in the hot sunshine for an X-certificate film, the men with jackets over their arms, braces [suspenders] showing; the women plucking at their shoulder straps. The man walking across the Square was eating a piece of wedding cake." (Eating, attempting to eat, refusing to eat or being unable to eat, the need to satisfy [or deny] appetites of one kind or another—all these are as much a preoccupation of the novel as of the film.) Of course, Hitchcock's prying camera had been leading us from public exteriors to private interiors for years (cf. the openings of *Blackmail, Shadow of a Doubt, Rope, Psycho*), but this time the movement was reversed (similar to a shot in *Mr. and Mrs. Smith*, of all films). The result not only provided *Frenzy* with perhaps its single most memorable sequence, but also achieved the perfect visual and emotional realization of La Bern's theme. Canny fans have long noted that Hitchcock actually accomplished the movement through two separate shots: one from inside the building—actually a **Pinewood Studios** set—and another from across Henrietta Street, the join being camouflaged by a man carrying a sack of potatoes past the camera. But this "trick" in no way detracts from either the impact of the sequence itself, nor from our appreciation of both the author and the auteur at their finest. Canny fans have also long noted Hitchcock's fondness for stairs, which appear more or less dramatically in the majority of his films. In fact, a *Frenzy* preproduction document of January 5, 1971 lists 10 "Possible Locations [for] Stairs," including the interiors of the pub, the marriage bureau, the Bayswater hotel, the **Old Bailey**, the prison hospital and, of course, Rusk's flat, all of which the director managed to incorporate into the finished film. As Hitchcock told Charles Thomas Samuels, "Staircases are very photogenic."

An unsuspecting Babs with serial killer Robert Rusk (Barry Foster) in *Frenzy*

Station: Covent Garden (Pl) Go R to the Market Building, where you will turn R and walk around the western side, to the SW corner and look for No. 3 catty-cornered across Henrietta Street. The directors of the publishing company, whose nameplate is clearly shown beside the door in several shots of this late 18th-century building, were apparently delighted to have their office appear as "the scene of the crime." They were not as delighted with the building itself, however, for they moved to 61 Frith Street, Soho, shortly thereafter. Interestingly, among the writers Duckworth had published was John Galsworthy, whose play *The Skin Game* Hitchcock filmed in 1931. Following Duckworth to No. 3 in 1972 was the book distributor Eurospan, who remain here to this day. The company specializes in scholarly and academic books and among the titles they distribute in Europe are several Hitchcock ones, including the Da Capo reprint of *The Dark Side of Genius* by Donald Spoto. In that very book, incidentally, Mr. Spoto offers another Hitchcock/Henrietta Street connection by way of author Clemence Dane, co-author (with Helen Simpson) of *Enter Sir John* (whence *Murder!*). Spoto (apparently quoting Hitchcock himself) claims that Miss Dane lived right here at No. 3, when, in fact, she maintained a flat in nearby Tavistock Street from the 1920s through the 1950s, her first and only residence in Covent Garden.

The MacGuffin: Also scripted (and shot at least in part) was an additional scene here at No. 3 Henrietta Street, in which a disheveled young girl runs out of the flat, closely followed by Rusk. A policeman happens to be on hand and Rusk coolly explains that he had just undone his tie when "the bloody little fool" bolted. The policeman laughs and suggests that, given the climate, Rusk should switch to "polo necked sweaters." Rusk agrees and the two men bid each other good night. This scene was to have punctuated the **Coburg Hotel** sequence, coming between Blaney sending his clothes off to the cleaners and Babs' trip to the loo.

6:8
ex Flower Market Building F
Covent Garden, WC2

Opened in 1872, the Flower Market provided the first permanent home for Covent Garden's bustling trade in flowers and plants. Nearly a century later, Alfred Hitchcock tracked his camera from one end of the building's interior to the other, as Bob Rusk led Babs from **The Globe** public house, down the garden path to his cozy bachelor pad in Henrietta Street (see 6:7). The 75-second sequence was done in one take on July 30, 1971. Three years later, the Flower Market relocated to New Covent Garden, Nine Elms, Battersea. Its refurbished former premises now house London's Transport Museum above and the National Theatre Museum below.

Station: Covent Garden (Pl) Go R to the Market Building, where you will turn L and walk around the eastern side, to the SE corner of the Piazza, where you will see the former Market Building.

Ask Mr. Memory 13: Where does Rusk suggest that Babs should travel?

Above: Flower Market Building
Below: Babs and Rusk in the Flower Market Building in *Frenzy*

6:9
The Nell of Old Drury F
29 Catherine Street, WC2

This Victorian-era public house (established on the site of a 17th-century inn frequented by actress—and Royal mistress—Nell Gwynn) appears near the beginning of *Frenzy*, just after the scene in which Blaney first meets Rusk in the **Central Market**. In a long shot, we see Blaney, with paper, grapes and jacket under his arm, stroll up

Catherine Street and pop into the "Sweet Smell of Old Brewery" (as Hitchcock himself referred to the pub; cf. Paul Kester's 1900 play, "Sweet Nell of Old Drury") for a quick one (or two, as it turns out). The pub interiors, including the comical discussion of the Necktie Murderer and his methods, were shot at **Pinewood Studios** on August 17 and 18, 1971. In fact, as production designer Syd Cain revealed, the Nell of Old Drury set was simply a "revamp" of **The Globe** interior, which Hitchcock had utilized on the 12th, 13th and 16th. It should be noted that Cain, presumably at Hitchcock's suggestion, cannily incorporated reproductions of the stairs from the real-life Globe for the first pub set and the doorway of the actual Nell of Old Drury for the revamp. It was also on the pub set—then dressed as the Globe—that Hitchcock celebrated his 72nd birthday, on August 13.

The Nell of Old Drury from the street

Station: Covent Garden (Pl) Exit for the Royal Opera in Bow Street; turn L into Russell then immediately R into Catherine Street. The pub is on the R, directly opposite its namesake, the Theatre Royal Drury Lane, and your view from this spot will approximate that of the film. Incidentally, if you wander into the Circle Rotunda of the theatre itself, you can see a bust of Ivor Novello (*The Lodger*, *Downhill*) sculpted by Winifred Ashton (a.k.a. Clemence Dane), co-author of *Enter Sir John*, whence Hitchcock's *Murder!*

Ask Mr. Memory 14: What does Blaney drink in the pub?

6:10
"Bob Rusk's Flat" (2) L
3 Endell Alley
Endell Street, WC2

In Chapter 13 of *Goodbye Piccadilly, Farewell Leicester Square*, we learn that Bob Rusk lives "on the top floor of an old building in an alleyway just off Endell Street. The other premises were let off as offices to fruit brokers and kindred traders, business mostly conducted in the early morning, so that by mid-afternoon the building was deserted." According to production notes, Hitchcock had originally envisioned the cinematic Rusk located in an "Endell Street flatlet" as well. At that point, January 1971, the screen story was still centered around **Piccadilly Circus** and **Leicester Square** and Rusk was a professional gambler, all as in the original novel. However, as mentioned above, Hitchcock ultimately decided to transfer much of the action to Covent Garden, with all its "fruit brokers and kindred traders," including Rusk himself, now safely ensconced in Henrietta Street (see 6:7).

Station: Covent Garden (Pl) Turn L out of the station then immediately R into Long Acre; Endell Street is ahead on the L. "Endell Alley" itself appears to have been a fictional street.

6:11
The Ivy H L
1 West Street, WC2

Located in the heart of the theatre district, this perennial West End favorite has attracted the rich and famous since it opened in 1911. Noël Coward was a regular, as was his good friend Ian Fleming, the creator of James Bond. Hitchcock, too, enjoyed the "Old World ambience" and eclectic British cuisine of the Ivy, whose décor runs to lots of wood (walls and floors), leather seats and stained glass windows. According to his daughter, Pat, it was one of the director's favorite London restaurants, along with

The Ivy

Simpson's, **Le Caprice** and **L'Etoile**. The Ivy was also just what the doctor ordered for the near-suicidal Lina Aysgarth and her sister, Joyce, after a day of "outrageously extravagant shopping" in Chapter 9 of *Before the Fact* (whence *Suspicion*). (For more on Lina's therapeutic trip to London—a detour omitted from the film—see **Lina Aysgarth's Home**.) Author Francis Iles doesn't tell us whether the two women spotted anyone rich or famous, but these days, if you're lucky to get a reservation, you might just espy Madonna and Guy, Elton John, Hugh Grant or even Tom Cruise.

Station: Leicester Square (NO; Pl) Exit R into Charing Cross Road East and walk N to Lichfield Street, where you will turn R. The restaurant is ahead on the L, at the corner of West Street. **Hours:** noon-3 pm (3:30 pm on Sun); 5:30 pm-midnight. Reservations are required—and as far in advance as possible.

The MacGuffin: It was at just such a "show biz" eatery (perhaps this very one) that Hitchcock found the inspiration—at least in part—for his infamous "actors are cattle" remark. As he told Truffaut "I think another reason [apart from their overly long lunches] ...that I resented actors is I would overhear two actresses in a London restaurant, talking. One would say to the other, 'What are you doing now, dear?' And the other one would say, 'Oh, I'm *filming*.' And she would use a tone of voice as though she were saying, 'Oh—oh, I'm *slumming*'."

7. FITZROVIA

7:1
L'Étoile H
30 Charlotte Street, W1

Founded in 1904, L'Étoile was one of Alfred Hitchcock's favorite restaurants. During his London days, the director savored many a fine French meal at this Charlotte Street institution. Actor Charles Laughton recalled lunching here with Hitchcock during the late 1920s, when the two men discussed the fact that they should some day like to work together. That day came, of course, in 1939, when Hitchcock directed *Jamaica Inn*, a picture produced by the actor's Mayflower Productions company and starring Laughton himself as an over-the-top 19th-century rogue. Hitchcock also paid a tribute of sorts to Charlotte Street itself in *Foreign Correspondent*, for which you should see the next entry.

Station: Goodge Street (NO) Go S in Tottenham Court Road then immediately R into Goodge Street. Turn L into Charlotte Street and look for L'Étoile ahead on the L.
Lunch: Mon-Fri noon-2:30 pm; **Dinner:** Mon-Sat 6 pm-11:30 pm.

L'Etoile was one of Hitchcock's favorite restaurants.

7:2
"Maison Rouge" F
242 Charlotte Street, W1

This is the Charlotte Street restaurant above which the bad guys hold Mr. Van Meer in *Foreign Correspondent*. The "typical foreign restaurant" (as the shooting script calls it) was fictional (and in earlier drafts was called "Maison d'Or" and located at No. 228), but the street, reproduced at the Goldwyn Studios, Hollywood, was not. Charlotte Street has long been famous for its fashionable foreign restaurants (e.g., **L'Étoile** [above] and Bertorelli's), most of which feature al fresco dining in the summer.

Station: Goodge Street (NO) Go R into Tottenham Court Road then immediately R into Goodge Street. Turn L into Charlotte Street. The buildings depicted in the film roughly correspond to those opposite Rathbone Street; or, alternately, north of Goodge Street, to those opposite Scala Street.

The MacGuffin: Watch closely as Stephen Fisher ascends the stairs to the room in which Van Meer is being held. A double for actor Herbert Marshall actually climbed the steps, Marshall's wooden leg (the result of a war injury) precluding a smooth ascent.

7:3
ex Scala Theatre F
60 Charlotte Street, W1

Built on the site of the old Prince of Wales Theatre in 1905, the Scala was used primarily for amateur productions and as the base for the United States Theatre Unit during World War II. In the summer of 1949, Alfred Hitchcock came here to rehearse and shoot Marlene Dietrich's "Laziest Gal in Town" number for *Stage Fright*. Actor Richard Todd (Jonathan Cooper) recalled that Dietrich insisted on having a live audience for the two weeks of rehearsals, as well as for the actual filming. The presence of so many people made Todd uncomfortable, but not Dietrich: "She wanted that audience." In addition to Dietrich's number, Hitchcock also shot the climactic chase through the theatre auditorium and backstage area, as well as the prop room, here on location. He was adamant, according to early production documents, that as much of this sequence as possible should be shot on location. Doing things like the prop room in a "real place" would save the cost of building a set, he told production supervisor Fred Ahern. In fact, only Charlotte's dressing room and the odd corridor were done as sets at **Elstree Studios**. Sadly, the Scala Theatre was pulled down in 1970 and replaced by a 10-story apartment building called Scala House.

Scala Theatre

Backstage at the Scala in a scene from *Stage Fright*

Station: Goodge Street (NO) Go S in Tottenham Court Road then immediately R into Goodge Street. Turn R at Charlotte Street and look for Scala House ahead on the R, between Scala and Tottenham Streets.

The MacGuffin: As with her fictional counterpart, a personal dresser assisted the glamorous Marlene Dietrich while she worked on *Stage Fright*. Babs Gray later revealed that Dietrich insisted upon a new pair of nylons each day (quite a luxury in a war-damaged country that still rationed such goods); that she wore a Dior perfume made especially—and exclusively—for her; that she never ate in the studio restaurant (preferring tea and biscuits alone in her dressing room); that she used a different cigarette holder for each new cigarette, which she smoked halfway down and then passed to Babs to finish; and that the otherwise meticulous star carelessly left thousands of pounds (in money, not weight) worth of diamonds and rubies lying about the dressing room, only to ask Babs some time later if the dresser had seen her jewelry. Peccadilloes aside, Dietrich was not an ungenerous boss: after shooting wrapped, she presented her dresser with a pair of black earrings and matching necklace that she had purchased especially for Babs in Paris.

Dietrich strikes a pose in Stage Fright

Ask Mr. Memory 15: Which literary character's mother is said to resemble Marlene Dietrich?

8. HOLBORN

8:1
Kingsway F
WC2

Alfred Hitchcock's meticulous attention to detail is, of course, legendary. What kind of house would a Santa Rosa bank teller occupy? What do **Scotland Yard** corridors really look like? How big is the charge room in the **Bow Street Magistrates' Court**? Where do the **Old Bailey**'s judges get the black caps they wear when handing down the death sentence? What is the precise route a taxi would take from the **Carlton Hotel** in the Haymarket to **The Savoy** in the Strand? These kinds of questions were asked, answered and the results transferred to the screen on countless occasions. There were, however, times when the director was willing to sacrifice accuracy for expediency. Thus, in the middle of the opening *Blackmail* Chase, we see one of Scotland Yard's

As shown in *Blackmail*, this photo is looking south toward Bush House.

"Flying Squad" vans tearing up Lower Regent Street in St. James's, then, after receiving orders to apprehend a suspect, making a dramatic U-turn in the middle of *Kingsway* in Holborn! Apparently the director wanted a wider venue for his turn than Lower Regent Street, and Kingsway, opened in 1905, spans more than 100 feet. Note that in the sound version of the film, the U-turn *appears* to have been faked by combining two subjective shots: one, looking north toward High Holborn, that pans approximately 160 degrees to the right; and a second, now from the other side of the road, that continues the pan around the remaining 20 degrees to Bush House in the south. However, in the silent version, the identical pan is, in fact, accomplished as a single shot. Why there is a cut in the sound version is unclear. (When asked for a solution to this mystery, Hitchcock scholar Ken Mogg suggested that the studio may have accidentally damaged the negative before the sound version was released and then simply printed the soundtrack over the damaged footage.) Note also that Hitchcock continues the chase back in Lower Regent Street, with the police van continuing north toward Piccadilly as if the U-turn had never happened. For another example of the director's "creative geography" (the term employed by Soviet film pioneer V.I. Pudovkin for the apparent spatial reality created by editing together pieces of film shot in widely disparate locations), see **Stevie's Final Journey**.

Station: Holborn (PI) Exit into Kingsway and walk south toward Bush House, the home of the BBC's international service. The pan begins on the western side of the street at Wild Court and stops on Bush House, which has been considerably enlarged since 1929. Kingsway also figures in the grand chase across London which climaxes the novel *Enter Sir John* (whence *Murder!*), a chase that begins in Shaftesbury Avenue (see the **Gielgud Theatre**) and finishes up in a Docklands police station. Bush House itself is mentioned in both *Man Running*, whence *Stage Fright*, and *Goodbye Piccadilly, Farewell Leicester Square*, whence *Frenzy*. In Chapter 19 of the former, Eve Gill claims it's where she worked with Jonathan (she didn't); in the latter, it's where Dick Blamey [*sic*] was awarded the DSO during World War II.

8:2
ex **Holborn Stadium (F)**
85 High Holborn, WC1

Opened as the New Royal Amphitheatre in May 1867, this massive auditorium went on to serve as the headquarters of everything from the National Sporting Club to the YMCA. Its greatest fame comes through its association with professional boxing, which began in England in the late 17th century and flourishes to this day. In fact, it was here at the Holborn (then still the National Sporting Club) that Eugene Corri became the first referee to officiate *inside* a boxing ring, at the Tommy Burns–Gunner Moir fight, in December 1907. It was also here at the Holborn, according to the poster in *The Ring*, that Jack Sander fought his last fight before the climactic battle royal staged at the **Royal Albert Hall**.

Jack Sander (Carl Brisson, center) with his trainer (Gordon Harker) and the barker (Harry Terry) in *The Ring*

Station: Holborn (Pl) The amphitheatre, which was pulled down in 1939, was on the N side of the street, on the site of present Templar House at 81-87.

Ask Mr. Memory 16: What is Sander's nickname?

8:3
Lincoln's Inn (F)
WC2

Lincoln's Inn is the oldest of London's four so-called "Inns of Court," the unincorporated law societies which, alone, have the power to call English (and Welsh) men and women to the Bar. (The other Societies are Gray's Inn, just to the north, and the Inner Temple and Middle Temple, just to the south.) In April 1946, Hitchcock's unit manager, Fred Ahern, and a small film crew prowled through the sprawling headquarters of the venerable society (founded before 1422), shooting both interior and exterior reference footage for *The Paradine Case*. As it turned out, Hitchcock wanted only two location shots for inclusion in the final film: a long shot of the "Lincoln's Inn terrace" (presumably looking across New Square), with doubles for Gregory Peck and Charles Coburn walking in the distance; and background plates of the same view for use in rear-projection set-ups with the actors themselves in Hollywood. This scene (in which Sir Simon briefs Keane on "the Paradine Case") was ultimately cut for time, the action now shifting immediately from the shower scene in the **Keane Home** to Keane's arrival at **Holloway Prison**.

Station: Chancery Lane (CE)
Take Exit 4 L into Holborn and turn L into Chancery Lane; look for the entrance to Lincoln's Inn ahead to the R. Enter and look for New Square to the R.

Lincoln's Inn

8:4
Ede & Ravenscroft Ltd. F
93 Chancery Lane, WC2

Robemaker to the Royal Family since the reign of George III, Ede & Ravenscroft is also the distinguished supplier of Legal London's judicial wigs and robes. The firm came to the aid of Alfred Hitchcock on at least two occasions, the first in April 1946. Approached by an emissary of Hitchcock and producer David O. Selznick, Ede & Ravenscroft gladly agreed to supply bespoke robes and wigs for both Gregory Peck and Charles Laughton, respectively the defense counsel and judge in *The Paradine Case*. As Leonard Leff notes (quoting the director himself): "[T]he little bay-windowed wigmakers shop" was part of the "characteristic background" that Hitchcock wanted to capture in this very British of films. (Having sacrificed a fair degree of authenticity in the casting of young American hunk Gregory Peck as a middle-aged English barrister [not to mention suave Louis Jourdan as an earthy, working-class valet], Hitchcock was apparently taking no chances with his costumes and sets [see the **Old Bailey**].) Two

Ede & Ravenscroft

A REFERENCE GUIDE TO LOCATIONS

kinds of wigs were used in the film: the "bar wig," worn by Peck, and the "bench wig," worn by Laughton. The former has a frizzed crown, several rows of larger curls, and two tails, looped and tied. The latter is frizzed all over, has two small ties at the back and no large curls. Both are made of bleached, white horsehair, with a few black hairs interspersed to give a gray, aged appearance (to the wig, not the person). Each wig is made by hand and takes four weeks to complete, following a technique patented by Humphrey Ravenscroft in 1822. Prior to that time (since at least 1670), British barristers wore wigs made out of black horsehair, which, following the fashion of the day, were powdered white—a decidedly messy job that had to be repeated each time the wig was worn. Hitchcock also consulted the firm on *Dial M for Murder*, in order to ensure the accuracy of the black cloth cap worn by the judge who hands down Margot's death sentence. I could find no record of Hitchcock having consulted the firm for *Frenzy*, although by that point he probably knew pretty much what was what when it came to wigs and robes. Today, Ede & Ravenscroft supply ceremonial robes to Elizabeth II; the Prince of Wales; and the Duke of Edinburgh (it is the only central London firm to hold all four Royal Warrants), as well as to Parliament and the Peerage. The firm also stocks simpler, but stylish, clothing for well-heeled professionals.

Charles Laughton in *The Paradine Case*

Hitchcock and Gregory Peck on the set of *The Paradine Case*

Station: Chancery Lane (CE) Take Exit 4 L into Holborn and turn L into Chancery Lane; the store is ahead on the R.

The MacGuffin: As to why Hitchcock employed Gregory Peck—an otherwise fine actor—in a part for which he was ill-suited, one has only to recall producer David O. Selznick's reaction to a preview of *Spellbound*: "We could not keep the audience quiet from the time [Peck's] name first came on the screen until we had shushed the audience through three or four sequences and stopped all the dames from 'ohing' and 'ahing' and gurgling…." As the "only…star of importance" (again, Selznick's words), Peck was clearly expected to carry the picture.

8:5
ex **HQ of the Air Ministry (F)**
Adastral House
Kingsway, WC2

The Air Ministry was created in January 1918 to administer the Royal Air Force, a new military service formed from the merger of the Army's Royal Flying Corps and the Navy's Royal Naval Air Service. A counterpart to the **Admiralty** and **War Office** departments in Whitehall, the Air Ministry took up residence here in Kingsway in 1919, where it would remain until 1955, when it relocated to Theobald's Road, WC1. At the conclusion of *Rich and Strange*, the **BBC** reports that "the Air Ministry issues the following gale warning: Strong northwesterly gales on all coasts of the British Isles. Rain in most districts....Channel crossings extremely rough." (This is something of an understatement, considering the film's proceedings.) In *The 39 Steps* the MacGuffin turns out to be the Air Ministry's secret formula for a device that renders aircraft engines completely silent. **Scotland Yard** tells Pamela that the Air Ministry "are positive no papers are missing about it" but, as Hannay later surmises, the plans were borrowed, memorized by Mr. Memory and replaced before anyone could find out. This updates the novel's concern over secret British naval dispositions, which were committed to memory by an enemy agent posing as the First Sea Lord (see **Home of the Foreign Secretary**), who now plans to leave the country via the title steps. The Air Ministry, along with the Admiralty and the War Office, was eventually absorbed by the **Ministry of Defence**, which is headquartered in the Board of Trade building, just off Whitehall.

HQ of the Air Ministry

Station: Temple (CI; DI) Go L out of the station and walk straight up Arundel Street and cross the Strand. On the other side of the street, veer to the L into the Aldwych and look for the large building at the corner of Kingsway, opposite the BBC. For another possible Hitchcock reference to the Air Ministry, see the **Royal Opera House**.

The MacGuffin: *Rich and Strange* concludes with Fred and Em bickering over whether or not to buy a bigger house, thus suggesting that their overseas adventures haven't changed them all that much. In the shooting script, however, Hitchcock gave his surrogates a happier ending: As the BBC announcer relays the Air Ministry's gale warning, Fred sits contentedly in front of the fire, smiling, as Emily moves in to kiss him. Fade out.

8:6
ex **Metropolitan Police Forensic Science Laboratory (F)**
Holborn Police Station
2 Richbell Place, WC1

The **Metropolitan Police Service** opened its first state-of-the-art forensic laboratory at the Hendon Police College on April 10, 1935. Its various branches were equipped to test fabrics, fibers, bloodstains, chemical compounds, etc., in murder, arson and other serious criminal cases, services previously rendered on behalf of the police by **Home Office** scientists. *Frenzy* preproduction notes of January 1971 list the "Hendon Science Laboratory" as one of the film's intended exterior locations. An interior set, to be built at **Pinewood Studios**, would show a technician comparing fingerprints on a potato with those on the cigar band of suspected killer Bob Rusk. This scene was subsequently dropped from the screenplay and in the finished film Chief Inspector Oxford simply directs Sgt. Spearman to get the clothes brush (whose potato dust will incriminate Rusk) "down to the lab as soon as possible." The omission of the name actually eliminates a potential error since by that time, 1971, the Science Lab had relocated from Hendon to Richbell Place, Holborn. The Lab's 200 scientists and technicians are today based at the Met's Lambeth Support Headquarters, 109 Lambeth Road, although they are no longer under the jurisdiction of the police. Since 1996, the Lab has been part of the Home Office's Forensic Science Service, which operates five other facilities in the U.K.

Station: Holborn (CE; PI) Exit the station and walk up Southampton Row to Theobald's Road, where you will turn R. Conduit Street, which leads to Richbell Place, is ahead to the L. The station was closed for extensive renovation in 2001 and reopened in 2002.

9. HYDE PARK

9:1
Hyde Park F L
W2, SW1, SW7

The largest of London's royal parks was once famous for the staging of duels but is today better known for the oratory at Speaker's Corner, boating on the Serpentine, horseback riding and even the playing of American baseball. In Chapter 18 of *The Paradine Case* barrister Sir Malcolm Keane (Sir Anthony in the film) takes a walk through the park prior to a "fateful talk" with Sir Simon Flaquer, while in Chapter 1 of *Rich and Strange*, Emily accuses Fred of listening to "those awful men" (Bolsheviks, don't you know) in Hyde Park. (As in the film, Fred is angry at his lot in life and resentful of all those who have wealth and the time to enjoy it.) In Chapter 9 of *Goodbye Piccadilly, Farewell Leicester Square*, Babs and Dick go for a casual walk in the Park, entering at Albion Gate and eventually settling down "on a bench, overlooking the Serpentine." For the film adaptation, *Frenzy*, Hitchcock brought the pair to the southeastern corner of the Park (actually a "wedge" between the north and south lanes of Park Lane) for a short but important scene. Here, after a rather more dramatic flight from the **Coburg Hotel**, Dick Blaney finally convinces Babs that he is not the Necktie Murderer, after which his old RAF chum Johnny Porter invites him to come up to his **London Hilton** suite.

At Pinewood Studios, doubling for Hyde Park, Dick tries to convince Babs he's not a killer in Frenzy.

Long shots of the park and hotel were filmed here on September 12, 1971; closer shots of Dick and Babs on the park bench were actually filmed in the gardens of **Pinewood Studios** the following day.

Hitchcock had also planned Hyde Park shoots for two of his most famous unrealized projects, *No Bail for the Judge* and *The Short Night*. In the former, baronet-cum-pimp (and suspected murderer) Sir Edward Devlin escorts heroine Elizabeth Proud (to have been played by Audrey Hepburn) through the Park and ultimately rapes her (although as scripted, the incident comes across more as Hepburn's character succumbing to Devlin's advances; see Appendix III for background on the story). *The Short Night* was, of course, the last production on which Hitchcock worked before his death in 1980. The film was to have chronicled the hunt for Soviet spy Gavin Brand (based upon the real-life double agent George Blake), who escapes from **Wormwood Scrubs** at the beginning of the film and is subsequently traced to Finland, from which he plans to escape to the Soviet Union. His pursuer, Joe Bailey, stops in Hyde Park, near the Albert Memorial, to ask directions to Earl's Court Road, where Brand's wife and children had been living. Production designer Robert Boyle recalled that while recces of the film's various London locations had been conducted, Hitchcock, then in failing health, ultimately planned to stage all these scenes in southern California, some with the use of matte paintings. Interestingly, the scenes set in Finland were to be filmed in Minnesota. "The general locale was similar," Boyle recalled, "with those 'scooped out' lakes. And also the weather and even the people—there are a lot of Finns and Scandinavians in that area—everything was very much like Finland." Sadly, Hitchcock's health continued to decline and *The Short Night* became "the film that never was." Boyle himself feels that this may not have been a bad thing given the Cold War themes that would, today, seem rather outdated. "In the end," he says, with all due respect to Hitchcock and his legacy, "it was probably fortunate that we didn't go forward with it."

Station: Hyde Park Corner (Pl) Exit for Park Lane and follow this N (away from Hyde Park Corner). The wedge is between Curzon Gate and Achilles Way, directly opposite the Hilton. It was returfed in the 1990s (when the underground garage was built), with the loss of the bench and stone terrace.

Ask Mr. Memory 17: Which two Hitchcock co-stars began their romance here in Hyde Park after having a snowball fight?

Hyde Park Corner

9:2
Hyde Park Corner (F) L
W1, SW1

Once the site of a tollbooth marking the western entrance to London, Hyde Park Corner is today famous for Constitution Arch, Apsley House (one-time home of The Duke of Wellington) and intense traffic congestion. It is also the spot to which *Man Running* hero Jonathan Penrose [*sic*] speeds and then ditches his car after noticing two policemen waiting to question him at his Cary Mews flat (Chapter 2). As in the film adaptation, *Stage Fright*, Jonathan (now surnamed Cooper) has just helped tidy things up at **Charlotte Inwood's Home (2)**, the site of a recent murder. Unlike the film character, however, Jonathan Penrose is actually innocent of the crime, the real killer being Charlotte Inwood's friend and lover, Freddy Williams (Freddie in the film). From Hyde Park Gate, Penrose will take to London's streets by foot, eventually running into a young woman named Eve, who will, perhaps against her better judgment, aid and abet the fugitive. In the film, of course, Eve and Jonathan are already well-acquainted, for which reason the fugitive speeds off from his mews flat (see 2:3) directly to **RADA**, trusting that the love-sick Eve will shelter him. Hyde Park Corner is also the spot where Tony Wendice claims to have picked up a taxi and then lost his small blue attaché case (the one with the £1,000) in *Dial M for Murder*. Mark, his wife's lover, has trouble believing this since he is in fact leaning on the case when Tony reports its loss to Inspector Hubbard.

Station: Hyde Park Corner (PI)

9:3
***ex* Regal Cinema (*now* Odeon Cinema) H**
Marble Arch, W2

On June 21, 1929, at a little after midnight, a new film debuted here at the Regal Cinema, Marble Arch. It was called *Blackmail* and its impact on both world cinema and the career of its young director would be enormous. *Blackmail* is generally described as "the first British talkie" or "the first real British talkie" (Taylor, p 97), but these statements require qualification. The "first British talking feature" (i.e., a full-length film as opposed to a short) was in fact Marshall Neilan's 1929 melodrama *Black Waters*, which was made in the U.S. for British and Dominion Sono Art World Wide. *Blackmail* was the first feature-length talkie actually made in Great Britain. Whether or not it is an "all talkie," as its poster proclaims, is still debated, since the first reel contains only incidental sound and music. This opens the door to British Lion's *The Clue of the New Pin*, also released in 1929, which *The Guinness Book of Movie Facts & Feats* describes as "Britain's first all-talking feature," the emphasis presumably being on the "all." It should be noted, however, that *Clue of the New Pin*, an adaptation of Edgar Wallace's novel, utilized the "sound-on-disc" system, in which a phonograph record was played (more or less) in synch with a silent film. *Blackmail*, on the other hand, employed a version of the modern optical "sound-on-film" recording system (which quickly supplanted its cumbersome rival) and thus may be regarded as the first *proper* talking feature film made in Britain.

In any case, Hitchcock had actually begun *Blackmail* as a silent film, with Polish-born Anny Ondra, so effective in the silent *The Manxman*, as the heroine who kills her would-be rapist. Then, sometime during filming (apparently fairly early on, according to Charles Barr's painstaking research), the decision was made to shoot both a silent and a sound version. Barr has demonstrated that for many *apparently* identical shots in the two films, Hitchcock did not simply reprint a single take but actually printed two separate takes. (Note, for example, the insert of Alice's watch, which indicates slightly different times in the two versions.) The **British Museum** shots also support Barr's thesis, since Tracy's movements throughout the building—courtesy of the Schüfftan process (see Appendix II)—differ slightly between the two versions. There are, however, shots from the silent footage that *were* simply reprinted for use

The Odeon now stands on the site of the Regal.

in the sound film, as in the **Blackmail** **Chase Routes**. Also, as Barr and others have reported, Miss Ondra's accent proved unacceptably "foreign" and post-synch looping (dialogue replacement) was not yet perfected. Therefore, another actress—Joan Barry (*Rich and Strange*)—stood just off-camera, reading Ondra's dialogue into a microphone as Hitchcock shot each take. A cumbersome solution, to the say the least, and one that, owing to Miss Barry's high-pitched voice and plummy accent, makes Alice's dialogue rather cringe-worthy today. In 1929, of course, talkies were still new enough (and many actors still theatrical enough), that none of this really mattered. Indeed, while modern viewers may find *Blackmail* somewhat slow and stilted, those who attended the Regal Cinema trade show[2] exalted the film to High Heaven. The *Daily Chronicle* (June 24) enthused that "after the nasal noises imported from America, the English voices in 'Blackmail'...are like music," while the *Sunday Express* (June 23) proclaimed it nothing less than "an epoch-making event in the history of British films." *To-day's Cinema* (June 24) noted that the Regal screening "was punctuated with at times almost continuous bursts of applause," one of which, according to *Daily Film Renter* (June 24), lasted for seven minutes. A number of critics singled out Hitchcock's treatment of London itself. The *Evening News* (June 22) described the film as "a brilliant picture of London," while *Sound Pictorial* enthused that "London has never been photographed so brilliantly." The *Daily Mail* (June 24) described *Blackmail* as "the first credible picture of London and its characteristic life" and noted that "London, indeed, is its leading lady." A notable exception in withholding its praise from both *Blackmail* in particular and sound films in general was *The Times*, whose August 29, 1929 editorial described the talkie as "an unsuitable marriage of two dramatic forms....We cannot believe that it will endure." Sadly, what did not endure was the Regal Cinema. Once the jewel in John Maxwell's cinema crown (see **Elstree Studios** for more on Maxwell), it closed in March 1964 and was subsequently demolished. In its stead was built the present 1,300-seat behemoth, said to contain the largest cinema screen in London. And that's about as close as you can get to the "birthplace" of British talkies.

Station: Marble Arch (CE) Exit R into Oxford Street and look for the cinema ahead on the R. The Regal's façade actually matched that of the adjoining building, which, apart from the McDonald's on the ground level, looks much as it did in the 1920s.

The MacGuffin: Hitchcock's next film, *Juno and the Paycock*, was also tradeshown here, on New Year's Eve 1929. The first "true" Hitchcock film, *The Lodger*, opened at the nearby Marble Arch Pavilion on January 20, 1927.

10. KENSINGTON

10:1
ex **John Galsworthy's Home (L)**
14 Addison Road, W14

Nobel-prize-winning playwright John Galsworthy (1867-1933) lived here from 1905 to 1913. Galsworthy, of course, wrote the 1920 play *The Skin Game*, which Hitchcock adapted for the screen in 1931. Galsworthy was also involved, at least tangentially, in the creation of another literary masterwork that Hitchcock would one day adapt. For Galsworthy was a life-long friend of Polish-born novelist Joseph Conrad (1857-1924), whose 1907 novel *The Secret Agent* Hitchcock filmed as *Sabotage* in 1936. In fact, Conrad finished that very novel here at No. 14, while sharing the home of his good friend Galsworthy. Galsworthy would later write of the "hard, unsparing light" his friend had used to show that "the irony of things is a nightmare weighing on man's life" (quoted in Kestner).

Station: Kensington (Olympia) (DI) Exit L out of the station into Olympia Way and continue to Hammersmith Road, where you will turn L. Addison Road is ahead to the L, just past the major traffic junction. The house at No. 14—on the L—was demolished long ago and replaced with flats.

10:2
ex **St. Mary Abbotts Hospital F**
Marloes Road, W8

Doubles as: Hammersmith Hospital, Shepherd's Bush, in *Frenzy*

St. Mary Abbotts Hospital actually began life as the Kensington Workhouse, a facility to house and treat the poor and infirm. The oldest building on the site was—and is—Stone Hall, a Jacobean-style brick mansion completed in 1846. It was here, on the night of September 16, 1971, that Alfred Hitchcock filmed: (1) the scene in which Dick Blaney walks out of the hospital, hotwires a car and drives off into the night and (2) the arrival of the prison ambulance bearing the injured Blaney. (Hospital interiors were filmed at **Pinewood Studios**: the ward itself was a set on D Stage, while the corridor was that linking the stages themselves.) Neither the shooting script nor the film actu-

St. Mary Abbotts Hospital Stone Hall is visible in *Frenzy* hospital scenes.

A REFERENCE GUIDE TO LOCATIONS

ally names the hospital, although the car theft is described as taking place in the road outside **Wormwood Scrubs**, thus indirectly identifying the facility as Hammersmith Hospital, which is next door to the prison. And Hitchcock himself made the identification clear in a 1973 interview with Arthur Knight. (In the novel, Blamey [*sic*] escapes from the Royal Northern Hospital, Holloway Road, which is now an apartment house.) Most of St. Mary Abbotts' buildings were demolished in the 1990s, including the low, white wing from which Blaney made his escape. Stone Hall Gardens now occupies that spot. Stone Hall itself, visible to the left of the screen in both hospital scenes, is now a high-priced apartment house.

Station: High Street Kensington (CI; DI) Exit L into the High Street and turn immediately L into Wright's Lane. Continue to Cheniston Gardens, where you will turn R, then L and continue into Marloes Road. Ahead, on the L, is an entrance to Kensington Green, through which you can see Stone Hall. (Access to the Hall, limited to residents, is via St. Mary's Gate, further on.) The hospital wing was parallel to Stone Hall, occupying the center of the present Stone Hall Gardens.

The MacGuffin: While shooting the hospital ward interiors, Hitchcock employed a nurse from Wexham Park Hospital, Slough, to provide technical advice on dressing wounds. She was paid £6 a day.

11. KNIGHTSBRIDGE
(BROMPTON)

11:1
Harrods L
87-135 Brompton Road, SW3

Founded by wholesale tea merchant Henry Charles Harrod in 1849, this colossal department store occupies one entire city block (4.5 acres), boasts 214 separate departments, a 35,000-square-foot Food Hall and a staff of some 4,000 people. That it can provide *Omnia Omnibus Ubique* ("Everything for Everybody Everywhere") is Harrods' humble—and, apparently, accurate—motto. This includes wedding presents for "discriminating" shoppers like Beatrice Lacy in Chapter 9 of *Rebecca*. Offering to buy a wedding gift for her brother Maxim and his new bride, Beatrice tells Mrs. de Winter that she recently gave the daughter of a friend "rather a nice standard lamp" as a wedding present. "Cost me a fiver at Harrods," she tactfully adds. That Harrods would esteem any of its wares as "standard" I doubt, though perhaps author du Maurier felt differently. (This exchange is omitted from the film, Beatrice being more concerned about Maxim throwing a party to introduce the new bride.) In Chapter 7 of *Man Running* (whence *Stage Fright*), Eve's Aunt Florence (with whom she stays while posing as Charlotte Inwood's maid) practically lives at Harrods. In fact, it is virtually all she thinks and talks about. Furthermore, in Chapter 15 she believes that she could actually get Eve a job at the megastore (in "Gowns and Mantles"), a far better position than working as a maid to a society woman. (In contrast to the cinematic Charlotte, this wealthy widow is an *ex*-actress and so requires a maid, not a dresser.) Eve doesn't take Aunt Florence up on her offer, but in Chapter 17 she does go to Harrods to buy the electronic equip-

Harrods

ment with which she plans to expose the real murderer of Charlotte's husband. Finally, in Chapter 8 of *The Rainbird Pattern* (whence *Family Plot*), wealthy spinster Grace Rainbird decides to put off thinking about the missing Edward Shoebridge in order to do a little redecorating at the family mansion. To that end, she goes up to London to buy curtains at—where else?—Harrods.

Station: Knightsbridge (Pl) The store is just down from the station in Brompton Road. **Hours**: Mon, Tue & Sat 10 am-6 pm; Wed-Fri 10 am-7 pm

11:2
Oratory of St. Philip Neri (Brompton Oratory) H
Brompton Road, SW1

This "most chic" of London's Catholic churches was commissioned by the Oratorian Order in 1880 and modeled upon its headquarters in Rome, the baroque Chiesa Nuova. Here, Alfred Joseph Hitchcock and Alma Lucy Reville, both aged 27, were married on December 2, 1926, more than two years after the announcement of their engagement. From here the wedding party, including Alfred's brother William and Alma's sister Eva, went to a reception in the Hitchcocks' new flat in the Cromwell Road (see entry 22:1). The year after the Hitchcocks were married, the church undertook a major scheme of "Roman" adornment, which included the marbling and

Brompton Oratory

A REFERENCE GUIDE TO LOCATIONS

gilding of the nave, mosaics beneath the dome, Stations of the Cross in high relief and the erection of the present, enormous pulpit.

Station: South Kensington (CI; DI; PI) Follow the signs for Ismaili Centre and Brompton Road. Turn R into Cromwell Road/Cromwell Garden (different names on either side of Exhibition Road) and follow this a short distance as it becomes Thurloe Place; the Oratory is across the street on the L.

The Paxton's Head

11:3
The Paxton's Head (L) (F)
153 Knightsbridge, SW1

Mention the words "Knightsbridge" and "pub" together in the same sentence—as Tony Wendice does in both the play and film *Dial M for Murder*—and most people who know the area—and its public houses—will immediately think of the famous Paxton's Head, a Victorian landmark run by the Nicholson brewing company. So, after a long, hard day of shadowing the Missus and her American lover, pop into *the* Knightsbridge pub, sit back with the beverage of your choice and ponder precisely how you might go about killing your adulterous bride. If you're lucky (or maybe if you're *un*lucky), an old college chum will turn up and suddenly everything will become quite clear....

Station: Knightsbridge (PI) Exit W into Knightsbridge and look for the pub ahead on the L.

Ask Mr. Memory 18: How much does Tony stand to inherit if his plan succeeds?

**11:4
"Robert Tisdall's Home" (L)
Yeoman's Row, SW3**

According to Chapter 8 of *A Shilling for Candles* (whence *Young and Innocent*), Robert Tisdall lived in this small street, one of the oldest in the area. Here Tisdall spent his time supporting dozens of spongers until one day, when his money was nearly gone, he had to make a decision. Should he now spend his time sponging off of *his* friends or should he simply disappear? "Disappearing seemed easier," Tisdall explains to Inspector Grant (Kent in the film), but first he had to do two things: spend his last five pennies and pawn his evening clothes for suitable tramping attire. Unfortunately, West End pawn shops weren't open on Saturday night and he certainly couldn't take to the road in evening clothes. Then, as he stood on a street corner, lost in thought, a car pulled up alongside and a woman smiled and asked, "Take you anywhere, mister?" Thus began Robert's short but dramatic interlude with actress Christine Clay, and for more of their story (background omitted from the film), you should now journey to the **Gaiety Theatre**.

Station: Knightsbridge (Pl) Exit for Harrods. Continue in Brompton Road past the store and Beauchamp Pont Street. Yeoman's Row is just ahead on the L.

12. LAMBETH

**12:1
County Hall F
Riverside Building
Westminster Bridge Road, SE1**

Completed in stages from 1911 to 1963, this monumental Thames-side complex (11 acres, 2.2 million square feet and 700 feet of river frontage) housed the London County Council and its successor body, the Greater London Council. Margaret Thatcher abolished the latter (for inefficiency in governing London) in 1986 and its lavish headquarters stood vacant for several years. Today, it is home to the London Aquarium, as well as several hotels and restaurants. Hitchcock apparently had quite a fondness for the riparian locale because he incorporated it, directly or indirectly, into four of his films, beginning with *The Lodger*. There, for the final shot, of Daisy and the Lodger embracing in front of the window, Hitchcock included a background image of

County Hall, *Frenzy* steps

Two of Hitchcock's cameos in *Frenzy* were filmed at the County Hall location.

the **Houses of Parliament** (complete with an incongruous "To-night Golden Curls" sign) taken from the steps of County Hall. Three years later in *Blackmail*, he included County Hall near the top of the frame of an aerial shot of the **Thames** during Alice's post-murder walk. Later in the film, he included a nice POV shot of the sprawling—and then relatively new—Edwardian complex as Alice stares out a **Scotland Yard** window. (In the silent version, she clearly stares out the window; in the sound version, she seems to be staring downward toward the floor. In either case, she is probably staring at nothing in particular, the intent being to show that the outside world proceeds apace, oblivious to her concerns.) In 1936, for a shot of the Houses of Parliament blacked out by Mr. Verloc's *Sabotage*, Hitchcock came to a spot on the County Hall river walk, hard by the steps leading down from **Westminster Bridge**.

Finally, and most prominently, Hitchcock showcased County Hall during the opening sequence of *Frenzy*, in which Sir George, the Minister of Health, proclaims a new scheme to eradicate pollution in the river, even as the Necktie Murderer's latest victim floats into view at the foot of the river steps. This relatively simple sequence was in fact filmed in three different locations, spanning a four-month period from August to December 1971, and that's not counting a restaging of the floating body for the theatrical trailer. The initial shoot, on August 2, included the actors and extras (as well as a **BBC** camera crew) in long shots and in closer shots that incorporated the **Houses of Parliament** and County Hall itself in the background. It also included an extended helicopter shot that began at **Tower Bridge** and finished at County Hall, where Sir George's speech was already in progress. (In the finished film, the helicopter tracks in to the bridge itself, from which there is a dissolve to County Hall. For the reasons behind the switch from a shot that began at the bridge and ended on the Hall, see the entry on Tower Bridge.) Stuntwoman Sylvia Hibbert was on hand, as was a dummy (if required), for shots of the victim in the Thames. The wardrobe department also provided foam rubber inserts to ensure that the strangler's necktie remained afloat in the water. The following day, Hitchcock restaged the action here at County Hall, *without* the helicopter shot, and then again, on the 26th, *with* the helicopter shot. As before, the helicopter began at Tower Bridge and finished at County Hall, but this time the director himself appeared in the conclusion of the shot, frame-left, leaning against the parapet. This would become the first of his three cameo appearances in the finished film (not two, as is usually claimed). On September 28, Hitchcock restaged the second portion of this sequence, this time near the paddock (exterior) tank at **Pinewood Studios**. It was here, not County Hall, that the onlookers debated the respective techniques of the Necktie Murderer and Jack the Ripper (see 58:2); that the Mayor of Lambeth urged Sir George to come away ("I say, that's not my Club tie, is it?"); and that Hitchcock made what would be his *third* cameo appearance (peering over the unseen parapet). Since the shot was a high-angle one, the only portion of the County Hall terrace that the art department had to reproduce was the paving stones on which the onlookers stood. The following day

The police on the County Hall steps in *Frenzy*

Hitchcock filmed the dead woman (now "played" by Judith Chisholme) floating into view in the studio tank, as well as the two policemen starting to raise her body. These shots had already been filmed at County Hall, but Hitchcock ultimately chose to use the studio tank footage instead of the location footage. This means that while the police rush down the steps at County Hall, they actually reach the body at Pinewood Studios, some 20 miles away. On December 16, the director restaged the action here at County Hall yet again, filming what would ultimately appear as his *second* cameo, standing near the railing of the terrace, as the crowd applauds the Minister's speech. Finally, on January 3, 1972, he filmed portions of the trailer here in the river, this time with stunt swimmer Roberta Gibbs playing the dead girl.

Station: Westminster (CE; DI; JU) Exit to Westminster Bridge and cross to the County Hall, which sits on the L. The shots of the *Frenzy* crowd, with Parliament in the background, were staged on the pavilion *between* the two sets of steps leading down to the river, while the Minister's speech was actually staged farther along, more or less opposite the second set of stairs down to the river. It was the second set of steps (closest to the London Eye) that the policemen descended. (Again, though, the body was actually lifted up at Pinewood.) The *Sabotage* view of Parliament is from the corner adjacent to the foot of the steps leading down from the Westminster Bridge. The view from *The Lodger* is from the first set of steps leading into the building, looking out across the first set of steps leading down to the river. The *Blackmail* view of County Hall is from the NE corner of the north wing of the Norman Shaw Building (see **Scotland Yard**). The concave colonnade in the center of the Riverside Building, so prominent in the *Frenzy* aerial shot, has since been obstructed by an oversized London Aquarium sign.

The MacGuffin: Hitchcock originally considered two other versions of the Thames-side "Prologue" in *Frenzy*. In one, a group of men walk along the river, boasting about the attack on pollution and the purity of the water—when a body suddenly floats into view. In the second, a politician pontificates to his cohorts about pollution when a woman's body suddenly falls out of a garbage heap.

Waterloo Station

12:2
Waterloo Station F L
Waterloo Road, SE1

Hitchcock told Truffaut that *Rebecca* didn't have an "authentic look" because, owing to the war, he could not shoot any actual English exteriors. The same problem pertained, he said, to *Suspicion* as well. In between these two films, however, Hitchcock *was* able to secure second-unit footage of the British capital for the Hollywood production *Foreign Correspondent*. This he skillfully combined with impressive studio sets for which producer Walter Wanger spared no expense. In fact, the art directors were able to construct nearly 100 three-sided sets, including the elaborate Amsterdam street and steps where "Van Meer" is assassinated (the famous umbrella sequence) and a 600 ft by 125 ft replica of Waterloo Station, where Johnny Jones arrives by train and has a drink with Stebbins in the station bar. The original Waterloo Station was built in stages between 1845 and 1898, by which time the hodge-podge result had earned a reputation as "the most perplexing railway station in London." A new station was begun in 1900 and finally completed in 1922. Its 21 platforms and massive concourse (120 ft wide and 770 ft long) made it the largest rail station in London. Something of its scale may be gleaned from the opening second-unit shot of Johnny's arrival, which shows an actual Southern Railway train pulling into Waterloo Station. The next shot, of Stebbins looking for Johnny, as well as the rest of the sequence (incorporating some 500 extras), was shot on the massive Hollywood set. Interestingly, the station also "appears" in *Suspicion*, which the director described to Truffaut as his "second English picture" in America (*Rebecca*, of course, being the first). Look closely at Lina and Johnnie's tickets in the opening scene: They are traveling from Waterloo to Hazledene, Sussex (presumably standing in for Haslemere, Sussex). The station also appears in the novel upon which

Waterloo Station in Foreign Correspondent

Suspicion was based, *Before the Fact*, as the setting for a short but poignant scene between Lina and Ronald, the man for whom she had planned to leave Johnnie (Ronald, sadly, is now engaged to someone else); and in *The Secret Agent* (whence *Sabotage*), as the starting point of Mrs. Verloc's trip to the Continent, a trip suggested, but never taken—as far as we know—in the film.

Station: Waterloo (BA; JU; NO; WC; NR) Exit for the National Railway (Waterloo Mainline Station) and look for Platform 14, still looking much as it did in *Foreign Correspondent*.

The MacGuffin: According to author Leonard J. Leff, the Waterloo Station scene earned the condemnation of the National Creamery Buttermakers' Association for suggesting (in reference to Stebbins reluctantly switching from booze to milk) "that milk drinking is an object of ridicule"!

12:3
Waterloo Underground Station F
Waterloo Road, SE1

Thanks to the detective work of Underground expert Richard Griffin it has been possible to identify not only the station but also the very platform on which Hitchcock "trained" his camera during the opening sequence of *Rich and Strange*. You may recall that the film begins with Fred Hill and his co-workers leaving their office at quitting time,

Waterloo Underground Station

opening their umbrellas (or, in Fred's case, *trying* to open his umbrella) and heading off for their respective homes. Next comes a shot of an Underground sign, followed by a shot of actual Underground escalators. A studio shot of Fred going down an escalator then precedes a shot of an actual Underground platform taken from inside the moving train. The shape of the platform, as well as information on the "Way Out" sign (visible as the train slows to a stop), provide the necessary clues to identify both the station and the platform: It is the southbound platform of the Bakerloo Line at Waterloo, one of the

Behind-the-scenes shot of the umbrella sequence from *Rich and Strange*

92 ALFRED HITCHCOCK'S LONDON

few sharply curved platforms in the whole of the Underground system. And, as Griffin pointed out to me, some things never change: The platform-edge lamps visible in the film are still there, some 70 years on. Interestingly, Hitchcock repeated the entire opening sequence of *Rich and Strange* (workplace, leaving work, taking the Underground, walking home from the station) in the New York-based *The Wrong Man*, with Henry Fonda—sans the uncooperative umbrella—recreating actor Henry Kendall's journey of a quarter-century earlier.

Station: Waterloo (BA; JU; NO; WC; NR)

12:4
"Gaynor Brand's Flat" L
32 Lincoln Street (*or* Lincoln Road)
Near Waterloo Road, SE1

According to Chapter 4 of *The Pleasure Garden*, chorus girl Gaynor Brand (*Patsy* Brand in the film) lives in a small flat in Lincoln Street (alternately called Lincoln Road in the novel), off Waterloo Road. There doesn't seem to have ever been such a street off Waterloo Road, so precisely what author "Oliver Sandys" (really Marguerite Florence Barclay) had in mind is uncertain. Hitchcock shows the interior of the flat (which was shot at the Emelka-Studios in Munich, Germany), but doesn't give any hint as to where in London it is supposed to be.

Station: Waterloo (BA; JU; NO; WC; NR) Exit for Waterloo Road.

13. MAIDA VALE

13:1
Maida Vale Underground Station F
W9

In *Downhill*, a disgraced Ivor Novello literally goes down in the world, via the escalator into the Maida Vale tube station. In an interview with Peter Bogdanovich, Hitchcock recalled the unusual circumstances under which he filmed the "key shot" on the escalator: "We couldn't shoot it until after midnight, after the last train had gone, so we went to the theatre first and in those days we used to go to a first night in white tie and tails and opera hats. So, after the theatre, I directed this scene in white tie and top hat. The most elegant moment in direction I've ever had." Photographs taken during the shoot not only confirm the story but highlight just how dramatically the top-

Ivor Novello at the Underground station in Downhill

Escalator where Ivor Novello went *Downhill* in the Maida Vale Underground Station

hatted director contrasted with the rest of the crew. The shoot actually took place on the night of Saturday, February 27, 1927, beginning just after midnight and continuing for nearly four hours. Notwithstanding the hour, a large crowd of extras gathered to watch matinee idol Novello, covered in yellow grease paint, enter the station; look at the Tube map and buy a ticket; and then descend the escalator, "a dwindling figure, borne down steadily until it disappears from the camera's view" (*Evening News*, February 28). Novello actually performed the descent five times before Hitchcock got exactly what he was after. The director was, in fact, extremely fortunate to have secured the cooperation of the Underground authorities, who agreed to keep their employees on after hours both here at the station and at the Kilburn and Baker Street switchboards. As the *Daily Mail* correspondent noted at the time (February 28), "The reluctance of official bodies to give facilities to film productions in this country has so long been a byword that the courteous and active aid of the Underground authorities…is to be commended." And, indeed it is, even if the onscreen result lasts barely 25 seconds.

Station: Maida Vale (BA) Ascend the escalator, then mirror the shot in the film by looking down the "Down" escalator, a modern replacement for the wooden conveyor shown in the film. Neither the interior nor the exterior has changed that much in 75 years, although the original green and white ceramic tiles were replaced by metal ones during the Second World War.

13:2
"Wendice Home" F
61A Charrington Gardens, W9

According to the address he gives Swann in both the play and the film *Dial M for Murder*, Tony Wendice and his wife live at 61A Charrington Gardens, Maida Vale, a two-minute walk from the Underground, presumably the **Maida Vale Station**, but possibly the Warwick Avenue Station. There is no such street as Charrington Gardens in Maida Vale, nor was there in 1954, although there is a Warrington Crescent, which may have been what playwright Frederick Knott had in mind. (Indeed, his screenplay indicates that the locale is near Maida Vale Road [*sic*], which also suggests Warrington Crescent.) Hitchcock apparently intended to film exteriors of the couple's home (for POV shots out the bedroom window, for Mark's view from the taxi, etc.) on location in Randolph Crescent, which is in fact one street over from Warrington Crescent. However, as the visitor to Randolph Crescent will quickly perceive, the street does *not* match the one shown in the film. Precisely where in London the exteriors were shot remains a mystery (although production notes do confirm that the footage was shot in London). Interiors, showing the couple's sitting room, bedroom, corridor and entrance were filmed at the Warner Bros. Studio in Hollywood. Hitchcock had actually wanted to base the entire production in London, but studio head Jack Warner turned him down. In fact, Hitch had to put up something of a fight just to get what little London footage there actually is. Warner tried to convince him that the old New York street on the studio backlot would make a perfectly acceptable—not to mention *cheap*—substitute for the genuine Maida Vale location. Hitchcock, of course, disagreed.

Station: Warwick Avenue (BA) Exit R out of the station and cross to Warrington Crescent.

Ask Mr. Memory 19: What false name does Tony use when he phones Swann?

13:3
"Maida Vale Police Station" (L) (F)
W9

In both the play(s) and the film *Dial M for Murder*, Tony Wendice phones the "Maida Vale police" after returning home to find Swann's body on his living room floor. Later, Inspector Hubbard arranges for that same station to help him expose the real criminal. According to Tony's conversation with Swann, the station is "opposite the church. Two minutes' walk." (It is "opposite the Tube" in the British original.) The trouble with all this is that there never was a Maida Vale Police station, opposite the Tube, opposite a church or anywhere else. Interestingly, though, there *was* a police station in nearby West Hampstead and according to Metropolitan Police historian Bernard Brown, its phone number was MAIDA VALE 1113.

13:4
"Mr. Pelham's Home" L
10 Montague Court, W9

The title character of Anthony Armstrong's short story "The Case of Mr. Pelham" occupies a flat at 10 Montague Court, Maida Vale. Here, he leads a simple, rather predictable bachelor's life, attended by his faithful manservant Peterson. In fact, the two men know each other so well—they've been together for six years—that when a double attempts to take over his employer's life, home, job and club, Peterson has no trouble at all identifying the real Mr. Pelham....There is no shortage of Montague (or Montagu) Places, Squares and Streets in Central London, but none, unfortunately, in Maida Vale. There are, however, a number of "Something-or-other Courts" in Maida Vale, most of them along Clifton Road and Maida Vale itself. (Indeed, the reference to "his bachelor flat in Maida Vale" could be taken to mean either the district or the street.) Hitchcock, of course, transposed the story to New York, where the Americanized title character lives on East 63rd Street.

Station: Warwick Avenue (BA) Exit into Clifton Gardens and continue into Clifton Road, which leads to Maida Vale, where you may turn R and wander among the haunts of the two Mr. Pelhams.

14. MARYLEBONE/REGENT'S PARK

14:1
London Zoo F
Regent's Park, NW1

The gardens of the Zoological Society of London were established here in the northern portion of **Regent's Park** in 1828. In fact, the London Zoological Gardens, to give the full title, was the world's first modern zoo, dedicated to both the display *and* study of "new and curious subjects of the Animal Kingdom." The society hired renowned Regency architect Decimus Burton to lay out their gardens, and several of his buildings, including the Clock Tower and Giraffe House, are still standing. The collection of curious animals (including kangaroos, llamas and emus) was augmented first by the Royal Menagerie, which arrived from Windsor Great Park in 1830, and then by the animals from the Tower of London, which were transferred in 1832-34. As one of the most popular educational and entertainment attractions in London, the Zoo provides an ironic backdrop for the meeting between Verloc the saboteur and his

The London Zoo looks much as it did in Sabotage.

superior, Vladimir, in *Sabotage*. (The meeting takes place at the **Russian Embassy** in the novel.) Verloc's initial act of sabotage—putting sand in the **Battersea Power Station** generator—resulted in a temporary blackout that left London laughing with amusement, not screaming in terror. Now, inside the Zoo Aquarium (completed in 1924 at a cost of £55,000), Vladimir tells Verloc that if he wants to receive the money owed him, he must strike terror in London's heart: He must detonate a bomb in the **Piccadilly Circus Underground Station** during the upcoming Lord Mayor's Parade. After the meeting with Vladimir, Verloc stares at the large glass side of an Aquarium tank and envisages the bustling circus literally dissolving in the wake of the explosion. Ironically, the Aquarium actually took a direct hit during World War II and suffered considerable damage.

Station: Camden Town (NO) Follow the signs to the Zoo, which is open every day except Christmas from 10 am-5:30 pm (until 4 pm in winter). The entrance—including the gate in which Verloc becomes entangled—has scarcely changed since 1936.

The MacGuffin: Scripted (and possibly shot) was an exchange on the bus that Verloc takes to the Aquarium. Having asked the conductor how much to the Zoo, the saboteur is told that the nearest stop is Gloucester Gate and that the fare is fourpence. Verloc pays and the conductor moves on down the bus, coming to Hollingshead, who holds up some coins and says simply, "Fourpenny." This, of course, lets us know that Hollingshead is following Verloc, but then we knew that anyway—which presumably explains why the sequence was dropped.

**14:2
Regent's Park L
NW1**

Occupying the site of one of Henry VIII's many hunting grounds, this elegant park was constructed by John Nash for the Prince Regent (later George IV) in 1817-1828. Less grandiose than originally envisaged, the 500-acre tract is still striking,

Hanover Terrace, Regent's Park

with Nash's impressive cream-colored stucco terraces and villas framing the western, southern and eastern sides of the horseshoe-shaped tract. No wonder it attracted the title character of Marie Belloc Lowndes' *The Lodger*, who, we are told in Chapter 5, is fond of going out "into the Regent's Park." Later we learn that he even favors a stroll through the park on very cold, snow-laden nights, when "everyone who could do so stayed indoors." In fact, it was on just such a night that Mr. Bunting—on his way home from a waiting job in Hanover Terrace—happened to spot the Lodger walking rather quickly down one of the short streets leading off Park Road. What could the Lodger be

A REFERENCE GUIDE TO LOCATIONS

doing out and about on such a night? What, indeed, since Belloc Lowndes' protagonist—unlike Hitchcock's—is actually the psychotic serial killer his landlady suspects him of being....It was also here, in Chapter 8 of *Marnie*, that Mark Rutland proposed to the title character. Actually, as they drive through the park en route to Mrs. Rutland's elegant flat "right in the centre of London," Mark simply announces that they should be married in November. Marnie is taken aback, to be sure, and asks if he is satisfied that he "really want[s] to marry a thief and a liar?" The lovesick scion explains, in a foreshadowing of the cinematic adaptation, that he is satisfied that he loves her and, "[a]nyway, who hasn't been a thief and a liar to some extent at some time of their lives? It's only a question of degree." Indeed. Later scenes are also set in Regent's Park, for it is here that Marnie comes to visit her psychiatrist. These scenes do not appear in the film, though some of the dialogue survives in the Mark-Marnie exchange during their honeymoon cruise.

Station: Baker Street (BA; CI; HC; JU; ME) Take the Baker Street North exit, turn R, follow Baker Street across Park Road and into Outer Circle, where, ahead on the L, you will see Hanover Terrace. Cumberland Terrace, where Mr. and Mrs. Bunting first met (at No. 90), is on the eastern side of the Park, between Cumberland Gate and Gloucester Gate. **Hours:** 5 am-dusk daily.

14:3
"Bunting Home" L
Marylebone Road, W1

According to the opening chapter, Mr. and Mrs. Bunting, landlords of *The Lodger*, occupy an "exceptionally clean and well-cared-for house" in "grimy, if not exactly sordid" Marylebone Road. From later descriptions, it is possible to locate the house on the north side of the road, just west of the present Landmark Hotel, between Lisson Grove and Cosway Street. In the film, the family appears to live in Bessborough Gardens, Pimlico (see 16:2).

Bunting Home

Station: Marylebone (BA) Exit R into Melcombe Place, then turn L into Harewood Avenue and R into Marylebone Road. The block is just ahead on the R.

14:4
Park Crescent F
W1

After disguising himself as a United Dairies milkman near the beginning of *The 39 Steps*, Richard Hannay leaves the real milkman's horse and cart around the corner from

Park Crescent as shown in *The 39 Steps*

his Portland Place flat (see below), in Park Crescent, an elegant semi-circle (originally envisioned as a full circle) completed in 1818. The shot of the crescent, which appears to have been filmed very early in the morning, immediately follows a sequence shot at **Lime Grove**, in which Hannay persuades the milkman to lend him his gear. The shooting script reveals that an additional sequence was to have appeared between these two scenes. First, Hannay was to have thrown the milk baskets onto the cart almost like a professional, then ridden off as the two enemy agents continued to watch his flat, completely unaware that he has just slipped through their fingers. The version of the crescent shot itself was also scripted a bit differently, with the abandoned horse going a bit wild and trying to climb onto the sidewalk as a curious policemen approaches to investigate. At this point, one might have wondered why the real milkman took so long to retrieve his cart, which may explain why the sequence was simplified to the present version.

Station: Regent's Park (BA) Exit for Great Portland Street/Albany Street, walk along Marylebone Road and take the first R into Park Crescent. The view is of the SE corner of the crescent, with the triangular pediment toward the extreme R of the shot.

Ask Mr. Memory 20: How much does Hannay offer the milkman for the use of his gear?

14:5
"Richard Hannay's Flat" F L
122 Portland Place, W1

In the opening of *The 39 Steps*, Canadian Richard Hannay escorts a mysterious brunette to his first floor flat in Portland Mansions, Portland Place, "by the BBC," as one of the traveling salesmen later remarks. The visitor turns out to be a spy-for-hire, temporar-

Portland Place, where Richard Hannay lived

ily in the employ of England. *Very temporarily*, as it turns out, since she is killed by enemy agents during the night. Hannay must now escape from his flat, unseen by the agents, which he does by disguising himself as a milkman (see above), a ruse actually employed in John Buchan's novel. Portland Place, which the director recreated on a **Lime Grove** soundstage, was laid out ca. 1778 and was then considered one of the grandest streets in London. Buchan himself lived at No. 76 Portland Place from 1912 to 1919, during which time he wrote *The Thirty-nine Steps* [*sic*] (as well as its first two sequels) and for which reason he presumably located his hero in a flat "near Portland Place…in a new block behind Langham Place." (In later novels, Hannay would take flats in Park Lane and Westminster.) Langham Place is, in fact, the short, curved "link" between Regent Street to the south and Portland Place to the north. It is dominated by All Souls Church and the southern end of the **BBC** itself. Portland Mansions appears to have been an invention—I could find no record of such a building in or around Portland Place in 1935—as is the number 122. Then, as now, the street numbers stop in the 90s. Hitchcock actually planned a return to the Buchan *oeuvre* in 1964, when he set about to film an adaptation of the author's 1924 novel *The Three Hostages*. Nothing came of the project, although, interestingly, *Frenzy* star Barry Foster would go on to play Hannay in a 1977 BBC TV adaptation of, what else, *The Three Hostages*. By the time of the later novel, though, Hannay had moved to Gloucestershire, with a St. James's club—possibly **White's**—serving as his temporary London base.

Station: Regent's Park (BA) Exit for Great Portland Street/Albany Street, walk along Marylebone Road and take the first R into Park Crescent. Follow this around to Portland Place, where you will turn L. As noted above, there is no 122 Portland Place, nor, unfortunately, does Buchan's attractive, Adam-style house remain at No. 76. It was demolished and replaced by the incongruous Institute of Physics.

The MacGuffin: Richard Hannay was based upon Field Marshal Lord Edmund Ironside, whom Buchan had met in South Africa. Ironside, who, at 6 feet 4 inches was known as "Tiny," fought in both the Boer War and World War I, did Intelligence work in German South-West Africa (now Namibia) and spoke 14 languages.

View of the Keane Home, shown in *The Paradine Case*

14:6
Keane Home F L
60 Portland Place, W1

As suggested above, Portland Place has always possessed a certain cachet, so it's perhaps no surprise to see yet another of Hitchcock's celebrated heroes located here: Anthony Keane, the lovesick barrister who defends *The Paradine Case*. And, as he had done with Buchan in the earlier work, Hitchcock simply followed the lead of *Paradine Case* author Robert Hichens, who located the barrister at No. 53. Keane, Hichens tells us, was "awfully fond of his big house, and proud of it, too. Its spacious beauty was a witness to his success." The same could be said of the film's interiors, built by art director Thomas Morahan at the Selznick Studios in Hollywood. Morahan also built a small portion of the exterior of the home, for the rainy, night scene in which Simmy drops Keane off near the beginning of the film. (For the longer version of this scene, see **St. Martin's Theatre**.) A later exterior was actually shot here on location by the second unit and includes the equestrian statue of Field Marshal Sir George White (John Tweed, 1922) lying opposite the house. The statue, per Hitchcock's explicit instructions, is silhouetted against the headquarters of the Royal Institute of British Architects, an impressive Portland stone building just across Weymouth Street at No. 66. Another establishing shot, looking down Portland Place toward the Langham Hilton Hotel, was filmed at night, in the rain. It was to have preceded Keane's arrival with Sir Simon but was ultimately cut for time.

Station: Regent's Park (BA) Exit for Great Portland Street/Albany Street, walk along Marylebone Road and take the first R into Park Crescent. Follow this around to Portland Place, where you will turn L. No 60 is ahead on the L.

**14:7
British Broadcasting Corporation (L) F
Broadcasting House
Portland Place, W1 (at Langham Street)**

The BBC is, of course, a British national institution, although it actually began as the privately owned British Broadcasting *Company*, on October 18, 1922. The original BBC transmitted its first domestic radio broadcast from Marconi House, Strand, on November 14, 1922, moving the following year to 2 Savoy Hill, near the famous hotel (see 23:5). In 1927, the BBC was reconstituted by Royal Charter as the British Broadcasting Corporation, now—and forever after—a state firm. In 1932, the "Beeb" moved to the present curved, Art Deco building, from which it began transmitting on May 12 and where portions of the Home Service are still based. (Other radio programming, including the famous *Today* show, are now based at the BBC's Television Centre, Shepherd's Bush.) Both BBC programming and the BBC itself are mentioned or depicted in a number of Hitchcock's films and literary sources. In the film *The Pleasure Garden* (longer version), Patsy's landlord listens to the wireless using a then state-of-the-art headset. In *The Lodger*, an intertitle describing "Murder Hot Over The Aerial" precedes a sequence in which a BBC announcer is shown reading his copy in the studio, while his headset-equipped listeners (including someone who looks suspiciously like Alma Reville) react to the news from the safety of their homes. In *Murder!*, Sir John shaves and reflects upon the Baring case while listening to a performance by the BBC's then newly formed Radio Symphony Orchestra (a full orchestra played just out of camera range, as Herbert Marshall's previously recorded "reflection" ran simultaneously in the background). In *Rich and Strange*, a frustrated Fred Hill turns off the radio before a Mr. Baker begins his twelfth talk on accountancy. (The first of the famous BBC "talks" had been broadcast on December 23, 1922.) At the end of the film—after a series of harrowing adventures—Fred again switches on the "wireless," this time to hear an **Air Ministry** warning about coastal gales, rain, sleet and rough channel crossings. Truly, there's no place like home. In *The 39 Steps*, one of Hannay's train companions reads about Annabella Smith's murder in the newspaper and notes that the crime occurred in "Portland Mansions, Portland Place." "By the BBC," says the second man, adding "That's a nice, quiet place to put someone to sleep." "Good night, everybody, good night," says the first, in imitation of BBC news reader Frank Phillips' well-known sign-off, after which both men enjoy a hearty laugh. All of this is lost, of course, on Hannay, who is obliged to take the Portland Place murder a bit more seriously. *Foreign Correspondent* concludes with Johnny Jones' heartfelt broadcast from the BBC, punctuated by the sound of Hitler's bombs raining down around him. A number of contemporary reviewers noted the aptness, even the uncanny accuracy of this scene since, at the time the film played in London, bombs were indeed raining down upon the city. *Cinema* (October 2, 1940), however, couldn't help complaining that the scene was historically inaccurate, since no bombs fell during the opening hours—or, indeed, months—of the war. In fact, the closing scene at the BBC takes place sometime *after* April 9, 1940 (the date of Jones' newspaper report on the invasion of Norway) and the bombing of London began in September 1940. Nothing, as far as I can tell, precludes the final scene from being set in September 1940—apart from the fact that it was shot two months earlier! *Foreign Correspondent* was, of course, inspired by American journalist Vincent Sheean's 1935 memoir *Personal History*. As a later volume, 1939's *Not Peace but a Sword*, revealed, Sheen himself was no fan of the BBC. He scolds the broadcasting giant for being blissfully unaware of Hitler's true intentions in the lead-up to the war, claiming (with respect to the Munich Agreement): "In the political disaster of 1938, the worst of modern times, the British Broadcasting Corporation did its bit." The film would thus seem to reflect (and reinforce) Sheean's views, inasmuch as it depicts an *American* broadcasting the war news, not an Oxford-accented Briton. The BBC also features indirectly in *Dial M for Murder*. There, Tony's best laid plans to have his wife murdered depend upon Margot staying home alone and listening to *Saturday Night Theatre* on the radio. This perennial BBC favorite debuted on April 3, 1943 and is still airing today, more than 60 years on. Finally, in Daphne du Maurier's story "The Birds," protagonist Nat Hocken notes that the BBC's Home Service had abandoned the usual programs and was playing dance music. This only happened "at exceptional times," like elections and, say, unprecedented attacks by masses of birds all over England. Interestingly, though the film adaptation takes place during the 1960s, Hitchcock still chose to have his protagonists monitor the bird attacks through the old-fashioned "wireless," heightening the sense of isolation and helplessness in a way that an "up-to-the-minute" television broadcast could not.

Station: Oxford Circus (BA; CE; VI) Take Exit 1 R into Regent Street and continue through Langham Place into Portland Place. BBC Radio is the curved building directly ahead. The BBC's television center is located in Wood Lane, Shepherd's Bush, while the Foreign Service is headquartered at Bush House (see **Kingsway**). For other Hitch-related BBC sites, see **Alexandra Palace** and **Lime Grove**.

The MacGuffin: According to the *Rich and Strange* shooting script (dated April 16, 1931), the initial sequence in the Hills' suburban home was to have been a bit longer, incorporating additional dialogue from the Dale Collins novel. After his "Damn the pictures—and the wireless," a line retained in the finished film, Fred begins a rant about "heroes and heroines…[having] fine fun…just flinging us shadows and echoes while the big world's living in flesh and blood….I tell you I want some life—I want to live—like the Prince of Wales—Charlie Chaplin—the Dolly Sisters—Bernard Shaw and Lady Di…[sic] Life I tell you—like that!" At this point, the novel, the script and the film cut to Fred's view of Thomas Somerscales' painting *Off Valparaiso*, after which comes the legacy. The return to London at the end of the story is an invention for the film: The novel concludes in Singapore, where author Dale Collins himself learns that the Hills have inherited yet *another* legacy, with which they plan to open a book shop on the South Coast of England.

14:8
Madame Tussaud's Wax Museum (F) L
Marylebone Road, NW1

Madame Tussaud's Wax Museum

Hitchcock's wax figure at Madame Tussaud's captures his *Psycho*-era appearance.

Founded by Marie Tussaud in 1835 (and located here in Marylebone Road since 1884), this perennial tourist favorite contains life-sized wax figures of the famous and infamous, including the Beatles, Agatha Christie, the British Royal Family, Jack the Ripper (see 58:2), Saddam Hussein, **Dr. Hawley Crippen** and even Alfred Hitchcock himself. (Hitchcock's figure captures his likeness in the *Psycho* era. The director was unable to attend the unveiling, but did send a telegram: "From the flesh to the wax—Good luck.") It was, of course, the infamous figures that fascinated Hitchcock, hence his desire—as he noted in 1937—to film the story of Edith Thompson and her young lover Freddy Bywaters, convicted murderers whose effigies were enshrined here at the museum from 1922 until 1981. (See the **Old Bailey** for more on the pair and their connection to *Stage Fright*.) Hence also the humorous reference to Tussaud's in *The 39 Steps*. There, hero Richard Hannay, handcuffed to—and on the lam with—the beautiful Pamela, explains to his reluctant companion that, "in years to come, you'll be able to take your grandchildren to Madame Tussaud's and point me out." In fact, talking of Tussaud's, that's how Hannay's career in crime began—through his descent from a murderous great-uncle, "the Cornish Bluebeard," who is himself displayed in the famous waxworks. "We must go down and see him sometime," he tells Pamela, who is by this time relaxed enough to fall asleep. A generation earlier, Marie Belloc Lowndes staged the suspenseful climax of her 1913 novel *The Lodger* in Tussaud's famous Chamber of Horrors. This sequence, rife with cinematic possibilities, was omitted from the film, as in the novel it confirms our belief that the title character is indeed the serial killer known as "The Avenger." In the film, of course, the lodger is ultimately proved innocent, so there could hardly be such a scene at the venerable tourist attraction. In Chapter 6 of *Malice Aforethought*, which Hitchcock adapted as a radio pilot in 1945, milquetoast Dr. Bickley and his domineering wife, Julia, consult a specialist in nearby **Harley Street** (see below) and then visit Tussaud's Chamber of Horrors. The doctor is especially interested in the Chamber, as he is planning to murder his wife! Finally, the museum is also mentioned in Chapter 21 of *Goodbye Piccadilly, Farewell Leicester Square*, when Dick Blamey jokes about selling his suit "to Madame Tussaud's for a tidy sum, so that they can dress my wax effigy in it."

Station: Baker Street (BA; CI; HC; JU; ME) Exit for Madame Tussaud's, which will be just ahead. **Hours:** Mon-Fri 10 am-5:30 pm; Sat-Sun 9:30 am-5:30 pm.

Ask Mr. Memory 21: A scene from one of Hitchcock's early films was first shown here at Tussaud's. What was the film?

14:9
Harley Street L
W1

Elegant Harley Street is the preserve of London's prestigious *private* medical practitioners and specialists, physicians to be distinguished from those in the National Health Service, who are remunerated by the Government and provide *free* medical care. In Chapter 6 of Francis Iles' *Malice Aforethought* (see above), Dr. Bickleigh takes his wife to a specialist here, knowing all along that what ails her is the drug he has been secreting in her morning grapefruit. The Harley Street specialist promptly concludes that the suffering spouse simply needs to have her tonsils removed! In Anthony Armstrong's story "The Case of Mr. Pelham," the title character fears for his sanity when a "double" appears to be taking over his life and so he visits a "mental specialist" here in Harley Street. The doctor avers that Pelham is sane, that the double is real, and that Pelham should vary his habits in order to throw off the impostor. Famous last words.... In the TV adaptation, Hitchcock switches the setting from London to New York and sets the patient-doctor conference in Mr. Pelham's club. A vestige of the original meeting place is retained, though, in the TV character's name: "Dr. Harley."

Harley Street

Station: Regent's Park (BA) Exit to the L into Marylebone Road, cross Park Crescent and look for Harley Street just ahead to the L.

A REFERENCE GUIDE TO LOCATIONS   **105**

14:10
Wigmore Street (F)
W1

According to *Personal History*, a 1939 film treatment by Alfred Hitchcock and Joan Harrison, there is a London-based organization called the World Peace Movement, located in Wigmore Street and headed by a politician named Buxton. A young American reporter pays Buxton a visit here in Wigmore Street, convinced that the politician may know something about the kidnapping of an important Dutch diplomat in Holland....This, of course, was the basis for *Foreign Correspondent*, an extremely loose reworking of Vincent Sheean's memoir *Personal History* (see **Gordon Square**). In the finished film, whose script is credited to Charles Bennett, Joan Harrison, James Hilton and Robert Benchley, the WPM has become the Universal Peace Party, Buxton has become Fisher and the reporter has acquired a name, Johnny Jones. The location of the party's headquarters is never specified in the film, nor need it be: The scene in which the reporter questions Buxton/Fisher about the Dutch diplomat now takes place in **Stephen Fisher's Home** in Smith Square, Westminster.

Station: Bond Street (CE; JU) Exit into **Oxford Street**, note the view eastward à la *Frenzy*, cross the street and take any of the little streets north to Wigmore.

14:11
Oxford Street F L
W1

The famous shopping thoroughfare—London's longest—was known as "the Road to Oxford" from at least 1682; the present name evolved in the 18th century after Edward Harley, 2nd Earl of Oxford, acquired the land on the north side of the road. Today, Oxford Street is routinely disparaged for its crass commercialism and the attendant bourgeois architecture, a notable exception being **Selfridges'** colossal colonnaded department store (see next entry). Yet there is a something undeniably vibrant and exciting about this hustling, bustling street. Maybe it's the aggressive determination with which the myriad merchants (from McDonald's to the Virgin Megastore) and street vendors try—and usually succeed—in separating the average consumer from his paycheck. Or perhaps it's the "familiar-yet-foreign" combination of American-style, in-your-face retailing set against a classic English backdrop of red double-decker buses and traditional black cabs. In any case, the street is a perennial tourist draw, one that Hitchcock chose to display on more than one occasion. In *Sabotage*, he dramatizes the effect of Verloc's actions at **Battersea Power Station** through a high-angle night shot of Oxford Street (at Selfridges), fully illuminated, bustling as ever. Suddenly, after the sabotage—sand in the power station works—all the lights go out, the frame goes black and London has seemingly just died. (For London's reaction to the sabotage, see the **London Zoo** and **Piccadilly Circus**.) Hitchcock returned to the street some 35 years later in *Frenzy*, which sees Dick Blaney turning off Oxford Street into Dryden Chambers (between Dean and Wardour Streets), en route to the **Blaney Bureau**. Immediately prior to this, he included an establishing shot of Oxford Street itself, looking east, from the Bond Street tube. The street visible in the background is Stratford Place, with the Berkshire

Oxford Street as shown in *Frenzy*

Hotel and Debenhams department store just beyond. Assistant director Colin Brewer actually filmed this shot (on October 15, 1971), as well as an *alternative* establishing shot of Oxford Street. The latter, which Hitchcock obviously rejected, was taken from the southeastern corner of Oxford Circus, looking west toward Debenhams et al. Interestingly, the call sheets—which list the day's filming set-ups—describe the Oxford Circus shot as the primary one and a shot of Marble Arch at the Cumberland Hotel as the alternative. It was also in—or, rather, just off—Oxford Street, near the Oxford Circus Underground Station, that Eve Gill first met Jonathan Penrose, the truly innocent man wrongly accused of murder in *Man Running*. At this point (Chapter 1), in fact, Jonathan is literally a "man running" from the law (as well as a man trying to "outrun the constable," the novel's American title) and is just about to be apprehended. In an instant, "a kind of reflex instinct...demanded that [Eve] protect this man from the hated police" and so she puts her arms around his neck and kisses him—a neat reversal of Hannay's trick on the train with Pamela in *The 39 Steps*. Hitchcock's adaptation of the novel, *Stage Fright*, presents us with characters who already know each other when the story begins and, indeed, are involved in something like a one-sided romance. Also, according to Chapter 16 of *Marnie*, the title character, having been identified by Strutt at a party, plans to flee to the Continent, stopping first at a Cook's travel agency (there was one at 86, near **St. Giles Circus**, and one at 416, near Selfridges), then dashing "straight into one of those quick places in Oxford Street where you can have your photo done in a few hours." In the film, Mark stops her long before she gets this far and simply carries on with the fox hunt, as he *eventually* does in the novel.

Station: Bond Street (CE; JU) Exit into Oxford Street and look east, toward Debenhams for the *Frenzy* view. Selfridges is just behind you and the Blaney Bureau is ahead to the right. Note that today Oxford Street is restricted to buses and taxis from 7 am-7 pm.

Ask Mr. Memory 22: In which film does a character pick up a plane ticket at a Cook's? Hint: The Cook's is in a hotel.

Selfridges

14:12
Selfridges F L
400 Oxford Street, W1

Opened on March 15, 1909 (but not completed until 1928), Gordon Selfridge's magnificent retail palace boasts what is undoubtedly the grandest shop façade in London: massive Ionic columns stretching from Duke to Orchard Streets, punctuated by bronze and glass interstices and ornamented with the distinctive Queen of Time clock over the main entrance. And the American retailer (retired from Chicago's famous Marshall Field's department store) didn't stop there; *inside* the store he installed over a hundred departments, a Hollywood-style soda fountain, a barbershop and a series of magnificent Art Deco lifts. The man himself boasted that "Selfridge's [sic] is for everyone," but it was the rich and famous who put the store on the map. Indeed, such was the immense appeal of the store that, after the adventures described in *The Wheel Spins* (a.k.a. *The Lady Vanishes*), the indomitable Miss Froy tells Iris that before she returns home, she plans to stop over for a few hours in London: "Selfridges, my dear. Just wandering. Topping." Hitchcock himself employed two exterior shots of Selfridges (the apostrophe was dropped in the 1960s) in the opening montage of *Sabotage*: one showing the brightly lit store majestically presiding over the hubbub of **Oxford Street** and a second showing the store and the street plunged into total darkness, the result of Verloc's sabotage at **Battersea Power Station**.

Station: Bond Street (CE; JU) Exit for Selfridges.

The MacGuffin: Although never mentioned in the film, Miss Froy's first name, according to the novel, is Winifred—ironically the same as that of the literary Mrs. Verloc. *Her* cinematic counterpart bears no first name either, although the shooting script calls her Sylvia, presumably after the actress who played her.

15. MAYFAIR

15:1
St. George's Hanover Square (F) L
2a Mill Street, W1

Built in 1721-24, St. George's boasts the first portico ever constructed for a London church. It also boasts a history of fashionable weddings among the rich and famous, including that of Percy Bysshe Shelley to Harriet Westbrook in 1814, Benjamin Disraeli to Mary Lewis in 1839, Theodore Roosevelt to Edith Carow in 1886, John Galsworthy (*The Skin Game*) to Ada Cooper in 1905 and John Buchan (*The Thirty-nine Steps*) to Susan Grosvenor in 1907. St. George's *was* to have hosted another prominent wedding on Thursday, July 26, 1938: that of Iris Matilda Henderson to Sir Charles Fotheringail, according to *The Lady Vanishes*. Iris doesn't seem particularly thrilled at the prospect, sighing to her friends that "this time next week, I shall be a slightly sunburnt offering on an altar in Hanover Square." Little wonder, then, that after the adventure—and romance—she enjoys in the Balkans, Iris returns to **Victoria Station**, takes one look at the stuffy Charles and renounces him for the dashing Gilbert. Whether Iris ever made it to the altar of the elegant St. George's is, unfortunately, one question the film leaves unanswered. The church is also name-dropped in Chapter 12 of Francis Beeding's *The House of Dr. Edwardes* (whence *Spellbound*), when asylum patient Miss Truelow asks if she can be a bridesmaid at Constance's wedding (to a devil worshipper!). Miss Truelow would know exactly what do, she explains, because she has "frequently been a bridesmaid at weddings at St. George's, Hanover Square." No trace of this character survives in the film, although early versions of Ben Hecht's script included a megalomaniac called "Mr. Trulow."

St. George's Hanover Square

Station: Oxford Circus (BA; CE; VI) Take Exit 3, go S in Regent Street to Maddox Street, where you will turn R. The church is ahead to the L, between Mill, Maddox and Saint George Streets.

The MacGuffin: We know that *The Lady Vanishes* takes place in July from the reference to the Test Match [cricket] in Manchester over which Charters and Caldicott obsess throughout the film. That match, between England and Australia, was scheduled for July 8-12, but was in fact, canceled on account of heavy rains—just as the newspaper headline reports at the end of the film. Yet, Hitchcock wasn't recreating history, he was prophesying it: The film was shot seven months before the actual match!

Bond Street

15:2
Bond Street L (F)
W1

London's most fashionable shopping street is in fact two streets: Old Bond Street, laid out in 1686 and stretching north from Piccadilly; and the larger New Bond Street, laid out in 1720 and continuing on to **Oxford Street**. As the site of so many exclusive shops and firms—Cartier, Tiffany, Asprey, Sotheby's, Gucci, et al.—Bond Street is an obvious reference whenever writers discuss the shopping habits of the rich and famous. Thus, the street is name-dropped into several Hitchcock source stories, though interestingly, only once in a Hitchcock film (*Downhill*, as the address of Roddy's solicitors). In Chapter 6 of *The Pleasure Garden*, Jerrie and Gaynor (Jill and Patsy in the film) visit a fortune-teller here in Bond Street (one Madame Ziska) and receive a startlingly accurate vision of their respective futures. (No such scene occurs in the film.) In *Rebecca* we learn that at the prompting of Mrs. Danvers, the second Mrs. de Winter has her party dress made by the fictional "Voce" of Bond Street (with the same disastrous results as in the film), while in *The Trouble with Harry* Sam asks Wiggy if she thinks his paintings would sell better in Bond Street, a venue altered to "Fifth Avenue" in the Americanized film. In *The Paradine Case* Sir Simon Flaquer's office is located in Bewly Place, a small cul de sac near Bond Street (we see only his private residence [1:2] in the film); later in the novel, the Keanes attend a showing in an art gallery (Sampson's) in Bond Street and later still, Keane meets with Lady Horfield at the same Bond Street gallery to discuss her husband's sadistic proclivities. This last scene was actually scripted and shot for the film, although the Bond Street setting was not specified. In the end, as with so much of the material planned or shot for this film, the art gallery sequence was cut for time. It does, however, appear in the original U.S. lobby card set of promotional photos. Interestingly, the novel *No Bail for the Judge*, which Hitchcock *almost* made into a film in 1959, contains a scene in which one of Mr. Low's agents picks up a prostitute here in Bond Street and the two of them then stop at an art gallery. Finally, in the short story "The Crystal Trench," the love-struck narrator takes Stella shopping in Bond Street, an episode omitted from Hitchcock's 1959 TV adaptation. Ironically, while the literary character lives in Dorset, her television counterpart must live fairly close to Bond Street as Cavendish tells us that she invited him "to have tea with her in her house in Mayfair."

Station: Bond Street (CE; JU) Exit R into Oxford Street; New Bond Street is just ahead, on the R. In the 1920s (when Robert Hichens wrote *The Paradine Case*) there were a number of art galleries in the vicinity of Sotheby's (No. 34-35), on both sides of New Bond Street, including Lewis and Lewis at No. 37 and Arthur Tooth at 155. Old Bond Street—farther on—was loaded with art galleries, including the Arlington Gallery and Gieves Art Gallery, both at No. 22.

The MacGuffin: Hitchcock himself invoked the famous street in a 1964 interview on the Canadian television program *Telescope*: "The most important moment [in a film is] when the man is buying a hat in the store in Bond Street when the gun is thrust into his ribs....[I]t's the juxtaposition of the norm of the accurate average against the fantasy.... That's what makes the thing interesting."

15:3
West End Central Police Station (F)
27 Savile Row, W1

In *Man Running*, whence *Stage Fright*, Ordinary Smith is assigned to the **Chelsea Police Station** in Lucan Place. In the shooting script for the film adaptation, Smith's card reveals his office as the "Criminal Investigation Dept., Scotland Yard, S.W.1.," which, of course, sounds far grander in the whole scheme of things.

West End Central Police Station

In the film itself, though, Smith's card locates him at the West End Central Police Station in "Saville Row" [*sic*], then and now, the headquarters of the Met's C Division. Geography—and technical advice from **Scotland Yard** itself—presumably prompted the change. Inwood's murder takes place in Mayfair (a setting clearly established by Eve's visit to **Shepherd's Tavern**), so it would have been from West End Central that Smith, et al., would have been dispatched.

Station: Oxford Circus (CE; PI; VI) Take Exit 3, go S in Regent Street to New Burlington Place, where you will turn R. The police station, little changed since Smith's day (at least on the outside), is straight ahead.

A REFERENCE GUIDE TO LOCATIONS

15:4
Claridge's H *(L)*
Brook Street, W1

Founded as Mivart's in 1812, this Brook Street landmark was acquired by William Claridge in 1854, sold to the Savoy Group in 1894 and rebuilt in its present seven-story, red brick form over the next few years. Since its patronage by the Royal Family in the 1860s, it has been considered one of the classiest hotels in London. Claridge's was, of course, Hitchcock's favorite hotel and he used it as a base of operations for virtually every trip back to London from the 1940s on. In the winter of 1943-44, for example, he stayed here while working on the two French-language shorts *Bon Voyage* and *Aventure Malgache* for Sidney Bernstein and the Ministry of Information (see **Welwyn Studios** and **University of London**); and again in July 1945, while working on the concentration camp documentary (eventually titled *Memory of the Camps*), also for Bernstein. In January 1955, he and writer Angus MacPhail worked here on the script for the new version of *The Man Who Knew Too Much*. Later that year, during production of that film, Hitchcock booked star Doris Day and her family into Claridge's, where they became virtual prisoners, thanks to the hordes of fans camped outside the hotel. (The singer/actress was then near the peak of her popularity.) In her autobiography, Day recalled that the hotel manager eventually asked her to leave "out of consideration for the...other guests." And so she did. In fact, she moved on to Paris (for wardrobe fittings) and Morocco (for location filming), before returning to London. This time, though, she was safely ensconced in **The Savoy**, just like her reel-life counterpart. In fact, Hitchcock had originally intended to base the McKennas at Claridge's, in accommodations similar to his own (suites 221 and 222). However, since no filming could be done at the hotel itself, the director planned to stage these scenes at **Forbes House**,

Claridge's

where the embassy ballroom sequence would also be filmed. In the end, however, it was decided to base the couple in the Savoy (Hitchcock's old haunt) and simply shoot the entire thing in Hollywood. Hitchcock and Alma returned to Claridge's in June 1956 when they conducted preproduction research at the **Colonial Office** for the ultimately aborted *Flamingo Feather*, this time staying in suites 418 and 419. In January 1959 and then again in April the couple settled into suites 318 and 319 while carrying out preproduction research for *No Bail for the Judge*, a project that also fell through, in this case because star Audrey Hepburn pulled out (see Appendix III). The Hitchcocks visited the hotel a number of times in the 1960s, notably during July-August 1968, when the director ensconced himself in suite 412 for a frantic rewrite of the *Topaz* script (the film was already in production) with screenwriter Samuel Taylor. Three years later, Hitchcock was back at work on another script here at Claridge's, this time collaborating with writer Anthony Shaffer on an adaptation of *Goodbye Piccadilly, Farewell Leicester Square*. During the preproduction and production of *Frenzy*, as the film itself was called, Hitchcock went on to spend over five months in the hotel, from mid-May until late October 1971, in suites 318 and 319. It was also here, in June of that year, that Alma Hitchcock suffered her first stroke. The director was, of course, devastated but Alma recovered fairly quickly (she was walking again by the 16th) and even popped onto the set from time to time. Associate producer Bill Hill recalls her humorous take on the situation: "Well, if I'm going to have a stroke, I can't imagine a better place to have it!" (At her daughter, Pat's, urging, Alma finally returned home to California.) Hitchcock's final visit to the hotel was in September 1972, when he visited London en route to the various European premieres of *Frenzy*.

Station: Bond Street (CE; JU) Walk S in Davies Street and look for the hotel ahead on the L, at the corner of Davies Street and Brook's Mews. Oh, and if you plan on attending any parties here, be aware that, according to Chapter 3 of *Rebecca*, it was at Claridge's that the boorish Mrs. Van Hopper first foisted herself on poor Maxim de Winter.

Ask Mr. Memory 23: Which Hitchcock actor once worked as a bill clerk at Claridge's?

15:5
"The Drummond (and Lawrence?) Home" L
Brook Street, W1

Though never as fashionable as nearby Grosvenor Street, this Mayfair thoroughfare has attracted its share of notables, including statesmen, prime ministers and even a legendary filmmaker (see previous entry). Brook Street also attracted the adventurous Hugh "Bulldog" Drummond and his wife, Phyllis, starting with *The Black Gang*, the second novel of the famous series by H.C. McNeile (Sapper), and continuing thereafter. (In the first novel, *Bulldog Drummond*, the bachelor protagonist—he has yet to meet Phyllis—lives at 60A Half Moon Street, which is not *too* far from Brook Street. In the fifth novel, *The Female of the Species*, the pair are inexplicably located in nearby Upper Brook Street. Whether Sapper intended to suggest that the Drummonds had moved from Brook Street, or whether he simply made a mistake, is unclear.) The Drummonds were the inspiration for the husband and wife protagonists of *The Man Who Knew Too Much*

(34), the original idea for the story being inspired by the notion of the couple's child being kidnapped. (The sole reference, veiled or otherwise, to the Drummonds having been so blessed, occurs in Chapter 1 of *Temple Tower*, the sixth in the Drummond series, when narrator Peter Darrell says of Hugh's ugly face that "even his wife admitted that she only used it to amuse the baby.") Additional elements from the Drummond canon appear in *Man Much*, as well as other Hitchcock films, and are discussed in Appendix I. One element from *The Black Gang*, however, is especially noteworthy in the context of the 1934 film—the setting at the **Royal Albert Hall**.

Station: Bond Street (CE; JU) Walk S in Davies Street and look for Brook Street ahead, where you will turn L. The Drummonds apparently lived near Bond Street, given details provided in Chapter 6 of *The Black Gang*. Upper Brook Street, where the couple is said to have lived at No. 5A in *The Female of the Species*, is on the western side of Grosvenor Square, in essence, a "continuation" of Brook Street itself.

The MacGuffin: The Drummond-Lawrence connection nearly came full circle in 1937, when Leslie Banks, star of *The Man Who Knew Too Much* (34), was asked to play the hero in *Bulldog Drummond Hits Out*, a stage adaptation penned by McNeile and his friend Gerard Fairlie. Banks turned down the part on the grounds that it was too physical. The part eventually went to actor-director Henry Edwards, who opened at the Savoy Theatre on December 21, 1937. McNeile himself died of lung cancer on August 14, 1937, with Fairlie continuing the Drummond series under the pen name of Sapper.

15:6
Grosvenor Square (L)
W1

Long known as "Little America," massive Grosvenor Square (the second largest in London, after Lincoln's Inn Fields) was laid out in the 1720s and, sadly, retains but a few of its original 18th-century homes on the north, east and south sides. (The fortress-

Grosvenor Square

like American Embassy wiped out all the houses on the west side in the 1950s.) The square has always been home to the rich and powerful, most of them titled, so it's no surprise to find that Sir Johnstone Kentley, father of *Rope* murder victim Ronald Kentley, lives here with his ailing wife. Playwright Patrick Hamilton describes Sir Johnstone as "a decidedly pleasant old gentlemen, slightly bent...[whose] listlessness and gentleness...derive not alone from a natural kindliness, but also from the fact that he has been in a position of total authority throughout the greater part of his life, and has no need to assert himself." The description equally applies to Hitchcock's own knight, Sir Cedric Hardwicke, who played the role to understated perfection in the film adaptation. The play's protagonists—Brandon and Granillo (Philip in the film)—also live in Mayfair, although Hamilton doesn't say precisely where.

Station: Bond Street (CE; JU) Walk S in Davies Street, then turn R into Brook Street and follow this to the square. No. 9, at the northeast corner of the square, was the residence of John Adams when he served as "minister plenipotentiary" of the United States in 1785-88.

Connaught Hotel

15:7
The Connaught H
Carlos Place, W1 (at Mount Street)

Built during the closing years of the 19th century, the former Coburg Hotel is one of several ornate terracotta-tiled buildings that line elegant Mount Street. Anti-German sentiment prompted the Coburg's change of name during World War I; a desire to preserve the hotel's distinctive "C" monogram inspired the actual replacement (after the Earl of Connaught and the various London locales named for him). Apart from its luxurious accommodations—and the Connaught is ranked as one of the leading hotels of the world—the establishment is also famous for its elegant restaurant, as well as the more intimate Grill Room, considered to be among the finest dining establishments in London. Both serve the same superb classic French dishes, as well as select traditional British fare. Not surprisingly, Alfred Hitchcock was a frequent restaurant patron during his London days, often dining here with London-based friends like Sidney Bernstein, his **Transatlantic** partner. Hitchcock had even planned to install the protagonists of the second *Man Who Knew Too Much* in the Connaught, according to the film's preproduction documents. In the end, he decided to base the McKennas in **The Savoy**, another of his London favorites.

Station: Bond Street (CE; JU) Go S in Davies Street then R into Mount Street. The hotel is straight ahead. **Restaurant hours:** Mon-Sun *Luncheon* 12:30 pm, last orders 2:30 pm; *Dinner* 6:30 pm, last orders 10:45 pm. Jacket and tie are required.

Berkeley Square

15:8
Berkeley Square F L
W1

This fashionable square, originally laid out in the 1730s, takes its name from the 1st Lord Berkeley of Stratton, the Royalist commander during the English Civil War. The elegant houses that once lined its eastern side are now gone, but the western side retains several fine buildings dating from the mid-18th century, including No. 44, which, though modest in appearance (at least on the outside), was once described as the finest terrace house in London. Perhaps even more striking than its buildings are the square's majestic plane trees, over 30 in all, which are believed to have been planted in 1789. This elegant setting forms a backdrop for an intriguing scene in Chapter 5 of John Buchan's *The Three Hostages*, arguably the best of his Richard Hannay novels, and one which Hitchcock considered filming in 1964. Here, Hannay and a new friend, the charming Dominick Medina, MP, cross the square en route to the latter's home in Hill Street. (For more on Hill Street, see **Lady Devlin's Home**.) As they do so, Hannay recalls the queer places he has visited and the adventures he has shared with their mutual acquaintance Sandy Arbuthnot. At first, Berkeley Square strikes him as a stark and refreshing contrast to those queer places:

> The West End of London at night always affected me with a sense of the immense solidity of our civilization. These great houses, lit and shuttered and secure, seemed the extreme opposite of the world of half-lights and perils in which I had sometimes journeyed. I thought of them as I thought of [my home], as sanctuaries of peace. But tonight I felt differently towards them. I wondered what was going on at the back of those heavy doors. Might not terror and mystery lurk behind that barricade as well as in tent and slum?

Might, indeed, for the well-connected Medina turns out to be the mastermind of a diabolical criminal conspiracy, the very prototype of Hitchcock villains in *The 39 Steps*, *Foreign Correspondent*, *Saboteur* and *North By Northwest*. And his "substantial house in Hill Street" is, in fact, the innocent-looking base from which he directs his operations, again, foreshadowing the establishment homes (and their secrets) of Jordan, Fisher, Tobin (as well as Mrs. Sutton) and Vandamm. Indeed, Hannay's musings here in the heart of London's most fashionable and respectable neighborhood could have easily been written of Hitchcock himself, whose interest in the chaos and darkness that lie beneath the surface or behind ordinary, respectable façades is well-documented. So, was it with a certain sense of irony that the director chose this setting for the home of *Murder!* protagonist Sir John Menier? Upon our return to London from the country district where the title crime takes place, Hitchcock establishes our new locale through a shot of a traditional street sign; it indicates that we are in "Berkeley Square, City of Westminster." The shooting script goes even further, locating the great actor-manager in "flat 2" of a "fashionable" apartment block. For some reason, Hitchcock chose not to include a scripted insert shot revealing the number and, beneath it, Sir John's name on an engraved plaque. Interestingly, authors Clemence Dane and Helen Simpson also indicate the number of Sir John's Berkeley Square flat, but not in *Enter Sir John*, the novel upon which the film *Murder!* was based. Rather, in the follow-up novel, *Re-enter Sir John*, the authors install their hero and his wife in No. 102 Berkeley Square (although then and now, the numbers stopped in the fifties). The sequel was published in 1932, two years after the film, and presumably follows the lead of *Murder!* itself. (For another of Sir John Menier's haunts, see **Her Majesty's Theatre**.)

Elsewhere, in Chapter 27 of *The Paradine Case*, Sir Malcolm Keane is walking home from Sir Simon's office near **Bond Street** when he finds himself inexorably drawn to a snow-covered Berkeley Square. The square is not on his way home, but *is* on his way to the St. James's Club where he believes he will find the odious Judge Horfield. Keane fears that his wife may have insulted Lord Horfield at the **Adelphi Theatre** and now wonders whether to face the old man, flatter him and try to make amends for Gay's actions (all in the interest of saving Mrs. Paradine's life), or to simply turn around and go home to Portland Place (see **Keane Home**). He decides, predicatably, to go suck up to Horfield. The film adaptation omits all of this business, merely suggesting that

Horfield may be fond of imposing the death penalty. (A scene in which Lady Horfield implored Keane to be nice to the judge in order to save Mrs. Paradine was filmed, but ultimately dropped. For more on this, see **Bond Street**.) Berkeley Square was also the setting for Brenda Blamey's [sic] club in the novel *Goodbye Piccadilly, Farewell Leicester Square*, a setting that Hitchcock actually considered for the film adaptation, *Frenzy*. In fact, he had reference photos taken of the Clermont Club at No. 44, as well as the elegant stucco house at No. 1 Tilney Street. In the end, however, he plumped for Universal Pictures' London office in Piccadilly (see **Brenda Blaney's Club**) for the club's exterior and the Green Room at **Pinewood Studios** for the interior.

Station: Green Park (JU; PI; VI) Exit on the North Side and go L (East) in Piccadilly, then L into Berkeley Street. Follow this to Berkeley Square. Brenda Blamey's club appears to have been located on the western side of the square, opposite Barclay's showroom, as is No. 44 itself.

The MacGuffin: The literary Sir John's surname—*Saumarez*—more closely approximates that of his real-life prototype, Sir Gerald du Maurier (see 17:8). The name may also recall that of Admiral Lord James (de) Saumarez, a hero of the Battle of Trafalgar. The de Saumarezes were a distinguished Anglo-French family of Guernsey, Channel Islands. They were connected by marriage to another distinguished local family, the de Havillands. Alfred Hitchcock twice directed a member of the latter family—Joan Fontaine, née de Havilland.

Ask Mr. Memory 24: Sir John Menier also maintains an elegant office—with impossibly plush carpeting. Where is it located?

15:9
"Edgar Brodie's Home" F
84 Curzon Street, W1

Hitchcock's 1936 thriller *Secret Agent* (adapted from Somerset Maugham's novel *Ashenden*) opens at "84 Curzon St. W.1.," the home of the "late" novelist Edgar Brodie. (An early version of the script located him at 21 Bruton Street, just off **Berkeley Square**.) Mourners have assembled to pay their respects to the celebrated author, whose one-armed servant attends the coffin. After the mourners have left, the servant struggles to remove the coffin, which he tips over to reveal that it is in fact empty. Brodie, it seems, is very much alive and on his way to a meeting with Secret Service chief "R" (for "rhododendron," of course), who assigns him a new name—Richard Ashenden—and a mission vital to Britain's efforts in the War (the time is May 1916). In the novel, Brodie's real name *is* Ashenden (he later poses as "Somerville"), he lives at 36 Chesterfield Street (see **Ashenden's Home**), meets "R." [sic] at a party, then journeys to his secret headquarters, presumably in the **War Office**. The fake funeral bit was invented for the film and later appropriated by Hitchcock source author Roald Dahl for the James Bond thriller *You Only Live Twice*. Also invented was the address "84 Curzon Street." Then as now, the numbers of this fashionable Mayfair venue stopped at 72.

Station: Hyde Park Corner (PI) Exit for Park Lane, walk N (away from Hyde Park Corner) and then turn R into Curzon Street.

The MacGuffin: Curzon Street was also the home of another fictional character of interest to Hitchcock: the incomparable Duke de Reichleau. Hero of a series of novels by British author Dennis Wheatley, De Reichleau debuted in *The Forbidden Territory* (1933), along with Simon Aron, Richard Eaton and Rex Van Ryn—a modern day three, or, rather, four musketeers. Hitchcock knew Wheatley and, shortly after the novel's publication, told the author that he was anxious to film *The Forbidden Territory*, a Buchanesque adventure set largely in the Soviet Union. Unfortunately, after his move to **Lime Grove Studios** that same year, Hitchcock lost his chance to direct the film, the job ultimately going to Russian-born Phil Rosen. Still, there remains an important Hitchcock connection to the film, for its screenplay was written Alma Reville.

Ask Mr. Memory 25: To what did the late Captain Brodie succumb, according to *The Evening News*?

**15:10
Shepherd Market (F)
W1**

The "village center" of Mayfair, Shepherd Market was the site of the 17th-century "May Fair," the frequently riotous annual event from which the district itself took its name. The present network of narrow streets and alleys was laid out by architect Edward Shepherd in 1735, with the majority of buildings—food shops, restaurants and pubs—having been rebuilt in the 19th century. It was in this traditional London setting

Shepherd Market

that Hitchcock chose to set portions of his unrealized 1959 film *No Bail for the Judge*. Near the beginning of the film, the title character, Sir Edwin Proud, was to witness here an unpleasant fight between two streetwalkers, one of whom is aided by another prostitute, Flossie. The judge, who had merely been out for his evening constitutional, retires from the distasteful scene and continues along Curzon Street, eventually turning into a deserted street. There, while attempting to save a dog from a speeding car, he falls, hits his head and, as he regains his precarious balance, appears for all intents and purposes as if he were drunk. (In the novel, it is a small child and the judge doesn't strike his head, but rather suffers a small stroke.) To his rescue comes Flossie, who takes him to her flat, puts him in her bed and promptly pockets his money. The next morning, the judge awakes to find himself lying across Flossie's dead body, his distinctive Club tie knotted tightly around her throat. In this departure from Henry Cecil's novel, in which Flossie is knifed through the heart, Samuel Taylor's script clearly anticipates *Frenzy* serial killer Bob Rusk's modus operandi, as well as the look of his victims, with their open mouths and "staring, bulging eyes." Later scenes, in which one of the central characters picks up prostitutes who may have known Flossie, were also to be set here in Shepherd Market. Production designer Henry Bumstead scouted the (in)famous district in the spring of 1959, taking dozens of reference photos for a planned recreation back in Hollywood. "I was there [in London] a month," he told me, "and I saw Hitch two times: once in Shepherd Market, where all the prostitutes hung out, and then in **Epsom Downs**, which was to be [the setting for] the end of the picture." And both times, the highlight of the day was "a great big lunch!" The setting for the former was nearby Cunningham's, where Bumstead and the director were joined by associate producer Herb Coleman. "My God, we were there two or three hours! And then Hitch says, 'Bummy, you look like you're still hungry. You want dessert, don't you?' And I said, 'Hitch, I couldn't eat another thing.' And with that Herbie Coleman kicked me under the table. Then Hitch asked me again and I said, 'Hitch, I just can't.' Later, Herbie said, 'You idiot! Hitch wanted dessert but he wasn't going to order any unless you ordered it too. You deprived him of his dessert!' But Hitch still liked me well enough to keep me on the picture!" Indeed, and, as related under the Epsom Downs entry, Bumstead was ready to begin set construction in Hollywood when the production was abruptly canceled. For more on the *No Bail* story, see Appendix III.

Station: Green Park (JU; PI; VI) Exit on the North side and go R in Piccadilly, then R into White Horse Street, which leads to Shepherd Market.

**15:11
Shepherd's Tavern F
50 Hertford Street, W1**

It is to this 300-year-old Mayfair institution that Eve comes to prize information out of **Scotland Yard** detective Ordinary Smith in *Stage Fright*. The scene is drawn from Chapter 7 of the source novel, *Man Running*, in which Eve follows Smith from **Charlotte Inwood's Home (2)** to the Four Feathers, a fictional pub in Chelsea. Hitchcock includes an exterior shot of the actual building, but the interior, with its fabled leather seats and bow window, was created on an **Elstree** soundstage.

Shepherd's Tavern

Station: Hyde Park Corner (PI) Exit for Park Lane, walk N (away from Hyde Park Corner), then turn R into Hertford Street and follow this as it curves to the L; the tavern is straight ahead, at the intersection with Shepherd Street.

15:12
"Ashenden's Home" (L)
36 Chesterfield Street, W1

In Chapter 7 of *Ashenden*, British Intelligence chief "R." learns to his amazement that the title agent has never heard of the infamous Indian agitator Chandra Lal. "Where have you been living all these years?" he demands impatiently. "At 36, Chesterfield Street, Mayfair," Ashenden impertinently replies. It's funny (in more ways than one) that Ashenden should say this, since his creator, William Somerset Maugham, also lived here in Chesterfield Street, an 18th-century setting that remains one of the least altered in Mayfair. Maugham actually lived at No. 6 (there is no 36 in this very short street) from 1911-1919, during which time he was recruited by Sir John Wallinger, an

Somerset Maugham's Home/Ashenden's Home

officer of the **War Office's** Intelligence Branch. Maugham, then 41 and already a successful author, was sent to Switzerland in September 1915 in order to reestablish contact with other British agents. His subsequent adventures both in Western Europe and Russia, as well as those of his fellow agent Gerald Kelly, were the inspiration for *Ashenden* (whence Hitchcock's *Secret Agent*), which, upon its publication in 1928, prompted Winston Churchill to declare the novel to be in violation of the Official Secrets Act!

Station: Hyde Park Corner (Pl) Exit for Park Lane, walk N (away from Hyde Park Corner) and then turn R into Curzon Street. Chesterfield Street is just ahead, to the L. Maugham's house is marked with an English Heritage Blue Plaque.

The MacGuffin: Curzon Street boasts a number of espionage-related sites: Leconfield House, at the corner of South Audley Street, was the HQ of MI5 (counterintelligence) from 1945 to 1976 (it is visible in the background of a shot of the police outside **Charlotte Inwood's Home (1)** in *Stage Fright*); Curzon Street House, at No. 1-4, was the MI5 Registry (administrative office) from 1976 to 1995; and No. 36 was the home of the Director of Naval Intelligence (Ian Fleming's boss) during WWII. Curzon Street House was demolished in 1996 but the other sites remain.

15:13
"Charlotte Inwood's Home" (1) F
78 South Audley Street, W1

In the novel *Man Running*, Charlotte Inwood lived in "Cary Gardens," a fictional South Kensington street linking Brompton and Fulham Roads (see **Charlotte Inwood's Home [2]**). Hitchcock's adaptation, originally called *Man Running* but ultimately retitled *Stage Fright*, would relocate Charlotte to tonier digs here in Mayfair. Specifically, Hitchcock wanted a house near Piccadilly, between **Hyde Park Corner** and **The Ritz**,

Charlotte Inwood's home as seen in *Stage Fright*

one with enough steps so that people could be seen going in and out above the heads of the onlookers. Production supervisor Fred Ahern eventually found the perfect house here in South Audley Street, just a short walk from Curzon Street (as well as the headquarters of MI5). Hitchcock incorporated exteriors of the actual building, as well as shots of the façade built at **Elstree Studios**. A double for actress Jane Wyman was brought to the location; Wyman herself performed only

Hitchcock's cameo in *Stage Fright*

on the studio set. Thus, when Eve first approaches Charlotte's home, Wyman is standing—courtesy of rear-projection—in Curzon Street, near Curzon Place. (Note that her view of No. 78 is, in fact, impossible from this vantage point.) Later, as she telephones her father from a callbox across from Charlotte's home, rear-projection footage accurately portrays Hill Street in the background. Another rear-projection shot—Eve's POV of Ordinary Smith in the crowd—accurately portrays the view looking south toward Curzon Street, including the large MI5 building to the left of the frame. Eve then follows Smith past No. 80 South Audley from which we jump immediately to **Shepherd's Tavern**, in Hertford Street, the actual route presumably being telescoped for the sake of pace.

Station: Hyde Park Corner (Pl) Exit for Park Lane, walk N (away from Hyde Park Corner) and then turn R into Curzon Street. South Audley Street is ahead to the L. Interestingly, in the novel, Charlotte's friend Freddy Williams (Freddie in the film), lives in North Audley Street, opposite the big chemist's.

The MacGuffin: Just to the south of Charlotte's house is No. 1 Tilney Street, a stylish Georgian mansion that Hitchcock had photographed as a possibility for the exterior of Brenda's club in *Frenzy*. In the end, he chose Universal's London office in Piccadilly (see **Brenda Blaney's Club**), although the scene was ultimately cut for time.

15:14
"Lady Devlin's Home" (F)
20 Hill Street, W1

Baronet-cum-pimp Sir Edward Devlin lives here, with his society hostess mother, according to the script for Alfred Hitchcock's unproduced 1959 film *No Bail for the Judge*. Hitchcock had originally considered **Albany**, the exclusive apartment block off Piccadilly, but ultimately decided to locate the action closer to **Hyde Park**, where a pivotal encounter precedes the sequences set in Lady Devlin's home. (Hitchcock may have also recalled the Hill Street home of the mother-son team of villains in John

Buchan's *The Three Hostages*, a Richard Hannay thriller which the director considered filming in 1964.) Heroine Elizabeth Proud, posing as a prostitute to uncover the murderer of a Mayfair streetwalker (with whose death her father has been wrongly charged), has just allowed herself to be "taken" in the park by Sir Edward, whom she believes to be the killer. She then accompanies him to his mother's home, where she is summarily chucked out by the not-so-grande dame. It seems Lady Devlin is, in fact, no lady at all. Rather, she is a former streetwalker who married a peer for his money, only to find out upon his death that the man had been cut off without a cent. She and her son now run a profitable ring of call girls and, twigging Miss Proud's purpose, decide to arrange a convenient "suicide" in the young woman's home. At this point, Elizabeth's "partner in crime," Anthony Low, decides to break into the Hill Street house through a fanlight in the roof. Unfortunately, he is too late—the Devlins have already drugged poor Elizabeth and are now heading for **Edwin Proud's Home**, to which you should turn for the rest of the story....

Lady Devlin's Home

Station: Hyde Park Corner (Pl) Exit for Park Lane, walk N (away from Hyde Park Corner), turn R into Curzon Street, then L into South Audley Street. Hill Street—visible in the rear-projection background plates for Eve Gill's phone call from a box opposite **Charlotte Inwood's Home (1)** in *Stage Fright*—is just ahead to the R. Lady Devlin's house is on the L (although, frankly, the house next door at No. 22, looks more attractive). Coincidentally (?), Julia Fotheringale, the conniving gold digger who contributes to Roddy's ruin in *Downhill*, also lived in Hill Street.

15:15
The Dorchester H L
53 Park Lane, W1

One of the most luxurious hotels in London (and consistently rated as one of the best hotels in the world), the fabulous Dorchester opened its doors with great fanfare on April 18, 1931. Since then, the "perfect hotel" (as its founders envisioned it) has hosted a star-studded clientele that includes General Dwight Eisenhower (whose two-room accommodation is today called—what else?—the Eisenhower Suite), the Duke of Edinburgh, Mikhail Gorbachev, George Bush, Noël Coward, Somerset Maugham, Ian Fleming, Pierce Brosnan, James Mason, Julie Andrews, Marlene Dietrich and, on at least one occasion during the late 1940s, Alfred Hitchcock himself. In fact, it was here in the Dorchester that Hitchcock discovered straight-faced comic actor Naunton Wayne in 1937. Wayne was then working as a compère, or emcee, at some of London's poshest nightspots, including the Ritz, the Café de Paris and, of course, the Dorchester. "He announced each act and said a few words between turns," Hitchcock recalled in a 1957 interview. And the director apparently liked what he saw (presumably the understated, deadpan delivery) for he cast him as the second half of the inimitable Charters and Caldicott in his next film,

The Dorchester

The Lady Vanishes. The slightly more animated Charters, of course, was played to perfection by Basil Radford, who had just appeared in Hitchcock's *Young and Innocent* opposite Mary Clare (who also appeared in *The Lady Vanishes*). Radford and Wayne would go on to play C & C in both Carol Reed's *Night Train to Munich* (1940), starring Margaret Lockwood and Rex Harrison, and *Crooks' Tour* (1940), all three films being written by Frank Launder and Sidney Gilliat. (In 1942, the two actors fell out with Launder and Gilliat over the size of their parts and so said goodbye to the names—if not the characters—of Charters and Caldicott. They continued as a team in both radio and films until Radford's death in 1952.) Years later, Hitchcock wanted to base *Frenzy*'s Hetty and Johnny Porter here at the Dorchester (according to exterior location notes of December 31, 1970), à la their literary counterparts in the Arthur La Bern novel. Production associates recommended a more modern hotel, Hitchcock consented, and so the Porters ended up in the **London Hilton** just down Park Lane.

Station: Hyde Park Corner (PI) The hotel is just up Park Lane, on the R. Afternoon tea is served on the Promenade each day from 3 pm-5 pm.

15:16
ex **Park Lane House F**
45 Park Lane, W1

Doubles as: Unnamed Embassy in *The Man Who Knew Too Much* (56)

Built for diamond magnate Barney Barnato in the 1890s, Park Lane House was a flamboyant French-style chateau whose roof originally boasted a gaggle of gargoyles. (These were subsequently pulled down by banker Sir Edwin Sassoon, who acquired the house from Barnato.) In May 1955, Alfred Hitchcock selected this imposing mansion as one of four London buildings that would double as the foreign embassy in *The Man Who Knew Too Much* (56). (For the other sites, and other candidate sites, see **Forbes House**.) So it was here, on June 7, 8 and 9, 1955, that the Draytons cooled their heels while waiting to meet with the ambassador; where the McKennas arrived for the reception (for which they retire to the ballroom of Forbes House); and where Drayton ultimately took his fatal fall down those plushly carpeted steps. The upstairs corridor and room (where Hank is held) were built in Hollywood; the switch from the studio to Park Lane House footage occurs as Drayton, Ben and Hank approach the upstairs landing. Hitchcock also photographed an establishing shot of the front of Park Lane House to be combined with footage of the McKennas entering the embassy on the Paramount backlot. This sequence was cut from the finished film, presumably for time. Sadly, PLH was demolished in 1964 and replaced with a glass and steel tower that went on to house Hugh Hefner's London Playboy Club from 1966 to 1981. That building is today owned by the Sultan of Brunei, one of the richest men in the world.

Station: Hyde Park Corner (Pl) The site is up Park Lane, on the R, just before the Dorchester. Hitchcock had planned to shoot the front of the "embassy" exterior from across the street (which was then much narrower), in Hyde Park.

The MacGuffin: Publicity materials for *The Lodger* indicate that the film's finale takes place in the title character's "Park Lane mansion." However, given the view of Parliament from his window, the location seems more like **County Hall**, Lambeth!

15:17
London Hilton on Park Lane F
22 Park Lane, W1

Although it is today considered the flagship property of Hilton International, this 30-story "Manhattanism" was thoroughly disparaged when it opened in 1963. Towering above Park Lane and **Hyde Park**, the hotel was said to "ruin" the local skyline. Alfred Hitchcock exploited that very effect in *Frenzy*, when he crafted the scene in which Babs and Dick meet up with the latter's old RAF comrade Johnny Porter in the park. As Dick explains his situation to Johnny (on the run as the suspected Necktie Murderer), we literally look down upon the trio from the lofty Hilton, the POV being that of Mrs. Porter, who thoroughly disapproves of (if not outright despises)

London Hilton on Park Lane

Dick Blaney. Indeed, she eventually convinces her husband to abandon "old Dicko" in his hour of need, an action that prompted Hitchcock himself (in an interview with Peter Bogdanovich) to describe the Porters as "a couple of shits." (Interestingly, in the Arthur La Bern novel [see Appendix I], the Porters do *not* betray Dick and, significantly, are based at a more traditional luxury hotel, **The Dorchester**, just up Park Lane from the Hilton.) The Hilton sequence, including the Hyde Park footage, was filmed on Sunday, September 12, 1971. Hetty's POV was shot from the window of suite 508/509, which also served as the makeup and hair room for actors Jon Finch and Clive Swift. (Anna Massey and Billie Whitelaw were readied at the **Coburg**.) Hotel interiors were filmed at **Pinewood Studios**.

Mrs. Porter looks down into the park from the Hilton in *Frenzy*.

Station: Hyde Park Corner (PI) The hotel is just up Park Lane, on the R. Look for the spot in the middle of Park Lane, directly opposite the hotel, where Dick and Babs meet Johnny.

Ask Mr. Memory 26: What is the name of the English pub that Johnny is opening in Paris?

15:18
Royal Air Force Club (L)
128 Piccadilly, W1

The RAF Club was founded here in 1918 as a gathering place for serving and former officers of the Royal Air Force. Arthur La Bern mentions the club in Chapter 4 of *Goodbye Piccadilly, Farewell Leicester Square*, when down and out ex-Squadron Leader Richard Blamey considers dropping by to put the touch on one of his old comrades. (His ex-wife has just given him dinner at her Mayfair club [see **Brenda Blaney's Club**], but now, as in the film *Frenzy*, he has to find somewhere to bed down for the night.) Blamey himself is not a member of the RAF Club, but is sure that someone at the bar would be good for a fiver. In the end, however, he cannot bring himself "to put the bite on old friends," and wanders off through Piccadilly Circus, eventually taking shelter at the **Salvation Army Hostel** in Middlesex Street. Loyalty, here reflected in Blamey's estimation of his old RAF comrades, is one of the novel's central concerns and it is interesting that, unlike his cinematic counterpart, Johnny Dring-Porterhouse (simplified to Porter in the film) stands by Blamey in his hour of need, testifying (along with his wife, Hetty)

Royal Air Force Club

that Blamey was with him at the time of Babs' murder (see the **Old Bailey**). That Johnny could or would let down his old Air Force comrade is literally unthinkable in La Bern's fictional world, which esteems the old order and its values and repudiates the new. Hitchcock's London, by contrast, is largely anachronistic: **Scotland Yard**, old Covent Garden, traditional pubs and references to Jack the Ripper (see 58:2) scarcely locate us in post-War Britain. Thus, since he has no axe to grind with the modern age (which, for all intents and purposes, does not exist), Hitchcock has no "old order" to uphold in contrast and can thus engineer Porter's abandonment of his old comrade. (And since the protagonists fought during the Suez crisis of 1956, not World War II, Hitchcock avoids aspersing the veterans whom La Bern celebrates.) With the Porters' betrayal (and the elimination of Blaney's alibi), Hitchcock can now effect a reasonably tight case against his hero while at the same time sparing us the extended and largely anti-climactic trial of the novel (in which the couple's testimony is ultimately discounted in any case). For all this, it is worth noting that Hitchcock actually had reference photos taken of the RAF Club and sent to him in California in January 1971. Did he envision a scene set in the club itself, or did he merely want background information (as he often did) to help with some detail of Blaney or Porter's character? Unfortunately, the answer was nowhere to be found in the *Frenzy* production notes at the Academy Library, so, for now, we can only speculate.

Station: Hyde Park Corner (PI) Exit for Piccadilly and look for the RAF Club on the L.

15:19
***ex* American Club (F)**
95 Piccadilly, W1

This was the club where Johnny Jones intended to have lunch in *Foreign Correspondent* but, of course, thanks to Rowley, he never made it (see **Westminster Cathedral** for the site of their fateful detour). The American Club was founded by a group of American businessmen (who else?) at **The Savoy** in October 1918. The club relocated to No. 95 Piccadilly, a late

American Club

19th-century mansion owned by Sir Henry Falle and his American-born wife, Lady Falle, a short time later. Having never attained anything like the devoted membership of the more traditional London clubs (see **White's**), the American closed its doors in the 1980s.

Station: Green Park (JU; PI; VI) Exit on the North Side and go R (West) in Piccadilly. No. 95 is just past the Naval and Military Club at No. 94.

15:20
May Fair (Intercontinental) Hotel (F)
Stratton Street (at Berkeley Street), W1

The elegant May Fair Hotel, along with its sumptuous Le Chateau restaurant, has been a favorite of the famous and fashionable ever since its high-profile opening by King George V in 1927. In a 1986 interview, screenwriter Charles Bennett recalled that during his collaboration with Hitchcock in the 1930s, the two men would stop working around 1:00 p.m. and then go to lunch, "always at the Mayfair [*sic*]." Biographer John Russell Taylor also noted, in reference to the collaboration on *The 39 Steps*, that Bennett would pick Hitchcock up at the latter's Cromwell Road home (see 22:1), drive to **Lime Grove Studios**, discuss the script, then lunch "in great comfort at the Mayfair [*sic*] hotel or the Kensington Palace Hotel" after which they would return "grandly to the studio for an afternoon session." It was also here, at the Institute of Amateur Cinematographers' annual dinner, on the night of November 3, 1936, that Hitchcock and actor Charles Laughton first discussed collaborating with producer Erich Pommer on a film project. Two years later, as a result of that conversation, Hitchcock directed (or at least *tried* to direct) Laughton in an extremely loose adaptation of Daphne du Maurier's *Jamaica Inn*, his last film before moving to Hollywood.

Station: Green Park (JU; PI; VI) Exit on the North Side and follow Stratton Street to the hotel.

15:21
"Johnnie Aysgarth's Flat" (F)
Albany
Albany Court Yard
Piccadilly, W1

Albany (*not* "The Albany," as it is often rendered) is an exclusive apartment complex centered around the former Melbourne House, a Palladian-style mansion built for the 1st Viscount Melbourne in the 1770s. Melbourne sold the house in 1802 and the new owner, Alexander Copland, converted the mansion (to which he added two rows of flats) into a bachelors' chambers. (It eventually went "co-ed.") Among Albany's roster of famous residents (which includes a virtual Who's Who of poets, playwrights and politicians) was the author J. B. Priestley, who collaborated with Hitchcock on *Jamaica Inn*, Sidney Bernstein, Hitchcock's **Transatlantic Productions** partner, and the fictional jewel thief A.J. Raffles, the unofficial inspiration for the protagonist of *To Catch a Thief*. (See

Johnnie Aysgarth's Flat in Albany

Appendix I for more on the latter.) According to the telephone directory Lina consults near the beginning of *Suspicion*, Albany is also home to London playboy Johnnie Aysgarth, who lives in Apartment A11. (Bernstein occupied 11A.) Now Albany is sometimes described as London's most exclusive address, so at first it would appear that our hero must be a man of quite some means. However, as we (and Lina) soon learn, Johnnie is broke and unemployed, a perennial ne'er-do-well who sponges off his friends and relatives. So just how does he afford to live in such opulent quarters? Perhaps Johnnie and Raffles have more than an address in common....

Station: Green Park (JU; PI; VI) Exit on the North Side and go L (East) in Piccadilly. Albany Court Yard, the entrance to the Albany, is ahead on the L.

Ask Mr. Memory 27: What is John Aysgarth's middle initial?

15:22
"Brenda Blaney's Club" (F)
138 Piccadilly, W1

On the evening of September 15, 1971, Alfred Hitchcock filmed two takes of Brenda and Richard Blaney exiting her exclusive "Women's Club" and hailing a taxi here in Piccadilly. (The first take was spoiled because the taxi driver waited too long to pull up to the curb.) This brief scene never made it to the film *Frenzy*, but it is noteworthy for two reasons. First, it reveals the address of Brenda's flat—31 Berkeley Mews; and second, it takes place in front of the London office of Universal Pictures, the company which distributed the film. The actual exterior of Brenda's flat was filmed in Ennismore Gardens Mews (see 22:4), while the Club's interior was filmed in the Green Room at **Pinewood Studios**. For another brief exterior sequence deleted from *Frenzy*, see **Chief Inspector Oxford's Flat**.

Station: Green Park (JU; PI; VI) Exit on the North Side and follow Stratton Street to the hotel.

Brenda Blaney's Club was cut out of *Frenzy*.

16. PIMLICO

16:1
The Lodger's Plan of the Avenger Murders F
SW1

In the novel he cuts a swathe (literally) between **St. Pancras** and **Regent's Park**, but Hitchcock's "Avenger" prefers an altogether different postal code. According to the map drawn up by the title character (who, unlike his literary counterpart, proves to be innocent of the crimes), the Avenger has struck in the following places: **Trafalgar Square**; **Charing Cross Station**; **St. James's Park** (twice: near the northeast corner and the southwest corner); **Victoria Embankment** (near **Westminster Bridge**); Storey's Gate (opposite Westminster Abbey); the top of Horseferry Road; Millbank at Lambeth Bridge; and Eccleston Square, behind Victoria Station. From this "pattern," **Scotland Yard** has concluded that the next attack will occur near a particular group of lodging houses, an assumption also shared by the Lodger, who has drawn a new triangle near the point where Vauxhall Bridge Road becomes Bessborough Gardens, just before Vauxhall Bridge. The implication is that the Bunting home is located here, at No. 13, which, at the time, was located at the corner of John Islip Street. (The house has since been demolished.) Charing Cross Station is actually announced as the site of the third murder in one of the Lodger's newspaper clippings; the film opens with the discovery of the Embankment murder; and the dancer is killed near **St. Margaret's Church**, although whether this is the Storey's Gate murder or the Millbank murder is unclear. Interestingly, the final (attempted) murder should have been the ninth, according to the narrative, although the map shows 10 separate triangles. Incidentally, all of this should refute the claim, beginning with the earliest commentators and continuing through, e.g., Yacowar (1977), that the cinematic Buntings lived in Bloomsbury. (Hitchcock himself made the claim in a 1970 interview.) For, as mentioned here, the Lodger's map clearly sets the action in Pimlico, the Avenger having worked his way south through Westminster via Charing Cross, the Embankment and St. Margaret's Church. Nor can the Bloomsbury tradition be traced to the source novel, because there the Buntings are specifically located in Marylebone (see entry 14:3). It may be that the script or some other early studio materials referred to Bloomsbury, although, interestingly, the version of the story released to *Picturegoer* magazine (February 1927) is silent, so to speak, on the precise location of the Buntings' "suburban" home.

Station: Station: Pimlico (VI) Exit for Bessborough Street (North) and veer around to the L into what is now Drummond Gate but—in the Buntings' day—was Bessborough Gardens. Around to the R, leading out to Vauxhall Bridge, is the present, abbreviated version of Bessborough Gardens, at the top of which, on the NE corner (at John Islip Street), stood No. 13. For other Avenger sites, see individual entries.

16:2
"Roddy Berwick's Flat" F
37 Bessborough Road, SW1

This, according to the letter from his solicitor, is the address of the dingy lodging to which Roddy Berwick retreats after his initial "fall" in *Downhill*. There never was a Bessborough Road in London, but here in Pimlico there *was* a Bessborough Street, a Bessborough Gardens *and* a Bessborough Place, each with a No. 37. The entire area has been heavily rebuilt since the War, but Bessborough Street still retains its No. 37. Interestingly, and presumably not coincidentally, the Buntings of *The Lodger* also live in this area, specifically in Bessborough Gardens, according to the Lodger's map of the Avenger killings (see previous entry). Neither location is mentioned in the respective literary sources, so one wonders whence Hitchcock's fascination for this particular part of Pimlico.

Station: Pimlico (VI) Exit for Bessborough Street (North) for a nice view of the older buildings across the street. Incidentally, it was to a "crummy" teashop here in Pimlico that *Dial M for Murder*'s C.A. Swann took "poor Miss Wallace," who was eventually "found dead due to an overdose of something," presumably not the tea!

17. St. JAMES'S

17:1
The Ritz, London (F) L
150 Piccadilly, W1

Bearing what is undoubtedly the most famous name in the business—that of Swiss hotelier César Ritz—this magnificent, French-styled hotel opened with great fanfare on May 24, 1906. It quickly established itself as one of the most fashionable social settings in London—*the* place to see and be seen. It was thus evoked with great irony in the film *Rebecca*, when Maxim seeks a private room in the local inn to discuss his "business" with Favell. "I hope this will do, Mr. de Winter," offers the innkeeper. "It's splendid, splendid," enthuses the smarmy Favell. "Exactly like the Ritz." The line has no precedent in the novel because the correspond-

The Ritz

ing scene takes place at Manderley, whose rooms presumably do look like the Ritz. It was also at the Ritz that Bulldog Drummond (whence Bob Lawrence of *The Man Who Knew Too Much* [34]) had a fateful encounter with arch-fiend Carl Peterson in *The Black Gang*. And it was just past the Ritz, at the entrance to Green Park, that Mrs. Lake was murdered in *Re-enter Sir John*, the 1932 sequel to *Enter Sir John*, which Hitchcock filmed as *Murder!*

Station: Green Park (JU; PI; VI) Exit on the South Side for the Ritz, which is just E of the station. Afternoon tea is served daily from 2 pm-5 pm. The park itself—from which the murderer appears in *Re-enter Sir John*—is open daily from 5 am to midnight.

17:2
Le Caprice (F)
Arlington House
Arlington Street, SW1

During the filming of *Stage Fright*, Alfred Hitchcock regularly brought his actors to this chic, "jet set" favorite, where he treated them to expensive steaks flown in specially from New York. Actress Marlene Dietrich speculated that as Hitchcock seldom commented on his actors' performances, the dinners at Le Caprice were his way of showing "that he was not really disgusted with our work." The original Caprice closed in 1974; the present restaurant, located on the same site and using the same name, opened under new management in 1981.

Station: Green Park (JU; PI; VI) Exit on the South Side and go R in Piccadilly. Turn R into Arlington Street and look for the restaurant at the bottom of the street, on the R. **Hours:** Mon-Sun 12 pm-3 pm; 5:30 pm-12 am

17:3
White's (F)
37-38 St. James's Street, SW1

Founded as White's Chocolate House in 1693, this St. James's institution is the oldest, most prestigious and most exclusive of London's traditional gentlemen's clubs. White's moved to its present home in 1788, where, in addition to its arch-conservative politics, it gained a reputation for high stakes gambling and a membership that would bet on literally anything. The most infamous example of the club's betting mania, as I noted in *James Bond's London*, occurred in 1750, when a man collapsed on White's doorstep and was then carried inside; the members wagered on whether the stricken man was already dead or merely unconscious! Thus, in *Jamaica Inn*, when Sir Humphrey boasts that he is "the only man below the rank of marquis who ever gambled 10 years at White's Club and kept his estate out of the hands of the moneylenders," we can certainly applaud the accomplishment (if not the man himself).

Station: Green Park (PI; VI; JU) Exit on the South Side and walk E in Piccadilly, then turn R into St. James's Street. No. 37 is on the E side of the street, unmarked, of course.

17:4
ex St. James's Theatre H
King Street, SW1

Built in 1835, the St. James's Theatre hosted a number of important and popular plays over the years, including Oscar Wilde's *The Importance of Being Earnest* (1895) and Agatha Christie's *Ten Little Indians* (1943). Hitchcock himself came here in the autumn of 1925 to see Frederick Lonsdale's comedy *The Last of Mrs. Cheyney*, which, to the extent that it involves sex and theft, has been suggested (by biographer Donald Spoto) as an inspiration for both *To Catch a Thief* and *Marnie*, notwithstanding the fact that both films were adapted from novels. The play starred Gladys Cooper (*Rebecca*) as Mrs. Cheyney, May Whitty (*The Lady Vanishes, Suspicion*) as Mrs. Ebley and, as Lord Dilling, Hitchcock's actor-manager friend Sir Gerald du Maurier, who had just moved here from **Wyndham's**. The St. James's was also the setting for one of Hitchcock's most infamous practical jokes, committed on Christmas Eve 1932. The victim was du Maurier himself, then appearing in John Van Druten's *Behold, We Live*. The joke was a cart-horse, carefully installed in the actor's dressing room. Around its neck hung a sign reading: "A Merry Christmas and a Happy New Year." Years later, in an interview with *The Guardian*, Hitchcock's daughter, Pat, recalled that upon seeing the horse, Sir Gerald deadpanned simply, "Oh, hello, old boy." In fact, the horse became something of a theatrical legend, as du Maurier then sent it along to Herbert Marshall's (*Murder!, Foreign Correspondent*) dressing room at the Lyric and Marshall, in turn, sent it along to that of another actor and so on. The original incident may well have inspired the scene in *Jamaica Inn*, in which Sir Humphrey—played by Charles Laughton—has his beloved horse brought into the dining room. (There is no precedent for such a scene in the novel.) Indeed, the scene may be considered as something of a "tribute" to the late, great actor-manager, who had died in 1934 and was a friend of both Hitchcock and Laughton. Laughton actually met du Maurier (whom he idolized) in the latter's dressing room here at the St. James's in 1928. Laughton had come to ask for the part of Hercule Poirot in du Maurier's production of *Alibi* (based on the Agatha Christie novel *The Murder of Roger Ackroyd*), as well as to confront the elder man over rumors that Sir Gerald had been calling him a "pervert" (Laughton was, of course, gay). "Well are you?" Sir Gerald asked. "No," the young actor replied. "Good, have a drink." Laughton got the part and thus began a short, but extremely close friendship. The actor debuted in *Alibi* under du Maurier's direction at the Prince of Wales Theatre on May 15, 1928.

St. James's Theatre

Station: Green Park (PI; VI; JU) Exit on the South Side and walk E in Piccadilly, then turn R into St. James's Street. Sadly, the birthplace of this delightful theatrical "tradition" was demolished in 1957, over the heated public protests of its husband and wife managers, Sir Laurence Olivier and Vivien Leigh. It was replaced by St. James's House, an office block at Nos. 23-24, in 1959.

The MacGuffin: John Van Druten, a Hitchcock family friend, actually cast 13-year-old Patricia Hitchcock in his play *Solitaire*, which opened on Broadway in early 1942 and, alas, ran for only 23 performances. The director, busy shooting *Saboteur* in Hollywood, never saw his daughter's professional acting debut. Sixteen years later, a film adaptation of Van Druten's *Bell, Book and Candle* would reunite *Vertigo* stars James Stewart and Kim Novak—this time with a happy ending.

17:5
Fortnum & Mason Ltd. (L)
181 Piccadilly, W1

Founded in 1770 as a purveyor—and deliverer—of posh goods to posh people, Fortnum & Mason remains one of the most exclusive department stores in London. Indeed, the firm's high-class clientele includes not only members of the Royal Family, but also the snooty Whittaker clan, who, according to the play *Easy Virtue* (Act II), hire Fortnum's to cater the party during which Larita chooses *not* to remain upstairs with a "headache." The film is silent, so to speak, on the name of the caterer.

Station: Piccadilly Circus (PI; BA) Exit for Piccadilly (South side), go L in Piccadilly and look for Fortnum's ahead on the L. Although it looks old, the present building actually dates from the 1920s. **Hours:** Mon-Sat 9:30 am-6 pm.

The MacGuffin: Behind Fortnum's is tony Jermyn Street, famous for its exclusive shops, restaurants and tailors. Jermyn Street is also famous, or perhaps infamous, for its

Fortnum & Mason Ltd

association with British occultist Aleister Crowley (1875-1947), who occupied assorted flats here in the 1930s and '40s. Crowley was known as "the Great Beast" and "the wickedest man alive" because of his occult (some said Satanic) beliefs and practices, illegal drug use, pornographic publications, and promotion of sexual promiscuity. Perhaps not surprisingly, he found a ready devotee in one Norman Bates, who, according to Chapter 9 of *Psycho*, has read Crowley and all the modern mystics, learning the secrets of time, space, dimension and being. Unfortunately for Norman, his mother did not approve of such books: they were not only "against religion," but also threatened to turn her little boy into a grown man and that, of course, would never do....

17:6
St. James, Piccadilly L
Piccadilly, SW1

Built to the design of Sir Christopher Wren (architect of **St. Paul's Cathedral**) in 1676-84, St. James became the prototype of the 18th-century urban church (its most famous American descendants may be found in Boston, Massachusetts, and Newport, Rhode Island). In *Goodbye Piccadilly, Farewell Leicester Square* (whence *Frenzy*), Brenda and Richard Blamey [*sic*] stop here on the way from her **Leicester Square** office to her **Berkeley Square** club. Given the novel's bittersweet evocation of World War II and its heroes, this was a significant stop: In 1946, St. James's churchyard had been converted into a garden of remembrance to honor Londoners' courage during the Blitz. Ironically, and with seeming indifference, while Brenda goes inside to pray, the perpetually truculent Dick Blamey cools his heels outside. This would have certainly made an interesting cinematic detour en route to Brenda's club (see **Brenda Blaney's Club**) and according to the location notes of January 1971, Hitchcock intended to include just such a scene. Reference photos of the church were even mailed to him in California the following month. However, when he and scripter Anthony Shaffer later shifted the setting from the novel's Piccadilly and Leicester Square to Covent Garden (and moved Blaney's fighting days forward from WWII to 1956), the church was unceremoniously dropped.

Station: Piccadilly Circus (BA; PI) Exit for Piccadilly (South side), go L in Piccadilly and look for the church ahead on the L.

17:7
Theatre Royal (Haymarket Theatre) H F L
Haymarket, SW1

The Theatre Royal, popularly known as the Haymarket Theatre, was built by John Nash in 1820-21. It went on to host some of the most prestigious productions—and playwrights—in the West End, including works by Wilde, Ibsen, Barrie and Galsworthy (Hitchcock adapted the latter's *Skin Game* in 1931). Less famous, but for our purposes, far more important, was Horace Annesley Vachell's *Who Is He?*, which began a four-month run here on December 9, 1915. Sometime during that run, 16-year-old Alfred Hitchcock attended a performance of the play, an adaptation of Marie Belloc Lowndes' 1913 novel *The Lodger*. Hitchcock was quite taken with both the play and its source

Theatre Royal

novel, which, in turn, was inspired by the infamous Jack the Ripper murders of 1888 (see entry 58:2). A little more than a decade later, in 1926, the young director would helm a stunning, silent film adaptation of the novel, *The Lodger*, the first "true Hitchcock" film. In the meantime, Hitchcock had also seen another play that he would long seek to film, J.M. Barrie's fantasy romance *Mary Rose*, which ran from April 22, 1920 to February 26, 1921 and starred Fay Compton (*Waltzes from Vienna*). In fact, the closest Hitchcock came to realizing the project was the commissioning of a script in early 1964, when he planned to feature Tippi Hedren—then working on *Marnie*—as the title character. Unfortunately, as relations soured between director and star, Hitchcock ultimately dropped the project, never to resurrect it. Still, the examples of these and other English plays remind us of what film historian Geoff Brown has called the "lure of the theatre in Hitchcock's creative personality…[and] its possible influence on his striking sense of spatial manipulation." Thus, for example, do we have the "English Hitchcock" undertaking several notable theatrical adaptations in the 1920s and '30s (*Downhill*, *Easy Virtue*, *The Farmer's Wife*, *Blackmail*, etc.) and the "American Hitchcock" experimenting with continuous takes on the theatrical *Rope* and *Under Capricorn* and with 3-D on *Dial M for Murder*. Ironically, Hitchcock the theatre-lover passed on the chance to stage an important scene here at the Haymarket when he adapted *The Paradine Case*. In the source novel (Chapter 1), Sir Simon Flaquer first approaches Sir Malcolm Keane (Anthony Keane in the film) about the title case at this very theatre. The two men are attending a first night, as is their custom, and so, it turns out, are Lord and Lady Horfield, with whom the Keanes banter on their way out of the theatre. As fans of the movie will know, no such scene appears in the film—but it almost did. For more on that, see **St. Martin's Theatre**.

Station: Piccadilly Circus (BA; PI) Exit for the Haymarket, turn R and follow the Haymarket down toward Pall Mall; the theatre will be on your L.

The MacGuffin: Look closely as Tracy's taxi prepares to turn right into Pall Mall during the final chase scene of *Blackmail*: in the distance, on the right, you can spot the thick white columns of the Haymarket Theatre.

17:8
Her Majesty's Theatre F
Haymarket, SW1

The shooting script for *Murder!* (dated March 5, 1930) describes an exterior establishing shot of the fictitious "Sheridan Theatre," along with a poster announcing Sir John Menier's latest triumph. The finished film doesn't specify the theatre but there can be little doubt about the real-life location Hitchcock had in mind. Her Majesty's Theatre, the fourth theatre to be built upon this site, is perhaps most famous for its association with Sir Herbert Beerbohm Tree (1853-1917), the founder of the **Royal Academy of Dramatic Art** and, along with Sir Henry Irving (1838-1905) and Sir Gerald du Maurier (1873-1934), one of the great actor-managers of the English theatre. Tree actually financed the construction of Her Majesty's Theatre in 1896-97 with profits he had earned from his production of *Trilby* (adapted from a novel written by du Maurier's father, George) at the nearby **Haymarket Theatre**. Here he lived and worked, in an elegant office noted for, among other things, a magnificent domed ceiling and an impossibly thick carpet. Hitchcock, an avowed theatre buff, obviously knew Sir Herbert's office (if not the man himself), for he lavishes both the dome and the carpet upon the actor-manager hero of *Murder!* In fact, the character of Sir John Menier clearly evokes both Tree himself and, to an even greater degree, Hitchcock's friend Sir Gerald du Maurier. (The relationship to the latter may be even stronger in the source novel, *Enter Sir John* [see Appendix I], where the character's surname, *Saumarez*, more closely approximates the look and sound of *du Maurier*.) Interestingly, Hitchcock himself called attention to the connection between the film's Menier and du Maurier in a 1972 interview with Charles Thomas Samuels, although he locates du Maurier here at His Majesty's (the name changes in accordance with the gender of the monarch), when, in fact, it was Sir

Her Majesty's Theatre

Herbert who held court under the famous golden dome from 1897 until 1914. For more on Sir Gerald, see **Wyndham's Theatre** and the **St. James's Theatre**. For the literary character's base, see the **Gielgud Theatre**.

Station: Piccadilly Circus (BA; PI) Exit for the Haymarket, turn R and walk down the street; the theatre is toward the bottom, on the R, just before New Zealand House.

The MacGuffin: Tree had connections with a number of future Hitchcock stars. From 1901 to 1908, Constance Collier (*Rope*, also co-author of the play *Down Hill*, whence *Downhill*) starred in all of Tree's major productions here at His Majesty's. London-born Claude Rains (*Notorious*, "The Horseplayer") began his acting career here as a "call boy" (calling actors for their cues), then worked his way up as Tree's protégé. And among the bisexual Tree's lovers was *Murders!*'s own Handel Fane, Esmé Percy, who would have presumably felt right at home in the ersatz Tree's plush office.

17:9
ex **Carlton Hotel L F**
Haymarket, SW1 (at Pall Mall)

The magnificent building, whose interior was modeled after the Paris Ritz, was built in the late 1890s as the "twin" of **Her Majesty's Theatre** next door. It opened in 1899 under the direction of César Ritz himself, who had recently ended his tenure as manager of **The Savoy**. Apart from its sumptuous Grill Room, Dining Room and sunken Palm Court, the Carlton could boast a bathroom in every bedroom—a London first. It can also boast not one but two appearances in a Hitchcock film. In *Foreign Correspondent*, Hitchcock based both Johnny Jones and Mr. Van Meer at the Carlton, combining second-unit footage of the real hotel with first-unit footage of a Hollywood replica. In fact, Hitchcock staged his cameo outside the studio-built Carlton façade, complemented with rear-projected footage of Pall Mall in the background. A decade earlier, the director had incorporated the same corner—albeit from a different angle—in *Blackmail*: it is the spot where Tracy's taxi makes the turn before miraculously depositing him near the **British Museum** in Bloomsbury! (For more on this amazing sequence, see the ***Blackmail* Chase Routes**.) Sadly, the Carlton was heavily damaged by German bombs in 1940, then lay dormant until 1957, when it was demolished to make way for New Zealand House, the hideous, American-style tower that houses the New Zealand High Commission (i.e., embassy). Literary fans should also take note that Hugh Drummond and his future wife, Phyllis, the inspiration for Bob and Jill Lawrence of *The Man Who Knew Too Much*, first met at the Carlton (in Chapter 1 of *Bulldog Drummond*) and continued to rendezvous here throughout the series.

Hitchcock and Joel McCrea in *Foreign Correspondent*

Station: Charing Cross (BA; JU; NO) Take the Cockspur Street exit, turn L into Cockspur Street and continue to the corner of Pall Mall and the Haymarket; the Carlton was in the NW corner. Just N of New Zealand House is Her Majesty's Theatre, which, apart from the different signage, is literally the twin of the grand hotel, right down—or, rather, up—to its impressive golden dome.

17:10
Blackmail **Chase Routes F**
Waterloo Place, Lower Regent Street, The Haymarket, SW1

Both the silent and sound versions of *Blackmail* begin with a seven-minute "silent" sequence, showing the arrest, booking and incarceration of a criminal apprehended by the "Flying Squad" of **Scotland Yard**. From an extreme close-up of a spinning wheel hub (immediately after the opening titles), both versions cut to a trucking shot of the Flying Squad van speeding north through Waterloo Place and into Lower Regent Street. (The long, neoclassical building it passes was and is a bank, today, the Confederation of Spanish Savings Banks.) The wireless operator then receives instructions to proceed to "6 Cambrid—" (we cut away before the full address is revealed) and the van makes a dramatic U-turn—in the middle of **Kingsway**, Holborn! Even more confusing, the following exterior shots show the van again driving north through Lower Regent Street, as if it had never turned around at all. The only difference between the two films—which use exactly the same footage—comes as the van pulls up outside the Marine Stores, near the suspect's flat. The sound version *cuts* from the Lower Regent Street trucking shot to a shot of the van pulling up and stopping, after which the policemen exit; the silent version *dissolves* from Lower Regent Street to the policemen exiting the van in a cloud of dust. Later in the film, the Flying Squad van pursues Tracy's taxi from **G**.

Blackmail chase routes, Haymarket

140   ALFRED HITCHCOCK'S LONDON

White Newsagents, theoretically in Chelsea, to the **British Museum** in Bloomsbury. In fact, the two vehicles are driving around in circles here in St. James's. (Although rather strangely for a car chase, the two are never shown in the same shot nor passing the same landmarks.) In the sound version, the police van again travels north in Lower Regent Street and again defies the laws of continuity and geography. It is first shown traveling north past Nos. 27 through 35, between Jermyn Street and Piccadilly (north end of the street) and then (in three subsequent shots), traveling north past Nos. 15 through 19, Nos. 21 through 25 and Nos. 9 through 13—all between Charles II Street and Jermyn Street (south end of the street). Meanwhile, one street over, Tracy's taxi is shown heading *south* down the Haymarket toward Norris Street (where the pedestrian starts to cross then turns back) in one shot, then traveling between Norris and Charles II Streets in a subsequent shot. In both sets of shots, the camera is trained on the western side of the street. Tracy's cab is then shown at the bottom of the Haymarket, turning right into Pall Mall, as if he's following the police van! (Interestingly, this is the exact "spot"—at the site of the old **Carlton Hotel**—where Hitchcock would make his cameo 11 years later in *Foreign Correspondent*. The cameo, roughly, a "reverse angle" of the *Blackmail* shot, was, of course, filmed in Hollywood in front of a rear-projection screen.) In the silent version, the shot of the spinning wheel cuts to a "continuation" of the opening shot of the bank building, with the van then crossing Charles II Street. Subsequent shots of the police van are also from Lower Regent Street and utilize additional footage of the block between Charles II Street and Jermyn Street. This time, however, Tracy's taxi is to be found rounding **Eros'** island in **Piccadilly Circus**, opposite Swan & Edgar (today, the Tower Records Sore). (Eros itself cannot be seen in these shots because it was then resting in the Victoria Embankment Gardens pending the completion of the new Underground station beneath the circus.) And instead of turning from the Haymarket into Pall Mall, he is shown heading south in Waterloo Place, past the Athenaeum Club (on the left) and with that same bank building in the background. From St. James's, the chase continues on foot at the museum itself. (The POV shot of the policeman stopping the taxi was filmed at an undetermined location; the subsequent shot of Tracy actually exiting the cab—a different one, if you note the numbers—was probably filmed on the backlot.) The utter lack of continuity in such automobile sequences apparently didn't bother the director. As he wrote to *Vertigo* editor George Tomasini nearly 30 years later, "Ignore geography—consider length only regardless of turns." In other words, it was the pace of the scene that mattered, not the accuracy of the route. Moreover, in those days, police and other authorities seldom gave permission to film in London's streets (a fact Hitchcock himself noted in a 1937 article he wrote for *News Chronicle*), so the director presumably had to get his shots as quickly as he could, *wherever* he could. For another geography-defying sequence, see **Stevie's Final Journey**.

Station: Piccadilly Circus (BA; PI) Exit for the Haymarket, turn R and walk down the street; the buildings shown in the sound version of Tracy's ride are on the western side, from Jermyn Street and St. James's Market to the middle of the block between Norris and Charles II Street (just before the McDonald's). At Pall Mall, round the corner to the R, as the taxi did in the sound version, and continue on to Waterloo Place. Turn L here and walk past the statue of Edward VII, turn around and look back toward the Athenaeum on the L and toward the Spanish bank farther along on the L for the view from the silent version. Now walk back up Waterloo Place, past the long bank building

Blackmail chase routes, Plaza Cinema, Lower Regent St.

shown in the opening chases of both versions and at the beginning of the second chase in the silent version. Continue past Charles II Street (shown only in the silent version) and into Lower Regent Street. The building at Nos. 1-3 appears twice in silent Chase 2, while the next building—Nos. 5-11—appears twice in silent Chase 2 and once in sound Chase 2. (The façade has since been rebuilt so the visual match is not a good one.) Both versions also contain footage of the van passing the next building, Statoil House at 11A, which still retains its distinctive stone archways at either end. Just past this is the bright, white building at No. 15, which also appears in both versions of Chase 2 (it now has columns on either side of its entrance, in place of the lamps visible in the film). The Plaza Cinema is the last building before Jermyn Street and may be seen intercut between shots of Tracy's taxi in the Haymarket in the sound version. Across Jermyn Street is Barclays Bank, which is obscured by scaffolding in the sound version of film. It is, in fact, the *first* building to appear after the spinning wheel during the sound version of Chase 2, in a trucking shot that concludes as the van enters Piccadilly Circus. This building was also the inspiration for one that Hitchcock constructed in a Northolt field for the bus explosion scene in *Sabotage*. (See **St. Giles Circus** for more on this scene.)

17:11
Buckingham Palace (F)
The Mall, SW1

Acquired by King George III in 1762, "Buckingham House" was originally built for John Sheffield, the 1st Duke of Buckingham and Normanby, in 1702-1705. The king bestowed "Buck House" (as it is popularly known) upon his wife, Queen Charlotte, after whom it was named "The Queen's House." Their son, George IV, decided that, with a little work and a lot of money, a refurbished Buck House would make the perfect permanent residence for the British monarch. The job was still not finished in 1837, when the new Queen, Victoria, decided to make the rechristened Buckingham Palace her official London residence. It remains, along with Windsor Castle and the Palace of Holyrood House in

142 ALFRED HITCHCOCK'S LONDON

Buckingham Palace

Edinburgh, one of the three Official Residences of the Sovereign. Buck House is, of course, one of the biggest tourist attractions in London, along with **St. Paul's Cathedral** and the **Houses of Parliament**, all three of which Rowley wants Johnny Jones to see from the top of the **Westminster Cathedral** tower in *Foreign Correspondent*. Rowley is, of course, trying to get Jones to stand still long enough so that he can push him out of the window. But as fans of the film well know, things don't always go as planned....

Station: Green Park (VI; PI; JU) For a closer—and much safer—view of the Palace than Johnny Jones' would have had, exit on the South Side, go R in Piccadilly, then R through the iron gates into Queen's Walk and follow this to the Mall. Turn right into the Mall and look for the Palace straight ahead. The Changing of the Guard takes place at 11:30 am daily from April 1 to August 7 (on alternate days from August 8 to March 31) when the Sovereign is in residence. The State Rooms (including the Throne Room and the State Dining Room), Queen's Gallery and Royal Mews are open in August and September Mon-Fri 9:30 am-5:30 pm daily. The royal standard flies from the palace mast whenever the sovereign is in residence.

The MacGuffin: Just around the corner from Buck House, in Palace Street (off Buckingham Gate), is the Westminster Theatre, which has a number of indirect Hitchcock connections. From 1938-40, it was home to the Mask Theatre, directed by J.B. Priestly (*Jamaica Inn*), while from 1943-45, it was managed by actor Robert Donat (*The 39 Steps*). The theatre's most important Hitchcock connection comes by way of Frederick Knott's play *Dial M for Murder*, which opened here on June 19, 1952 and ran for 425 performances. (It had originally aired as a **BBC** television drama on March 23.) The following year, Hitchcock directed a screen adaptation of the play written by Knott himself and featuring John Williams as Inspector Hubbard, a role the English actor had played to great acclaim during the play's New York run in 1952-53.

18. St. PANCRAS

18:1
St. Pancras Station L
Euston Road, NW1

Constructed in the 1860s as the terminus of the Midland Railway, St. Pancras Station is a marvel of Victorian engineering and construction. It is fronted by the former Midland Grand Hotel, an imposing Victorian palace designed by Sir George Gilbert Scott and now used for offices, while its massive glass and iron train once boasted the widest span in the world (689 feet). (It was eclipsed by Jersey City, New Jersey's Pennsylvania Station in 1888.) Sadly, Hitchcock never found an opportunity to film at the historic station, but St. Pancras does pop up in a number of the director's source novels. *The Lodger* begins with the discovery of another Avenger victim near the station, while in *The Thirty-nine Steps*, Richard Hannay departs from here for Galloway, Scotland, where he plans to hide out until he can effect a plan to stop the foreign spies. Hitchcock, in contrast, sent Hannay to *Edinburgh* from nearby **King's Cross Station**, a journey that the literary character actually made in the novel *Mr Standfast*.

St. Pancras Station

Station: King's Cross St. Pancras (CI; HC; ME; NO; PI; VI; NR; Thameslink)
Follow the signs from the Underground to the St. Pancras railway station.

18:2
King's Cross Station F L
Euston Road, NW1

Named for a monument to George IV (that stood near the crossroads here between 1830 and 1845), the London terminus of the Great Northern Railway was completed in 1852, at which time it was the largest rail station in England. Ten years later, King's Cross became the starting point for the famed "Flying Scotsman" express train service to Edinburgh, a 393-mile journey that in the 1930s constituted the longest nonstop run in the world (and at locomotive speeds of up to 100 mph, the fastest). It was precisely this journey that *39 Steps* hero Richard Hannay had to undertake in order to stop the foreign spy ring and clear himself of the murder of Annabella Smith. After making a comical escape from his flat (see entries 14:4 and 14:5), Hannay makes his way to King's Cross Station, literally a few steps ahead of the police. Hitchcock shows us footage of locomotive No. 2595 (the Trigo) preparing to depart, then actually steaming out of the

King's Cross Station

station. (The platform, as shown in the film, was No. 10; the time, not indicated, would have been 10:00 a.m.) These location shots punctuate footage of actor Robert Donat on the rail carriage set at **Lime Grove Studios**. Incidentally, engine No. 2595 was one of some 70 members of the famous A3 Class of steam locomotives, also known as "Pacifics," built in the 1920s and '30s. All but one of the powerful Pacifics were scrapped in the early 1960s. The sole survivor, the Flying Scotsman (named after the train route itself) has recently undergone a meticulous three-year restoration process and, as "the most famous steam engine in the world," makes public and private runs to a variety of destinations in southern England. King's Cross is also the site of not one but two Avenger murders in the novel *The Lodger*. For Hitchcock's murder venues, see **The Lodger's Plan of the Avenger Killings**.

Station: King's Cross St. Pancras (CI; HC; ME; NO; PI; VI; NR; Thameslink) Exit for the National Rail platforms and walk out to Platform 10; apart from newer trains and signage, the overall effect is still very much as in the film. For more of Hitchcock's railway shenanigans in the King's Cross area, see **Copenhagen Tunnel**.

A REFERENCE GUIDE TO LOCATIONS 145

Euston Station

**18:3
Euston Station F L
Euston Road, NW1**

London's oldest mainline rail terminus opened here in 1837 in an area then known as Euston Grove; it was enlarged and expanded throughout the 19th century, the most notable improvement being the massive Great Hall, a combination concourse and waiting hall, in 1849. As the London terminus of the London Midland and Scottish Railway, Euston Station is mentioned in Chapter 23 of *The Paradine Case*, when Keane departs from here for Hindley Hall (see entry 65:7). The station also appears briefly in the film version, after Keane has returned from Cumberland and hires a taxi to take him to **Holloway Prison**. A stand-in doubling for actor Gregory Peck appears on the No. 2 arrival platform here at the station, while Peck himself is shown in front of rear-projected footage. Sadly, "the railway station…without equal" (as it was dubbed in 1849) was swept away in the 1960s to make way for the new Euston Station, a sleek but decidedly bland replacement.

Station: Euston (NO; VI; NR)
Exit for the mainline station; there is still a Platform 2, but little recalls the images from the film.

Hitchcock's cameo in *The Paradine Case*, exiting the Cumberland train station.

146 ALFRED HITCHCOCK'S LONDON

19. SMITHFIELD

19:1
St. Bartholomew's Hospital (L)
West Smithfield, EC1

London's oldest and most famous hospital—popularly known as Bart's—was founded by an Augustinian monk in 1123 as a sanctuary for the poor and sick. Henry VIII re-founded the hospital in 1544 (after the Dissolution of the Monasteries); the first physician—Dr. Roderigo Lopez—was appointed in 1568; and William Harvey—discoverer of the circulation of blood—was chief physician from 1609-33. The oldest surviving buildings—the chapel tower and vestry—date from the 15th century, with the remainder of the complex dating largely from the mid-18th century. With such an exemplary history and reputation, Bart's naturally attracts the best and brightest physicians, including one Dr. Murchison, according to Chapter 13 of *The House of Dr. Edwardes* (whence *Spellbound*). Unlike his cinematic counterpart—who turns out to be the murderer—the literary Murchison is the *victim* of a diabolical madman, the emphasis being on the *diabolical* (the man is literally a devil-worshipper). Poor Murchison—much younger than the film's Leo G. Carroll—is drugged and held in isolation at the title asylum, while the madman—Geoffrey Godstone (ironic name, that)—takes control and converts the patients to devil worship. To Murchison's aid will come Dr. Constance Sedgwick (renamed Petersen in the film, presumably to accord with actress Ingrid Bergman's Swedish background)—but not before the doctor comes to doubt his own sanity, having to remind himself that it was he "who had done so well at Bart's, and had been offered this excellent job...."

St. Bartholomew's Hospital

Station: St. Paul's (CE) Exit the station L into Newgate Street then turn R into Giltspur Street, which leads to the hospital.

20. SOHO

20:1
Piccadilly Circus Underground Station (F) L
Piccadilly Circus, W1

Opened in 1906 to accommodate the new Bakerloo subway line, Piccadilly Circus Underground Station underwent a massive overhaul in the 1920s, with the entire booking hall relocated underground. In addition to the booking hall, the new circulating area—roughly, but not quite circular—also included telephone booths, automatic ticket machines and a cloak room for checking parcels. And it was here that young Stevie was to leave Verloc's deadly package in *Sabotage*. The bomb was set to explode at 1:45 p.m., which meant that Stevie had to deliver it by 1:30. Unfortunately, Stevie took his own sweet time in getting to the station (see **Stevie's Final Journey**) and the consequences were devastating. It was also here, according to Chapter 2 of *Man Running* (whence *Stage Fright*) that Jonathan Penrose [*sic*] deposited the suitcase containing Charlotte Inwood's bloodstained dress and from which Eve Gill would later retrieve it. In the film, you will recall, Jonathan takes it to the Commodore's home and burns it in the fireplace.

Station: Piccadilly Circus (BA; NO) The cloakroom/left-luggage room was closed some years ago out of concern that a real terrorist might attempt to succeed where Verloc failed.

20:2
Stevie's Final Journey F
SE5 to W1

According to the newspaper shown in the film, *Sabotage* hero Stevie's final journey culminates "in **Piccadilly [Circus]**" with the explosion of a "fully laden" bus. That journey began in Camberwell, south of the **Thames**, at his brother-in-law's **Bijou Cinema**, continued through a crowded market, across the river via an unspecified bridge, past some shops, along the Strand and thence, via the bus, to Piccadilly. There, in the Underground Station (see above), the unwitting Stevie was to have left a package containing a time bomb set to explode at a certain hour. Hitchcock needed to prolong the boy's journey both to maximize the suspense and to ensure that Stevie did not, in fact, make it on time. (For critical reaction to this, see **St. Giles Circus**.) Thus, Stevie is delayed by a barker in the crowded market, by the Lord Mayor's Parade opposite the **Law Courts**, near **St. Clement Danes**, and by an interminable traffic jam in the heart of London. However, a closer look at the locations involved reveals the "real" reason the journey took so long. In happy defiance of any rational plan of travel from Camberwell to Piccadilly, Stevie's *first* stop is **Chapel Market**, a mile and a half *north* of the river, after which he crosses **Blackfriars Bridge** heading *south*, as if back to Camberwell! He then passes some unidentified shops before pausing opposite the Law Courts to watch the parade. Catching a westbound bus in the Strand—as he finally does—*would* be a logical choice for Piccadilly Circus, except that the ensuing traffic jam occurs *northeast* of Piccadilly, in **St. Giles Circus**. The climactic explosion—or at least its aftermath—was staged neither in Piccadilly nor St. Giles Circus, but rather on the same exterior set as the Bijou (see entry 20:15). Obviously, in this case, an accurate reproduction of a journey from SE5 to W1 was not a primary concern of Hitchcock's. As mentioned elsewhere (see ***Blackmail* Chase**), filming on location in London wasn't always easy in those days, so presumably it was another case of getting shots where one could and hoping the audience wouldn't notice the decidedly idiosyncratic route taken by the ill-fated boy.

Station: Piccadilly Circus (BA; NO)

**20:3
Piccadilly Circus F
W1**

When describing the advantages of the talking film over the theatre in a 1929 interview, Hitchcock remarked, "I can put Piccadilly Circus on the films." And indeed he could. This world-famous intersection, once known as the "Hub of the British Empire," conjures up the glitz, glamour and congestion of London as readily as its American counterpart, Times Square, does New York City. The intersection was laid out in 1819 and was then a true circle, or circus, similar in appearance to the majestic Oxford Circus just to the north. In the 1880s the northeast block was destroyed to make way for Shaftesbury Avenue and the "circus" took on its present, roughly triangular shape. Then in 1910 came the ads—garish, gaily lit electric signs overwhelming the northeastern side of the intersection and promoting everything from gin to jewelers. Countless filmmakers have trained their cameras on these (in)famous signs, including, of course, Hitchcock. In *Downhill, Rich and Strange, The Man Who Knew Too Much* (34) and *The 39 Steps,* he incorporates ordinary night shots of the signs to establish

Piccadilly Circus

that the heroes have returned home, to London. (Indeed, some or all of these may have simply been "stock shots," as suggested by the shooting script for *The 39 Steps*.) The shooting script for *Murder!* (dated March 5, 1930), indicates that Hitchcock planned to mark Sir John's return to London (after the trial) by showing streets and flashing signs around Piccadilly, including a prominent sign mentioning Sir John's latest stage success. In the finished film, we instead see images of Sir John's apartment, inside and out, preceded by a **Berkeley Square** sign. In other films, Hitchcock exploits the circus for more sinister purposes. In *The Lodger*, bystanders read of the latest Avenger murder on the electric sign above the circus, even as newspapers and the radio saturate London with their versions of the story. In another night sequence, *Blackmail* heroine Alice White wanders, trance-like, from the murdered artist's flat in Chelsea (see **Crewe's Studio**) to the West End. At Piccadilly Circus, ablaze with illuminated ads, she stops and looks at the **Café Monico**, then shifts her gaze across Shaftesbury Avenue to the Gordon's Gin sign on the London Pavilion. As she stares at the sign, transfixed, a studio-made insert shot of a moving cocktail shaker suddenly transforms into a stabbing knife, thrusting downward into an unseen victim. As a revelation of her state of mind—and Hitchcock's incomparable technique—the effect is quite stunning, at once shocking, haunting, bizarre and even amusing. An equally effective image of the circus, this time by day, occurs in *Sabotage*, as Verloc stares into an aquarium at the **London Zoo** and visualizes the people and traffic of the bustling intersection dissolving in the wake of his carefully planted bomb. Hitchcock's original treatment also called for a parallel shot to take place at the Circus itself, where Verloc would stand before a red pillar-box (the traditional English mail box) and again contemplate the prospective devastation, this time with a brief overlay of the Aquarium fish swimming off in all directions. In the end, neither Verloc—nor his agent, Stevie—would make it to Piccadilly Circus (see the previous entry). In fact, *Sabotage* marks the Circus's last appearance in a Hitchcock film. (A nice high-angle establishing shot of the circus does appear, however, in the opening of "Murder Case," a non-Hitchcock-directed episode of *The Alfred Hitchcock Hour*.) In future London adventures, the director would incorporate shots of the **Houses of Parliament** (*Foreign Correspondent*), **Trafalgar Square** (*Stage Fright*) or simply abjure a London establishing shot altogether (*The Lady Vanishes*, *The Man Who Knew Too Much* [56]).

Station: Piccadilly Circus (BA; NO) Note that in Hitchcock's day, indeed until the 1980s, the famous Eros statue was in the middle of the intersection, with motor traffic passing on either side (see next entry).

Ask Mr. Memory 28: What does Vladimir—Verloc's paymaster—recall having seen on a sign in Piccadilly Circus?

20:4
Eros Statue F
Piccadilly Circus, W1

The aluminum statue popularly known as "Eros" surmounts the Shaftesbury Memorial Fountain, erected in 1893 in honor of the 7th Earl of Shaftesbury, a noted philanthropist. The statue was intended to represent the Angel of Christian Charity, but as anyone will tell you, it's "really" Eros, the God of Love. Hitchcock incorporates an eerie silhouette of the statue during the opening sequence of *Sabotage*, along with blacked-out images of Nelson's Column (see **Trafalgar Square**) and **Selfridges** to dramatize the effect of Verloc's handiwork at the **Battersea Power Station**. In 1986, Eros and the fountain (which hasn't pumped water since 1899) were removed from the center of the circus to the south side, in front of Lillywhite's sporting goods store.

Station: Piccadilly Circus (BA; NO) Take Exit 3 or 4 for Eros.

The Eros statue was shown in *Sabotage*.

20:5
ex **Café Monico F L**
46-48 Piccadilly Circus, W1

Founded in Shaftesbury Avenue in 1876, Café Monico proved an immediate success, expanding southwest to Piccadilly Circus by 1888. The Circus's famous Coca-Cola sign—a vestige of which still remains—was erected over the Monico's Piccadilly entrance in 1954, shortly before Forte's took over that part of the restaurant. The truncated Café closed its doors for good in 1960. As a fashionable dining spot, the Café is mentioned in a number of Hitchcock's source novels, including *Ashenden* (a minor character wants to dine there); *Before the Fact* (Lina dines here with her younger lover, Ronald, a character absent from *Suspicion*); and *Goodbye Piccadilly, Farewell Leicester Square* (Dick Blamey [*sic*] bemoans its replacement with cheaper eating places [see below]). And the café's neon sign appears, however briefly, in not one, not two, but *three* Hitchcock films: *Blackmail*, *The Man Who Knew Too Much* (34) and *The 39 Steps*, each time as a part of a traditional Piccadilly Circus establishing shot of London by night. (The clearest image of Café Monico appears in *Blackmail*, as Alice's POV, just before she looks across to the Pavilion and sees the stabbing knife.) It was also here, in September 1926, that producer Michael Balcon and future editor and script supervisor Ivor Montagu discussed the fate of *The Lodger* over a lunch of fried onions and mashed potatoes. **Gainsborough** honcho C.M. Woolf thought the picture too "high-brow" and intended to shelve it, but Balcon believed in both the film and Hitchcock (whom he had promoted to director on *The Pleasure Garden* the year before). Montagu, a co-founder of the prestigious Film Society (see **New Gallery Cinema**), agreed to take a look at the film and suggest any changes that might make it more acceptable to Woolf. Hitchcock "ungrudgingly" accepted—and adopted—all of Montagu's suggestions: reduce the number of intertitle cards (from more than 300 to 80); repeat the heroine's name "Daisy" in the title cards; add sinister backgrounds to some of the title cards (like the opening shot of the shadowy figure); and reshoot a few scenes that "had not quite come off." The result, of course, was hailed as a brilliant achievement, establishing Hitchcock's reputation as one of Britain's foremost directors. And just think, if it hadn't been for a luncheon here in **Piccadilly Circus**, the first "true" Hitchcock picture might have never made it off the studio shelf.

Station: Piccadilly Circus (BA; NO) Take Exit 1 for Regent Street (East side); look for Boot's drug store across the street, to the R of the Burger King. The Café's Glasshouse Street entrance—the one shown in the film—was located here.

20:6
Café Royal L
68 Regent Street, W1

This fashionable French café-restaurant, established in 1865, was frequented by a number of famous writers and artists, including Oscar Wilde, T. S. Eliot, James McNeill Whistler and Augustus John, as well as the future Edward VIII and George VI when they were still young princes about town. According to the novel *The Thirty-nine Steps*, the restaurant was also visited by a retired Scottish mining engineer on at least one occasion in 1914. For it was here that the literary Richard Hannay spent his last dull, but peaceful evening prior to the adventures described in John Buchan's classic novel. After dining at the Café Royal, Hannay "turned into a music-hall. It was a silly show, all capering women and monkey-faced men, and I did not stay long." For the screen adaptation, Hitchcock and writer Charles Bennett would skip the restaurant and instead concentrate on the music hall, where Hannay would stay long enough to encounter both Mr. Memory and the mysterious Annabella Smith. In the novel, Smith's counterpart—an adventurous young man named Scudder—accosts Hannay at his Portland Place home (see entry 14:5), not the music hall, although the end results are quite similar. (Where Annabella is knifed in the back, Scudder is skewered to the floor with a knife through the heart.) For Hannay's second visit to a music hall, see the **London Palladium**.

Station: Piccadilly Circus (BA; PI) Take Exit 1 into Regent Street (East side) and look for the restaurant ahead—and around—on the R. Lunch and

Café Royal

dinner are served Mon-Sat, with reservations recommended. While you're in the neighborhood, be sure to pop into some of the fine Regent Street shops. After all, it was here, according to *Suspicion*, that Johnnie Aysgarth acquired the necklace he gave to Lina after his supposed win at **Goodwood Racecourse**.

20:7
ex HQ of Transatlantic Pictures H
36 Golden Square, W1

In October 1933, cinema chain owner Sidney Bernstein moved from 197 Wardour Street (London's famous film district) to a new office here in Golden Square, just off **Piccadilly Circus**. The following July he created Granada Theatres, Ltd. to take over for the old Bernstein Theatres, Granada going on to become one of the most famous names in British show business. (Apart from the famous theatre chain, the name is enshrined in that of Granada Television, the pioneering independent broadcasting company Bernstein founded in 1955.) Bernstein was also one of the founders of the prestigious Film Society, which held monthly screenings at the **New Gallery Cinema** in Regent Street. Here he developed his friendship with novice director and film buff Alfred Hitchcock, whom he had met two years earlier at **Islington** and whose path he would cross both personally and professionally for many years to come. An early "collaboration" saw Bernstein paying a visit to the British Censor, Brooke Wilkinson, to plead Hitchcock's case for retaining the strong language of Sean O'Casey's play *Juno and the Paycock*, which the director adapted for the screen in 1929. Little seems to have been accomplished at the meeting, which O'Casey himself attended, although the Censor eventually passed the film. A far more important collaboration during the war years saw Hitchcock crafting two short films and a documentary for the Ministry of Information, of whose films division Bernstein was the head. (See the **University of London**, the wartime

Transatlantic Pictures

headquarters of the Ministry of Information, for more on these films.) Finally, in April 1946, Bernstein and Hitchcock formed a production company, Transatlantic Pictures Corporation, whose London office would be located here in Granada's Golden Square headquarters. Transatlantic marked a welcome change for Hitchcock, who had been working under contract to producer David O. Selznick since 1939. Now, he would be his own boss, in partnership with an old friend, and could choose projects that excited *him*, projects like Patrick Hamilton's 1929 play *Rope*. Unfortunately, Transatlantic's initial effort, famous for its uninterrupted (and somewhat cumbersome) 10-minute takes, met with "mixed reviews and a lukewarm public response" (to quote Donald Spoto), not to mention the scorn of the play's author, who had worked on the initial treatment with Bernstein in the latter's Arlington House flat. (Hamilton's blunt assessment: "[Hitchcock] produced a film which *I* think…was sordid and practically meaningless *balls*.") The next Transatlantic project, an adaptation of Helen Simpson's 1937 novel *Under Capricorn*, would be based at **MGM-British Studios**, near Hitchcock's old **Elstree Studios** home, with exteriors shot on location in California. It, too, featured a number of long, difficult takes, which greatly unnerved the film's star, Ingrid Bergman. (To make up for the ordeal, Bernstein threw a large party for the actress at **The Savoy**.) And it, too, would receive a less than enthusiastic reception upon its release in September 1949. In fact, Bergman's highly publicized romance with Italian director Roberto Rossellini during and after the production of *Under Capricorn* (she was, of course, a married mother), led to the costume melodrama being banned by the Roman Catholic Church and to Miss Bergman herself being denounced by the U.S. Congress. Perhaps understandably, this was to prove Transatlantic's last project: *I Confess*, which was begun under the auspices of both producers in 1951, saw Bernstein's withdrawal as production difficulties mounted. (One such difficulty involved the casting—and *un*casting—of Swedish actress Anna Bjork in the role eventually assumed by Anne Baxter. Bjork, her lover and their "illegitimate" child were simply more than the distributors, Warner Bros., could bear in the wake of the recent Bergman-Rossellini scandal.) So, the troubled Transatlantic partnership was dissolved and *I Confess* was sold to Warner Bros., which released it to generally unenthusiastic reviews and box office in 1952. In the meantime, of course, Hitchcock had directed the masterful *Strangers on a Train* for Warner Bros., and was about to embark on his most critically and commercially successful period as a director. Bernstein, of course, went on to found the Granada Television empire and, happily, both men remained friends until the end of their days.

Station: Piccadilly Circus (BA; PI) Take Exit 1 L into Glasshouse Street, turn R into Sherwood Street and follow this to the square, which is today home to the Sony entertainment conglomerate's British office. No. 36 is on the opposite side.

**20:8
New Gallery Cinema H (L)
121-125 Regent Street, W1**

Originally a restaurant, the New Gallery Cinema seated its first filmgoer on January 14, 1913. Following a massive overhaul in 1924 the New Gallery reopened as a 1,400-seat luxury theatre on June 12, 1925. A few months later, the "most comfortable cinema" in London became the venue for the Sunday afternoon screenings of the new Film Society, which counted Alfred Hitchcock among its many distinguished members. The Film Society had been founded in June 1925 by writer (and former zoologist) Ivor Montagu, actor Hugh Miller, film director Adrian Brunel, film critics Iris Barry and Walter Mycroft, sculptor Frank Dobson and cinema exhibitor Sidney Bernstein. It was officially based at 56 Manchester Street, Marylebone, the office of its first secretary, Miss J.M. Harvey. The Society's purpose was to exhibit uncut foreign films (principally German, French, Italian and Russian), along with full orchestral accompaniment, as well as experimental works and revivals of old favorites. Its membership was to consist of "serious" filmgoers starved for something beyond the ordinary American and British fare. (Of the 625 films released in Britain in 1925, 577 were American, 25 European and only 23 British, the latter representing less than four percent of the total.) Montagu, who would work with Hitchcock on *The Lodger* and the mid-1930s thrillers (see **Café Monico**), secured the patronage of such artistic and intellectual luminaries as H.G. Wells, George Bernard Shaw, John Maynard Keynes, Julian Huxley, Augustus John, Bertrand Russell and J.B.S. Haldane. Bernstein, who would work with Hitchcock on a number of projects in the 1940s (see **University of London** and **Transatlantic Pictures**), facilitated the actual renting and exhibition of the films, as well as the use of the New Gallery. The Society's inaugural event was held here at the cinema on October 25, 1925, with some 1,400 people in attendance—900 members and their 500 guests. The program included Chaplin's *Champion Charlie* (1915; U.S.: *The Champion*), Paul Leni's *Waxworks* (1923; German: *Das Wachsfigurenkabinett*) and several shorts. Everyone in attendance loved the experience; everyone else hated it. The Press labeled the Society "snobbish" and "intellectual" (always a damning epithet), Brooke Wilkinson, the British Censor, decried the content of *Waxworks* and the film trade itself blasted the whole venture as an unwarranted attack on its own standards in choosing what films to exhibit. Yet, the Film Society not only survived the assault, it prospered, going on to exhibit some 39 films that first season. The following year it screened the seminal works of the European masters Fritz Lang, Erich von Stroheim, René Clair, Luis Buñuel and G.W. Pabst, while in the 1928-29 season it showcased the films of Soviet pioneers Lev Pudovkin and Sergei Eisenstein, both of whom addressed the Society on their respective visits to

New Gallery Cinema

London. Not surprisingly, the latter events provoked the ire of both the censor and the press, which denounced the Society for trying "to communise the country by showing Soviet films." But, again, none of the charges stuck. The Film Society had become "a force in the British film world" (to quote Bernstein's biographer Caroline Moorehead) and anyone connected to the film business who wished to be taken "seriously" attended the monthly screenings here in Regent Street.

Hitchcock, a commercial artist to be sure, but one who nonetheless wished to be taken seriously, joined the Society during its first season and attended many of its monthly showings, often in the company of his fiancée (and future wife), Alma Reville. The novice director had long been fascinated by international cinema, even observing first-hand the technique of F.W. Murnau on the set of *Der letzte Mann* (English: *The Last Man*) in 1924. That he was influenced by European "art films" (not to mention, horror of horrors, American popular films) is well documented. Yet Hitchcock also seems to have been inspired by the documentary films then being made in both Britain and Europe. Film historian Tom Ryall, for example, relates the opening sequence of *Blackmail* to "documentary cinema," noting its "realistic" attention to detail (of the pursuit, arrest, booking and incarceration of a criminal suspect) and the "social commentary" in the scene of the women and children at work and play in the seedy alley. He also quotes director Lindsay Anderson's 1949 encomium to Hitchcock's authentic use of "everyday locales" and "minor characters." In fact, documentaries had been a Film Society staple from the beginning and, indeed, would provide the basis for one of the Society's more interesting experiments. This took place during the 1936 season, when the Society screened two documentaries on the Ethiopian war, one Italian, the other Soviet, back to back. The notion that documentary films were somehow "objective" was quickly and dramatically dispelled when the "flower-like" explosions from the bomber pilot's perspective in the Italian film were contrasted with the death and devastation depicted in the Soviet film. Hitchcock, of course, not only infused many of his films with a documentary-like feel (*The Wrong Man* is probably the most obvious example) but also supervised the compilation of an actual documentary, *Memory of the Camps*, as part of his work for the British Ministry of Information during the war (see **University of London**). Ironically, Hitchcock's departure from the British film world, in March 1939, roughly coincided with the demise of the Film Society itself, whose last showing took place on April 23 of that year. There was to have been a new season the following October, but the war put an end to those plans. In addition to its impact on the filmmakers and theorists who attended its 108 screenings, perhaps the most enduring legacy of the original Film Society is the popularizing of both "art films" and "art cinemas," which continue to thrive today on both sides of the Atlantic. Indeed, a New London Film Society was organized in 1947 and it is today part of the British Federation of Film Societies based in Swansea. The New Gallery itself closed in 1953, was subsequently used as a religious center, then closed for good in 1990. (A 50th anniversary celebration was held here in Regent Street in 1975, with founder Ivor Montagu, among others, in attendance.) It became a Grade II listed building (i.e., protected by the government) in 1992.

Station: Piccadilly Circus (BA; NO) Take Exit 2 for Regent Street (West side), turn L and continue on to 121-125, ahead on the L. The Film Society's alternate—and larger—venue, the 1,500-seat Tivoli cinema at 65-70 Strand, was not as fortunate as The New

Gallery: it closed in 1956 and was subsequently demolished. The Tivoli, which hosted the Film Society showings from late 1929 to 1935, also hosted the British premiere of *Spellbound* on May 19, 1946. For more on this site, see the **Tivoli Music Hall**.

The MacGuffin: The New Gallery is mentioned in Patrick Hamilton's play *Rope* as the venue for an unnamed film that two of the party guests have seen and liked. The conversation is replicated in Hitchcock's adaptation, where the theatre is called the Strand. (Even the bit about a recent Cary Grant–Ingrid Bergman film called "just plain *something*" has a precedent in the play, with different stars, of course.) The New Gallery has yet another important Hitchcock connection in that it was also the setting for the premiere of *The 39 Steps* on June 6, 1935. In attendance were author John Buchan and his family, Hitchcock and Alma, and the film's stars, Robert Donat and Madeleine Carroll. Buchan's wife, Susan, hated the introduction of a heroine, but Buchan himself modestly claimed to prefer Hitchcock's version of the story to his own. Indeed, by this point in the Hannay novels, Buchan had already married off his hero and given him a son.

20:9
ex Lyons Corner House F
7-14 Coventry Street, W1

Owned by the firm of J. Lyons and Co. Ltd, this massive West End favorite (built in 1907; expanded in 1921-23) had a seating capacity of some 4,500. (Lyons' other Corner Houses, in the Strand and Oxford Street, by comparison, could seat a "mere" 2,500.) The capacious restaurant forms the backdrop for an important scene in *Blackmail*, when Alice and Frank quarrel over whether or not to see a new film called *Fingerprints*. In fact, Alice is awaiting the arrival of a secret admirer, for whom she plans to ditch Frank. The admirer eventually turns up, Alice leaves with him (Frank had earlier stormed out in a huff over her indecisiveness) and accompanies him to his Chelsea apartment (see entry 4:7), where things turn decidedly ugly. Hitchcock actually filmed the restaurant exteriors, including the various attempts to get in, here in Coventry Street. The extended dialogue scene, in which Alice says first one thing and then another, was shot at **Elstree**. Hitchcock also name-drops the restaurant chain in *Sabotage*, when Mrs. Verloc initially rejects Ted's offer to take her to **Simpson's**, saying that she and Stevie would go instead to "the Corner House or a tea shop."

Station: Piccadilly Circus (BA; NO) Exit for Shaftesbury Avenue, walk past the London Pavilion into Coventry Street and look for Planet Hollywood ahead on the L. This is the site of the Corner House.

The MacGuffin: Behind the Corner House, at the corner of Shaftesbury Avenue and Great Windmill Street, Lyons operated another famous restaurant, the Trocadero, which opened in 1896. Here, Hitchcock, a friend of the owner's son, staged one of his most famous practical jokes: a dinner party in which every item on the menu was blue! Among the guests was his old friend and fellow practical joker, Sir Gerald du Maurier. (See **St. James's Theatre** for more of their ongoing "battle.") The restaurant closed in 1965 but the building still stands, a repository for trendy (i.e., touristy) shops and restaurants.

Ask Mr. Memory 29: Who is the thriller writer Alice credits with popularizing Scotland Yard?

20:10
Gielgud Theatre (*formerly* Globe Theatre) (F)
33 Shaftesbury Avenue, WC2

Opened in 1906 as the Hicks Theatre, the Globe was the setting for the brief, but important, London run of Charles Bennett's play *Blackmail*, which opened on February 28, 1928 and closed after 38 performances on March 31, 1928. (The play would also run for a week at the Regent Theatre the following June, with Bennett himself playing the artist.) Produced by Raymond Massey (whose daughter Anna would appear in *Frenzy*), the play featured Tallulah Bankhead (*Lifeboat*) as Daphne Manning (renamed Alice Jarvis for the Regent run and Alice White for the film), Reginald Gardiner ("Banquo's Chair") as Alice's brother Jimmy (a character absent from the film), Frank Vosper (*Waltzes from Vienna, The Man Who Knew Too Much* [34]) as the blackmailer Tracy, and Alexander Onslow as the artist Peter Hewitt, called Crewe in the film. At this time, Hitchcock was working for British International Pictures at **Elstree Studios** and whether or not he actually saw the play is uncertain. His boss, producer John Maxwell, apparently did, for he acquired the screen rights and assigned the project to Hitchcock in the autumn of 1928. The result, of course, was Britain's first feature-length talkie (see **ex Regal Cinema**) and a true milestone in Hitchcock's career. (For more on the adaptation, see Appendix I.) Bennett himself was subsequently hired as a screenwriter for BIP and went on to collaborate with Hitchcock on the 1930s thrillers, starting with *The Man Who Knew Too Much*, as well as on the U.S.-made *Foreign Correspondent*. The Globe—renamed on the occasion of Sir John Gielgud's 90th birthday in 1994—has a number of other associations with Hitchcock collaborators: Gerald du Maurier starred in *Brewster's Millions* here in

Gielgud Theatre

1907; Noël Coward's comedy *Nude with Violin* ran here from 1956 to 1958; and Gielgud himself starred in *The Lady's Not for Burning* in 1949.

Station: Piccadilly Circus (BA; PI) Exit for Shaftesbury Avenue—the "heart of Theatreland"—and turn L at the top of the stairs then R into Shaftesbury Avenue; the theatre is ahead on the L. Shaftesbury Avenue was also the location of the fictional "Sheridan Theatre"—Sir John Saumarez's base—in the novel *Enter Sir John* (whence *Murder!*). For the cinematic Sir John's base, see **Her Majesty's Theatre**.

The MacGuffin: Next door to the Gielgud is the Queen's Theatre, where Ivor Novello starred in the play *Down Hill* in the summer of 1926 (Hitchcock adapted it the following year) and where Daphne du Maurier's own adaptation of *Rebecca* ran for 181 performances in 1940 (the year of the film's release). The theatre was the first to suffer a direct hit during WWII and was not rebuilt until 1959. John Gielgud (*Secret Agent*) debuted his *Hamlet* here in 1930; Marlene Dietrich (*Stage Fright*) staged her one-woman show here in 1964; and Noël Coward (*Easy Virtue*) made his last theatrical appearance here in 1966.

**20:11
Leicester Square F
WC2**

Laid out as a high-priced residential area in the 17th century, Leicester Square is today the "cinema center" of London, boasting four large movie palaces on its north, east and south sides (see also the **Odeon**). The square is linked, via Coventry Street, to London's "true" center (see entry 20:3) and the two together form the title backdrops

Leicester Square

of the novel *Goodbye Piccadilly, Farewell Leicester Square* (whence *Frenzy*). Indeed, Leicester Square is literally the scene of the crime, for it is the site of the Matrimonial Agency where Necktie Murderer Bob Rusk rapes and murders poor Brenda Blamey [*sic*]. Although Hitchcock shifted the renamed **Blaney Bureau** northward to **Oxford Street**, he did permit Leicester Square a brief cameo in the film. Here, on the eastern side of the square, opposite the Odeon, Dick Blaney waits for Babs to bring him his clothes from the **Globe**. When Babs' taxi pulls up in front of the cinema, Dick crosses over, hops in the cab and the pair ride off to the **Coburg Hotel**. Hitchcock shot the brief scene from the cover and security of a GPO (General Post Office) tent on August 5, 1971. Also shot here (and in the neighboring streets) were the rear projection process plates for the background of the scene *inside* the taxi. In fact, this constitutes the first footage actually shot for the production, by the second unit, on Wednesday, July 21, 1971. Hitchcock began principal photography the following Monday, July 26, at **Russell Street** in Covent Garden.

Station: Leicester Square (NO; PI) Take the Charing Cross Road (West) exit to Leicester Square. Literary Brenda's office would have been ahead, on the north side of the square, probably in the building at the corner of Leicester Street. The film rendezvous took place on the east side, with Blaney waiting on the Leicester Fields side, directly opposite the Odeon. Their taxi's route to the Coburg was: down the eastern side of the square, L into Irving Street, R into Charing Cross Road and thence into St. Martin's Place near **Trafalgar Square**. Note that the square is now open to foot traffic only, so if you want to recreate the journey to the Coburg, you'll have to start in Charing Cross Road.

20:12
Odeon Cinema F
22-24 Leicester Square, WC2

Built on the site of the old Alhambra Theatre, this famous Art Deco style cinema celebrated its 60th anniversary in 1997. It is perhaps most famous for the many royal charity film premieres held here, including those for nearly all the James Bond films. Hitchcock and Alma attended the London premiere of *To Catch a Thief* here in 1955, with no less than Queen Elizabeth herself in attendance. For the London premiere of *The Birds* in August 1963, the director arranged to have two black mynah birds— Alfie and Tippi—placed in

Odeon Cinema

the Odeon's foyer. Eight years later, Hitchcock managed to work the cinema itself into *Frenzy*. You will recall that Dick Blaney rings Babs from a Soho Square phone booth (see entry 20:17) and asks her to meet him opposite the Leicester Square Odeon at 4 o'clock. Hitchcock's camera catches a brief glimpse of the cinema's distinctive *moderne* black façade when Dick crosses to the cab that will take them to the **Coburg Hotel**, Bayswater. The cinema underwent an extensive renovation in 1998 but is still recognizably the same as in the '70s.

Station: Leicester Square (NO; PI) Take the Charing Cross Road (West) exit to Leicester Square. Turn L into the Square and look for the cinema on the L.

The MacGuffin: The Alhambra Theatre itself has an indirect Hitchcock connection: It was the venue for the year-long, 1931-32 run of *Waltzes from Vienna*, a musical which the director adapted for the screen in 1933.

20:13
Wyndham's Theatre H (F)
Charing Cross Road, WC2

Built by actor-manager Charles Wyndham in 1899, this famous West End theatre is connected with Alfred Hitchcock primarily through Sir Gerald du Maurier (1873-1934), the legendary producer, director, playwright and actor who co-managed Wyndham's from 1910 to 1925. Du Maurier was the son of the celebrated cartoonist and novelist Sir George du Maurier (*Trilby*), as well as the father of novelist Daphne du Maurier, three of whose stories Hitchcock would adapt into films (see **Menabilly**). Sir Gerald was considered the living embodiment of the English stage, idolized by an entire generation of theatre-goers and actors alike, including future Hitchcock collaborator Charles

Wyndham's Theatre

Laughton. He was the world's first "Captain Hook," in the December 1904 stage debut of J.M. Barrie's *Peter Pan* and only the fifth actor in British history to receive a knighthood. (Henry Irving was the first, in 1895.) Du Maurier was also the principal inspiration for the character of Sir John Saumarez in the 1928 novel *Enter Sir John*, which Hitchcock adapted as *Murder!* in 1930. (Another inspiration was actor-manager Sir Herbert Beerbohm Tree, who is discussed under **Her Majesty's Theatre**.) In fact, authors Clemence Dane and Helen Simpson reinforced the connection between Sir John and Sir Gerald in their follow-up novel, *Re-enter Sir John*, which was published in 1932. Here, the title character takes up film acting under the guidance of a "fat little director" named Rupert Lowstoft, who also happens to be bald, to smoke cigars and to have known Sir John for many years. That same year, 1932, Sir Gerald essayed one of his infrequent film roles in *Lord Camber's Ladies*, a picture produced—but not directed—by a "fat little director" named Alfred Hitchcock. (Dane and Simpson also put words like "ain't" and constructions like "that don't look comfortable" in the mouth of their little director, an allusion, apparently, to Hitchcock's comparatively humble East London origins.) Of course, Hitchcock and du Maurier had known each other for years, ever since the budding film director began attending plays here at Wyndham's during Sir Gerald's tenure as manager. The two friends were famous (or *infamous*) for the elaborate practical jokes they played on each other, the most notorious of which occurred at the **St. James's Theatre** in King Street, to which you should turn for the rest of the story. In addition to meeting du Maurier, Hitchcock also made a number of important acting discoveries here at Wyndham's. The most notable were Gordon Harker, whom he saw in Edgar Wallace's 1926 mystery *The Ringer*, and whom he would go on to feature in *The Ring*, *The Farmer's Wife*, *Champagne* and *Elstree Calling*; and Tallulah Bankhead, who dazzled him in Sir Gerald's own 1923 play *The Dancers* (co-written with Viola Tree) and whom he would later star in *Lifeboat*. Indeed, Hitchcock was not the only one impressed with the flashy Alabama flapper: du Maurier himself engaged in a brief but torrid affair with Bankhead shortly after her arrival here in January 1923.

Sir Gerald du Maurier

Station: Leicester Square (NO; PI) Exit into Charing Cross Road (South) and look for the theatre just ahead on the L. Fans of the du Maurier family may wish to visit Sir Gerald's London home (commemorated by an English Heritage Blue Plaque) at Cannon Hall, 14 Cannon Place, NW3.

The MacGuffin: From December 1922 to February 1923, Sir Gerald starred as *Bull-dog* [*sic*] *Drummond* here at Wyndham's, in a play he co-wrote with Drummond's creator H.C. McNeile, a.k.a. "Sapper." Whether or not Hitchcock saw the play is not known, although he was certainly a Sapper fan and, indeed, found the inspiration for *The Man Who Knew Too Much* (34) in the Drummond stories (see Appendix I).

20:14
London Hippodrome L (F)
Hippodrome Corner
Cranbourn Street, WC2

Built to the design of architect Frank Matcham (who also designed the **Coliseum Theatre** and the **Palladium**), the Hippodrome opened in 1900 as a combination music hall and circus, complete with a massive built-in water tank for aquatic spectacles. It was reconstructed internally in 1909 and went on to host a series of famous musical comedies, including *Sunny* (1926), *That's a Good Girl* (1928) and *Stand Up and Sing* (1931), all of which starred Jack Buchanan and Hitchcock friend Elsie Randolph (*Rich and Strange, Frenzy*). Several of Hitchcock's early films were trade-shown to exhibitors here, including *The Lodger*, on September 14, 1926, *The Mountain Eagle*, on October 1, 1926, *Downhill*, on May 27, 1927, *Easy Virtue*, on August 30, 1927 (at 3:00 p.m.), and *Champagne* on August 20, 1928. The Hippodrome is also mentioned in Anthony Armstrong's story "The Case

London Hippodrome

of Mr. Pelham." A friend who claims to have seen him at the Hippodrome the previous night accosts the title character, but, in fact, "Mr. Pelham hadn't been inside the Hippodrome for many months." In the Americanized television episode, the meeting is now alleged to have taken place "at the Garden," i.e., Madison Square Garden, New York. (The original Madison Square Garden, ironically, was built on the site of an arena also known as the Hippodrome.) In 1958, the Hippodrome was converted to a restaurant/cabaret called The Talk of the Town, which closed in 1982. It has since been reopened in yet another guise, as "the world's most famous discotheque." In other words, it's beloved of tourists but avoided by Londoners.

Station: Leicester Square (NO; PI) Exit for the Hippodrome.

Ask Mr. Memory 30: Which Hitchcock heroine made her stage debut as a singer here at the Hippodrome in 1947?

20:15
St. Martin's Theatre L H (F)
West Street, WC2

Built in 1916 as a companion to the neighboring Ambassadors Theatre, St. Martin's is perhaps best known as the home of the world's longest-running play, Agatha Christie's *Mousetrap*, which opened here in 1974 after a 22-year run at the Ambassadors itself. In 1920, the St. Martin's hosted a rather more serious play, John Galsworthy's *The Skin Game*, which Alfred Hitchcock apparently saw here at some point during its nine-month run. The original cast included a number of actors who would eventually appear in Hitchcock films: Mary Clare (*Young and Innocent*, *The Lady Vanishes*),

St. Martin's Theatre

Malcolm Keen (*The Lodger*, *The Manxman*) and Edmund Gwenn and Helen Hayes, the only performers who actually reprised their roles in Hitchcock's film adaptation of the play. Interestingly, the same year he shot *The Skin Game*—1930—Hitchcock also saw a young performer here at St. Martin's in the play *Honours Easy*, which ran from February 7 to May 31. Her name was Ann Todd and he would cast her some 17 years later as Gay Keane in *The Paradine Case*. In fact, for that very film, Hitchcock assigned a second unit to film a short exterior sequence here at St. Martin's. The bit showed a taxi pulling up in front of the theatre and a double for actor Charles Coburn (Sir Simon Flaquer) getting out of the car and entering the building. The ensuing interior—never filmed—was to replicate a scene from the novel in which Sir Simon first approaches Keane about "the Paradine Case" at the **Haymarket Theatre**. Hitchcock ultimately replaced this scene with one in which Sir Simon and Judy drive to an Assize Court in Lincoln, where Keane is defending a murder case before none other than Lord Horfield ("one of our most distinguished justices," Flaquer calls him). Keane's impressive theatrics earn his client—who had actually confessed to the crime—a relatively light sentence from the judge, who, as it happens, is stuck in Lincoln without a car. After trying to persuade Tony to take on the Paradine Case (which Keane claims that anyone could handle), Flaquer offers Horfield a ride back to London. This entire sequence, which concluded with the lecherous Horfield cozying up to Judy in the back seat, was ultimately cut for time. In the finished film, the action switches from Mrs. Paradine in custody at the **Bow Street Police Station** to the Flaquers dropping off Keane in front of his Portland Place home (see entry 14:5). We thus lose not only the background for Simmy's "Think it over, Keane" (as Keane exits the car) and Keane's later "You might ask me if I won my case" (to Gay), but the triumphant introduction of Keane himself in a courtroom setting before the imperious Horfield.

Station: Leicester Square (NO; PI) Take the Charing Cross Road (East) exit L into Cranbourne Street, then turn L into St. Martin's Lane. The theatre is ahead on the L. Directly across the street is the legendary show biz haunt, **The Ivy**, which along with **Simpson's** and **Le Caprice** was one of Hitchcock's favorite London restaurants.

**20:16
St. Giles Circus F
W1, WC1, WC2**

Doubles as: Lower Regent Street near Piccadilly Circus in *Sabotage*

In one of Hitchcock's most suspenseful sequences, Stevie, the young hero-cum-sacrificial lamb of *Sabotage*, takes an interminably slow bus from **St. Clement Danes** to **Piccadilly Circus Underground Station**, unaware that he is carrying a time-bomb set to explode at 1:45 p.m. Street clocks along the Strand indicate that it has already passed 1:30 and Stevie's bus is soon hopelessly mired in traffic in what (according to Hitchcock's treatment of April 17, 1936) is supposed to be Lower Regent Street, just below Piccadilly Circus. (The newspaper reports indicate that the bus actually exploded *in* Piccadilly Circus, although you can't tell that from the film.) Then, after what must rank as the longest red light in British history, Stevie's bus finally begins to crawl

St. Giles Circus

through the intersection, but, of course, it's too late. The clock strikes 1:45, the bomb explodes and the boy is killed—a powerful scene, a powerful statement. In fact, some 70 years on, it's hard to imagine just how scandalous this scene was in 1936. For one thing, there was the idea of the bombing itself—a fairly rare occurrence at the time. As an exasperated Will Hay exclaims in 1939's *Ask a Policeman*, "This is England. They don't throw bombs here!" (Worth mentioning: *Policeman*'s screenplay was co-written by Hitchcock collaborator Sidney Gilliat, who evoked comedian Hay himself in *The Lady Vanishes*.) Even more shocking, of course, was that Hitchcock had killed young Stevie. Important London critics, notably C.A. (Caroline) Lejeune, excoriated the director for this, completely overlooking the dramatic impact—and dramatic necessity—of the scene. Hitchcock took the criticism to heart and forever after repudiated his decision to let the bomb explode. (Lejeune herself did not hold a grudge, going on to say upon the release of *Rebecca* that Hitchcock was "our Number One director, and the most consistent genius who has ever worked for the cinema in this country" [*The Sketch*, July 10, 1940].) Interestingly, some 20 years after *Sabotage*, Hitchcock directed "Four O'Clock," an episode of the television anthology series *Suspicion*, in which a watchmaker plants a time bomb to kill his (apparently) adulterous wife, is tied up by burglars and, believing that he is about to be hoist by his own petard, loses his mind. The episode was based on the story "Three O'Clock" by "Rear Window" author Cornell Woolrich and, in turn, recalls a similar incident in an early Bulldog Drummond novel, *The Black Gang*. Hitchcock was, of course, a fan of Sapper's Drummond series, elements of which inspired the original *Man Who Knew Too Much*. Returning to *Sabotage*, the "Piccadilly Circus" traffic jam was actually filmed in Charing Cross Road, just below St. Giles Circus (then and now a horribly congested intersection), while the shots of the traffic light were made in the northwest corner of the intersection itself, looking south toward 7 Oxford Street, then a J. Sears True-Form shoe outlet (whose sign is visible in the film as the buses pass from west to east along Oxford Street).

The aftermath of the explosion was filmed at the bottom of the exterior High Street set Hitchcock built in Northolt, with background façades to approximate those of the buildings in Lower Regent Street, buildings that the director actually incorporated in the *Blackmail* **Chase Routes**.

Station: Tottenham Court Road (CE; NO) Take Exit 2 for the view across to 7 Oxford Street (the traffic lights have since been repositioned). For the traffic jam, take Exit 1 R into Charing Cross Road, walk down to the bus stop, take a No. 24 bus (at rush hour!) and enjoy the ride through the circus. For more on the boy's route through London, see **Stevie's Final Journey**.

The MacGuffin: Discussion of the traffic jam scene reminded Desmond Tester (Stevie) of the day in 1937 when he was driving down a London street, came to a red light, and happened to glance up toward a massive sign. It was an advertisement for Hitchcock's new adaptation of the novel *A Shilling for Candles*. As the 18-year-old Tester digested the film's title, partly blocked by a light pole, he saw the words "Young and In-," then the pole, followed by "-cent." "I thought, Shit! They've called the bloody thing *Young and Indecent*!" When the light changed and he drove on, Tester was quickly disabused of his fantasy. "But that," as he explained, nearly 65 years later, "is just the way boys think."

20:17
"Frenzy **Telephone Booth Site"** F
31 Soho Square, W1

Laid out in the late 17th century, this former residential square is now largely occupied by business and other professional offices, including a number of film companies. Fittingly, Soho Square was chosen as the site of Dick Blaney's phone call to Babs at **The Globe** in *Frenzy*. The sequence had originally been slated for July 30, 1971, then August 3, but time, weather and the lack of a suitable site delayed its filming. Finally, on August 4, a construction van carted a dummy telephone booth (with "operational phone") here to Soho Square and Hitchcock filmed the short scene in which Dick arranges for Babs to bring his belongings to **Leicester Square**.

Station: Tottenham Court Road (CE; NO) Take Exit 1 L into Oxford Street. Turn L into Soho Street, which takes you into Soho Square. The phone booth was set up in the southwest corner, with the camera facing out into the garden, opposite No. 31.

20:18
"Blaney Bureau" (*ex* **Castano Employment Agency) F**
Dryden Chambers
119 Oxford Street, Suite 3, W1

Frenzy victim Brenda Blaney's matrimonial agency—ultimate satisfaction: the bringing together of two lonely people—was located just off **Oxford Street**, as suggested by an establishing shot of the intersection of that street and Stratford Place in the film itself. In the novel *Goodbye Piccadilly, Farewell Leicester Square*, Brenda Blamey's [*sic*] matrimonial agency was located in **Leicester Square** and, in fact, Hitchcock initially envisioned the film character in a Coventry Street office, on the north side of the square. However, when he and scriptwriter Anthony Shaffer shifted the action of Arthur La Bern's novel eastward to Covent Garden, Brenda's office no longer necessitated a Leicester Square setting. Associate producer Bill Hill recalled that Hitchcock knew exactly what he wanted instead, an alley off Oxford Street, something quieter and perhaps a bit more "down-market" than bustling Leicester Square. The location manager duly found the Castano Employment Agency in Dryden Chambers, just off Oxford Street, to which Hitchcock gave an instant thumbs-up. Filming commenced here on Wednesday, August 4, 1971, with the shot of Blaney walking past the Ronald Keith Shoe Store and turning left into Dryden Chambers (shot with a hidden camera in a camera tent). Interestingly, the dark brick building at the end of the passage—visible when Blaney leaves the agency just before Miss Barling's arrival—was a Victorian brothel. (Do you suppose Hitchcock knew?) Office interiors, including the stairs, were shot at **Pinewood Studios**. (See **Bob Rusk's Flat** for more on Hitchcock's stairs.) For these scenes, Hitchcock took precisely the opposite approach to that of novelist Arthur La Bern, who emphasized the myriad external sounds that could be heard in Brenda's office. According to the Final Dubbing Notes of November 26, 1971, Hitchcock wanted no external sounds whatsoever, in order to preserve the "remoteness" and "isolation" of Brenda's office. In this way, he would "reassure the audience" that no one outside could possibly hear Brenda's screams during the attack. Sadly, Dryden Chambers was obliterated in 1984, much of the block between Oxford and Wardour Streets being replaced by the massive Quadrangle building.

Station: Tottenham Court Road (CE; NO) Take Exit 1 L into Oxford Street. The entrance to Dryden Chambers was at 119, just before Wardour Street. The archway and iron latticework visible near the top of the shot of Blaney walking down the alley toward the agency *is still here*, above the entrance to 119—now a Legends Boutique. Across Oxford Street, at No. 100, is the 100 Club, a fashionable jazz venue since the 1930s. The club served as the *Frenzy* production base while shooting in and around Oxford Street.

The MacGuffin: Trimmed from the scene in which Chief Inspector Oxford interviews Miss Barling *after* Blaney's trial and sentencing was the reason Miss Barling was still working at the Blaney Bureau: She had actually taken over the agency after Brenda's murder.

20:19
London Palladium F
8 Argyll Street, W1

This luxurious music hall opened on December 26, 1910, when it was known simply as "The Palladium." At that time there were some 60 music halls in and around London, serving up roughly the same kind of variety acts as vaudeville in America. Talking pictures led to the decline of variety shows in the late 1920s, when a number of music halls, including the Palladium, were converted into cinemas. The turnaround came in 1932, when theatrical manager George Black (1890-1945) reinvented variety entertainment through his popular "Crazy Gang" shows here at the Palladium. These were lavish revues, featuring popular comedy teams, rapid pacing, outlandish skits and, of course, the ever-popular men-in-drag routines! Black renamed the theatre the London Palladium in 1934, just in time for the finale of Hitchcock's *The 39 Steps*. Fans of the film will recall that it is here, during one of those very Crazy Gang shows, that Richard Hannay finally exposes "the Thirty-Nine Steps" as a spy ring, through the timely help—and ultimate murder—of "Mr. Memory." In fact, much of this sequence was shot in either of two different studios: **Lime Grove** for the theatre interiors (including Pamela's search for Hannay, Hannay's recognition

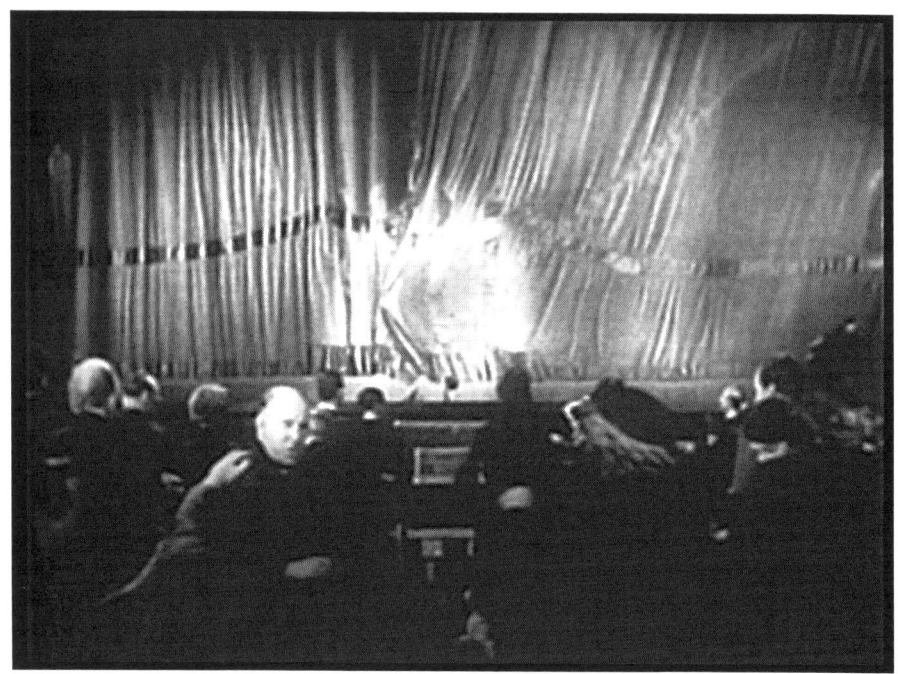

The secret spy ring is revealed in the finale of *The 39 Steps*.

of Memory, and the encounter with the police) and **Welwyn** for the exteriors (including Pamela's arrival by taxi and the police van arriving at the rear entrance). Several bits were staged at the actual theatre, though, including Memory's introduction and the Professor's dramatic jump onto the stage. In addition, Hitchcock apparently indulged in at least one Schüfftan shot of the theatre. The shooting script describes the long shot of the audience watching the performers on the stage as a Schüfftan shot (see Appendix II for more on this special effects process). However, the long shot of Hannay breaking free from the police to ask Memory about the Thirty-Nine Steps may also have been accomplished in this manner (note its "static" look). Speaking of Hannay and Memory, the shooting script also reveals that their original exchange went a little differently: "What are the Thirty-Nine Steps?" Hannay demands. "Come on! Answer up—Where [*sic*] are the Thirty-Nine Steps?" The slightly shaken Memory replies: "The Thirty-Nine Steps lie at the North Foreland—four miles the other side of—," at which point the Professor shoots him, as in the film. This, of course, was precisely the set-up of the novel, in which the steps were real steps, located on the North Foreland (see **The Site of "the Thirty-nine Steps"**), via which the spies would reach the ship that would whisk them out of the country. Hitchcock's switch from a "where" to a "what," making "the Thirty-Nine Steps" an organization, truly seems to have been a last minute decision, possibly to heighten the dramatic impact of the title, the enemy operation, or both. The original exchange was filmed in semi-long shots, with Hannay demanding his answer at Lime Grove and Memory actually responding here at the Palladium. The modified exchange substitutes an extended close-up of Memory, apparently filmed at Lime Grove, during which we hear Hannay's revised question, after which Memory gives the new answer and is shot. Apart from a few extraneous bits and lines (notably in both music hall sequences [see 58:2]), which were obviously dropped for time or pace, the shooting script is quite close to the finished film and it is remarkable to think that but for the change of two lines near the end, the film's title would have had an entirely different meaning. Then, again, considering the lack of importance Hitchcock attached to the MacGuffin, maybe it isn't so remarkable after all.

Other Hitchcock connections with the Palladium include the 1929 short, *An Elastic Affair*, which was shown here on January 19, 1930. Hitchcock made the film at **Elstree** to showcase two young film scholarship winners, Aileen Despard and Cyril Butcher. No copy of *An Elastic Affair*—which was shot with sound but shown silent—is known to have survived. In *Saboteur*, Barry dances with Pat under the watchful eyes of Mrs. Sutton and her Fifth Columnists, then laments that the pair can't "go on dancing like this were Saturday night at the Palladium." Hitchcock also indirectly alludes to the Palladium in *The Man Who Knew Too Much* (56), when the McKennas' friends try to figure out why Ben and Jo keep running in and out of their **Savoy** hotel room. Val Parnell (played by English character actor Alan Mowbray) says, "It must be a new American gag. I'll ask Danny about it." The "Danny" is American entertainer Danny Kaye, who had played the Palladium for six weeks in 1948 and was a certifiable sensation. Parnell himself was the managing director of the Palladium, having succeeded George Black upon the latter's death. He ensured the survival of Black's dream through a scheme of hiring top American film stars such as Kaye, Mickey Rooney, Bob Hope, Judy Garland and others to headline here at the Palladium. Both Parnell and his wife, Helen Howell (played by Alix Talton in the film), consented to their "characterizations" in *The Man*

Who Knew Too Much. In fact, the Parnells recorded an interview in July 1955, which Hitchcock used to ensure accuracy in their portrayal.

Station: Oxford Circus (BA; CE; VI) Take Exit 8 for the Palladium. **Tours:** M-T, Th-F 5:30 pm; W, S 12:30 pm.

Ask Mr. Memory 31: Which Hitchcock heroine played Peter Pan at the London Palladium in December 1935?

20:20
"Adolf Verloc's Shop" L
32 Brett Street, W1

According to the novel *The Secret Agent* (whence *Sabotage*), Adolf Verloc, his wife Winnie, her brother Stevie and her mother live in a grimy brick house at 32 Brett Street—a "sullen, brooding, and sinister" street (Conrad at his Dickensian best)—in Soho. Verloc's stationery shop (and pornography emporium) occupies the front of the building, which is not far from the corner fruit stand. This sounds very much like Brewer Street, the archetypal Soho street, today laden (or bedecked, depending on your perspective) with sex shops and call girls.

Brewer St., possible site of Adolf Verloc's shop

Station: Piccadilly Circus (BA; NO) Exit for Shaftesbury Avenue and turn L at the top of the stairs then R into Shaftesbury Avenue. Cross to Great Windmill Street and follow this to Brewer Street.

Ask Mr. Memory 32: What was the American title of *Sabotage*?

21. SOUTH BANK

21:1
Royal Festival Hall F L
Belvedere Rd, SE1

Alfred Hitchcock originally planned to stage the climax of the second *The Man Who Knew Too Much* at the sleek, new Royal Festival Hall, not the **Royal Albert Hall**, which he had used in the original film. The former, built in 1951 as part of the Festival of Britain celebration, was used for concerts, recitals, film and ballet performances and, indeed, had been intended to supersede the acoustically questionable Albert Hall

Royal Festival Hall

(which, in fact, it never did). In February 1955, Hitchcock sought permission to film (unobtrusively) during an actual concert, as well as to shoot selected bits here with his principal actors. Production documents indicate that the Festival Hall management was interested in accommodating the director and in March Hitchcock had photographic tests made to determine if there was sufficient light from the house lights to actually film inside the Hall. As of April 26, Festival Hall had been booked for May 26, 27 and 28, when composer Bernard Herrmann would conduct recording sessions with the London Symphony Orchestra and the Covent Garden Choir. Unfortunately, as the expanding shooting schedule evolved, it became clear that Herrmann and Hitchcock would need more time in Festival Hall than the facility could grant them—hence the decision to switch to the Albert Hall. Still, the Royal Festival Hall does make an "appearance" of sorts in the 1956 film: If you look closely through the window of the McKennas' **Savoy** hotel room, you will spot the hall's distinctive curved roof to the right of the shot. (The tall, chimney-like structure to its left, Shot Tower, a part of the original 19th-century exhibition, was torn down in 1967.) Festival Hall was also the setting for a concert attended by Mark and the title character in Chapter 12 of *Marnie*, a scene with no counterpart in the film but which would have occurred shortly after their marriage. The evening out constitutes something of a break during Marnie's rather intense sessions with a psychiatrist (see **Regent's Park**) and, while the first part of the program bores her, the finale, Brahms' *Fourth Symphony* (she thinks), positively enraptures her.

Station: Waterloo (BA; JU; NO; WC) Exit into York Road and turn L; look for Sutton Walk ahead on the L. Follow this under the bridge and then turn L into Concert Hall Approach, which leads to Festival Hall.

22. SOUTH KENSINGTON

22:1
Alfred Hitchcock's Home H
153 Cromwell Road, SW5

In preparation for his December 1926 wedding to Alma Reville (see **Brompton Oratory**), Alfred Hitchcock leased the top two floors of No. 153 Cromwell Road, just along from the Natural History Museum and other South Kensington landmarks. It was his—and Alma's—first home away from their respective families (see also 44:1). Notwithstanding the director's later success, the family—including daughter Pat (born here on July 7, 1928)—resisted the move to larger, more stylish digs in Mayfair or Kensington, remaining here until their move to America in 1939. The reason, according to Pat herself, was quite simple: Her mother and father loved this house and the quiet life they had here. "I don't remember an awful lot [about the house]," Pat told me,

On August 13, 1999, the 100th birthday of Alfred Hitchcock, Patricia Hitchcock prepares to unveil the blue plaque on her family's home.

"[because] I was only 10 when we left....But the bedrooms were on the top floor and the living room and dining room were on the lower floor." The dining room was, arguably, the most important room in the house, the place where the Hitchcocks entertained both family and friends. The latter included such celebrated writers as James Hilton, George Bernard Shaw and John Galsworthy, whose play *The Skin Game* Hitchcock adapted for the screen in 1931. It was also in the dining room that Hitchcock worked with writers and collaborators on the screenplays for his films (there was no den or study, according to Pat). During preproduction of *The Lady Vanishes*, for example, he and Sidney Gilliat worked there on the script that Gilliat and his partner, Frank Launder, had written more than a year before Hitchcock himself became involved with the project. (Launder later recalled that the differences hammered out here in Cromwell Road were primarily in the opening, which was now faster paced, and the last reel, which, with the addition of more twists and turns, "was certainly more exciting.") In 1999—60 years after the move to America—Pat

Hitchcock O'Connell returned to London to take part in the celebrations honoring the centenary of her father's birth. Among other tributes (notably that of the National Film Institute), the English Heritage organization erected one of its famous blue plaques here, on August 13, 1999, with Pat herself in attendance. The plaque reads simply: "Sir ALFRED HITCHCOCK 1899-1980 Film Director lived here 1926-1939."

Station: Gloucester Road (CI; DI; PI) Exit L into Cromwell Road; the house is just ahead on the L. For the family's other English home, see **Alfred Hitchcock's Country Home**.

22:2
Royal Albert Hall F L
Kensington Gore, SW7

Doubles as: Unnamed Embassy, London, in *The Man Who Knew Too Much* (56)

Opened in 1871, this magnificent concert hall put in a number of notable appearances in the life and work of Alfred Hitchcock. In March 1971, for example, Princess Anne awarded Hitchcock the first honorary membership in the Society of Film and Television Arts at a ceremony here. Years earlier, Hitchcock attended the Chelsea Arts Ball here at the Albert Hall and "got very drunk." As he told Truffaut, "I always remember everything going away—so far away." The sensation so impressed him that he sought for years to represent it onscreen, e.g., in *Rebecca*, where it would have served as Mrs. de Winter's POV before she faints at the inquest. He finally achieved success in *Vertigo*, in which reverse track/forward zoom shots of a miniature staircase dramatized Scottie Ferguson's debilitating condition. (Hitchcock's account of the evolution of the famous "Vertigo shot" rings true enough, although author Dan Auiler has suggested that the credit may instead belong to the film's unbilled second-unit cameraman, Irmin Roberts.) On celluloid, the director would commemorate the hall in no less than three films, most famously in *The Man Who Knew Too Much* and its American remake. The first ap-

Royal Albert Hall

Royal Albert Hall, where Doris Day waited, in *The Man Who Knew Too Much* (1956)

pearance, however, was in his 1927 silent *The Ring*, which chronicles the rise of boxer "One Round" Jack Sander. Hitchcock himself had attended a number of championship fights at the Albert Hall, so it's no surprise that his one cinematic foray into the world of boxing should contain a climactic scene set in the venerable hall. (The preclimactic bout occurs at the old **Holborn Stadium**.) Hitchcock did not, however, film inside the hall itself, relying instead upon studio sets and the Schüfftan process to create the illusion (see Appendix II). He also employed the Schüfftan process for the 1934 version of *The Man Who Knew Too Much*, although after initially obtaining (and customizing) the photographs he wanted, Hitchcock returned to the hall to stage limited portions of the action, the crowd itself being largely supplied through special effects. (In fact, the audience members were painted onto the photos by renowned Italian illustrator Fortunino Matania.) Arthur Benjamin's magnificent cantata "The Storm Clouds," composed especially for the film, was also recorded here, with H. Wynn Reeves conducting the London Symphony Orchestra. (It is perhaps worth noting that the film was inspired by Sapper's Bulldog Drummond novels [see Appendix I], the second one of which, *The Black Gang* (1922), concludes with a gala scene at the Albert Hall.)

For the 1956 remake, Hitchcock filled up much of the hall with extras and staged a longer version of the cantata, this time with Bernard Herrmann conducting the LSO and the Covent Garden Chorus. (See **Royal Festival Hall** for the venue Hitchcock had originally intended for the

The finale of *The Ring* occurred at Royal Albert Hall.

Bernard Herrmann directs the LSO at Royal Albert Hall in *The Man Who Knew Too Much*. (1956)

film's climactic setting.) Filming took place in the main lobby (Door 6), the corridor, and auditorium throughout the month of June. High-angle matte shots, completed in Hollywood, would emphasize the vastness of the Hall. (Note the second extreme long shot of the auditorium, after Jo enters; the brightly lit portion of the image "jumps" a bit.) Portions of the Hall, including the PM's box, the assassin's box, the box office, the Green Room, the upper corridor, the passage where Jo tearfully reacts, and the stage where the cymbalist clashes, were all recreated by art director Henry Bumstead in Hollywood, Hitchcock again preferring to stage the more "intimate scenes" in the controlled studio environment. In addition, after searching all over London for an appropriate "embassy kitchen and corridor" (for the scene in which the guard rousts the staff out of the kitchen and the staff then muse upon the strange comings and goings at the embassy), Hitchcock wound up using the kitchen and staff canteen here at the Albert Hall. As production manager Doc Erickson explained, "We were doing a lot of filming at the Hall, so it just made sense to do the kitchen scenes there as well." (Incidentally, if you watch this sequence closely, you'll notice that the guard is played by two different actors: an American, Milton Frome, in the Hollywood close-up, saying, "Wait till I clear the kitchen"; and a Briton, Walter Gotell, in the London long shot, ordering, "Everybody out!" Pretty cheeky, eh?) Both the kitchen and canteen have since been refurbished (almost beyond recognition) but with canny guides—which I was extremely fortunate to have—you can actually locate the precise spots where Hitchcock shot the two short scenes. The Albert Hall also pops up in *Dial M for Murder* (both the play and film), when Tony misreads an engagement at the hall in Margot's diary as one with an "Al Bentall" ("Another one of your boyfriends?" he asks). Interestingly, Hitchcock skipped yet another chance to evoke the famous landmark in adapting the novel *Topaz*, where we learn that during the War, Devereaux and Granville attended a meeting of the Free French Forces at the Albert Hall.

Station: South Kensington (CI; DI; PI) Follow the signs to the Royal Albert Hall, which will lead you into Exhibition Road. Turn L and follow this to Prince Consort

Road, where you will turn L then R into the curved Albert Court. For the view in the 1956 film (an establishing shot taken by the second unit in July 1955), cross to the neo-Gothic Albert Memorial and stand just back from the Europe statue, which is on the left, as you face the memorial. (The memorial itself—or, rather, a photographic cut-out of it—can be seen through the office window during the scene in which Ben and Jo confer with Buchanan after the assassination attempt. Of this ersatz medieval shrine—built in homage to Queen Victoria's deceased consort—Hitchcock source author Edmund Crispin aptly noted: "[It is] intrinsically graceless, but so uncompromising as to compel respect.") You will not be able to replicate Doris Day's entrance since the portico of Door 6—where Hitchcock parked two black limousines—has since been enclosed with glass. In the 1934 film, the "exterior" view (after the assassination attempt) is from outside Door 4, looking across to Albert Hall Mansions, although as the "Stalls K" sign suggests, the corridor and lobby are based upon Door 6, as in the later film. Just west of the Hall, in De Vere Gardens, is the Kensington Palace Hotel, where Hitchcock and screenwriter Charles Bennett often lunched together in the 1930s.

The MacGuffin: The Royal Albert Hall isn't the only South Kensington locale associated with a political assassination at a concert. Just south of the Hall is the Imperial College of Science, Technology and Medicine, which occupies the site of the former Imperial Institute. (The 287-ft Queen's Tower is all that remains of the original neo-Renaissance building.) On July 1, 1909, the Imperial Institute was host to a lavish concert and reception as part of the National Indian Association's annual celebration. Among the prominent persons in attendance was the association's treasurer, Sir William Curzon Wyllie, also the political Aide-de-Camp to Lord Morley, the Secretary of State for India. Just after the concert, at approximately 11:00 p.m., a Punjabi student named Madanlal Dhingra shot and killed Curzon Wyllie, as well as another man—an Indian—who tried to intervene. (Scotland Yard had been monitoring the activities of Indian dissidents, including Dhingra, and had warned the government of a plot to kill Morley himself, as well as Lord Curzon, the former Viceroy of India.) Although widely hailed as a hero in the struggle for Indian independence, Dhingra was tried for murder at the Old Bailey, sentenced to death, and hung at Pentonville Prison on August 17, 1909.

22:3
ex **Thorney Court F**
Palace Gate, W8

Doubles as: Unnamed Embassy in *The Man Who Knew Too Much* (56)

According to *The Man Who Knew Too Much* continuity reports, Alfred Hitchcock shot the scene in which the Draytons bring Hank to the rear entrance of the embassy on June 10, 1955, the same day he shot the kitchen sequence at the **Albert Hall**. Frustratingly, the documents do not specify precisely where Hitchcock shot the brief sequence. Production designer Henry Bumstead recalled that it was near the Albert Hall, but neither he nor production manager Doc Erickson could remember the exact location. Well, it turns out that the street was Palace Gate and the building was an apartment complex called Thorney Court. The original Thorney Court, a Georgian structure similar in appearance to the still extant Zambian Embassy next door, was pulled down in the early

Thorney Court: view across the street as shown in *The Man Who Knew Too Much* (1956)

1980s and replaced with a far larger luxury apartment complex, also called Thorney Court. The saving grace is that the buildings directly opposite the entrance—visible in the film when the car pulls into the drive—have scarcely changed since 1955. For the other buildings that doubled as the embassy, see **Forbes House** and **Park Lane House**.

Station: High Street Kensington (CI; DI) Exit R into Kensington High Street and continue through Kensington Road to Palace Gate, where you will turn R. Look for the Thorney Court entrance across the street—and the stucco houses directly opposite. The Thorney Court gateposts clearly resemble those in the film, although they are in fact later replacements. Incidentally, if you're interested in accommodation in Thorney Court itself, a 2-bedroom apartment will run you around £2,000 a week and that doesn't include VAT [value-added tax]!

22:4
"Brenda Blaney's Home" F P
31 Ennismore Gardens Mews, SW7

Doubles as: 37 Berkeley Mews, Marylebone, in *Frenzy*

According to the *Frenzy* shooting script—and a scene actually shot but omitted from the finished film (see entry 15:22)—Brenda Blaney lives at 37 Berkeley Mews. There is no indication that Hitchcock ever planned to shoot in that small Marylebone mews, located in back of the Churchill Hotel. Rather, production records indicate that Hitchcock had selected Kynance Mews, Kensington, on the western side of all the museums, to double as the exterior of Brenda's home. So how did he—and the Blaneys—end up in Ennismore Gardens Mews, to the east of Museumland? Nothing in the production documents confirms this, but it is possible that Hitchcock's attention was drawn to the new location by actress Eileen Atkins, whom he had originally sought for the part of

Brenda. The actress, who politely turned down the director's request, then lived in Ennismore Gardens, which adjoins Ennismore Gardens Mews. In any case, it was to the latter that Hitchcock brought his crew on the night of September 15, 1971, the same night he shot exteriors of **Wormwood Scrubs**. Later, afraid that filmgoers might think Brenda lived "in some remote spot" (Final Dubbing Notes, November 26, 1971), Hitchcock instructed his sound editor to "have some distant motor horns to remind the audience that they are still in the city...." That said, such sounds are not especially audible in the finished film.

Brenda Blaney's home

Station: South Kensington (CI; DI; PI) Follow the signs to the Royal Albert Hall, exit into Exhibition Road and cross to Princes Gate Mews. Follow this as it veers to the L and continue in the footpath that leads into Ennismore Gardens Mews. The house is ahead on the L.

Ask Mr. Memory 33: In his first visit with Brenda, Dick mentions that they were married for nine years. How long were they actually married? A Bonus Point if you know how long they've been divorced.

22:5
"Florence Webster's Home" LP
Thurloe Square, SW7

According to Chapter 7 of *Man Running*, Eve Gill's Aunt Florence lives in Thurloe Square, an area of attractive terraced houses laid out in the 1840s. In fact, Aunt Florence is seldom found in Thurloe Square, at least during the day, her "true" home and family being those located under the **Harrods** sign in Brompton Road. Eve comes here to stay with her aunt while posing as Charlotte Inwood's new maid, a deception replicated in the film *Stage Fright*, but with a change of venue to Hampstead (see the **Gill Home**).

Florence Webster's home

Station: South Kensington (CI; DI; PI) Exit into Thurloe Street, which leads directly to the square.

A REFERENCE GUIDE TO LOCATIONS 179

22:6
"Charlotte Inwood's Home" (2) L P
4 Cary Gardens (i.e., Cranley Gardens), SW7

According to Chapter 1 of *Man Running*, newly widowed Charlotte Inwood lives at No. 4 Cary Gardens, in a road that connects Brompton and Fulham Roads and that is near (Old) Church Street. Opposite her house is a gardens and behind her house is Cary Mews, where her friend and protector Jonathan Penrose lives at No. 21. Author Selwyn Jepson clearly had in mind the parallel streets of Cranley Gardens and Cranley Mews, which match the novel's settings perfectly. It is here that Eve Gill watches the crowd of curious spectators the day after the murder, first espies police inspector Ordinary Smith, and later poses as a maid to obtain information about Charlotte. Hitchcock, for the film adaptation *Stage Fright*, chose to relocate Charlotte to Mayfair (see **Charlotte Inwood's Home [1]**) and Jonathan to Eaton Mews North (see 2:3), while Eve now poses as Charlotte's dresser.

Charlotte Inwood's home

Station: South Kensington (CI; DI; PI) Exit into Old Brompton Road and continue on to Cranley Gardens, which will be on the L. Cranley Mews is the next street on.

22:7
ex John George Haigh's Workshop C P
79 Gloucester Road, SW7

The modus operandi of widow-killer John George Haigh would seem the perfect inspiration for that of Uncle Charlie—if not for the fact that Haigh's crimes only came to light six years *after* the release of *Shadow of a Doubt*. Yet, Haigh personified precisely the kind of charming villain, one who could truly get close to his victims, that Hitchcock so often extolled. In September 1944, the 35-year-old forger and confidence man dissolved his first victim in a bath of sulfuric acid here in the basement of No. 79. The following summer, Haigh disposed of the young man's parents in a similar way, then, using the son's name, sold off the parents' real estate and securities. Over the next few years, he continued to worm

79 Gloucester Rd., workshop of serial killer John George Haigh

his way into the hearts—and bank accounts—of affluent people, each of whom ended up in the acid bath. His last victim, a widow named Olive Durand-Deacon, proved his undoing. A friend from the nearby Onslow Court Hotel—where all three principals, as well as a plethora of wealthy widows, were living—reported the woman's disappearance. Haigh's new "workshop," in Crawley, Sussex, was investigated and, lo and behold, bits of Mrs. Durand-Deacon's false teeth and other accessories were found in the acid sludge. Haigh was arrested, claimed he drank his victims' blood (vainly hoping to bolster an insanity plea), was tried and hanged in August 1949. Hitchcock related this story to Andy Warhol in great detail, comparing the killer not only to Joseph Cotten's character in the earlier film, but also to his—Hitchcock's—ideal murderer. In fact, there's more than a little of Haigh in C.A. Swann, a.k.a. Lesgate, and his story, also known as *Dial M for Murder*, definitely postdates the crimes of the "Acid Bath Murderer." Indeed, one of the aliases Haigh assumed was that of his first victim—W.D. McSwan.

Station: Gloucester Road (CI; DI; PI) Exit into Gloucester Road. Cross Cromwell Road and look for No. 79 ahead on the R.

23. STRAND

23:1
Charing Cross Station L (F)
WC2

Opened in 1864, Charing Cross Station was and is the major railway terminus nearest to the heart of London. It is mentioned—but not shown—in *The Lodger*, where we are told that the Avenger's last victim was a fair-haired waitress killed at Charing Cross Station. His latest victim, revealed as the film opens, was killed on the **Embankment**,

Charing Cross Station

near **Westminster Bridge**. It was also here at Charing Cross Station, as we learn near the end of both the play and film *Dial M for Murder*, that Tony Wendice kept the small blue attaché case containing the £1,000 with which he intended to pay off Swann. He later tells Inspector Hubbard that he first took the money to the station *after* Swann's death, the implication being that Margot had had the money (to pay off the blackmailing Swann) all along. Yet, as his earlier conversation with Swann himself made clear, the money was already safely ensconced in the checkroom of an as yet undisclosed railway station *before* the fateful night. It was also from Charing Cross Station that the Green Line's coach excursion to Brentwood, a town some 20 miles northeast of London, departed in the early 1930s. It was a Bentwood-bound Green Line bus that Barton hijacked in *Number Seventeen* ("These coaches can travel, can't they?!"), the final destination being the train ferry at Harwich. Finally, in Chapter 5 of *Goodbye Piccadilly, Farewell Leicester Square*, Richard Blamey [*sic*] has a shoe shine here at the station, the morning after his rather miserable night in the **Salvation Army Hostel**. He watches the first rush of harried commuters surge out of the station, concludes that these wage-slaves are the misfits, not he, then rings Brenda's office from a public phone inside. Hitchcock apparently liked the scene, for Charing Cross Station appears on the *Frenzy* location list of January 4, 1971 (although apparently the shoe shine already took place in Covent Garden). As the screenplay evolved away from Arthur La Bern's novel, the scene, as with a number of others (see, for example, **St. James, Piccadilly**) was dropped.

Station: Charing Cross (BA; JU; NO)

23:2
Coliseum Theatre (London Coliseum) (L)
St. Martin's Lane, WC2

London Coliseum

Built in 1904, London's largest theatre (now home to the English National Opera) boasts a magnificent Edwardian interior and exterior, the latter surmounted by the famous—and formerly revolving—globe. *Rope* victim Ronald Kentley attended a performance here on the day of his untimely demise, according to the Patrick Hamilton play. Indeed, it was here, outside the theatre, that Granno (Philip in the film) picked up Kentley to escort him back to the Mayfair house that he—Granno—shared with Brandon. There, as in the film, the partners strangle young Kentley, dump him in a chest, then host a dinner party over his cooling corpse. Later, Sir Johnstone, Ronald's father, mentions that his son had rushed off to the movies at the

Coliseum, a misstatement that prompts Granno to explain that the Coliseum is, in fact, a music hall—not that he'd know, or anything, since he's never been there. In fact, it was young Kentley's blue ticket stub from that day's performance that Granno has tucked into his jacket pocket—and which almost gives the game away during the party.

Station: Charing Cross (BA; JU; NO) Exit on the Strand (North) side and turn R into Duncannon Street and R again into St. Martin's Place. Follow this to the R into St. Martin's Lane and look for the Coliseum on the R.

23:3
Adelphi Theatre L
Strand, WC2

Rebuilt three times since it opened in 1806, the Adelphi (also called the Sans Pareil, the Century and the Royal Adelphi, at one time or another) is famous for its dramatizations of Dickens' works in the 1830s and '40s; its Shakespeare revivals in the early 20th century; and its musical comedies in the 1920s and '30s. It was presumably one of the latter that Gay Keane attended with the odious Judge Horfield, according to Chapter 26 of *The Paradine Case*, while her husband was off visiting the Cumberland haunts of Mrs. Paradine. Keane is mildly shocked to learn of the event upon his return to London, all the more so since his wife had apparently intended to keep the information from him. He later concludes that Horfield is after Gay, but to the extent that he must suck up to the man who will preside over the Paradine Case, Keane actually facilitates the judge's efforts! Some of Horfield's lechery does make it to the film adaptation, but Keane's dubious complicity, thankfully, does not.

Adelphi Theatre

Station: Charing Cross (BA; JU; NO) Exit on the Strand (North) side and go L (East) in the Strand; the theatre is ahead on the L. True-crime buffs take note: On December 16, 1897, Adelphi actor-manager William Terriss was stabbed to death outside the theatre by a deranged former protégé named Richard Prince.

A REFERENCE GUIDE TO LOCATIONS

The MacGuffin: Like many London theatres, this one has a number of indirect Hitchcock connections. One of the musicals which Gay and Horfield could have seen was *Ever Green*, which starred Jessie Matthews (*Waltzes from Vienna*) and was written by Benn Levy (*Blackmail, Lord Camber's Ladies*). Another was Noël Coward's revue *Words and Music* (1932). Ivor Novello's *The Dancing Years* (1942) subsequently ran for nearly 1,000 performances.

23:4
Simpson's-in-the-Strand F L
100 Strand, WC2

The original Simpson's Divan and Tavern was opened here by caterer John Simpson in 1848. It quickly found favor with the rich and famous, attracting everyone from Charles Dickens to members of the Royal Family. The tavern was demolished in 1900 when the Strand was widened, but a new restaurant was built on the site by the **Savoy Hotel** and opened with great fanfare in 1904. Alfred Hitchcock seems to have discovered Simpson's in the early 1920s and the restaurant remained one of his favorite London dining spots. Thus, when *Sabotage* hero Ted Spencer wanted to treat Mrs. Verloc and Stevie to a truly swell lunch, it was to Simpson's that he insisted on taking them. (Mrs. Verloc demurs, at first, saying that she and Stevie will eat in either "the [Lyon's] **Corner House** or a tea shop.") Hitchcock abjured actual location work in the bustling Strand, recreating Simpson's staircase and large first floor (U.S.: second floor) dining room at **Lime Grove Studios**. In any case, the scene is clearly supposed to be set in Simpson's, a fact the press learned here on the night of May 13, 1936 after the premiere of *Secret Agent*. According to biographer Donald Spoto, Hitchcock spent a week's salary "entertaining the press in grand fashion" here at Simpson's. The Strand institution

Simpson's-in-the-Strand

184   ALFRED HITCHCOCK'S LONDON

was also the venue for the title character's meeting with the American businessman in the short story "The Case of Mr. Pelham." Here, James Mason (not, presumably, the actor) reassures himself that he and "Pell" are still on speaking terms after a recent incident in which Pelham had given the man "the dirtiest cut I'd ever seen." This exchange is replicated in the TV episode, with Mason's first name changed to Tom. The meeting-place, too, has been changed, to Mr. Pelham's club, since the setting has been transposed to New York.

Station: Charing Cross (BA; JU; NO) Exit on the Strand (South) side and go R (East) in the Strand; the restaurant is ahead on the R, just past Savoy Court.

Ask Mr. Memory 34: How much does Ted spend on the lunch date?

23:5
The Savoy H F L
Strand, WC2 (at Savoy Court)

Built as an annex to the Savoy Theatre in 1889, this world-famous luxury hotel is renowned for both its American Bar and Grill Room restaurant, the latter a perennial favorite of Parliament members. Indeed, the Savoy is one of the grandest and most expensive hotels in London, a fact not lost on Alfred Hitchcock. Hitch enjoyed the amenities of the Savoy during his English years and whenever he happened to be in London thereafter. He and Alma stayed here during the productions of both *Under Capricorn* (in 1948) and *Stage Fright* (in 1949), a fact sometimes overlooked in view of the Hitchcocks' subsequent switch to **Claridge's**. Thus, *Stage Fright* actor Richard Todd recalled meeting with Hitch and Alma at the Savoy in July 1949, when the director held a press conference here to "introduce" Marlene Dietrich as the star of his new

The Savoy

picture. (A Savoy event that Hitchcock did not attend but at which he would have presumably felt quite at home was H.G. Wells' 70th birthday party in October 1936. Among the guests honoring the celebrated author were J.B. Priestly [*Jamaica Inn*], John Galsworthy [*Skin Game*] and Somerset Maugham [*Ashenden*, which the director had recently filmed as *Secret Agent*].) On film, Hitchcock commemorated the hotel on four occasions. In *Foreign Correspondent*, title reporter Johnny Jones travels with Mr. Van Meer from the **Carlton** to the Savoy, where a luncheon is being held for the latter, and later asks Carol to have lunch at the Savoy. Notwithstanding his use of second-unit London footage elsewhere in the film, Hitchcock included no actual shots of the Savoy itself. Instead, he recreated the hotel's entrance, foyer, cloakroom and reception rooms at the Goldwyn Studios in Hollywood. Following a brief mention in *Suspicion* (where we learn that Johnnie had dined here with Beaky the night before Beaky left for Paris), Hitchcock returned to the Savoy in *The Paradine Case*. Here, Judy and Gay take tea in the beautiful River Restaurant, which, again, was recreated in the studio (this time, **Elstree**), and enhanced with a rear-projected view of the **Embankment** and Waterloo Bridge, visible through the window behind them. Finally, in *The Man Who Knew Too Much* (56), the McKennas stay at a luxury hotel in London—revealed in the shooting script as the Savoy and confirmed as such in the film, through the view out their third-floor window of the **Royal Festival Hall** across the river. (The number of their room, as shown on the door, is 392. In fact, the Savoy's third floor only goes up to 363 and the view actually corresponds to that from Room 316.) Again, after first considering a location shoot at **Forbes House** (never at the hotel itself), the director chose to recreate the Savoy on a Hollywood soundstage. The Savoy was also Jerrie Cheyne's choice for one of London's "best [dining] places" in Chapter 7 of *The Pleasure Garden*; Richard Hannay's choice for "a very good luncheon" and "the best cigar the house could provide" after his return to London in Chapter 8 of *The Thirty-nine Steps*; and Universal Studios' choice for the *Frenzy* post-premiere party, which was held in the Savoy's River Room (not to be confused with the River Restaurant) on the night of May 25, 1972. Finally, mention should be made of the "scandal of the decade"—a true crime that occurred at the Savoy on a stormy July night in 1923. Beautiful French-born Marguerite Fahmy shot and killed her Egyptian husband, millionaire playboy Prince Ali Fahmy, and—in a scene more or less replicated in *Murder!* seven years later—was literally found holding the murder weapon over the body. Madame Fahmy was later defended at the **Old Bailey** by Sir Edward Marshall Hall, a handsome barrister noted for his defense of beautiful women in fashionable society. Marshall Hall was, of course, the inspiration for Sir Malcolm Keane, the barrister hero of the novel *The Paradine Case*. And in the Fahmy case, he fared much better than his literary and cinematic incarnations. Relying on repellant racist and sexist innuendo, as well as excruciating personal details from the lives of both the deceased and the defendant, Marshall Hall was able to secure an acquittal on the grounds that the woman was defending herself from her husband's "unnatural desires."

Station: Charing Cross (BA; JU; NO) Exit on the Strand (South) side and go R (East) in the Strand; look for the entrance to the Savoy on the R, just past Shell-Mex House and nearly opposite the Strand Palace Hotel. Afternoon tea is served each day in the Thames Foyer from 3 pm-5:30 pm. The River Restaurant is open for lunch every day from 12:30 pm-2:30 pm.

The MacGuffin: Vincent Sheean, author of *Personal History*, the memoir that inspired *Foreign Correspondent*, would probably have been pleased with Jones's restaurant selection, if not with the Savoy's theatrical association. In *Not Peace but a Sword*, the 1939 follow-up to *History*, he remarks: "I have a great deal more to say for the Savoy Grill than for Gilbert and Sullivan ... [whose] operas were mostly produced at the Savoy Theatre." Sheean goes on to excoriate the music of Sullivan, the lyrics of Gilbert and the philosophy of both ("that everything is very funny, especially in foreign countries, and that everything will be all right if you laugh at it") and the pernicious effect this has had on the British governing class!

23:6
Cleopatra's Needle F
Embankment, WC2

Erected at Heliopolis (a suburb of Cairo) by the Egyptian pharaoh Thutmose III, this 185-ton red granite obelisk was later transplanted to Cleopatra's palace at Alexandria, from which site it received its present name. (There is no other connection to the famous ruler, who was dead and buried when the Romans relocated the obelisk.) In 1819, Egypt's Ottoman viceroy, Muhammad Ali, presented the 3,500-year-old monument to the British in commemoration of their ouster of the French from Egypt. More than half a century of planning and dithering passed before the obelisk (which had long since toppled over) was finally encased in a specially constructed iron cylinder and towed out into the Mediterranean. (Its twin was sent to New York City, where it now stands in Central Park, behind the Metropolitan Museum of Art.) After having been lost and eventually recovered in the Bay of Biscay, the obelisk, now slightly damaged, arrived in London in January 1878. It *was* to have been erected in front of the **Houses of Parliament**, but surveyors discovered that the chosen site was subsiding. *Finally*, on September 13, 1878, amidst much fanfare, Cleopatra's Needle—really, Thutmose's Obelisk—was erected here on the Adelphi Steps of **Victoria Embankment**, between the Waterloo and Hungerford Bridges. The famous, and somewhat foreboding, monolith pierces the lower central portion of a shot of London by night during a montage sequence in *The Paradine Case*. Included in the still, somber shot, taken from Savoy Hill (at **The Savoy**), are the Embankment itself, the Hungerford Bridge, the **Westminster Bridge**, the **Houses of Parliament** and, far in the background, **Westminster Abbey**. In the lower left foreground of the shot, a barge slowly makes its way down the River Thames, while in the lower right foreground, motor traffic hums routinely along the Embankment, oblivious presumably to the stark, silent sentinel surveying them both.

Cleopatra's Needle

Station: Embankment (BA; CI; DI; NO) Exit to the Embankment and follow the signs to the Needle, which is just downriver from the station.

Site of the Gaiety Theatre

23:7
ex **Gaiety Theatre F L**
335 Strand, WC2

Opened near here in 1868, the original Gaiety Theatre was famous for its chorus of beautiful singer/dancers known as—what else?—the Gaiety Girls. (One of those Gaiety Girls, ca. 1898, was none other than Constance Collier, future co-author [with Ivor Novello] of *Down Hill* and co-star of *Rope*.) The theatre was demolished in 1903 (as part of the Strand widening scheme) and a smaller venue, called the New Gaiety Theatre, was opened on the present site later that year. It went on to host a number of successful productions, including Novello's *Theodore and Co.* (1916), *Love Lies* (1929), starring Cyril Ritchard (who opened here during the middle of the *Blackmail* shoot) and *Hold My Hand* (1931), featuring Jessie Matthews (*Waltzes from Vienna*). The Gaiety was also the setting for *The Lodger*'s "Golden Curls" show, at least according to the film's publicity materials. For some reason the theatre's name was omitted from the finished film, the insert shots simply indicating 'To-night "Golden Curls."' (Note that the top half of all the 'To-night "Golden Curls"' shots is mysteriously blank.) *English Hitchcock* author Charles Barr suggests that in omitting any explicit reference to the theatre itself, the sign has "the effect of a direct address to the film's own audience...who [in addition to the film's male protagonists] are 'keen on golden curls'...." It was also here, on the sidewalk in front of the Gaiety, that a near-penniless Robert Tisdall first met the actress Christine Clay, according in Chapter 4 of *A Shilling for Candles* (whence *Young and Innocent*). Chris was actually in her car, stopped for the "traffic lights at the Aldwych, just before you turn round into Lancaster Place...." Taking pity on the young man (see entry 11:4), Chris offers him a ride and eventually a whole lot more—a formula certain to end with an innocent man wrongly accused of her murder. Sadly, the Gaiety was demolished in 1957 (the site is today occupied by Citibank House), but the Strand still switches from two ways to one at the Aldwych, where you can indeed turn right into Lancaster Place.

Station: Charing Cross (BA; JU; NO) Exit on the Strand (North) side and go L in the Strand; the theatre was located in the "island" between the Strand and the Aldwych. Also located somewhere in the Strand, according to Chapter 9 of *The Pleasure Garden*, was the Huguenot Theatre, a fictitious venue which Hitchcock called simply "the Pleasure Garden Theatre" for the film adaptation. For yet another connection, follow the Aldwych around toward Drury Lane and look for the Strand Theatre, just ahead on the L. Here, in a flat above the theatre, the legendary actor/composer/playwright Ivor Novello (*The Lodger*, *Downhill*) lived from 1913 until his death in 1951.

The MacGuffin: In the crossroads scene in *Young and Innocent*, Robert whistles a tune while Erica decides which way to turn (in more ways than one). The tune is "Keep the Home Fires Burning (Till the Boys Come Home)," a perennial favorite dating from World War I and written by none other than the Lodger himself, Ivor Novello.

23:8
St. Clement Danes F
The Strand, WC2 (near Chancery Lane)

The original church on this site was apparently founded by the Danes toward the close of the ninth century. The present building dates from the late 17th century and was designed by the Baroque genius Sir Christopher Wren, whose most famous achievement is **St. Paul's Cathedral**. It was here, near the western end of the church, that Hitchcock trained his camera for Stevie's view of the Lord Mayor's Parade in *Sabotage*. Or, rather, it was near a *mock-up* of the western end of St. Clement Danes, that Hitchcock staged the parade. Sadly, the precise location of the spot cannot be identified. In *Film Making in 1930s Britain*, cinema historian Rachael Low claimed that the parade

On the set of the *Sabotage* parade

sequence was staged on the massive backlot of Shepperton Studios, then known as Sound City. However, neither the film's late star, Desmond Tester, nor books on Shepperton productions support this statement. (In all likelihood, Low confused Hitchcock's *Sabotage* with a 1934 Adrian Brunel film also called *Sabotage*, which was indeed shot at Sound City.) What Tester clearly remembered was his Underground trip each day to Isleworth, in the southwestern part of London, where, in an open lot, Hitchcock built his church. Behind the church, Hitchcock erected a spectacular full-scale photo cut-out of the **Royal Courts of Justice** (see next entry), then lined both sides of his faux Strand with hundreds of extras, horses and policemen, all the better to ensure that Stevie would not reach the **Piccadilly Circus Underground Station** on time.

Station: Temple (CI; DI) Go L out of the station and walk straight up Arundel Street to the Strand, where you will turn R. The first street you will come to is Milford Lane. Just before this, look to your left, past the church and across to the Law Courts, for the view from the film. You can even catch a Number 9 bus to Piccadilly Circus—but for goodness sake, don't bring any cans of film.

23:9
The Royal Courts of Justice F L
The Strand, WC2 (near Chancery Lane)

This magnificent, late-19th-century Gothic Revival complex of some 60 courtrooms (and a thousand rooms in all) is the headquarters of the Supreme Court of Judicature, Britain's highest civil—as opposed to criminal—court. The Supreme Court comprises three divisions: the Crown Court, the Court of Appeal and the High Court of Justice. The latter, in turn, comprises the Chancery, the Queen's (or King's) Bench and the Family Division. Prior to 1970, the Family Division included the Admiralty Court and

Royal Courts of Justice

was thus called the Probate, Divorce and Admiralty Division. And it was in Court II of *that* division that Larita Filton underwent her scandalous divorce proceedings in *Easy Virtue*—or, at any rate, in an impressive replica of the court, designed by art director Clifford Pember. Hitchcock originally asked Pember to make reference sketches inside the Divorce Court itself but court officials turned him down. Undaunted, Pember arranged to visit the court with a relative, memorized the interior and then ran to a nearby pub to make the sketch! (For an even more elaborate courtroom replica, see the **Old Bailey**.) Brief scenes in the short story "The Crystal Trench" and the novels *The Paradine Case* and *No Bail for the Judge* also take place here in the Law Courts. Indeed, Sir Edwin Prout, the title judge of the latter, sits in the High Court of Justice, "in the Law Courts, you know, in the Strand," as he explains to the prostitute who comes to his rescue in Curzon Street (for which, see **Shepherd Market**). In Hitchcock's adaptation, to have been filmed in 1959 (see Appendix III), Sir Edwin Proud [*sic*] was instead a High Court justice at the **Old Bailey**. For Hitchcock's use of the Law Courts as a backdrop in *Sabotage*, see the previous entry.

Station: Temple (CI; DI) Go L out of the station and walk straight up Arundel Street to the Strand, where you will turn R. As you pass **St. Clement Danes Church**, to the L, the Royal Courts of Justice will be directly across the Strand. **Hours:** Mon-Fri 10 am-1 pm and 2 pm-4 pm

23:10
Strand Palace Hotel (F)
372 Strand, WC2

This was Hitchcock's base of operations for the *Frenzy* Covent Garden shoot, which took place during the last week of July 1971. Each day, the director was driven to the Strand from his own hotel, **Claridge's**, in a rented Silver Shadow Rolls-Royce, which, in turn, was parked in nearby Southampton Street, awaiting his beck and call. (Hitchcock had also used the Rolls during his February-March trip to London; this time, though, he would request—and receive—a new driver, the old one having apparently proved unsatisfactory.) In addition to serving as a production office, Room 112 was also used for the actors' makeup, hair and wardrobe. And speaking of hair, actress Vivien Merchant, who did not appear in any of the Covent Garden scenes, dropped by the hotel on the 28th so that Hitchcock could inspect her new wig from Wig Creations of Portman Close, W1. (He approved.)

Strand Palace Hotel

Station: Charing Cross (BA; JU; NO) Exit on the Strand (South) side and go R (East) in the Strand; look for the entrance to the Savoy on the R, just past Shell-Mex House. The Hotel is just across the street.

23:11
***ex* Tivoli Music Hall (F)**
65-70 Strand, WC2

In "Banquo's Chair," former **Scotland Yard** inspector Brent explains to Major Cooke-Finch that they are lucky to have the help of Shakespearean actor Robert Stone, who, were it not Sunday, would be busy playing in *Macbeth*. (The trio, you may recall, are planning to shock a suspected murderer into confessing by staging the "appearance" of a ghost à la that of Banquo in *Macbeth*.) The major admits to having heard that *Macbeth* is a very good play, but confesses "that the Tivoli is rather more my style. I'm a great admirer of Gertie Gitana." The first reference is to the massive music hall built here in the Strand in 1890. Under the management of theatrical impresario Charles Morton, the Tivoli fast became one of London's premier social settings—notwithstanding its dearth of anything remotely Shakespearean. The second reference is to one of the most popular singers in the history of the British music hall. Performing as "Little Gertie," a male impersonator (!), by the age of four, Gertie Gitana made her London debut here at age 14 (in 1902, the year before the story is set) and went on to become the darling of the Armed Forces during WWI. She climaxed her career with a Royal Command Performance at the **London Palladium** in 1948. The Tivoli itself went out on a far less glorious note: It was closed in 1914 and ultimately replaced with a "super cinema" in 1923. (From 1929 until 1935, that cinema hosted the Sunday afternoon programs of the Film Society [see **New Gallery Cinema**].) Today, the site is occupied by a Chinese restaurant.

Tivoli Music Hall

Station: Charing Cross (BA; JU; NO) Exit on the Strand (South) side and go R (East) in the Strand; the Tivoli was ahead on the R, just past Adam Street.

24. VICTORIA

24:1
Victoria Station F L
Victoria Street, SW1

Victoria Station is actually an amalgam of two separate stations, built in the 1860s, remodeled in the early 1900s and first linked by the Southern Railway Company in 1924. The larger structure, the so-called Brighton Station (from its use by the old Lon-

Victoria Station

don, Brighton and South Coast Railway) comprises Platforms 9-19, while the smaller, more romantic Chatham Station (famous as the London terminus of the Orient Express) contains the first eight platforms. Establishing shots of the Brighton exterior (to the west) and a train pulling into the station mark our return to England near the end of *The Lady Vanishes*. Lovebirds—and temporary spies—Iris and Gilbert arrive here on the fabled express, at which point Iris decides to dump her stodgy fiancé for the dashing Gilbert. It was also during this sequence, filmed with rear-projection plates of the *Chatham* interior at **Islington**, that Hitchcock made his cameo appearance: smoking a cigarette and shrugging his shoulders as he walks alongside the train. According to the shooting script, it is also from Victoria Station that Fred and Emily depart for the Continent in *Rich and Strange*. Here, as with the opening sequence of Fred's humorous trek from his office in the City (Wotherspoon's, according to the novel) to his home in the suburbs (see **Waterloo Underground Station**), Hitchcock gives us some sense of the bustling London the Hills are leaving behind, in contrast to the novel, which opens with Fred already at home, jumps immediately to the boat at Dover, and may as well take place in New York or Liverpool. (An additional scene, scripted but apparently not shot, was to take place in the couple's Pullman en route from London to Dover. There, a flashily dressed, "Continental" woman passes their compartment, prompting Emily to straighten her hat so as not to look like a "fast" female. Fred apparently likes the faster look better because he immediately shakes his head and gestures for her to return the hat to its original position.)

Hitchcock's cameo in *The Lady Vanishes*

A REFERENCE GUIDE TO LOCATIONS   **193**

Hitchcock also invokes the station in two other London films, *Dial M for Murder* and *Frenzy*. In the former, we learn that Margot "lost" her handbag at Victoria Station the previous autumn, presumably in the tea-room (or restaurant, as the American version of the play renders it). In fact, her husband, Tony, actually pinched it in order to read—and exploit—the letter from her lover that she kept hidden inside. In the latter film, Dick Blaney arranges to meet Babs at Victoria the next morning "at eleven o'clock, by the flower stall" for their trip to the Continent with the Porters. Actor Jon Finch himself suggested the line "by the flower stall," as a replacement for the original "at the book stand," his objection being that were at least five book stands at the station (including the W.H. Smith's shown in *Rich and Strange*). Victoria Station, along with **Charing Cross**, is also mentioned in Chapter 6 of *The Secret Agent* (whence *Sabotage*) as one of the termini where **Scotland Yard** stations men to monitor the activities of Adolf Verloc, the title character. The station is also the setting for two short scenes in *Ashenden*, the Somerset Maugham novel upon which *Secret Agent* is based. The title character, a British writer turned spy, recalls how he had once fallen in love with an exiled Russian revolutionary named Anastasia Leonidov. Though married, Anastasia agreed to assay a trial period of living together on the Continent, after which she would give Ashenden her decision as to whether or not she would marry him. (Her decision to do so, it is explained, would impel her husband to suicide, thus removing *that* obstacle!) The pair meet at Victoria Station, from which they depart for Dover and thence cross the Channel to Paris. At the end of the week, they reverse their journey and alight in Victoria Station. Here, like Iris in *The Lady Vanishes*, Anastasia renounces her husband (fiancé in Iris's case) and agrees to marry the hero of the story instead. However, unlike Gilbert in the later adventure, Ashenden suddenly finds himself unable to imagine life as a married man and renounces Anastasia. Whether the contrasting outcomes reflect the differing concerns of a homosexual author—Maugham—on the one hand, and a heterosexual *auteur*—Hitchcock—on the other, I shall leave for the reader to decide.

Station: Victoria (VI; CI; DI) Exit into the main railway station, go outside and look for the white "Southern Railway" entrance (to the left, as you face the building). Go back inside to Platform 7 and look out toward the street: The view is remarkably close to that of the rear-projected image of the entrance in *The Lady Vanishes*.

Ask Mr. Memory 35: What does Fred Hill struggle to do at Victoria Station?

25. WESTMINSTER

25:1
Trafalgar Square F
WC2, SW1

Located in the traditional heart of London, Trafalgar Square commemorates one of the most famous naval victories in British history: that of Admiral Horatio Nelson over the combined French and Spanish fleets off the coast of Cape Trafalgar, Spain, on October 21, 1805. Nelson himself was mortally wounded during the fighting, yet emerged not only as the hero of the Battle of Trafalgar but also as the greatest naval

Trafalgar Square as shown in *Sabotage*

hero in British history. His monument, a fluted Corinthian column surmounted by a 17-foot statue of the admiral himself (overall height: 185 feet), is located on the south side of the square. Guarded by four massive bronze lions at its base, Nelson's column has become one of the most famous landmarks in London. Trafalgar Square appears in a number of Hitchcock films, starting with *Blackmail*. There, an early morning, nearly deserted square looms in the background as a dazed Alice walks down the eastern side of Whitehall following the encounter in **Crewe's Flat**. In *Sabotage*, Hitchcock includes a shot of Nelson's column, black against the day-for-night sky, the result of Verloc's sabotage. Later in the same film, Ted espies Mrs. Verloc and Stevie from a spot just west of the statue of General Charles James Napier, then crosses to join the pair at the base of the "northwestern" lion. The long shot, looking east toward South Africa House, was filmed on location with doubles; the footage of the actors themselves was shot at **Lime Grove Studios**. Four years later, in *Foreign Correspondent*, Hitchcock used rear-projection plates to guide Van Meer and Johnny's taxi around the eastern side of the square (the pair are traveling from the **Carlton Hotel** to **The Savoy**), the view of which prompts Van Meer to comment that "there must always be parks and places for the birds to live." For *The Paradine Case*, Hitchcock initially planned—but apparently never shot—a brief bit in which Mrs. Paradine's taxi passes the square en route to **Bow Street Police Station**. *Stage Fright* includes a "standard" high-angle shot, looking down on the square from the corner of The Mall and Spring Gardens, which marks Eve's return to London after the scenes in Essex Flats. Finally, in *Frenzy*, if you look closely, you can just spot the eastern edge of the square near the end of Babs' and Dick's cab ride from **Leicester Square** to the **Coburg Hotel**.

Station: Charing Cross (BA; JU; NO) Exit on the Strand (South) side and go L (West) in the Strand; the square is straight ahead. The *Sabotage* view is from just W of Spring

A REFERENCE GUIDE TO LOCATIONS **195**

Gardens in The Mall. Opposite the northeast corner of the square is St. Martin-in-the-Fields, architect James Gibbs' striking but functional synthesis of English and Italian design. A photo of the 18th-century church appears in the first of the newspapers shown near the beginning of *Young and Innocent*. The church is also visible in shots of the square in *Sabotage* and *Stage Fright*.

25:2
The National Gallery L F
Trafalgar Square, WC2

The National Gallery

Lina Aysgarth asks her brother-in-law Cecil to take her to the National Gallery in Chapter 9 of *Before the Fact* (whence *Suspicion*). Lina has been staying with her sister and brother-in-law in Hamilton Terrace (see 50:1), having finally—but temporarily, as it turns out—decided to leave her cad of a husband. During their visit to the art gallery, Cecil explains to his sister-in-law "quite vehemently why none of the pictures should be there at all," notwithstanding the fact that the gallery's collection of Western European paintings is considered one of the finest in the world. Hitchcock eliminated the entire subplot of Lina's London adventures, so naturally there is no trace of the National Gallery scene in *Suspicion*. The director did, however, capture the gallery's domed exterior in two other films: *Blackmail*, during Alice's early morning walk down Whitehall; and *Stage Fright*, during a brief establishing shot of "London." For more on these shots, see **Trafalgar Square**.

Station: Charing Cross (BA; JU; NO) Exit on the Strand (North) side and veer R into Duncannon Street, which leads directly to the gallery. **Hours**: Mon-Sat 10 am-6 pm (Wed until 8 pm); Sun noon-6 pm

25:3
ex **HQ of the War Office C F (?) (L)**
Old War Office Building
Whitehall, SW1

The War Office was the government department responsible for the administration and supervision of the British Army. Its counterparts were the **Admiralty**, which oversaw the Royal Navy, and, from 1918, the **Air Ministry**, which oversaw the RAF. Previously located in Pall Mall, the War Office moved to its purpose-built Victorian baroque headquarters here in Whitehall in 1906. Among its many sections was the Directorate of Military Operations (MO), originally founded as the Army Intelligence Branch in 1873. (What all this has to do with Hitchcock will become clear in a moment.)

War Office Headquarters

The MO Directorate was tasked with gathering strategic military intelligence during peacetime, i.e., spying, an important complement to the tactical or field intelligence operations that were generally set up on an ad hoc basis during wartime. Among the many offshoots of the MO Directorate were the predecessors of both MI5 (the Security Service, responsible for spy-catching at home); MI6 (responsible for spying abroad) and the GHQ Intelligence Branch, which was set up during the First World War to provide tactical intelligence from the European theatre. It was the latter organization, through Captain (later Major Sir) John Wallinger, that recruited 41-year-old writer William Somerset Maugham to spy for it in 1915. (We're getting closer to Hitchcock now.) Wallinger was head of the Intelligence Branch's network in Switzerland, which, at the time, was something of a disaster. Believing that a multilingual writer like Maugham might well improve the Swiss set-up, Wallinger offered him the job over dinner in London and Maugham, invalided out of the ambulance corps, accepted. His experiences in Switzerland over the next year, and in Russia in 1917, formed the basis of *Ashenden*, a very thinly disguised collection of related short stories subsequently adapted as both a play (by Campbell Dixon) and a film—*Secret Agent*—by Alfred Hitchcock (at last). Maugham describes Ashenden's chief as "a middle-aged Colonel…known in the Intelligence Department…by the letter R." This and subsequent passages clearly point to Wallinger as the model for "R," whom the War Office had recalled from Jamaica at the beginning of the War. (Wallinger had been recalled from India.) There is no evidence that Wallinger himself used his initial as a code name, but plenty of other people in British Intelligence did, including Sir Mansfield Cumming, the founder of what we now know as MI6 (or the Secret Intelligence Service), after whom all SIS chiefs are still known as "C." Indeed, Maugham's second foray into British Intelligence, in 1917, was undertaken at the request of William Wiseman, an officer in Cumming's organization (then headquartered in 2 Whitehall Court, which stands between the War Office and the

Embankment). Hitchcock, of course, replicated Ashenden's recruitment into Secret Service work in the film adaptation, staging a meeting between novelist Edgar Brodie and "R" (for "rhododendron") in a Whitehall office. (Brodie here becomes "Ashenden" as a cover; in the book, Ashenden is his real name, although he later poses as Somerville, which was in fact Maugham's own cover name.) In the novel, Ashenden is recruited in "R's" home/office, which, from the description, can scarcely represent a government building in Whitehall. (In real-life, Wallinger answered to his brother, Ernest, whose office was located in Basil Street, Knightsbridge.) That Hitchcock intended to suggest the actual War Office is clear enough, though, given the shot of Ashenden's (miniature) car traveling south in Whitehall/Parliament Street toward a photographic cut-out of the **Houses of Parliament**: The vantage point for the shot is just below the War Office, on the western side of the street. (For an earlier version of the scene with "R," see **Tower Bridge**.) It was also here at the War Office, according to Chapter 9 of *Man Running*, that hero Jonathan Penrose (transformed into villain Jonathan Cooper in *Stage Fright*) worked for Military Intelligence during World War II.

Station: Charing Cross (BA; JU; NO) Exit on the Strand (South) side and go L, past **Trafalgar Square**, then L into Whitehall. The building is on the E side, just past Whitehall Place. The *Secret Agent* shot of Whitehall itself (looking S toward Parliament) is from the W side of the street, at No. 68, just S of the War Office.

Ask Mr. Memory 36: When "R" asks Ashenden if he loves his country, what is the agent's reply?

25:4
Horse Guards (F)
Whitehall, SW1

Constructed in the 1750s, Horse Guards (barracks) serves as the headquarters of the Household Division of the British Army. The Household Division includes the two regiments of the Household Cavalry, whose soldiers provide mounted escorts for the Royal Family and carry out a variety of ceremonial duties, including the Trooping the Colour. Each day, members of the Household Cavalry ride the one and a half miles from Hyde Park Barracks, Knightsbridge, to Whitehall, where they take up sentry posts at Horse Guards Arch, the official entrance to **Buckingham Palace**. It is this procession to which the bungling assassin Rowley calls Johnny Jones' attention in *Foreign Correspondent*. The pair are at the top of the **Westminster Cathedral** tower and Rowley, poor devil, needs to distract the man who knows too much just

Horse Guards

long enough to push him over the edge. "Oh, and look, look, there's the 'Orse Guards approaching Buckingham Palace," Rowley helpfully points out. "Oh, you must see the 'Orse Guards." And indeed you must. But for goodness' sake, mind your step or you may end up just like Rowley!

Station: Charing Cross (BA; JU; NO) Exit on the Strand (South) side and go L, past **Trafalgar Square**, then L into Whitehall. The building is on the W side, just past the Old Admiralty complex (see next entry). The two mounted sentries, or "boxmen" (so called from their stations inside boxes outside the Arch), are posted from 10 am to 4 pm. The Changing of the Guard takes place daily at 11 am and Sundays at 10 am.

25:5
ex HQ of the Admiralty L
Old Admiralty Building
Whitehall, SW1

The British government traditionally maintained three separate departments to oversee the nation's armed forces: the **War Office** to run the Army; the **Air Ministry** to run the Air Force and the Admiralty to run the Navy. The latter was headquartered in the purpose-built Admiralty Building, constructed in the 1720s and today known as the Old Admiralty. The Admiralty is the setting for an important scene in John Buchan's *The Thirty-nine Steps*, which Hitchcock adapted in 1935. Here, in a scene missing from the film (although a rough counterpart may be said to take place at **Scotland Yard**), Hannay and an assortment of government officials (see **Home of the Foreign Secretary**) determine that the foreign spy ring plans to escape from England by means of a set of "thirty-nine steps" located near Bradgate, Kent (actually Broadstairs). Hannay and Company then race to intercept the spies at the **Site of The Thirty-nine Steps**, to

Admiralty Headquarters

which you should turn for the rest of the story. The Admiralty department was abolished in 1964, when administration of the three services was transferred to the new Ministry of Defence, located just off Whitehall in Horseguards Avenue. Its former HQ is now used by the Foreign Office.

Station: Charing Cross (BA; JU; NO) Exit on the Strand (South) side and go L, past **Trafalgar Square**, then L into Whitehall. Continue to **Horse Guards**, pass through the arch and enter the Parade. The Admiralty is to the L.

The MacGuffin: James Bond creator Ian Fleming served as Personal Assistant to the Director of Naval Intelligence here in the Admiralty during World War II. Fleming was actually a casual acquaintance of Alfred Hitchcock's and plugged the director's film *North By Northwest* in the novel *Thunderball*. Hitchcock, according to legend, was asked to direct the first Bond film, *Dr. No*, in 1962, but declined the offer. However, in a 1965 letter to Fleming's biographer John Pearson, Hitchcock explained that while, yes, he knew the late author, he could not recall ever having been offered—or declining—a directorial job on a Bond picture.

25:6
Foreign (& Commonwealth) Office F L
King Charles Street, SW1

Designed by Sir George Gilbert Scott, the palatial Foreign Office complex was constructed between 1861 and 1875 and actually comprises four distinct buildings, each with its own courtyard. References to the Foreign Office, the government department responsible for overseas relations and foreign affairs (roughly equivalent to the U.S. State Department) occur in several of Hitchcock's films, beginning with *The Man Who Knew Too Much* (34). There, Gibson, secretary to Sir Norman Wood of the Foreign

Foreign Office

Office, solicits Bob and Jill's help in preventing the assassination of a foreign diplomat in London. Gibson further explains that Louis Bernard, the Frenchman whose dying words involved the Lawrences in the whole spy plot to begin with, was also an agent of the FO. Miss Froy, the delightfully dotty governess of *The Lady Vanishes*, turns out to be a secret agent in the employ of the Foreign Office (code for **MI6**), where she is reunited with the young lovers, Iris and Gilbert, at the end of the film. In *Foreign Correspondent*, we learn that Fisher was at the Foreign Office "with Ainsworth" and that "they're taking the whole [Van Meer affair] over." For the second *Man Who Knew Too Much*, Hitchcock actually contemplated a shoot at this magnificent building, having reference photos taken and queries made as to permission and availability. But then he had second thoughts. Would the Foreign Office take responsibility for the international conspiracy, or would some other governmental department? In the end, he learned that the Special Branch of **Scotland Yard** would actually handle such an affair (and, incidentally, control Bernard), thus precluding the need for any filming at the Foreign Office. The department is also mentioned in Chapter 7 of *The Thirty-nine Steps*, where Richard Hannay meets with Foreign Office official Sir Walter Bullivant (with whom he will again work in subsequent novels); and in Chapter 19 of *The Short Night*, where we learn that Soviet mole Garvin [*sic*] Brand had worked as an "unestablished civil servant" in the Foreign Office, from which he betrayed his country for money. In reality, double agent George Blake, upon whom Brand was clearly based, worked for **MI6**, the British Secret Service department supervised by the FO, and apparently did so not for money, but out of principle. For more on Blake/Brand and Hitchcock's plans for the film version of the story, see **Wormwood Scrubs**, **Gavin Brand's Flat** and **Gavin Brand's Safe House**.

Station: Charing Cross (BA; JU; NO) Exit on the Strand (South) side and go L, past **Trafalgar Square**, then L into Whitehall. The building is on the W side, just past Downing Street.

Ask Mr. Memory 37: What old Foreign Office proverb does Gilbert quote in *The Lady Vanishes*?

25:7
ex **Home Office (L) (F)**
Foreign & Commonwealth Building (Southeast Wing)
Whitehall, SW1

The Home Office is the government ministry responsible for the administration of law and order, immigration, community relations and other matters of public order. Its functions roughly coincide with those of the United States Department of Justice, State

Foreign & Commonwealth Building

A REFERENCE GUIDE TO LOCATIONS

Department and Department of the Interior. Its minister, the Secretary of State for Home Affairs, or Home Secretary, also oversees the internal Security Service, or MI5, an approximate counterpart to the American FBI. In *Murder!*, Sir John receives official permission from the "Prison Commissioner, Home Office, Whitehall, S.W.1.," to visit Diana Baring in "Melhurst Prison" (see **HMP Holloway**) on weekdays between 9 a.m. and 11 a.m. and between 2 p.m. and 4 p.m. (In the source novel, *Enter Sir John*, it is explained that Sir John knew the Home Secretary's *wife* and through her, got to the man himself.) In *Sabotage*, Ted's **Scotland Yard** superior, Talbot, tells him that "the Home Office has been on [about the sabotage at **Battersea Power Station**]. They're scared something worse than tonight's job may happen." In *Jamaica Inn*, it is the Home Office that dispatches Jem to investigate the mysterious shipwrecks near the title locale. In the play *Dial M for Murder*, the **BBC** announces that the Home Secretary has decided there are not sufficient grounds to recommend a reprieve for Sheila (i.e., Margot). (In the film, Mark asks if Tony has gotten any news from the Home Secretary, to which the answer is negative.) Finally, in the short story "The Birds," the BBC reports that the Home Office has issued a statement saying that birds are attacking all over the British Isles, a scene replicated (with appropriate geographical adjustments) in the film adaptation. In 1978, the Home Office relocated from the southeast wing of the **Foreign Office**, to 50 Queen Anne's Gate, just up from the St. James's Underground station.

Station: Charing Cross (BA; JU; NO) Exit on the Strand (South) side and go L, past **Trafalgar Square**, then L into Whitehall. The building—now exclusively occupied by the Foreign and Commonwealth Office—is on the W side, just past Downing Street.

25:8
ex **HQ of the Metropolitan Police Service (*informally* Scotland Yard) C F**
Norman Shaw Building (*formerly* New Scotland Yard)
Victoria Embankment, SW1

Established in 1829, London's Metropolitan Police Service was originally headquartered at 4 Whitehall Place, on the site of the present Ministry of Agriculture (just off Whitehall). The adjoining "A" Division police station had its own entrance—the so-called Back Hall—onto Great Scotland Yard, a small square apparently named after the old lodgings for the kings of Scotland. The back entrance quickly superceded the front and thus did the name of "Scotland Yard" extend to the headquarters itself. (For more on London's early police forces see, **Bow Street Magistrates' Court**.) In 1890, the Met relocated to a new building here, on the **Victoria Embankment**, which, appropriately enough, was named *New* Scotland Yard. (Equally appropriately, the Baroque fortress—designed by Richard Norman Shaw—was partly faced with granite quarried by convicts from **Dartmoor Prison**. And, in an ironic twist quite worthy of Hitchcock himself, the initial excavation of the site revealed the dismembered body of a young woman—whose murder Scotland Yard was never able to solve.) The Met is, of course, the most famous police force in the world: Its constables, detectives, inspectors and superintendents have been depicted in countless novels, plays, films and television shows, attracting the talent and attention of writers as diverse as Charles Dickens (*Bleak House*, 1852), Wilkie Collins (*The Moonstone*, 1868), Agatha Christie (*The Secret of Chimneys*, 1925, et al.) and Ian Fleming (*Moonraker*, 1955, et al.), not to mention a host

Former home of the Metropolitan Police Service–New Scotland Yard

of Hitchcock literary sources (*The Lodger, The Thirty-nine Steps, The Secret Agent, A Shilling for Candles, Before the Fact, Man Running, The Rainbird Pattern*, etc.) The Yard's most famous department, beloved of mystery writers (and fans) everywhere, is undoubtedly the Criminal Investigation Department, or CID, which was established in 1878 as a replacement for the old (and corrupt) Detective Department. "Today," as its former head, Sir Ronald Howe, wrote of this department in 1965, "when speaking of Scotland Yard it is generally taken as referring to the CID." This, indeed, is the referent in *Foreign Correspondent*, when Jones, speaking of the Nazi Krug, asks Fisher, "What do we do now—call in Scotland Yard?" and later, in the same film, when ffolliott laments that he can't get his "fool brother" to do anything about Fisher and asks, rhetorically, "what is the good of being related to Scotland Yard?" Within the CID itself is the Special Branch, charged with investigating espionage and other plots against the State (originally from Irish terrorists known as the "Fenians," whence the old name Special *Irish* Branch). Mr. Buchanan, the sympathetic inspector in *The Man Who Knew Too Much* (56), works in this department. Another famous CID department, the Flying Squad, was formed in 1919 "to deal with smash and grab raids and sudden outbreaks of crime" (Howe). Its unmarked cars (made by the Crossley Aircraft Company, whence the name "Flying Squad") were equipped with concealed radios and collapsible antennas that enabled the motorized patrol to communicate via Morse code with the control room at New Scotland Yard. Hitchcock shows one of the Flying Squad's original Crossley tenders, shorn of its rooftop antenna, in the opening of *Blackmail* (see entry 17:10), as well as a later model in *Sabotage*. Unfortunately, he errs in showing the telegraph operator sending and receiving messages in the earlier film. Not only could this not be done without an antenna, but the vehicle also had to be stopped in order to make the transmission. On a more sensational note, Scotland Yard is also famous for its "Black Museum," a collection of criminal artifacts and exhibits (photos, poisons, death masks,

A REFERENCE GUIDE TO LOCATIONS

pieces of incriminating evidence—like Belle Crippen's hair curler [see 37:2]) that was first assembled in the Whitehall Place HQ in 1875 and has intrigued visitors ever since. Among those to visit the Black Museum here in the Embankment were Harry Houdini, Arthur Conan Doyle and the teenage Alfred Hitchcock, who discovered, to his lasting delight, that the color of a Victorian-era prostitute's shoes revealed her "specialty." (The museum, today housed at **New Scotland Yard**, is now closed the public.)

As an adult, Hitchcock retained his fascination with the police, their methods and procedures (not to mention the crimes they investigated), even as he harbored an intense fear of their power to arrest and incarcerate. (A famous, perhaps apocryphal anecdote he repeated to the press and others was that, as a boy, he had been briefly locked in a jail cell, on his father's instructions, as "punishment" for some childish offense. He also claimed that the reason he never drove a car was that he was afraid of getting a ticket.) Something of this "mixed" attitude is reflected in his English films, where Scotland Yard's finest run the gamut from effective to ineffectual: from the masterful Chief Inspector Hubbard of *Dial M for Murder* to the oafish Joe of *The Lodger*. Interestingly, both of these supporting characters "double" the heroes of their respective films: Hubbard is ultimately smoother and smarter than the dapper Tony Wendice, whom he rightfully accuses; Joe is downright crude and common next to the sophisticated Lodger, whom he wrongfully accuses. In most cases, though, especially when the detective himself is the hero of the story, the treatment is more objective. For example, *Blackmail* begins with a documentary-style sequence depicting the apprehension, arrest, charging and incarceration of a criminal suspect, a sequence possibly inspired by a scene from the *Lodger* novel, in which Joe takes Daisy and her father on a tour of the Yard, with stops at the Fingerprint Department and the Black Museum. One of the policemen involved in the arrest turns out to be Frank Webber, the film's hero. Obviously, he is a man who knows his job and does it. Which means, of course, that before the end of the film he will be forced to choose between public and private duty—between arresting his fiancée for murder and saving her for himself. And while Frank does what most of us would probably do—cover for the person we love—this is no easy choice. The couple, though united in the end, still faces an uncertain future. Ted Spencer confronts exactly the same dilemma in *Sabotage* and with exactly the same outcome. Yet the fact that these men would waver in their duty, even abjure their duty, only makes them stronger, more sympathetic characters. Hitchcock's interest is in the personal dilemma, not in "policemen gone bad."

In subsequent films, Hitchcock largely eliminated this kind of "hard choice," whether his policemen were the romantic leads or not. In *Young and Innocent*, for example, *Blackmail*'s John Longden turns up as yet another Scotland Yard inspector, but this time he has no romantic connection to the heroine. He simply follows police procedure and pursues the only logical suspect—the man who ran from the scene of the crime, the man whose raincoat belt was found with the body of the murdered woman and the man who gained financially by the woman's death. That Inspector Kent is wrong—that suspect Robert Tisdall is relatively young and innocent—is irrelevant. Kent does his duty, as does Chief Constable Burgoyne. These are intelligent, noble men, no matter how "obvious" the innocence of Tisdall to the audience. As the inspector tells Burgoyne, "These Scotland Yard men have their own methods," methods which Hitchcock obviously admired. In the second *Man Who Knew Too Much*, for example, Buchanan's methods include not only an impressive knowledge of the affair but also a

Hitchcock's cameo in *Young and Innocent* was outside a Police Court.

sympathetic treatment of the McKennas. He rightly warns them that if they do not reveal what they know they will be accessories before the fact in a murder. However, as a father himself, Buchanan can identify with the anguished parents and accepts that they must follow their own course. And, yes, Buchanan is ultimately aided by "gifted amateurs," as also happens in *The 39 Steps*, *Young and Innocent*, *Foreign Correspondent* and *Stage Fright*. But again, these are conventions of the thriller genre and remarks such as Scott ffolliott's should not be taken as a serious indictment of the police. In fact, in at least two notable cases, the police redirect *themselves*. Both Chief Inspector Hubbard and Chief Inspector Oxford of *Frenzy* come to realize their mistakes and attempt to redress the wrongs they have caused, even as they are chided by some of those famous gifted amateurs (Mark in *Dial M*; Mrs. Oxford in *Frenzy*). In so doing, both Hubbard and Oxford (two of Hitchcock's most appealing and sympathetic characters) commandeer center stage and assume the role of "hero." They even get to chide the chiders: "[Proof] takes a little longer to acquire than intuitive insights," Oxford reminds his wife. And, as if to refute Bob Rusk's assessment that "the police, as usual, have the whole thing arse about face," Hitchcock literally gives the two chief inspectors the last word (or at least the last shot) in their respective films.

There are, of course, a number of films in which the police are simply there, more or less in the background, doing their duty (arresting suspects, questioning witnesses), as in *The Paradine Case* and, to reference the American films, *Spellbound* and *North By Northwest*. Sometimes the police go above and beyond the call of duty. In "Banquo's Chair," a dogged Scotland Yard inspector (again played by *Dial M*'s John Williams) pursues his quarry even after he has officially retired from the force. In *The Man Who Knew Too Much* (34), the police emerge from the background to reenact the famous "Siege of Sidney Street" (see entry 54:1), a scene which the British censor challenged because it depicted English policemen using guns. Hitchcock, of course, was not dissuaded, insisting, as usual, upon verisimilitude in his recreation of actual events and locales. This insistence extended to the depiction of something as basic as the interior of Scotland Yard, which, in the case of *Blackmail*, he had meticulously recreated at **Elstree Studios**. The sets—a corridor and office—were vetted by an actual policeman, "Ex-Det. Sergt. Bishop," who appears in the opening of *Blackmail*, as well as the end of *The 39 Steps*. Twenty years later, Hitchcock again insisted upon realism in the depiction of police procedures in *Stage Fright*, for which he sought technical assistance from the Yard. So, in the end, François Truffaut's assessment of Hitchcock's "half-hearted approach" toward the police (who, the French director claimed, "never get things straight"—a claim echoed in Patrick McGilligan's recent Hitchcock biography) doesn't bear close scrutiny. Hitchcock himself may have feared the police (and incarnated that fear on occasion), but clearly he also respected them. Just ask Inspector Hubbard....

Station: Westminster (CI; DI) Exit L into Victoria Embankment; the complex—South Wing to the L, North Wing to the R—is just ahead on the L. In *Blackmail*, Hitchcock includes an actual exterior shot of the South Wing courtyard entrance, complete with bobby and passing police van. This appears just before studio footage of the "same" van disgorging Frank and the detective sergeant. A later shot of Frank and Alice leaving the building apparently depicts the same entrance, but was actually filmed on the studio backlot. In *Sabotage*, Ted exits his taxi on the Embankment side of the South Wing (note Big Ben in the background), then, after a quick insert of the New Scotland Yard sign, passes through the same entrance shown in *Blackmail*. The *Blackmail* view *from* Scotland Yard across the river to **County Hall** (Alice's POV, near the end of the film) replicates that from a window at the NE corner of the North Wing (although it was probably made from outside the building). Note that there is also a splendid establishing shot of both buildings, from the Embankment (looking south toward **Parliament**), in "The Avon Emeralds," a non-Hitchcock-directed episode of *Alfred Hitchcock Presents*.

Ask Mr. Memory 38: What is the surname of the Chief Inspector in *Blackmail*? A Bonus Point if you know what is unique about this role.

25:9
Houses of Parliament F
Parliament Square, SW1

Britain's two Houses of Parliament meet in what is officially known as the Palace of Westminster, a massive Victorian Gothic complex built between 1835 and 1860. Along with **St. Paul's Cathedral** and **Tower Bridge**, the Palace and, in particular, St. Stephen's Clock Tower (a.k.a. "Big Ben," after its massive bell), is perhaps the most recognizable symbol of the British capital. Not surprisingly, it appears in a number of Hitchcock's films, starting with *The Lodger*, where a shot of the Clock Tower indicates that the time (11:27 p.m.) for "the Avenger" to strike is drawing near. We then see a

Houses of Parliament

young couple walking north along Margaret Street, stop, quarrel and finally storm off in opposite directions. The brief scene takes place in front of the 14th-century Westminster Hall, one of the few surviving portions of the original medieval palace. A fuller view of the entire complex appears in the background of the final shot of the film, in which the Lodger and Daisy share a romantic embrace. (See **County Hall** for more on this shot.) In *Blackmail*, Hitchcock again employs the famous clock to tell us the time (11:45) during Alice's post-murder walk through London; and later startles us with an impressive aerial shot of the Palace, **River Thames** and surrounding area to reveal that a gray dawn has broken—and Alice is still not home. For the next seven years, the closest Hitchcock would come to the Palace was a reference in *The Skin Game* (as in the play) to the fact that the parvenu Hornblower plans to stand for Parliament. Then in 1936, he resurrected the landmark for the last London shot of *Secret Agent*, thereby indicating that Edgar Brodie's meeting with Secret Service chief "R" has taken place in Whitehall, apparently at the **War Office**. (The shot appears to be of a back-lit photographic cut-out, with a model of Ashenden's car driving toward the building.) In *Sabotage*, a silhouette of the darkened Palace against a night sky (really a day-for-night shot made from the terrace of County Hall) demonstrates the effectiveness of Mr. Verloc's treachery at **Battersea Power Station**, while later, when Ted pulls up to **Scotland Yard**, the Clock in the background shows the time as 8 p.m. In *Foreign Correspondent*, we actually get the classic (almost cliché) shot of the Clock Tower as seen from the steps of the **Embankment**, with Boadicea's horse rising up in the lower right corner of the frame. Hitchcock uses this image twice in the film, both times as an establishing shot for London itself. Another establishing shot of London, this time from Broad Sanctuary, opens *Bon Voyage*, and includes Parliament Square, the buildings at the corner of Bridge and Parliament Streets, as well as—you guessed it—the Clock Tower and northern end of the Palace. (Clearly, Big Ben equals London.) Finally, fittingly, Hitchcock includes the Palace in the background of two shots of the crowd assembled across the river at County Hall in the opening of *Frenzy*, his last English film.

Station: Westminster (CI; DI) Exit for the Houses of Parliament.

**25:10
Westminster Bridge F
SW1, SE1**

In the opening of *The Lodger* the Westminster Bridge is in the background when the Avenger's victim is found.

The first Westminster Bridge was officially opened in November 1750; prior to this, the only way to cross the river in central London was via **London Bridge** in the City. The present Westminster Bridge was completed a century later, its extra-wide (84 feet) cast-iron structure being considered exceptional at the time. The bridge appears in the background in the opening of *The Lodger*, when the Avenger's latest victim is discovered on the **Embankment** (see next entry) at Whitehall Stairs. Had Hitchcock gotten what he originally wanted, however, we would have seen not Westminster Bridge but Charing Cross Bridge silhouetted against the night sky. That's because, as he recalled in a 1937 piece for *News Chronicle* (see *Hitchcock on Hitchcock*), the director planned to place powerful arc lights on Westminster Bridge, pointing down toward the Embankment, where the action itself would be staged. All went well for the closer shots, but somehow, for the long shot, "the big scene," as Hitchcock called it, the cameraman forgot to put a lens on the camera—and so there was nothing. Why he restaged the action looking in the other direction, toward Westminster Bridge, is left unexplained.

Station: Station: Westminster (CI; DI) Exit for the Bridge.

The MacGuffin: It was here beneath the bridge, at Westminster Pier, that Alfred Hitchcock began what was supposed to be an inspirational journey down the Thames on a drizzly, dark December day in 1934. Hitchcock had long believed that fresh ideas were to be found in dreary, unattractive places such as "seaside resorts looking their worst in winter." On this particular day, his "search for the dreary" led him to a river taxi, which, for two pounds ten shillings, would take him to Greenwich and back. The purpose of the trip, as the director himself related in a short, 1962 film made for the Westcliff Cine Club of Essex, was to work with his screen collaborators (presumably writer Charles Bennett and, possibly, producer Ivor Montagu) on the script for *The 39*

Steps. So, after a lunch in the West End, the trio took a taxi to the bridge, alighted beneath the famous statue of Boadicea (shown in *Foreign Correspondent*) and then climbed aboard a 300-seat steamer that immediately struck Hitchcock as "a bit large for our purpose." The collaborators duly spread out over the 300 seats and slowly made their way down the river. In the event, the afternoon proved too dreary for any inspiration (by three o'clock it was already nearly dark) and so the trio spent their time holed up below, drinking tea with "horrible" condensed milk!

25:11
Victoria Embankment F
SW1, WC2, EC4

Commonly known as "the Embankment," this pleasant riverside road extends from **Westminster Bridge** to **Blackfriars Bridge** in the City. It contains a number of Victorian buildings and monuments, including the famous statue of the ancient Celtic queen Boadicea, which is generally photographed from below, with the clock tower of the **Houses of Parliament** in the background. The Embankment appears in a number of Hitchcock films, including *The Lodger*, where the first of the Avenger's onscreen victims is discovered near the southern end of the road, at the Whitehall Stairs, with Westminster Bridge visible in the background of the shots. Both the newsroom teletype and the electric street sign specifically mention the Embankment, although the former says that the body was found "early this evening" and the latter that it was found "late this evening." (See also **The Lodger's Plan of the Murders**.). In *Blackmail* Alice stands at a **Scotland Yard** window and looks out across the Embankment to the **County Hall** on the other side of the river; and in the *Paradine Case* we look down upon **Cleopatra's Needle** from **The Savoy**, with the river and the Embankment stretching out before us.

Victoria Embankment as shown in *The Lodger*

Station: Westminster (CI; DI) Exit for the Embankment.

The MacGuffin: Among the statuary along the embankment is an 1877 bronze of Victorian engineer Isambard Kingdom Brunel, famous for the design of London's Paddington Station among others. Brunel's assistant—according to Chapter 2 of *The Rainbird Pattern*—was one Henry Rees Morton, who, long after his death, came to the aid of self-proclaimed psychic Blanche Tyler. So, the next time you're watching *Family Plot* and wondering who the heck *Henry* is…now you know!

The Thames is the background for the opening credits of *Frenzy*.

**25:12
River Thames F
SW1, WC2, EC4**

"I dare say you are wondering why I am floating around London like this. I am on the famous Thames River investigating a murder. Rivers can be very sinister places…" So begins Alfred Hitchcock's personal introduction to the *Frenzy* trailer and, of course, he knew whereof he spoke. Hitchcock managed to weave the river into a number of his London films, starting with *The Lodger* in 1926. Indeed, *The Lodger* actually opens with the discovery of the latest Avenger victim along the **Embankment** at Whitehall Stairs, near **Westminster Bridge**, **Scotland Yard** and the **Houses of Parliament**. In *Blackmail* Hitchcock includes a dramatic daybreak shot of the Thames near Parliament as part of Alice's long walk home from the artist's studio (see entry 4:7). In *The Man Who Knew Too Much* (34), a twilight shot of the Thames and **Tower Bridge** indicates that the heroes have passed from the safety of central London to the wilds of Wapping in search of Betty, while in *Sabotage,* the river—actually **Blackfriars Bridge**—marks Stevie's passage from South to Central London on his long and fateful journey to **Piccadilly Circus**. In *The Paradine Case*, Hitchcock includes another twilight shot of the river, this time from the 8th floor of **The Savoy**, looking down on **Cleopatra's Needle** and the Embankment. Finally, there is *Frenzy*, which, as with *The Lodger* some 45 years earlier, begins with the discovery of a murdered woman's body in the Thames. Actually, the film begins with a sustained tracking shot on to **Tower Bridge**, to which you should turn, along with **County Hall**, for the development of this signature opening. The famous river is also mentioned in the novel *The Trouble with Harry*, where we learn that Captain Wiles is in fact a "retired lighterman of the Thames barges," who has "killed more rats than anyone else between Battersea and Woolwich." (A lighterman works on a *lighter*, a small, flat-bottomed boat used to transfer cargo from ship to wharf or to another ship.) He is, thus, not strictly a captain at all, having been accorded the title when he moved to the "captain's bungalow" in Sparrowswick Heath. In the Americanized film, Wiles says that he was the captain of a tugboat on the East River before he moved to "Mansfield Meadows."

Station: See the entries mentioned above for relevant Underground directions.

25:13
St. Margaret's Church, Westminster Abbey F
Parliament Square, SW1

Founded in the 12th century (and since rebuilt many times), St. Margaret's is famous as the "parish church" of the House of Commons and as the venue for the "celebrity weddings" of people like John Milton, Samuel Pepys and William Shakespeare. The back of the church and its fence—unchanged to this day—appear briefly in *The Lodger*, when the crowd of onlookers spies the second Avenger murder victim. This suggests that the scene in which the girl is murdered and where Daisy and the Lodger eventually encounter Joe take place on the grounds of the church itself, although they were actually filmed on a set at **Islington Studios**. This is also, apparently, where the Lodger is nearly killed by the frantic mob in the film's climax.

Station: Westminster (CI; DI; JU) Exit for Westminster Abbey. The church is in St. Margaret's Street, between Parliament Square and the Abbey. Walk just a bit past it and look back for the view in the film.

25:14
Caxton Hall (F)
Caxton Street, SW1

Built as the Westminster City Hall in 1878, Caxton Hall, as a nearby plaque proclaims, is famous for its association "with women's suffrage meetings and deputations to Parliament." It was also famous for its registry office, which, until 1977, provided the setting for many a notable wedding, including that of Elizabeth Taylor to Michael Wilding (*Under Capricorn, Stage Fright*) in 1954 and that of Richard Starkey, a.k.a. Ringo Starr, to Maureen Cox in February 1965. Another notable union took place here 31 years earlier, during the shooting of *The Man Who Knew Too Much*. According to Alfred Hitchcock himself, actor Peter Lorre wanted time off from filming his role as the villainous Abbott to marry

Caxton Hall

his fiancée, Celia Lovsky. Hitch obliged, but only for an hour. Lorre thus left the **Lime Grove Studios** in Shepherd's Bush, rushed here to Caxton Hall in full make-up (gray streak in his hair, horrible scar over his right eye), said his "I dos," kissed his new bride and rushed back to the studio to complete the day's filming! Sadly, the marriage did not survive the couple's move to Hollywood, where the two were divorced in 1945. (Prior to his marriage, Lorre had been living with Hitchcock's friend and future partner, Sidney Bernstein, in the latter's Albemarle Street home.) Lorre, of course, went on to achieve cult status for his roles in *The Maltese Falcon*, *Casablanca* and other celebrated films, while Lovsky may be most familiar for her role as the high-ranking Vulcan official T'Pau in the *Star Trek* episode "Amok Time" (the one where Spock undergoes the Vulcan mating ritual).

Station: St. James's Park (CI; DI) Exit into Palmer Street and look for the hall ahead to the left, at Caxton Street.

The MacGuffin: Actress Celia Lovsky actually appears, unbilled, in the Tabernacle of the Sun sequence in *The Man Who Knew Too Much*. She is the woman sitting across from Leslie Banks at the back of the chapel as Clive is being hypnotized onstage. Other famous couples to appear—separately—in Hitchcock's films include Herbert Marshall and Edna Best, Claude Rains and Isabel Jeans, Hume Cronyn and Jessica Tandy, John Hodiak and Anne Baxter, George Sanders and Benita Hume, Bernard Miles and Josephine Wilson, Laurence Olivier and Jill Esmond, Brian Aherne and Joan Fontaine, and Oscar Homolka and Joan Tetzel. Michael Wilding and Margaret Leighton actually appeared in the same film—*Under Capricorn*—made over a decade before their 1960 marriage.

**25:15
St. James's Park (F) L
SW1**

In *Foreign Correspondent*, a distracted Van Meer comments on the birds in **Trafalgar Square** as he and Jones ride to **The Savoy**, then mentions that he had been "walking through the Park this morning." The reference is to London's oldest and most ornamental royal park, which is just down Waterloo Place and across the Mall from the **Carlton Hotel**, in which the two men are staying. Later, when Rowley has taken Jones to the top of the **Westminster Cathedral** tower, he points out the **Houses of Parliament** and St. James's Park. The Park is also notable as the site of not one but two Avenger murders in *The Lodger*. This is not stated in the film (as with **Charing Cross Station**), but rather shown—on the Lodger's map. (For more on his "plan of the murders," see entry 16:1.) In John Buchan's *The Thirty-nine Steps*, hero Richard Hannay is strolling along Jermyn Street when, at the corner of Duke Street, a group of young men identify him as "the Portland Place murderer." A policeman is soon on the scene, but Hannay breaks free of the group and sprints down Duke Street to Pall Mall (presumably through King Street and Pall Mall Place), from which he turns into Marlborough Road and thence continues across the Mall and into St. James's Park. He crosses the park itself—via the bridge over the lake—and then enters the "quiet thoroughfare" of Queen Anne's Gate. (The reason for his mad dash is explained under

St. James's Park

ex Home of the Foreign Secretary.) Also, according to Chapter 1 of *The Rainbird Pattern* (whence *Family Plot*), Grandison's offices are located "in Birdcage Walk, not far from Wellington Barracks, and with a pleasant view over St. James's Park and its lake." Author Victor Canning does not name the actual organization for which Grandison works, although he does tell us that the small, super-secret department "sat on top of [the police], using a power that came straight from the Prime Minister." This strongly suggests the British Security Service, or MI5, which was, indeed, a truly secret service (along with **MI6**, the Secret Intelligence Service) until the 1990s. (That Canning indeed had MI5 in mind is effectively confirmed in his 1979 novel *The Satan Sampler*, in which Grandison's high-ranking secret organization is said to be "concerned with the internal security of the country.") Appropriately, Hitchcock's Grandison works for the FBI, the approximate American counterpart to MI5. In 1972, the year of the novel's publication, the Security Service was headquartered at Leconfield House in Curzon Street, for which see **Charlotte Inwood's Home (1)**.

Station: St. James's Park (CI; DI) From the station walk straight up Queen Anne's Gate, across Birdcage Walk and into the park. Continue straight ahead to the bridge and lake. **Hours:** 10 am-9:30 pm daily in summer; 10 am-4 pm daily in winter

The MacGuffin: In Chapter 7 of *The Rainbird Pattern*, Shoebridge writes of Grandison being "at the Home Office," which could have been his departmental cover, but not the man's actual location. At that time (1972), the Home Office was located in Whitehall in part of the massive **Foreign Office** complex. Ironically, though, in 1978, the Home Office *did* move to a new building in Queen Anne's Gate, quite close to the Birdcage Walk locale described in the novel. Perhaps Canning shared some of Madame Blanche's psychic abilities.

A REFERENCE GUIDE TO LOCATIONS

25:16
Metropolitan Police Service C F
New Scotland Yard
10 Broadway, SW1

In 1967, the Metropolitan Police Service, a.k.a. Scotland Yard, moved from **Victoria Embankment**, near Whitehall, to No. 10 Broadway, the site of the former Vickers head office. The new, rather nondescript complex, like its distinctive, 19th-century predecessor, was called New Scotland Yard. (The Victoria Embankment building [see entry 25:8] is now called the Norman Shaw Building or *Old* New Scotland Yard.) The revolving "New Scotland Yard" sign outside the granite and aluminum façade of the present building has been seen in countless movies and television programs, many of which continue to appear on the PBS series *Mystery!* Hitchcock employed a shot of the modern sign only once, in his 1972 thriller *Frenzy*, all his previous Scotland Yard adventures having taken place at the Embankment location. Chief Inspector Oxford's office was based on Room 1118, right down to the view out the 11th floor window of Methodist Central Hall.

Station: St. James's Park (CI; DI) Exit for New Scotland Yard; the building—along with its famous sign—will be across the street.

25:17
ex **Colonial Office H**
Church House
Great Smith Street, SW1

The Colonial Office was one of three government departments concerned with Britain's external relations, the others being the Foreign Office and the Commonwealth Relations Office. This particular department was responsible for the administration of Britain's many colonies, protectorates and other dependent territories, which numbered more than 50 in the mid-1950s. Alfred Hitchcock came here in late June of 1956 to discuss the logistics of shooting a new film, *Flamingo Feather*, in the African territories of Swaziland, Nyasaland (modern Malawi) and Tanganyika (now part of Tanzania). The film was to be based upon a novel by soldier-statesman-author-philosopher Laurens van der Post (later Sir Laurens) and, in its story of African hunters caught up in political intrigue in southern Africa, would have presumably evoked comparisons with the recent remake of *The Man Who Knew Too Much*. After his consultation here in Church House, Hitchcock and his entourage (including wife Alma and long-time collaborator Angus MacPhail) set off for Africa, visiting locations in Eastern and Southern Africa and even meeting with van der Post himself in Johannesburg. During the trip Hitchcock realized that the film would simply be too costly and difficult to mount and so decided to abandon the project, which was to have followed *The Wrong Man*. (Fans of *Vertigo* may be glad that he did.) The Colonial Office was subsequently merged with the Commonwealth Relations Office and, as the Commonwealth Office, relocated to the Foreign Office building in Whitehall. The Commonwealth and Foreign Offices were themselves merged into a single ministry, the **Foreign & Commonwealth Office**, in 1968.

Station: St. James's Park (CI; DI) Exit the station into Petty France/Broadway (opposite the new Home Office), turn R and follow this straight into Tothill Street. At Victoria Street, cross toward Westminster Abbey and look for the small archway (and security cabin) leading into Dean's Yard. Enter through into Dean's Yard and look for Church House straight ahead.

25:18
"Stephen Fisher's Home" F
36 Smith Square, SW1

According to the shooting script for *Foreign Correspondent*, Stephen Fisher, head of the Universal Peace Party (and undercover *Nazi agent*), lives in this quiet square (laid out in 1726), just a short walk from Westminster Abbey. The latter, in fact, appears in the background of the establishing shot of Smith Square in the film itself. Opposite the house, though not visible in the film, is St. John's Public Hall, originally a Baroque church (built 1713-28), but now a concert hall. The subsequent shot, of actors Joel McCrea and Laraine Day embarking from their cab, were filmed at the Goldwyn Studios in Hollywood, as was the scene in which Rowley pushes Jones in front of the oncoming truck. Hitchcock also envisioned Smith Square as the setting for Mrs. Gill's home in *Stage Fright*, but in the end, found his location in Hampstead (see entry 34:1).

Stephen Fisher's home in *Foreign Correspondent*

Station: St. James's Park (CI; DI) The location is a bit of hike from any direction, but this route will allow you to approach the square from the angle shown in the film. Exit the station into Broadway, continue S across Victoria Street (which is shown in rear-projection in the film, when Johnny and Rowley are en route to **Westminster Cathedral**) and into Strutton Ground, which becomes Horseferry Road. Follow the latter around to the L, past Marsham Street, and look for Dean Bradley Street, to the L. Turn here and continue on to Smith Square. Veer to the L and look for Dean Trench Street to the L and, just past this, the location itself. Interestingly, Robert Hichens located *Paradine Case* protagonist Malcolm Keane (Anthony in the film) in nearby Cowley Street, prior to his move to a much larger home in Portland Place (see 14:6). Also, be sure to pop over to St. John's itself, a building architectural historian Nikolaus Pevsner described as "the boldest manifestation of an English Baroque in Inner London," but which Charles Dickens (in *Our Mutual Friend*) pronounced "a very hideous church"![4]

Ask Mr. Memory 39: Fisher explains to Krug that he—Fisher—is only a politician (in a sense) and that politicians aren't usually called upon to do what?

25:19
Royal Horticultural Society Hall L
Greycoat Street, SW1

Built in the 1920s as a larger companion to the Society's hall in nearby Vincent Square, the imposing Greycoat Street facility hosts a broad range of trade fairs, exhibitions and, of course, flower shows. Among the latter have been those of the prestigious Royal National Rose Society, the oldest and largest such society in the world. The Society's shows attract rose enthusiasts from all walks of life, including lovesick businessmen and the compulsive thieves whom they would reform. Thus, in Chapter 4 of *Marnie*, the title character accepts Mark Rutland's invitation to attend the National Rose Society Show in London (the actual venue isn't mentioned but this is where it was held), although she herself used to wonder "why anyone should bother to go nasal and wet-eyed about a plant as feeble" as a rose. In the event, she is rather impressed by the roses, and by Mark, too, who invites her to tea "just round the corner." This is, in fact, their first "date," and the prelude to one of the most interesting relationships in the Hitchcock literary canon. The scene was omitted from the film, wherein the two first get acquainted in Mark's house one stormy Saturday afternoon.

Royal Horticultural Society

Station: St. James's Park (CI; DI) Exit for New Scotland Yard, continue in Broadway across Victoria Street and into Strutton Ground; at Greycoat Place turn R and look for Greycoat Street just ahead to the L. The hall is at the end of the street on the L.

25:20
Westminster Cathedral (Cathedral of the Most Precious Blood) F H
Francis Street, SW1

London's preeminent Roman Catholic cathedral was the setting for one of the more dramatic scenes in *Foreign Correspondent*. Here, Johnny Jones and his "body-

Westminster Cathedral

guard," Rowley (actually Johnny's would-be-assassin), attempt to lose their "pursuers" (Rowley's invention) inside the cathedral. In a rear-projection shot, we first see them riding down Victoria Street (having turned from Buckingham Gate) and then having their cabbie take the next left, which deposits them (accurately then; impossibly now) in Ashley Place (note the street sign in the background). Rowley then glances up to the cathedral's 273-foot bell tower, which, for some reason, Hitchcock chose to show in reverse. (The tower should be to the left of the frame from that angle. In the subsequent newspaper photo, it's the right way around.) Jones and Rowley then enter a Hollywood mock-up of the cathedral and ascend to the top of the tower, the set being rather larger than its real-life counterpart. Rowley then waits for the perfect opportunity to push Johnny over the edge, but, as you will recall, his plans go rather seriously awry. Forty years later, in June 1980, the life of Alfred Joseph Hitchcock was commemorated by a Requiem Mass at Westminster Cathedral, the director having died on April 29 in California. Among those in attendance were Ingrid Bergman, Ann Todd, Barry Foster, Lord Bernstein and John Mills. The memories they must have shared....

Jones (McCrea) and Rowley (Gwenn) atop the cathedral tower in *Foreign Correspondent*.

Station: Victoria (CE; DI; VI) Exit for Victoria Street, turn R and look for the cathedral ahead on the R. Be sure to take the lift to the top of the tower and don't worry about following in Rowley's "footsteps"—the windows are barred. You might also note that when looking north from the tower, as the characters do in the film (note the massive, domed Methodist Central Hall in the background), you can certainly see both **St. James's Park** and the **Horse Guards'** route. But by no stretch (well, perhaps, quite a stretch) can you see **St. Paul's Cathedral** in that direction, as Rowley says. He may be "quick," but his geography is a bit dodgy.

The MacGuffin: In Hitchcock's original screen treatment, written with Joan Harrison, the foreign correspondent was to have had an "accident" while traveling by taxi along the **Embankment** past **The Savoy**. Here, the murder plan went awry when the Fisher character learned that his daughter would be accompanying the reporter and stopped the whole thing.

25:21
ex **Home of the Foreign Secretary L C**
3 Queen Anne's Gate, SW1

Home of the Foreign Secretary

Following his hurried sprint through **St. James's Park**, Richard Hannay enters the "quiet thoroughfare" of Queen Anne's Gate in Chapter 8 of *The Thirty-nine Steps*. Here, he barges into the home of Sir Walter Bullivant, a high **Foreign Office** official to whom he has confided information about enemy spies and "the thirty-nine steps." Assembled in Bullivant's home ("in the narrow part" of the street) are the War Minister, an Admiralty official, a general, a French military official and the First Sea Lord—who actually turns out to be the head of the spy ring in disguise! (As in the film, the spy will memorize the content of important military documents, in this case naval dispositions along the British coasts.) At the time the novel was written (1914), No. 3 was home to Sir Edward Grey, who served as Foreign Secretary (head of the FO) from 1905 to 1916. Across the street at No. 16 lived Admiral of the Fleet Lord Fisher, who served as 1st Sea Lord (head of the Admiralty) from 1905 to 1910. (Both addresses are commemorated by English Heritage Blue Plaques.) From here, the action switches to the **Admiralty** and thence to the Kentish **Site of the Thirty-nine Steps**, where the climax of the novel takes place.

Station: St. James's Park (CI; DI) Walk straight up Queen Anne's Gate and follow it around to the R. The building is just ahead on the R.

25:22
ex **HQ of MI6 (F) L C**
Broadway Buildings
54 Broadway, SW1

From 1926 until 1967, one of the most famous espionage organizations in the world was headquartered in this narrow, nine-story building opposite the St. James's Park Underground station. The British Secret Service—once thought to be among the six most powerful institutions in the world[5]—was established by the **War Office** in 1909 to address the growing military threat from Germany, a threat then being dramatized in widely read books by E. Phillips Oppenheim, William Le Queux, Erskine Childers and others. The task of the Secret Service, also known as "MI6" or today, officially, the "Secret Intelligence Service (SIS)"—was to gather foreign intelligence on behalf of the Army, Navy and, later, the **Foreign Office**. This "foreign section" was initially paired with a "home section" tasked with counter-espionage, i.e., spy-catching within the British Isles; the latter evolved into a separate organization, the Security Service, or, popularly, "MI5" (The cover names "MI5" and "MI6" reflect the agencies' *former* classification within the War Office Bureaucracy as Military Intelligence, Section Five and Military Intelligence, Section Six, respectively. Both MI5 and MI6 have been independent, civilian agencies since the inter-war years.) The Secret Service settled here in 1926, after its new chief, Admiral Hugh Sinclair, took a flat in nearby Queen Anne's Gate, which, in turn, was connected via secret passage to Broadway Buildings; previous headquarters were located in Victoria Street, Whitehall Court and West Kensington. Hitchcock, of course, was fascinated by espionage and foreign intrigue, as evidenced by an even dozen of his films from *The Man Who Knew Too Much* in 1934 to *Topaz* in 1969. (That number would have grown to a baker's dozen, if ill health hadn't forced him to abandon *The Short Night* in 1979 [see below].) Hitchcock flirted with the British Secret Service itself in his first two spy films, deploying—and quickly killing off—its *foreign-born* agents in both *The Man Who Knew Much* and *The 39 Steps*. (In the former, Bernard is said to work for the Foreign Office, which in fact means MI6; in the latter, "Annabella Smith" is clearly a foreign-born free agent, temporarily in the employ of England. This suggests that she was recruited overseas, which, again, points to MI6.) Then, in *Secret Agent*, Hitchcock settled down to a depiction of the life and work of an actual *British* agent called "Ashenden." The film was based upon the semi-fictional *Ashenden* stories of author Somerset Maugham, who had spied for both the War Office and SIS during World War I. The film is in many ways a forerunner of the James Bond series, from Ashenden's initial briefing by "R," who explains the assignment

Secret Agent **Ashenden (John Gielgud) and the Hairless Mexican (Peter Lorre) spying in a bell tower.**

and then dispatches the agent to a scenic foreign locale, to the explosive climax and fade-out with a beautiful woman at the end. Here, though, Ashenden's employer appears to be the War Office (see that entry for details), rather than SIS. Thus, it was not until *The Lady Vanishes* that Hitchcock first deployed an actual *British* Secret Service agent in the person of a little old lady named Froy. And don't let her reference to the Foreign Office fool you; Miss Froy works for MI6, plain and simple. And, following established procedure, she instructs Gilbert and Iris to deliver the coded message *not* to SIS headquarters in Broadway, which was *never* revealed to the British public, but rather to the Foreign Office in Whitehall. In this, screenwriters Gilliat and Launder came very close to the truth, for outsiders having any business along these lines were then directed to Room 070 of the War Office. (Incidentally, for those who haven't read the source novel, *The Wheel Spins*, the literary character really is an innocent governess; the possibility that she might be a spy is suggested once, but only as a joke.)

Hitchcock continued his association with spies and foreign intrigue in Hollywood, first in *Foreign Correspondent* (partly set in England, on the eve of World War II), next in *Saboteur* (a loose remake of *The 39 Steps*) and then in *Notorious*, set just after the war. The latter deals with the attempts of an unnamed U.S. intelligence agency to penetrate a German lair in Rio de Janeiro and find out what they're up to. Hitchcock's early draft treatments and screenplays indicate that the intelligence agency was supposed to be the FBI. But surely the FBI engages in *spy-catching*, not spying, and this only *within* the United States. Right? Wrong. Whether they knew it or not, Hitchcock and screenwriter Ben Hecht had come all too close to the truth: In June 1940 the FBI had established a "Special Intelligence Service" to round up German spies in Latin America. The unit was still operational in May 1945 when producer David O. Selznick submitted the *Notorious* shooting script to FBI director J. Edgar Hoover. Hoover had no choice but to object to the depiction of an FBI presence in Brazil; Hitchcock had

Hitchcock would use spies as a subject once again in *Notorious* with Claude Rains and Ingrid Bergman.

no choice but to eliminate all references to the FBI from *Notorious*. (The film's other, more famous topical reference, was the use of uranium ore—and its implications for atomic weaponry—as the MacGuffin.) Now, all this has little or nothing to do with the *British* Secret Service—*except* for the following. First, the film is actually based on a relatively obscure WWI-era story called "The Song of the Dragon," in which the American "Secret Service Department" recruits a young woman to do just what Alicia will do in *Notorious*: infiltrate and help expose a band of German agents by romancing their leader, a well-bred ladies' man and "supposed Englishman" who is actually a big shot in the German Foreign Office. (Claude Rains was the perfect choice to play such a character.) The problem with the story, at least from a factual standpoint, is that author John Taintor Foote's vaunted "Secret Service Department," which "could not be matched the world around," simply did not exist. America's so-called "Secret Service" was in fact a Treasury agency, founded in 1865 to combat counterfeiting, and later tasked with protecting the President and other government officials. The espionage (really *counter*-espionage) that did take place on behalf of the United States at that time was conducted by relatively small, ad hoc units of the Army, Navy, State and Justice Departments, as well as the Treasury's Secret Service. Thus, Foote very likely confused or deliberately conflated the powerful British intelligence organization (and its global reputation) with one or another of the smaller U.S. agencies. This opinion is reinforced near the beginning of the story, when one of the characters compares the spymaster's briefing to "a plot for a moving-picture scenario or a tale by Oppenheim." (Oppenheim's pre-war spy stories have been alluded to above; his praised and popular *The Kingdom of the Blind* (1917) and *The Great Impersonation* (1920) were very possibly on Foote's mind as he wrote in 1921. Another possible influence may have been Buchan's 1919 novel *Mr. Standfast*, in which the future Mrs. Richard Hannay is used as bait to trap a German villain.) The case for a connection between *Notorious* and MI6 is, admittedly, something of a stretch; but the background story nicely illustrates Hitchcock's ongoing fascination with spying and the consequences for those (like the "woman with a past" in both "Dragon" and *Notorious*) who conduct it. Hitchcock pursues this theme again in the second *Man Who Knew Too Much*, as well as *North By Northwest*, which contains perhaps his strongest overt indictment of the espionage business. The message, conveyed through the Cary Grant character, is simply this: If the United States cannot win a war openly and properly, without employing beautiful women to sleep with foreign enemies (cf. *Notorious*), then it should learn to start *losing* a few wars—a truly radical notion given the Cold War climate of the day.

Hitchcock directed two more spy films, back to back, in the 1960s: *Torn Curtain* and *Topaz*. Of the former, Hitchcock told Truffaut: "I got the idea from the disappearance of the two British diplomats, Burgess and MacLean [sic], who deserted their country and went to Russia. I said to myself, 'What did Mrs. MacLean [sic] think of the whole thing?'"[6] Cambridge graduates Donald Maclean and Guy Burgess had begun spying for the Soviets in the 1930s. Both secured important posts within the Foreign Office (Burgess had also worked briefly for MI6) in order to better serve their Communist masters. Maclean's cover was blown in 1951 and, thanks to the timely warning of the as yet unidentified "third man," Kim Philby of MI6, Burgess was able to whisk Maclean out of England and ultimately to Moscow—a defection not officially confirmed until 1956. Hitchcock's concern about Mrs. Maclean, the unsuspecting wife who was left behind, provided the ostensible setup for *Torn Curtain*, yet the "defection" turns out to have been faked and the "wife" who was left behind *wasn't*. (The real Melinda Maclean seems to have known about her husband's life as a double agent and, indeed, eventually joined him in Moscow.) Unfortunately, Hitchcock seems to have grown somewhat bored with the plight of his 1960s spies and neither *Torn Curtain* nor its rather muddled follow-up contribute very much to his ongoing commentary on espionage.

After recharging his batteries on the superior *Frenzy* and *Family Plot*, the director planned to revisit his original *Torn Curtain* set-up—what happens to the wife who is left behind? Now, he would employ two literary sources: Ronald Kirkbride's novel *The Short Night* (which was also to provide the film's title) and Sean Bourke's non-fiction account of *The Springing of George Blake*. Here, Hitchcock would have come very close indeed to the venerable British Secret Service and its Broadway Buildings headquarters. George Blake, a Royal Naval officer of Dutch and Egyptian-Jewish ancestry, had joined the Secret Service in November 1944. He was assigned to the Dutch section and based on the eighth floor of Broadway Buildings. Following distinguished service in the war, he was offered permanent employment as an MI6 officer, eventually being sent to South Korea as the Head of the Seoul Station. During the ensuing war, Blake was captured by the North Koreans, underwent a conversion to Communism (a result of his own reflections and Russophilia, *not* brainwashing, according to his autobiography) and duly offered his services to the Soviet Union. He was returned to London (and Broadway Buildings) in 1953 and promptly embarked upon one of the most damaging careers in the history of espionage. Over the course of the next seven years, Blake exposed (and undermined) a number of important Allied intelligence operations against the Soviets and, most significantly, revealed the names of nearly 400 British agents operating in the Eastern Bloc—many of whom were believed to have been killed. In his autobiog-

Broadway Buildings, former HQ of MI6

raphy, Blake claims that none of those he betrayed were actually killed; former KGB officers have claimed otherwise. Blake also specifically denies the charge—widespread in intelligence circles—that his information led to the arrest and execution of Lt. Col. Pyotr Popov, a Soviet GRU (military intelligence) officer who spied for the CIA in the 1950s. Popov, by the most reliable accounts, was thrown live into a blazing furnace in front of several of his GRU colleagues. It was apparently just this kind of barbarism that inspired Kirkbride's graphic descriptions of the fates of those betrayed by Brand in Chapter 23 of the novel. Finally, his cover blown through information supplied by a Polish defector in 1961, Blake was arrested and interrogated by MI6, to whom he ultimately confessed. He was quickly tried and convicted at the **Old Bailey**, where he was given the longest sentence in the history of peace-time espionage—42 years. He was sent to **Wormwood Scrubs** (to which you should turn for more details), where he spent five years before being "sprung" by Bourke, a convicted Irish terrorist whom he had befriended in prison. Additional sympathizers hid Blake in London for the next two months (see 47:1), then smuggled him to East Germany, whence he was taken to Moscow. Kirkbride's novel details the pursuit of the escaped double agent (renamed Garvin Brand) by Joe Baird, the vengeful brother of one of the betrayed agents, as well as the painful reunion of Brand with his wife and children in Finland. (In this, Kirkbride comes closer to the story of Maclean, than to Blake. Gillian Blake had already begun divorce proceedings against her husband while he was still in prison and certainly never joined him in Europe or anywhere else. Other details—such as Brand's capture and imprisonment by the North Koreans and his language studies at Cambridge—more clearly recall Blake.) Hitchcock's screenplay retained much of the novel's action, including a climactic train chase (all fictional, of course), but added a suspenseful opening sequence derived from Bourke's account of the real-life "springing" (see also Appendix III). Sadly, Hitchcock's final assault on espionage—on the very real price paid by spies and those who loved them—was not to be. As revealed in David Freeman's *The Last Days of Alfred Hitchcock*, the director's deteriorating health forced the cancellation of the production in May 1979 and Hitchcock died the following April.

Station: St. James's Park (CI; DI) The building is opposite the Broadway exit.

The MacGuffin: Interestingly, another GRU double agent who feared his cover was blown by George Blake (but apparently not) was Col. Oleg Penkovsky, who in 1961-62 passed classified information to the U.S. and Britain about Soviet missiles in Cuba. This revelation was incorporated into the novel (and film) *Topaz*, which was more directly inspired by the defection of KGB agent Anatoly Golitsyn. It was the latter who revealed the existence of a Soviet spy ring (codenamed "Sapphire") operating within the highest levels of the French government.

OUTER LONDON

26. BATTERSEA

26:1
Battersea Power Station F
Battersea Park Road, SW8

Rather oddly, this former power station, closed since 1983, has become one of London's most famous—and beloved—landmarks. The building's exterior was designed by Sir Giles Gilbert Scott (Liverpool Anglican Cathedral, Bankside Power Station, Waterloo Bridge and even London's classic red telephone box) and is today considered the epitome of 20th-century industrial architecture. Station A, with a 337-ft-high fluted chimney at either end, was completed in 1933; Station B, with two matching stacks, was opened in 1953. Hitchcock incorporates a miniature of Station A in the opening montage of *Sabotage*, thereby indicating the site of Verloc's perfidy. (Neither the film nor the shooting script names the station, though Hitchcock's treatment of April 17, 1936 does, even having Vladimir threaten to expose Verloc over "the Battersea Power Station job.") An interior shot of the station's massive turbine hall was combined with studio footage of the actors through the Schüfftan Process so beloved of the director (see Appendix II). The detail-obsessed Hitchcock even shows the station's famous clean, white smoke belching from one of the model's chimneys (emissions were treated to prevent sulfur and other impurities from polluting Central London). The only real snag is that sabotage at Battersea

Battersea Power Station

would not have resulted in a shutdown of the Underground system (as shown in the film), since the Underground receives its electricity from the Lots Road Power Station in Chelsea (and has done so since 1905). Why Hitchcock chose a famous power station is uncertain (there is no precedent in the source novel, *The Secret Agent*), although he may have recalled the sabotage of power stations in the Bulldog Drummond novel *Black Gang*. (See also **St. Giles Circus** for more on this connection.) In any case, after years of neglect—and near destruction—Battersea Power Station, now a Grade II listed building, is being developed as a hotel/entertainment complex.

Station: Vauxhall (VI; NR); The station is probably best viewed from across the river, in the Chelsea Embankment near Chelsea Bridge.

The MacGuffin: Hitchcock actually omitted a reference to the famous landmark in one of his most faithful adaptations, *Dial M for Murder*. In the Frederick Knott play, Max (our Mark) recalls the night that Sheila (our Margot) said her final "goodbye," exactly one year ago. He then walked along the Chelsea Embankment (not far from his "ramshackle studio") and stared at the Battersea Power Station across the river. (In the American version of the play, Knott changed this to Chelsea Gas Works, which lies just beyond the Embankment.) Was he thinking of the power station or her, Sheila asks? Neither. He was writing a new story, "a triumphant story" of his "returning from America with his pockets full of coin—to snatch his lady love from the arms of her jealous husband." In the film, their last night in Mark's apartment is recalled (we later learn, from Tony, that it was in Chelsea), but without the reference to the power station or to the story.

26:2
"Chief Inspector Oxford's Flat" (F)
York Mansions
Prince of Wales Drive, SW8

Doubles as: Ashley Gardens, Westminster

On the night of September 21, 1971, Alfred Hitchcock shot two versions of *Frenzy*'s Chief Inspector Oxford arriving at York Mansions, bidding his driver good night and entering the building. (In one take the car pulled up in front of the building; in the other the car pulled up across the street.) This brief bit, including a shot of the Chief Inspector exiting the lift and crossing the corridor to his flat (also filmed here that night), was to have appeared immediately before the first scene in which Oxford reviews the Blaney case with his wife. (The interior of the

Chief Inspector Oxford's Flat

Oxford flat, with a door based on those of York Mansions, was filmed at **Pinewood Studios**.) Hitchcock's original location notes (December 1970) indicate that the Chief Inspector lived in a semi-detached home in the North London suburb of Winchmore Hill, as in the Arthur La Bern novel. However, the shooting script of July 21, 1971, indicates that the house is located in Ashley Gardens, "alongside Westminster Cathedral," a landmark Hitchcock had showcased in *Foreign Correspondent* (see 25:20). Neither York Mansions nor Ashley Gardens is mentioned in the novel.

Station: Victoria (CI; DI; VI); Transfer to British Rail and take this to Battersea Park. Turn R out of the station, R again into Queenstown Road, then L at the roundabout into Prince of Wales Drive. The building is ahead on the L, at Macduff Road, the corner used for filming. For a glimpse of how the building looked in the 1970s, including the lift and corridor that Hitchcock photographed, check out the 1975 John Wayne thriller *Brannigan*, in which the Duke takes up temporary residence in York Mansions.

The MacGuffin: In 46-year-old Alec McCowen Hitchcock undoubtedly found the perfect actor to play Chief Inspector Oxford. However, the director may have originally had someone rather younger in mind. Among the questions he researched during the preproduction of *Frenzy* was the minimum age for a Scotland Yard detective chief inspector. The answer: 30 years.

Ask Mr. Memory 40: How long have the chief inspector and his wife been married?

27. BRIXTON

27:1
HM Prison Brixton C L (F)
Jebb Avenue, SW2

Opened in 1820, London's famous Brixton Prison became the first of Richard Blamey's two temporary homes near the conclusion of the novel *Goodbye Piccadilly, Farewell Leicester Square*. Location notes of December 1970 indicate that Hitchcock intended that the cinematic Blamey (eventually renamed *Blaney*) would also be remanded here, before his trial at the **Old Bailey**, but, in the end, this sequence was dropped. Instead, we see Blaney in only one prison, **Wormwood Scrubs**, following his murder conviction. (See also **Pentonville**.) Some years earlier, Hitchcock had also planned to film prison exteriors here in Jebb Avenue, for a sequence in the film *No Bail for the Judge*. The title character, having been charged with the murder of a prostitute, is remanded to Brixton, where, given the bad fall he has suffered, he is then treated in the prison hospital. (In the novel, he is treated here in Brixton for a stroke.) As mentioned in Appendix III and elsewhere, the film was eventually abandoned and Hitchcock turned from a psychopathic young English murderer to an even more bizarre American killer.

Station: Brixton (VI) Exit L into Brixton Hill—and walk till you drop. Or better, take a bus—Jebb Avenue is nearly a mile from the station, on the R.

HM Prison Brixton

The MacGuffin: The shooting script for *Rich and Strange*, for which Hitchcock received one of his rare screenwriting credits, marks the Hills' return to London with a shot of "a typical London high road, such as Brixton High Street [*sic*; presumably, for Brixton Road]," after which there would be a dissolve to the suburban street shown early in the film. In the event, he settled for stock shots of **Piccadilly Circus**.

27:2
"John S. King" L (F)
23 Newport Street, SW9

This is the address of the little shop to which Margot was directed to send the "blackmailer's" money in the film *Dial M for Murder*. (In the British version of the play the name is "N. S. King," it is a tobacconist's, and Margot is, of course, "Sheila.") As with a number of other places mentioned in the play/film, it is a fictional one: There has never been a Newport Street in Brixton. *Nevertheless*, Margot herself went to the shop, where she learned that "people use it as a forwarding address." (From the play: "They act as agents for forwarding letters and advertisements.") The blackmailer, of course, turns out to be her husband, who was simply trying to manipulate her into the murder scheme that constitutes the film's plot.

Station: Brixton (VI)

27:3
***ex* St. Saviour's Church Hall F**
Vicary Street, SW2 (now part of the Blenheim Gardens Estate)

Doubles as: Ambrose Chapel in *The Man Who Knew Too Much* (56)

A REFERENCE GUIDE TO LOCATIONS   **227**

St. Saviour's Church

The parochial rooms and Sunday School of a nearby Anglican church doubled as the "real" Ambrose Chapel in *The Man Who Knew Too Much* (56). (For the *other* "Ambrose Chappell," see entry 29:1.) Here, Ben and Jo McKenna rendezvous in an attempt to locate and rescue their young son, Hank, who, as it happens, has been kidnapped by a "vicar." (In fact, one of the Paramount censorship department's concerns during production was that Drayton be exposed as a fake early on, lest any "religious-minded group" be offended.) The chapel scenes combine footage of actors James Stewart and Doris Day shot here on location in June 1955, with interiors, matte and rear-projection shots (of Ben escaping through the belfry, for example) created "back home" in California in August. Art director Henry Bumstead recalled the intensive search that led up to the discovery of the Brixton building and how it exasperated director of photography Bob Burks. "'Bummy,' he says, 'if you stop and take one more picture [of a prospective location], I'm going back to the hotel and to hell with it!' He was a wonderful guy!" (Burks, who worked on a number of Hitchcock films in the 1950s and '60s, died in a house fire in 1968.) Fortunately, Bumstead and Burks found just what the director ordered here in Brixton. In her autobiography, Doris Day recalled her scenes here with fondness, due to the kindness of the locals, who, "between takes…invited us for tea." Sadly, the hall—to which Bumstead's art department added the belfry—has since been demolished, as has the entire street on which it stood.

Station: Brixton (VI) St. Saviour's Church itself—now the New Testament Church of God—is in Lambert Road, Brixton Hill; behind the church (parallel with Lambert Road) is Glanville Road, which replaced the earlier Bartley Road. Vicary Street started approximately two blocks ahead, on the L. It ran through to Blenheim Gardens (a portion of which is still extant) and the church hall itself was on the R. In the film, the police car turns from Bartley Road, R into Vicary Street and pulls up opposite the church, about three quarters of the way down. The phone booth Jo used was on the NE corner of Vicary Street and Blenheim Gardens. (It is thus just out of camera range, screen left, as the police car pulls away toward Blenheim Gardens at the end of the scene.) If you turn R out of Glanville Road, go R into Halliwell Road then R again into Blenheim Gardens, you can actually reach the "spot" where the telephone booth was located. Walk to the end of Blenheim Gardens, then around the apartment building directly in front of you. On the other end of the building is a small courtyard that leads into Ramilles Close. It was here, in a spot corresponding to the SW corner of the courtyard, that the phone booth stood. Today, Ramilles Close continues straight out to Lyham Road; in the 1950s, Blenheim Gardens curved around to the N before it reached Lyham Road, a curve actually visible in the background as Jo leaves the phone booth and crosses Vicary Street. Incidentally, knowing all this about the original layout actually allows you to identify a "continuity error" in the film: When Jo exits the phone booth and crosses to the W side of Vicary Street, she is actually on the same side of the street as the church hall; in the next shot, however, she is on the E side of Vicary Street and must *again* cross over to the chapel.

28. CAMBERWELL

28:1
"Bijou Cinema" F
Plouthorp Road, SE5

The postcode SE5 corresponds to the South London district of Camberwell, which according to his letterhead, would be the location of Verloc's cinema in *Sabotage*. As far as I can determine, there was never a "Plouthorp Road" in Camberwell or anywhere else in Greater London. For the cinema exteriors, Hitchcock actually utilized three different locations: a full-sized street mock-up near Northolt; Wood Lane (for the scene in which Verloc catches the bus to the

A police detective (John Loder) talks to Mrs. Verloc at her husband's ticket booth in *Sabotage*.

Zoo), just outside the studio; and, of course, **Lime Grove** itself. Now, over the course of two pages in *Hitchcock's Notebooks*, author Dan Auiler refers to the location of the Bijou façade as the backlot of both "Lime Phane Studios" (he presumably means Lime *Grove*) and **Elstree Studios**. Neither statement is correct. The film was, of course, shot at Lime Grove, but the street was built on a remote site between Northolt and Harrow, one that producer Michael Balcon sometimes used for exteriors. Actor Desmond Tester (Stevie) recalled the daily Underground trip he took from Central London to Northolt, although he could not remember the precise location of the shoot. (The area has long since been redeveloped.) There is, however, no question that the street scenes (apart from the Lord Mayor's sequence, for which, see **St. Clement Danes**) were shot in the Northolt/South Harrow area. Hitchcock, himself, in a 1937 article called "Search for the Sun," refers to the location as simply "a field near Harrow." For the location of the literary character's business, see **Adolf Verloc's Shop**.

29. CAMDEN TOWN

29:1
"Ambrose Chappell" F
61 Burdett Street

This is the address of the Camden Town taxidermist that Jimmy Stewart visits in a futile attempt to find his kidnapped son in *The Man Who Knew Too Much* (56). Burdett Street was fictional—the 61 was not. See the next entry.

29:2
ex **Edward Gerrard & Sons F**
61 College Place, N1

Doubles as: Ambrose Chapell, Taxidermists, in *The Man Who Knew Too Much* (56)

Taxidermist's sign from *The Man Who Knew Too Much*

This was the actual site of the taxidermist Ben visits with unintentionally humorous results in *The Man Who Knew Too Much* (56). (The film gives the location as "61 Burdett Street, Camden Town," the street being fictional, the number real.) In the film, of course, the taxidermist is "Ambrose Chappell," but the route Jimmy Stewart followed to the shop was legitimate. He exited the taxi in Royal College Street, turned west into Plender Street, at the end of which, to the left, sat the entrance to the taxidermist. Hitchcock had been alerted to this rather unlikely Camden Town locale by scriptwriter Angus MacPhail, who recalled having read a magazine article about "the last stronghold in Britain of taxidermy." (The corresponding scene in the original film takes place in a sinister dentist's office and is arguably more effective. Indeed, prior to MacPhail's discovery, Hitchcock had intended to stage this scene in a dentist's office, the question being which of the principals, Doris Day or Jimmy Stewart, should have a tooth pulled, à la Uncle Clive in the 1934 version.) Associate producer Herb Coleman and unit manager Doc Erickson actually found *two* taxidermists in London: Gerrard's, the one mentioned in the *Illustrated London News* article, and another who proved to be "most disagreeable." Photographs were taken of both establishments and

Plender Street still looks much as it did in *The Man Who Knew Too Much* (1956)

Hitchcock ultimately selected Gerrard's, the more cooperative of the two. Director of photography Robert Burks then paid a visit to 61 College Place and determined that Hitchcock could actually film *inside* the building *if* the director could accommodate his action to the existing structure. He could and he did, shooting the interiors here on June 2, 3 and 4, 1955. (Insert shots of stuffed animal heads were actually filmed at **Forbes House**, although this footage never made it to the finished film.) Art director Henry Bumstead recalled an amusing incident during the filming here in College Place. Apparently while Hitchcock and the real taxidermist were engaged in conversation, Burks took note of his surroundings and asked Bumstead why anyone would want to stuff so many rabbit heads. The sharp-eared Mr. Gerrard turned away from Hitchcock and icily interjected: "They are not rabbits, they are *hares*." Bumstead and Burks had to stifle their laughter! Sadly, as Camden Town resident and Hitchcock buff Danny Nissim alerted me, the buildings in the relevant portions of Plender Street and College Place have been demolished and replaced with a housing estate and a playground (for the Richard Cobden Primary School), respectively. Still, the approach is roughly the same as in the film and the view down Plender Street toward Royal College Street will certainly look familiar.

Station: Mornington Crescent (NO) Exit R into Crowndale Road and walk E. Turn L into Royal College Street, then L into Plender Street, just as Stewart did 50 years ago. At College Place, look across the street to the L for the site of the taxidermist (now a playground); turn around and look back toward Royal College Street for the view of Stewart's approach. To return to the station, continue along Plender Street to Camden High Street, turn L and look for the station straight ahead.

Ask Mr. Memory 41: With an insert shot of what animal does the taxidermist's shop sequence conclude?

30. EARL'S COURT

30:1
"Gavin Brand's Flat" (F)
Earl's Court Road, SW5

Hogarth Road, to have been used as Gavin Brand's flat

The villain of Hitchcock's last—unrealized—film, *The Short Night*, was Soviet mole Gavin Brand, a character based upon real-life British traitor George Blake (see **MI6**). The film was to have begun with Brand's escape from **Wormwood Scrubs** and subsequent exfiltration from Britain, after which the focus would shift to hero Joe Bailey's pursuit of the fugitive from London to Finland. Along the way, Bailey visits Brand's old flat, which production documents (as well as the published script) locate in Earl's Court Road. The documents indicate that in May 1978 art director Robert Boyle and longtime Hitchcock associate Hilton Green scouted a number of possible locations for the flat, including Onslow Gardens, Redcliff Road and Cromwell Place, all of which are located just to the east of Earl's Court in South Kensington. The only actual Earl's Court locale they scouted was Hogarth Road, which connects Earl's Court Road to Cromwell Road.

Station: Earl's Court (DI; PI) Exit into Earl's Court Road and look for Hogarth Road directly across the street.

31. FULHAM

31:1
"Harry Worp's Home" (L)
87 Eastfield, SW6

Fans of the film *The Trouble with Harry* may recall that dotty old Captain Wiles discovers an envelope identifying the body before him as that of "Harry Worp, 87 Maple Avenue, Boston, Massachusetts." Given the film's New England setting, Harry's address isn't particularly surprising. However, as the setting of Jack Trevor Story's novel was actually *old* England, you shouldn't be surprised to find that the troublesome corpse hailed not from Boston, but from London. In fact, he lived at "Eighty-seven, Eastfield, Fulham," at least according to the original author. In fact, there doesn't appear to be any such street in Fulham, although there are a few Eastfields elsewhere in London

Station: Putney Bridge (DI) Exit for Fulham Palace Gardens (the palace is the old seat of the Bishops of London) and stroll along the river or up in Fulham Palace Road for a taste of Harry's old neighborhood.

32. GREENWICH

32:1
Royal Observatory Greenwich C L
Greenwich Royal Park, SE10

One of the most powerful scenes in the Hitchcock canon is the explosion of the bomb on a crowded bus near **Piccadilly Circus** in *Sabotage*. The explosion results in the tragic death of one of the film's major characters—young Stevie—and sets in motion all the action that follows. The scene was adapted from a similar explosion in Joseph Conrad's 1907 novel *The Secret Agent*, which in turn was based on a real-life incident here at the Royal Observatory, Britain's preeminent seat of astronomy since 1675. The date was February 15, 1894; the time was approximately 4:45 p.m. Workers in the Observatory heard the sound of a "sharp and clear detonation" and rushed outside. There, in the park below, they saw the shattered body of a young man, later identified as French anarchist Martial Bourdin. Bits of Bourdin were scattered for yards in every direction, yet, astonishingly, he survived for some 30 minutes after the blast. Precisely what he had hoped to accomplish at the Royal Observatory and what went wrong—for presumably he was not intending to blow *himself* up—have never been determined. Bomb-wielding anarchists were then active in both Russia and France, but their targets were usually theatres, operas, government buildings and other gathering places of the rich and powerful. Some suggested that Bourdin's brother-in-law, H.B. Samuels, was a police informer and had himself instigated the bombing as an *agent provocateur*. Conrad, then living at 17 Gillingham Street, Victoria, considered the attempted sabotage "a blood-stained inanity of so fatuous a kind that it was impossible to fathom its origin by any reasonable or even unreasonable

Mrs. Verloc (Sylvia Sidney) with her young brother Stevie (Desmond Tester), who is the sacrificial lamb in *Sabotage,* and her husband, the terrorist Mr. Verloc (Oscar Homolka).

process of thought." Then a friend mentioned that the unfortunate bomber was "half an idiot…[whose] sister committed suicide afterwards," and Conrad knew he had a story. (Another staple of Edwardian crime fiction—duly adapted by Hitchcock—was also inspired by an anecdote, for which see, the **Site of Jack the Ripper's First Victim**.) Hitchcock knew it, too, but Conrad's motive for bombing the Observatory—to attack a symbol of scientific learning in hopes of prompting a police crackdown on anarchists—proved too esoteric for a film treatment. Instead, Hitchcock opted for a plan to distract London from events on the Continent by blowing up the **Piccadilly Circus Underground Station**, ironically, the very kind of simple butchery repudiated in the novel. Hitchcock, did, however, keep the younger brother as both sacrificial lamb and symbol, although not without alteration: Conrad's mildly retarded adult (who trips and falls and thus inadvertently detonates Verloc's bomb) becomes a winsome teenager whose tragic death—whose murder, in fact—impacts far more strongly than in the novel. (For more on this scene, see **St. Giles Circus**.) Returning to Greenwich, we should note that the anarchists' original target, the Royal Observatory, was actually transferred to Herstmonceux Castle, Sussex, in 1948 (and thence to Cambridge in 1990), London's skies having become so polluted that accurate astronomical observations were no longer possible. In 1998, the Royal Observatory ceased to operate as a research institution, merging its equipment and resources with those of the U.K. Astronomy Technology Centre in Edinburgh. It presently operates as a center for the public understanding of astronomy here in its original Greenwich home, the site of the famous Prime Meridian, from which the world calculates both time and distance.

Station: Bank (CE; CI; DI; NO; WC; DL), then transfer to **DLR** and exit at **Cutty Sark for Maritme Greenwich**. Turn L out of the station into Creek Road, then R into Greenwich Church Street, L into Nelson Road, then R into King William Walk, which leads to the Park and the Observatory. **Hours:** Every day, from 10 am to 5 pm (last admission 4:30 pm)

The MacGuffin: In the summer of 1948, during a delay in the production of *Under Capricorn*, star Ingrid Bergman accompanied Ann Todd (*The Paradine Case*) on a number of sightseeing excursions around London, including visits to Kew Gardens and the Greenwich Observatory.

32:2
R Division, Metropolitan Police, et al. (F)
10 Blackheath Road, SE10

In Victorian days, the Metropolitan Police Service comprised 23 Divisions in Greater London, including the R, or Greenwich, Division in Blackheath Road. This would have been the "Blackheath Police Station" that dispatched Sgt. Balter to aid retired **Scotland Yard** inspector Brent in "Banquo's Chair." The exact location of Major Cooke-Finch's home ("Blackheath, near London") is not specified, although Shooters Hill Road, with its handsome Victorian houses, would be a safe guess. In fact, Shooters Hill Road is actually a continuation, via Blackheath Hill, of Blackheath Road itself. (For the literary locale—leased not by the major, but rather by Brent himself—see **Miss Fergusson's Home**.) Blackheath also has another Hitchcock connection, apart from its "appearance" in "Banquo's Chair." In 1870, French composer Charles François Gounod stayed at No. 15 Morden Road, Blackheath, and Gounod, as every reader of this book should know, composed "Funeral March of a Marionette," which was adapted as the theme for *Alfred Hitchcock Presents* and *The Alfred Hitchcock Hour*. Gounod actually wrote the piece as a piano solo and published it in London under its English title in 1872. He published an orchestral arrangement under the title *Marche funèbre d'une marionette* in 1879.

Charles François Gounod

Station: Deptford Bridge (DLR) Exit into Blackheath Road and look for the station—now a magistrates' court—ahead on the L. The present Greenwich Police Station is located at 31 Royal Hill, Greenwich.

Ask Mr. Memory 42: Which Hitchcock film cameo is accompanied by strains of the TV show theme?

A REFERENCE GUIDE TO LOCATIONS

33. HAMMERSMITH

33:1
Olympia F (L)
Hammersmith Road, W6

Founded as the National Agriculture Hall in 1884, this large exhibition center went on to host some of Britain's most popular car, horse, dog and home shows, not to mention the famous "Paris Hippodrome," a circus spectacular featuring 400 animals, a chariot race, and a stag hunt. Although never stated in the film itself, the shooting script for *Murder!* reveals that it was here at Olympia that murderer Handel Fane performed his last act, at least in this world. (Note that the character's name is spelled "Handel" in the opening credits, but "Handell" in Sir John's notebook and in the source novel.) In fact, the script calls for an exterior establishing shot of Olympia, as well as a sign announcing "Claudette, the Mystery Woman, the Woman Trapeze Artist." (The sign goes on to boast: "Something you have never seen before. Something you may never see again.") Neither made it to the finished film, which cuts directly to the backstage area of the circus.

It is also to see the circus here at Olympia that Erica Burgoyne invites Inspector Grant at the conclusion of *A Shilling for Candles*, whence *Young and Innocent*. The inspector, renamed Kent in the film, accepts her invitation, suggesting that something of a romantic nature might develop between them. In the film, of course, the inspector is denied his chance for romance as Erica only has eyes for Robert. The hall is also mentioned in the play *Rebecca*, when Beatrice and Maxim argue about the weight of their respective horses, Maxim refers to that "half starved…idiot mare" of hers, and Beatrice snaps back that the "'idiot mare' won a first at Olympia last year." This exchange almost exactly replicates one in the novel, except the pair are arguing about weight of their dogs, with Beatrice maintaining that Jasper is too fat, Maxim disparaging her half-starved half-wit Lion, and Beatrice snapping back that "Lion won two firsts

Olympia

at Crufts' last February." The referents are, respectively, the International Horse Show, which began at Olympia in 1907, and the famous Crufts Dog Show, which began at the Royal Agricultural Hall, Islington, in 1891, transferred to Olympia in 1948, and is today held at the National Exhibition Centre in Birmingham. The only remnant of the "weighty" exchange in the film comes *after* Beatrice and Giles' visit, when Maxim and Mrs. de Winter go for a walk and Maxim orders, "Come on, Jasper! Come and take some of that fat off."

Station: Kensington (Olympia) (DI) Follow the signs to Olympia.

34. HAMPSTEAD

34:1
"The Gill Home" F
11 Church Row, NW3

In the novel *Man Running*, amateur sleuth Eve Gill stayed with her Aunt Florence in Thurloe Square (see entry 22:5). In Hitchcock's version of the story, retitled *Stage Fright*, Eve stays at her mother's Georgian home in Westminster (according to the script), more specifically (according to Hitchcock's instructions to production supervisor Fred Ahern) in the vicinity of Smith Square, which was also home to *Foreign Correspondent* villain Stephen Fisher (see 25:18). This way, Eve could conveniently meet Ordinary Smith in nearby Parliament Square for their romantic taxi ride to the **Roehampton Club**. In the end, though, Hitchcock's crew came up with a charming Georgian home for the Gill family in tony Hampstead, some five miles north of Smith Square. And, as with the Parliament Square sequence, Miss Wyman was again doubled on location. In fact, production documents indicate a mild disagreement on this point between Hitchcock and Ahern. The production supervisor felt that the brief scene in which Eve and her

Gill Home as shown in *Stage Fright*

father walk home from the theatre (after her faked fainting spell) should be filmed with the actors on location. Hitchcock insisted that it be done on a treadmill in the studio in front of a rear-projection screen because it was a "very important little scene" and there would be "difficulty with the acting of it on an exterior." The scene was duly shot on an **Elstree** soundstage, although there isn't much in the present version to suggest the importance Hitchcock originally attached to it. There is, however, a "mistake" in this sequence: The houses behind Eve and the commodore are in fact those from across the street, not those adjacent to Mrs. Gill's home, as the shots suggest.

Alastair Sim and Jane Wyman in *Stage Fright*

Station: Hampstead (NO) Exit the station straight into Heath Street and follow this to Church Row, where you will turn R. The house is ahead on the R, just before Holly Walk. Note that the view of Ordinary Smith walking away from Eve (toward the church) is actually from several doors to the R of No. 11. In other words, having taken leave of Miss Gill at No. 11, Smith is then shown approaching that very house. For the real-life home of actress Sybil Thorndike (Mrs. Gill), see **Peter Hewitt's Studio**.

Ask Mr. Memory 43: As you leave Church Row and enter Heath Street, look to the right. Heath Street becomes Fitzjohn's Avenue, toward the bottom of which is the street and district of Belsize Park. Which Hitchcock villain once lived in Belsize Park?

35. HIGHBURY

35:1
Arsenal Football Club (F)
Highbury Stadium
Avenell Road, N5

One of London's most famous football (i.e., soccer) teams, Arsenal was formed in 1886 and turned professional five years later. The club is mentioned during the meeting of the conspirators in Verloc's flat in *Sabotage*. One of the men, Michaelis (Torin Thatcher), notices an eavesdropper at the window (Ted) and abruptly shifts from talk of the upcoming terrorist plot to a more harmless topic: "Of course, if the Arsenal lose to Birmingham on Saturday I shan't be so pleased." "Pardon?" Verloc interjects, "I don't follow." "No, no, I know you don't follow Arsenal, but they're a good bet, believe me." And indeed they were, having won the 1st division League Championship title in 1931,

'33, '34 and '35. Arsenal, based here in Avenell Road since 1913, is scheduled to move to a new purpose-built stadium in nearby Ashburton Grove in 2006.

Station: Arsenal (PI) Follow the directions to the stadium.

36. HIGHGATE

36:1
ex **George Joseph Smith's Home   C (F)**
14 Waterlow Road (*formerly*** Bismarck Road), N19**

Here, on the night of December 15, 1914, Mr. John Lloyd returned to his top floor flat at No. 14 to find his new wife, Margaret, dead in the bathtub. A local doctor attested to Mrs. Lloyd's "dizzy spells," a verdict of "accidental death" by drowning was recorded and the dead woman was duly buried by her grieving husband. Oddly, though, the very same thing had happened to Mr. Lloyd's previous wife, Alice, as police soon learned from a member of the woman's family. Needless to say, the odds against such a coincidence were pretty large, so the police began a thorough investigation of Mr. Lloyd. In short order they learned that Lloyd's real name was George Joseph Smith, that he was a bigamist and a swindler, and that yet another of his wives had "accidentally" drowned in the bathtub. (Shades—or, rather, foreshadows—of C.A. Swann in *Dial M for Murder*.) Quickly dubbed the "Brides-in-the-Bath" murderer, Smith was arrested on February 1, 1915, charged at **Bow Street Court**, tried and executed for the murders of the three women. (The prosecution even demonstrated how Smith likely committed the crimes by pulling his victims' legs up out of the water as they lay in the bath.)

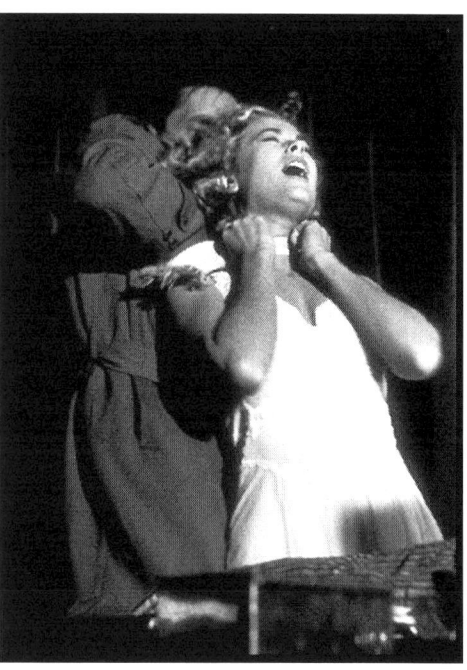

Anthony Dawson and Grace Kelly in *Dial M for Murder*

Hitchcock—ever the true crime buff—briefly invokes the sensational case in *Shadow of a Doubt* (during one of Joe and Herb's ongoing dialogues on the perfect murder) and, more significantly, in the sound version of *Blackmail*, during the scene in which the nosy neighbor chats with Mr. White about the knife murder. At first she cannot recall the killer's name (although eventually she does), but that doesn't stop her from going on about it. "Pushed 'is lady friends under the water when they was 'avin' a bath," she explains. "I think that was ever so beastly. Fair gave me the shivers. After I read about it I didn't dare have a bath for a month. And for weeks after that I only used to have a rinse down." And so we have a humorous contrast to and diversion from the more serious business at hand—a typical Hitchcock scene. (Cf. a remarkably similar scene, right down to the reference to a recent serial killer, in *Frenzy*, at the **Nell of Old Drury** pub.) Today, of course, the scene seems not just apt, but prophetic. After all, who scared a generation of moviegoers out of taking a shower?

Station: Archway (NO) Exit L into Holloway Road/Highgate Hill and look for Waterlow Road—its name was changed from Bismarck Road during WWI—ahead on the R.

37. HOLLOWAY

37:1
HM Prison Holloway C L F
Parkhurst Road, N7

The largest women's prison in Europe, Holloway was opened in 1852 and for the next 50 years accommodated both male and female prisoners. In 1903, the Victorian Gothic prison (partly modeled on the famous Warwick Castle in central England) was reconstituted as a women's facility, which it remains. Holloway has hosted a number of famous prisoners, including suffragette Sylvia Pankhurst, IRA supporter Roisin McAliskey and murderers Edith Thompson (see **Madame Tussaud's**) and Ruth Ellis, the latter—hanged here on July 13, 1955—being the last woman executed in Britain. Novelist Somerset Maugham invokes the foreboding prison in Chapter 7 of *Ashenden*, in which Secret Service Chief R. tells the title character about the arrest and imprisonment of an Italian spy named Giulia Lazzari, a dancer-cum-prostitute who may lead him to bigger fish. "Holloway's not a very cheerful place," R. notes with a rather sinister smile. "I imagine no prison is," deadpans the laconic Ashenden. After leaving her "to stew in her own juice for a week," R. frightens the woman into luring her lover—a powerful enemy agent—into a trap on the Continent, a trap to be sprung by Ashenden himself. Nothing of this scene makes it to Hitchcock's adaptation, *Secret Agent*, which was also set against a World War I backdrop. Hitchcock did make it to Holloway Prison, though, in 1946, for the scenes in which *Paradine Case* barrister Anthony Keane visits his beautiful client, Maddalena Paradine. The initial shot of the prison originally began in the street—Camden Road—as Keane's car approached the prison entrance. Hitchcock assigned this shot (and all other English footage) to his second unit, specifying that the prison gates should be open quickly enough to permit the car to

In *The Paradine Case*, Keane (Gregory Peck) visits his beautiful client Maddalena (Alida Valli).

enter the prison without having to stop outside the gate. In the end, apparently, things didn't move quite quickly enough and the shot was trimmed to its present form, which shows the car already inside the prison compound. Prison interiors, though filmed in Hollywood, were faithful recreations of the originals. (Precisely why a studio insert shot of the prison sign actually omits the name of the facility is unclear; that the prison is meant to be Holloway is clear from both the final shooting script (scene 37) and also from the film itself, when Keane tells his taxi driver to take him to Holloway Prison; (see **Euston Station**). The prison is also mentioned (but not shown) in *Stage Fright* when the Commodore warns Eve that if she tries to implicate Charlotte Inwood in the death of the latter's husband, she'll probably be tried at the **Old Bailey** and, if she's lucky, "might get off with a couple of years, which you will spend in Holloway Prison." Holloway also seems to have been the model for "H.M. Prison Melhurst," where Diana Baring awaits her execution in *Murder!* Unfortunately for Hitchcock buffs (not to mention those who actually reside here), reform-minded officials deemed the original prison too "grim" for women and so completely demolished it in the early 1970s. The replacement, a controversial, hospital-style facility where the inmates were treated not as prisoners, but as patients ("rehabilitation with a feminine touch"), opened in 1977 (but was not actually completed until 1985).

Station: Caledonian Road (Pl) Exit into Caledonian Road and turn L then L again into Hillmarton Road. The prison is straight ahead, in Parkhurst Road.

37:2
ex **Dr. Hawley Crippen's Home C (F)**
39 Hilldrop Crescent, N7

During the opening Music Hall sequence of *The 39 Steps*, a member of the audience challenges Mr. Memory with the question: "When was Crippen hanged?" In this way, Alfred Hitchcock introduces us to one of the most sensational murderers in British history and, indeed, to one of his own favorite real-life crime cases. The murderer was Hawley Harvey Crippen, a mild-mannered physician who had fallen on rather hard times; the victim was his unfaithful wife, Belle, a musical performer of questionable talent and profligate ways. Sometime during the early morning hours of February 1, 1910, Crippen first poisoned, then possibly shot and ultimately dismembered the woman who had been making his life miserable for years. Rather foolishly, Crippen then bestowed some of Belle's jewelry upon his

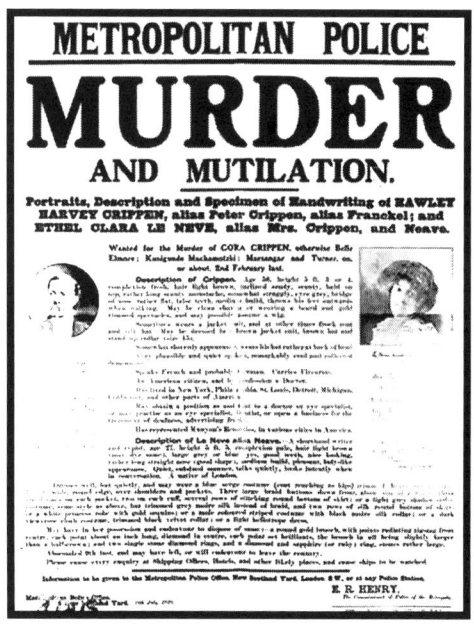

Wanted poster for Crippen

The Crippen case influenced *Rear Window,* starring Grace Kelly and Jimmy Stewart.

secretary—and mistress—Ethel LeNeve and actually moved Ethel into No. 39 itself, actions that naturally aroused the suspicions of his wife's friends—and the police. Crippen initially claimed that his wife had died in America, then, later "admitted" to the police that she had taken up residence there with an old lover. Chief Inspector Walter Dew of **Scotland Yard** was satisfied with the cuckolded husband story, but did insist that newspaper ads be run to try to locate Belle. (For more on Dew, see entry 58:2.) Knowing that the jig would soon be up, Crippen hauled Ethel (who was apparently unaware of Belle's true fate) off to **Liverpool Street Station**, where they boarded a train for Harwich (as the protagonists would do in *Number Seventeen*) on July 9. From Harwich they crossed to Antwerp and there—posing as "Mr. Robinson" and his "son"—boarded a ship, the *Montrose,* bound for Canada. When Dew learned of Crippen's disappearance, he instituted an immediate search of the house and, there, in the cellar, unearthed the de-boned torso of the late Belle Crippen. (Crippen had apparently dropped the rest of her—head and limbs—into the nearby canal.) An abdominal scar and a lock of hair wrapped around a curler provided the positive identification. (The curler is now displayed in Scotland Yard's famous Black Museum.) The press was immediately alerted of the find and the likely perpetrators. Fortunately, the captain of the ship, Henry Kendall, saw the newspaper photos and quickly recognized "the Robinsons" for who they really were. Captain Kendall wired his company's office in Liverpool and the company, in turn, made Kendall's observations known to Scotland Yard. Dew was duly informed and immediately secured passage on another ship bound for Canada; the press—and the world—awaited the outcome of the thrilling "sea race" across the Atlantic. In the end, as in the best pulp fiction, Dew's ship was faster: Crippen was arrested upon his arrival in Father Point, Quebec, and promptly shipped back to England. He was tried (sensationally, of course) at the **Old Bailey** and hanged at **Pentonville Prison** on November 23, 1910 (a date never actually revealed in *The 39 Steps*); Ethel was acquitted of being an accessory after the fact.

Hitchcock the true crime buff was, of course, fascinated with the Crippen case, relating a detailed version of the above story to Truffaut and explaining how it influenced the plot of *Rear Window*, where the late, dismembered wife's jewelry is also a clue to her fate. (He might also have mentioned *Vertigo*, in which Elster's bestowal of his late wife's jewelry upon Judy also gives the game away.) A further detail from the film—nosy neighbors engaged in "rear-window spying"—derives from the Cornell Woolrich short story *Rear Window*, but also from Crippen's life here at No. 39. Hitchcock may have also been thinking of the Crippen case in *Foreign Correspondent*, where authorities radio ahead to have the villain arrested upon his arrival in America; and in *Frenzy*, when Bob Rusk poses as "Mr. Robinson"—a detail absent from the source novel. (In fact, screenwriter Anthony Shaffer had visited Crippen territory in his 1953 short story "Larger than Life," in which a man's neighbors write to police about the strange disappearance of the wife, who is supposedly on holiday but is in fact buried behind the fireplace.) Hitchcock was clearly thinking of the case in *Stage Fright*, wherein the Commodore cheekily (and, as it turns out, prophetically) refers to Cooper as Crippen and Cooper himself uses the alias "Robinson" during his visit to the **Gill Home**. Aspects of the Crippen case also inspired two of the short stories the director adapted for *Alfred Hitchcock Presents*: John Collier's "Back for Christmas" and Arthur Williams' "Being a Murderer Myself." In the former, a doctor murders his wife, dismembers her body, buries it in the basement and then sets sail for America to be with his mistress. And like Crippen, the doctor (who becomes a metallurgist in the teleplay) is ultimately undone. In the second story, the title character decides that the best way to bring things to a climax between himself and the policemen who suspect him of murder "was to make Crippen's mistake, and run away." In Hitchcock's version, retitled "Arthur," this line was amended to: "was to appear to make Crippen's mistake, and run away," thus clarifying the narrator's true intent. ("Arthur" also recalls elements of the Norman Thorne case, for which see **Elsie Cameron's Home**.) Finally, the idea of a milquetoast doctor murdering his overbearing wife in order to be with his young girlfriend formed the basis of Francis Iles' 1931 classic *Malice Aforethought*, which Hitchcock long sought to film. (He filmed Iles' *Before the Fact* as *Suspicion* in 1941). In fact, Hitchcock adapted *Malice* for the radio in 1945, with Hume Cronyn as the mild murderer. As he explained to Truffaut, the radio play never aired and were he to have translated the story to film, a better choice than Cronyn would have been…Alec Guinness.

Station: Caledonian Road (Pl) Exit into Caledonian Road and turn L then L again into Hillmarton Road. At Camden Road turn L and look for Hilldrop Road, just ahead and across the street. This leads to Hilldrop Crescent, where you will again turn L. Crippen's three-story brick townhouse was destroyed during World War II but the neighboring buildings give something of the flavor of No. 39.

The MacGuffin: The poison Crippen administered to his wife—hyoscine—was commonly used in minute doses to calm violent mental patients—a use to which it is actually put in Francis Beeding's novel *The House of Dr. Edwardes*, whence *Spellbound*. Interestingly, celebrated British barrister Sir Edward Marshall Hall, the inspiration for Sir Malcolm Keane of the novel *The Paradine Case*, turned down the job of defending Crippen because the man had been "wrongly" charged with murder. Marshall Hall is said to have believed that Crippen simply administered the hyoscine as a "sexual depressant."

Ask Mr. Memory 44: Another ridiculously easy one: The captain of the *Montrose* shares his name with the star of a Hitchcock film. Name the film.

The McKennas arrive at Heathrow in *The Man Who Knew Too Much*.

38. HOUNSLOW

38:1
London (Heathrow) Airport F
Hounslow, TW6

Europe's busiest airport (and the fifth largest in the world) replaced **Croydon** as "London's airport" in 1946. Indeed, the new facility was then called simply "London Airport." Heathrow, the name of the ancient Iron Age settlement on this site, was adopted in the 1960s, after the opening of London's second major airport at Gatwick. Alfred Hitchcock determined to set the scene of Jo's arrival here for the second *The Man Who Knew Too Much*, even though airport officials were less than enthused about the prospect. They were then in the midst of a massive construction project (prior to this, London's airport accommodated passengers in an army surplus tent!) and the presence of a film crew headed by Alfred Hitchcock and featuring prominent movie stars would be a most unwelcome distraction. In the end, though, the director got his way, securing permission from the **Air Ministry** to shoot at the BEA Maintenance Depot, Staines Road, at the far side of the airport. Filming took place on June 12, 1955, when Hitchcock recorded the McKennas alighting from a Vickers Viscount, the crowd of cheering extras and onlookers, and Ben and Jo meeting the CID inspector and entering the administration building. Close-ups of the principals, as well as administration building interiors and Edna's telephone call, were filmed in Hollywood in late July. A second unit returned to Heathrow on June 26 to shoot background plates for the call box scene. Hitchcock had also planned to shoot *Short Night* hero Joe Bailey's arrival by Concorde here at Heathrow in 1978 or '79, but, sadly, it was not to be.

Station: Heathrow Terminal 1 (PI)

Ask Mr. Memory 45: Prior to June 1955, *The Man Who Knew Too Much* actually had a different working title. What was it?

39. HOXTON

39:1
ex **Islington/Gainsborough Studios F**
Poole Street, N1

Founded as the London base of Famous Players-Lasky Corporation/Company (the American parent of Paramount Pictures) in 1919, this former railway power station boasts the distinction of having been the very first film studio to employ Alfred Hitchcock. As the director told François Truffaut in the 1960s, "I started out, in 1921 [*sic*, for 1920], in an American studio that happened to be located in London and never set foot in a British studio until 1927." Indeed, as a student of American film technique, it never occurred to Hitchcock to seek employment at a British studio. He regarded American films as "truly professional" and "in advance" of those of other countries, especially his own. Thus, when he read that Famous Players-Lasky was opening a studio in London, he decided that he wanted to design title cards for the company. And that is precisely what he did. Here, as Tom Ryall notes, Hitchcock had "the opportunity to learn from American methods of production" and to work with "the latest American cinema technology and equipment." Hitchcock soon rose through the ranks, becoming head of the title department, then art director, screenwriter, and, by 1923, assistant director. Producer Michael Balcon gave Hitchcock his first real directing opportunity in 1925, Balcon's Gainsborough Pictures having bought the studio from Famous Players the year before. The film was *The Pleasure Garden*, based on Oliver Sandys' 1922 novel, and it was to be filmed on location in Europe and at the Emelka Studios in Munich.

Site of Islington/Gainsborough Studios

The Lady Vanishes, **with Paul Lukas and Mary Clare, was filmed entirely at the Gainsborough Studios.**

Hitchcock followed this up with another German-based production, *The Mountain Eagle* (of which no known print survives), and then, in 1926, the first "true Hitchcock film," *The Lodger*, which was shot here in Islington and on location in London. His next two pictures, *Downhill* and *Easy Virtue*, were also filmed here at the Gainsborough Studios, as well as on location in London and neighboring counties. Both were also adapted from popular stage plays, a practice that Balcon later repudiated. (In his autobiography he claimed that it was wrong for filmmakers to try to "bask in the reflected glory of people like Noël Coward," especially in the silent era since such films "deprived [the plays] of their very essence, the words.") By this time, Hitchcock had earned a reputation as one of Britain's finest directors and other studios duly came calling. The director opted for John Maxwell's British International Pictures at **Elstree Studios**, where he would go on to make 10 consecutive features, including Britain's "first talkie," *Blackmail*. Hitchcock returned to Islington in the autumn of 1937 to supervise the editing of *Young and Innocent* (a cheaper prospect here than at **Pinewood Studios**, where the film had actually been shot), after which he began work on *The Lady Vanishes*, his penultimate film before moving to America in 1939. Director Val Guest occupied the office next to Hitchcock's and recalled his colleague's famous "sadistic" humor: "He truly did call his actors cattle and he would bang a little gong, which meant that the 'cattle' had to move [to their places]. But the actors knew that it was all done with tongue in cheek." Guest also recalled another example of the Hitchcock humor, involving actress Linden Travers, who played "Mrs. Todhunter." "One day on the set, she asked Hitchcock which did he think was her best side and he replied: 'You're sitting on it.' That's the sort of humor he always had. Sadistic, yes, but also funny." Unfortunately, the fun stopped within a year of Hitchcock's departure. Islington/Gainsborough was closed for most of the War, reopened for a brief resurgence, then shut down for good in 1949. In the half century since, the building has been used as a warehouse, a theatre and even, briefly, a film studio, when director Guy Ritchie helmed the boxing scenes for *Snatch* here. In August 1999, Islington was the setting for a celebration honoring Hitchcock's centenary, with Patricia Hitchcock herself in attendance. In an interview at the time, the director's daughter recalled that the English film she remembered best was *The Lady Vanishes*, which was filmed almost entirely within the walls of the studio. Sadly, although the main building survives, the interior has been converted into luxury apartments, obliterating the stages that Hitchcock first called home.

Station: Old Street (NO) Exit into East Road and follow this N into New North Road; look for Poole Street—and the new "Gainsborough Studios," i.e., the apartments—ahead to the R.

40. ISLINGTON

40:1
"A.F. Chatman Bird Shop" F
465 Liverpool Road, N1

This was the address of the bird shop to which Verloc came for his bomb in *Sabotage*. The exterior does not suggest anything in the actual locale and was apparently filmed at **Lime Grove Studios**.

Station: Highbury & Islington (VI) Exit into Highbury Station Road, which leads to Liverpool Road, where you will turn R; 465 is ahead to the L.

40:2
Chapel Market F
N1

Designated an official street market (one of London's first) in the 1870s, Chapel Market (originally Chapel Street) remains a lively, thriving throwback to an earlier time. Hitchcock incorporates a high-angle establishing shot—probably stock footage—of the famous market near the start of Stevie's final journey in *Sabotage*. The bit where Stevie is pressed into a demonstration of "Salvodont" toothpaste was actually shot at **Lime Grove Studios**. Note that Chapel Street is miles away from the Camberwell district where Stevie theoretically began his journey (see **Bijou Cinema**) and well removed from the direct route to **Piccadilly Circus**. For more on this, see **Stevie's Final Journey**.

A REFERENCE GUIDE TO LOCATIONS

Chapel Market

Station: Angel (NO) Exit into Upper Street, veer L into Liverpool Road and immediately L into the Market. The 70-plus stalls (fruits and vegetables, household goods, shoes, clothing, linens, flowers, electrical goods, luggage, etc.) are open every day except Monday.

41. KENNINGTON

41:1
"The Markham Home" F
10 Primer Road, SW9

According to their ad in the April 24, 1930 issue of *The Stage*, Ted and Doucie Markham, the actors Sir John hires to trap the killer in *Murder!*, live at "10, Primer Road [*sic*], Stockwell, SW9." Southern English pronunciation being what it is, there was apparently a miscommunication between the director and the art department, with the correct form "Prima" being heard and spelled as "Primer." In the novel *Enter Sir John*, the Markhams live at 12 Ladbroke Grove, Notting Hill, an address slightly modified to 28 Ladbroke Grove in the script of March 5, 1930.

Station: Oval (NO) Tiny Prima Road is adjacent to/opposite the station, just off Clapham Road.

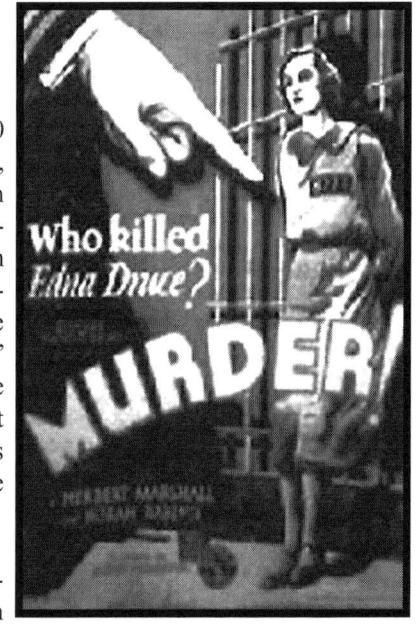

42. KENSAL GREEN

42:1
ex **Elsie Cameron's Home C P**
86 Clifford Gardens, NW10

This was the home of a young woman unfortunate enough to fall in love with one Norman Holmes Thorne—engineer, entrepreneur and eventual murderer. Elsie was a shy, rather neurotic 22-year-old typist (in appearance not unlike *Frenzy* star Anna Massey), when she met Thorne, aged 18, at the nearby Kensal Rise Wesleyan Church in 1920. The two began a courtship and eventually became lovers. When Elsie discovered that she was pregnant, she not unnaturally assumed that Norman would marry her. Norman, however, had other plans. After losing his engineering job, he had borrowed £100 from his father and acquired a field in Blackness, Crowborough, Sussex. There he set himself up as—what else?—a chicken farmer. The business was not quite the rousing success Norman had hoped but, more to the point, he had since met someone else—a fun-loving dressmaker named Bessie Coldicott. So, when Elsie showed up in Crowborough on Friday, December 5, 1924, to demand marriage or else, Norman decided to terminate the relationship…for good. The young woman was soon reported missing by her father, prompting a visit to Norman's farm by the local police. Cool as a cucumber under questioning, Norman simply explained that Elsie had never arrived. **Scotland Yard** stepped in next, searched the farm and, lo and behold, found a case and several small items belonging to Elsie Cameron. Norman, still as nonchalant as a chicken on its way to the chopping block, adjusted his story accordingly. Elsie *had* arrived at the farm, he had told her of his plans to marry another woman, and had then gone off to meet that woman at the train station. While he was away, the despondent bride-not-to-be found some rope and hanged herself from the beam of his shed. Unsure what to do upon discovering the body, Norman ultimately decided to dismember poor Elsie and bury the pieces under the chicken run—at a spot, indeed, where the police had earlier photographed him! If all this sounds a bit familiar (and it should), that is because the story of chicken farmer-cum-murderer Norman Thorne bears more than a passing resemblance to that of the title character in Hitchcock's teleplay "Arthur." The source story, "Being a Murderer Myself," was written by "Arthur Williams," the pen name of South African writer Peter Barry Way, as well as the name of the title character. (Note that the teleplay was transposed from South Africa to New Zealand.) Whether Mr. Way knew of Mr. Thorne is uncertain, but Alfred Hitchcock certainly did. Thorne's case was among those enshrined in his cherished "Famous Trials" series,[7] along with that of Hawley Harvey Crippen, whose tale most assuredly influenced both Williams and Hitchcock. (See **Dr. Hawley Crippen's Home** for more on the man and his murder.) And the results of his trial were pretty predictable: there being no evidence whatever that Elsie had hung herself, the Lewes Assizes jury found Norman guilty of murder on April 16, 1925. Six days later, Norman Thorne was hanged at Wandsworth Prison, ironically, the 27th birthday of Elsie Cameron.

Station: Kensal Green (BA) Exit for College Road and follow this to Clifford Gardens, ahead on the R.

43. LEYTONSTONE

43:1
Alfred Hitchcock's Birthplace H
517 The High Road, E11

Alfred Joseph Hitchcock was born here, above his family's greengrocer's shop, on August 13, 1899. Hitchcock's parents, William and Emma, already had two other children, William, age nine, and Ellen (Nellie), nearly seven. Young Alfred often rode on his father's horse cart when William delivered goods to his customers, including merchants in **Covent Garden**. (Fittingly, director Hitchcock would incorporate a horse and cart in *Stage Fright* [see **Jonathan Cooper's Flat**] and the famous market in *Frenzy*.) William had been Church of England, but young Alfred would be raised in his mother's Roman Catholic faith, attending her old church, **St. Francis**, in Stratford. The site is today occupied by a Jet petrol station; a plaque, erected by the Waltham Forest Heritage Commission, reminds us that "The famous film director was born near this site at 517 High Road Leytonstone on August 13th, 1899." From here, the family moved down the River Lea to Limehouse (see below).

Leytonstone Underground Station

Station: Leytonstone (CE) Take the Church Lane exit into the Leytonstone High Road, turn R and follow this to 517, on the R (the Jet petrol station). The main corridor of the station features 17 mosaic panels inspired by scenes from assorted Hitchcock films, including *The Skin Game* and *Suspicion*.

43:2
Sir Alfred Hitchcock Hotel H
147 Whipps Cross Road, E11

Opened on August 27, 1980, this combination pub/hotel/restaurant is also a shrine to the world's favorite director. Here you will find copies of Hitchcock's birth and marriage certificates, photos, posters and more. Not coincidentally, the hotel is also near the site of the Hitchcock family grocer's, where Alfred was born in 1899 (see above).

Alfred Hitchcock Hotel

Station: Leytonstone (CE) Take the Church Lane exit into the Leytonstone High Road, turn L and at the intersection, veer L into Whipps Cross Road. The pub is ahead to the L.

44. LIMEHOUSE

44:1
Alfred Hitchcock's Childhood Home H
175 Salmon Lane, E14

Successful greengrocer William Hitchcock moved his family from Leytonstone (see **Alfred Hitchcock's Birthplace**), where his youngest child Alfred had been born, south to Limehouse—the true East End of London—in 1907. Here, young Alfred would continue his education in nearby East India Dock Road, at the Howrah House Secondary School, a Catholic facility for both boys and girls run by the Sisters of the Faithful Companions of Jesus. William's thriving fish business was based here at No. 175, with the family living above the shop. His fried fish shop, opened a few years later, was located at No. 130. Alfred's next known move would be to Cromwell Road—as a newly married man (see entry 22:1).[8]

Station: Limehouse (DLR) Exit into Yorkshire Road and follow this to Salmon Lane. Howrah House, the late-19th-century mansion-cum-convent where Hitchcock went to school, stood at 83 East India Dock Road, just to the east of Salmon Lane. It was destroyed following heavy bomb damage during World War II. For Hitchcock's subsequent education, see **St. Ignatius College**.

45. LOWER HOLLOWAY

45:1
Copenhagen Tunnel F
N7

It's no secret that Alfred Hitchcock loved trains, nor that he featured them in a number of his films. Indeed, *The 39 Steps, The Lady Vanishes* and *North By Northwest* are not just classic films but also classic *train* films. Yet Hitchcock's first major cinematic train trip predates all these films, popping up at the climax of the comparatively obscure 1932 comic thriller *Number Seventeen*. The good guys and bad guys all scramble from a house—Number 17—in Anderson Road, Amhurst Park (see entry 54:1) to board an LNER (London North Eastern Railway) train bound for the Harwich ferry some 70 miles away. This route, which began at **Liverpool Street Station**, is confirmed by posters showing the train ferry at Harwich, as well as the Green Line bus's destination of "Brentwood," through which the train passed on the way to Harwich (see

Copenhagen Tunnel

A REFERENCE GUIDE TO LOCATIONS   251

The climax of Number Seventeen takes place on a train.

Charing Cross Station for more on Barton and the bus). Instead of the Great Eastern Line, however, Hitchcock actually shot his chase on the Great *Northern* line between **King's Cross Station** and Hertford, some 20 miles to the north. Thus, when the baddies first run out onto the tracks, the view is looking south from Copenhagen Tunnel. Shortly thereafter Barton tries to board the train as it enters the tunnel but is kicked off by one of the baddies. The action continues on the actual line, as well as in **Elstree Studios**, with both full-scale train cars and miniatures pressed into service. Later, the train is shown passing over the A119 at Hertford in the famous Hertford Loop. The final smash-up theoretically takes place at Harwich, but was of course done with miniatures at the studio.

Station: King's Cross St. Pancras (CI; HC; ME; NO; PI; VI; NR; Thameslink) Exit into York Way, catch a No. 10 bus, sit on the R side and watch for Copenhagen Street. Just past this, again, to the R, you will be able to see the tunnel and train yard where Hitchcock filmed. Unfortunately, there isn't a particularly good spot at street level from which to view or photograph the site.

The MacGuffin: Ealing comedy fans probably already know that Mrs. Wilberforce's home in the 1955 classic *The Ladykillers* was perched atop the southern end of Copenhagen Tunnel.

45:2

HM Prison Pentonville C L (F)
Caledonian Road, N7

HM Prison Pentonville

Built as a "model prison" in 1840-42, Pentonville became Richard Blamey's less-than-permanent home near the conclusion of the novel *Goodbye Piccadilly, Farewell Leicester Square*. Hitchcock, too, had initially intended to sentence Blaney, as he was now called, to Pentonville Prison in *Frenzy*, but in the end, permission was secured to film outside **Wormwood Scrubs** instead.

Pentonville is also where suspected murderer Jonathan Penrose spends the final portion of *Man Running* (whence *Stage Fright*), his friend Eve having turned him over to the police to protect him from the real killer. In Hitchcock's version, of course, Jonathan himself turns out to be the murderer.

Station: Caledonian Road (PI) Exit R into Caledonian Road; the prison is ahead on the L.

46. NEW CROSS

46:1
Goldsmiths College, University of London H
New Cross, SE14

During his tenure at **Henley's**, Hitchcock enrolled here at Goldsmiths College, a branch of the **University of London** famous for its classes in creative and performing arts. According to biographer Patrick McGilligan, the future director took art courses in which he "studied illustration and composition." His instructors also dispatched him to railway stations to sketch people in "various attitudes." This would be the last formal education that Hitchcock would receive.

Station: New Cross (EL) Exit here and follow the signs to the college. Note that Biographer Donald Spoto suggests that Hitchcock also took classes in electricity, drafting, mechanics and navigation at the University of London. However, as the director himself told Truffaut, these classes were taken at the London County Council School of Engineering and Navigation in Poplar High Street.

47. NORTH KENSINGTON

47:1
"Gavin Brand's Safe House" C (F) P
15 Highlever Road, SW10

This was the address of the small flat to which Soviet mole Gavin Brand fled in the opening of *The Short Night*, Alfred Hitchcock's final film project (see Appendix III). Here, according to the published screenplay, a sympathetic doctor (a member of the IRA) treats Brand's broken wrist, an injury sustained during his escape from nearby **Wormwood Scrubs**. Brand was modeled upon real-life double agent George Blake, who escaped from the Scrubs on October 22, 1966, did, indeed, break his wrist while doing so, and was, in fact, treated by a sympathetic doctor. (See **ex HQ of MI6** for more on Blake.) And Blake's accomplice, former fellow prisoner Sean Bourke ("Brennan" in the script), did stash him here in Highlever Road, although farther up, at No. 28. In his account of *The Springing of George Blake*, Bourke recalled the difficulty he and his accomplices (convicted peace activists Patrick Pottle and Michael Randle) had had in trying to lease "a good-quality flat" without proper references. "[I]t was easier for an ex-convict to break a spy out of jail than to acquire a reference," Bourke lamented, so the

Gavin Brand's safe house

trio had to settle for a more modest accommodation in which to hide their distinguished guest. This they finally found in Highlever Road, "virtually round the corner from...the prison." After three days at No. 28, Bourke and the others moved Blake first to one flat, then another (including one very near Hitchcock's old Cromwell Road home [see entry 22:1]!), before Randle and his family smuggled him to the Continent and thence to Berlin in a camping van in December. Bourke himself continued on and off at No. 28 until he joined Blake in Moscow in January 1967. Hitchcock, as part of his *Wrong Man*-style documentation of real-life locations, also planned to replicate the short car ride down Du Cane Road to Oxford Gardens, from which Blake and Bourke walked to the flat in Highlever Road. (Freeman's screenplay has the directions a bit muddled and describes Oxford Gardens as "Oxford Road"; the actual route from the prison is: left into Du Cane Road, left into Wood Lane, right into North Pole Road, right into Latimer Road, left into Oxford Gardens and then immediately left into Highlever Road.) This sequence, according to production designer Bob Boyle, would have been filmed by a second unit and would have probably included long shots of the car in transit, POV shots and footage for rear projection plates. Neither Bourke nor Blake (in his own version of the story, published in 1990) says anything about the escaped traitor strangling a young female acolyte here in Highlever Road—Hitchcock's first major departure from real-life events. (There was such an acolyte—Randle's wife, Anne—but while Blake clearly thought she was attractive, nothing suggests that he harmed her.) Hitchcock, as with Kirkbride before him, apparently wanted to dramatize the evil side of a man then believed responsible for the deaths of some 40 Western agents (see **MI6** for more on this). For Kirkbride, the assault came late in the story, in Finland, when Brand savagely rapes his unfaithful wife. Hitchcock cleansed the victim of her "sexual taint," but not her political one, for she greatly respects Brand and his service to the Communist Party. (This contrasts with Blake's real-life supporters, who were no fans of the Soviets.) He also "upgraded" the assault to murder and thrust it foursquare into the opening of the film, thus removing any doubt as to the kind of man he was dealing with—the kind of man who would betray Queen and Country.

Station: Latimer Road (HC) Exit R into Bramley Road, follow this under the motorway and turn L into Oxford Gardens and then R into Highlever Road. Both houses—15 to the L and 28 to the R—will be just ahead, near the bottom of the street.

The MacGuffin: Blake not only betrayed Queen and Country, but close friends, as well: He turned on Bourke once the two were safely ensconced in Moscow, suggesting that the KGB eliminate him if he did not agree to stay behind the Iron Curtain. Bourke was eventually returned to Ireland, where he wrote his account of the "springing." He died in January 1982, aged 47, of apparent alcohol poisoning. However, in the context of Bourke's early death, it should be noted that ex-KGB spymaster Oleg Kalugin has claimed that before he left Moscow, Bourke was given a drug to induce brain damage so that he would be unable to provide any useful intelligence to British authorities.

48. NOTTING HILL

48:1
ex **John Christie's Home C**
10 Rillington Place (*now* Ruston Mews), W11

Here, between 1943 and 1953, John Reginald Halliday Christie, a former postal worker and volunteer policeman, killed and concealed the bodies of at least six women, including his wife, Ethel. Three of the women were prostitutes; all except Ethel surrendered their sexual favors—*before, during or after death*. Christie was undone in March 1953 shortly after his departure from No. 10; his successor in the flat smelled something nasty in the kitchen, tore off the wallpaper and discovered three decomposing bodies in a concealed cupboard. Police were called in, the bodies removed (from the cupboard, as well as from the back garden and a space beneath the front room floor) and the manhunt begun. It didn't take long. Christie, broke and jobless, had simply wandered around London, sleeping on benches and in cinemas. He was spotted on Putney Embankment on March 31 and promptly arrested. He was tried at the **Old Bailey** in June and hanged the following month at **Pentonville Prison**, just as Hawley Harvey Crippen before him (see 37:2). Complicating the case is the fact that one of Christie's neighbors also claimed to have committed murders here at 10 Rillington Place. In November of 1949, Timothy Evans, a slow-witted truck driver, confessed to disposing of his wife's body in

Serial killer John Christie

the sewer drains below Rillington Place. The police searched the drains, as well as the house and garden of No. 10, but found no bodies. Reg Christie actually watched the proceedings, pausing momentarily to get rid of the skull that his dog had dug up in the back garden—all unobserved by the police! (Unlike *Rear Window*'s Thorwald, Christie did *not* kill the curious canine.) A subsequent search of the washhouse, however, uncovered the bodies of both Beryl Evans and the couple's baby daughter, Geraldine. Evans then confessed to killing his wife and child, but later recanted, claiming that Christie had committed both murders. Authorities didn't buy it and—with Christie as the chief prosecution witness—secured Evans' conviction on the charge of murdering his daughter; he was hanged on March 9, 1950. Crime buffs continue to debate whether Evans or Christie actually killed Beryl and the baby or whether one killed the mother and the other killed the daughter. The most likely scenario is that Christie killed and raped Beryl (after agreeing to perform an abortion), told Evans the abortion had failed and asked him to help dispose of the body (which prompted the younger man's initial "confession"); Christie then offered to turn the baby over to some friends, but instead simply killed it. The government officially resolved the matter in 1966 by issuing Evans a free pardon. (His sister filed a claim against the government for wrongful execution in May 2001.) The Christie case—in which a trusted man, friendly with the police, lured women back to his place for sex and strangulation—is thought to have been the inspiration for Arthur La Bern's serial killer in *Goodbye Piccadilly, Farewell Leicester Square*, whence *Frenzy*. (Another inspiration was apparently the murders committed by the sadist and ex-RAF officer Neville Heath in 1946. In addition, the film also recalls the "Jack the Stripper" murders of the mid-1960s, in which several of the victims' nude bodies were left in or near the **Thames**. Of course, Hitchcock's adaptation of *The Lodger*, in which the first onscreen victim is found along the river, is itself an obvious inspiration for *Frenzy*.) Hitchcock expounded on "that adorable Christie, a necrophiliac" in a number of interviews and explicitly acknowledged the killer in the scene set in the **Nell of Old Drury** pub. There, as Blaney sulks in his brandy, the doctor and lawyer discuss the Necktie murders and the lack of police progress in the case. The lawyer expresses the hope that the killer will slip up soon, but the doctor is not so sure: "In one way I hope he doesn't. Well, we haven't a good, juicy series of sex murders since Christie. And they're so good for the tourist trade." Indeed....

Station: Ladbroke Grove (HC) Go R out of the station into Ladbroke Grove then turn R into Lancaster Road. Follow this to St. Mark's Road, where you will turn R; Ruston Mews is ahead to the R. The house was at the end, on the L. The original Rillington Place was renamed Ruston *Close* shortly after Christie's execution. It was demolished in the 1970s and replaced with the present cul-de-sac, "quite unreminiscent" (as crime author Martin Fido notes) of the Christie-era setting.

The MacGuffin: Hitchcock actually planned to dramatize Neville Heath's story in a 1967 film called *Frenzy* (a.k.a. *Kaleidoscope*), which would have been transposed from London to New York. As is well known, scripts were written and test footage made but censorship problems forced the director to cancel the project. The title, of course, was saved for the 1972 film. And books on Heath—gifts from Hitchcock himself—were to serve as research material for actor Barry Foster.

49. ROEHAMPTON

49:1
Roehampton Club F
Roehampton Lane, SW15

To stage the *Easy Virtue* scene in which Larita and the Whittakers watch a polo match, Alfred Hitchcock approached a number of London-area racecourses. Each and every one of them turned him down flat. He then turned to the Roehampton Club, a prestigious sporting and leisure club founded in 1901. The Roehampton Club had generally been reluctant to permit filming on its grounds, but in this case they made an exception, providing "generous

Larita Filton (Isabel Jeans) is a woman of *Easy Virtue*. Hitchcock filmed a scene at the Roehampton Club.

assistance" as Hitchcock told the *Daily Mail* (June 8, 1927). And so on June 7, 1927, Hitchcock staged his polo match here, with actress Isabel Jeans and some 50 spectators in attendance. Two decades later, Hitchcock staged a return of sorts to the Roehampton Club, where the Theatrical Garden Party in *Stage Fright* takes place. As noted in the film, the Theatrical Garden Party was an annual charity event held to benefit the Actors Orphanage, of which Noël Coward was then president. During a preproduction discussion with production supervisor Fred Ahern, the director referred to this scene as "our *piece de resistance*," noting that the party had taken place at the Roehampton Club the year before and in **Regent's Park** years earlier, when Hitchcock himself had attended it. He went on to explain that the scene would be done in the rain because it would be fresher and more amusing than a garden party in the sunshine. He hoped to film an actual garden party, with real actors and, in order to secure permission from Coward, contemplated donating the film's London premiere proceeds to the charity. However, in shooting on location, he ran the risk—quite ironic in view of London's weather—that it might *not* rain during the party! One alternative was to bring a crowd of extras to the location the day *after* the party and *simulate* a rainy day in London with a combination of sprinklers and smoke pots (to black out the sun), as he had done for the assassination scene in *Foreign Correspondent*. Then again, he could simply stage the party at the studio and, in the end, using half an acre of real turf, that is exactly what he did. The Roehampton itself staged its last polo match in 1956 (the sport never really regained its foothold here following the war) and replaced the grounds—including the pavilion shown in *Easy Virtue*—with an expanded golf course.

Station: Waterloo (BA; JU; NO; WC; NR) Transfer to the National Rail at Waterloo Station and take this to Barnes; exit into Rocks Lane and follow this across Upper Richmond Road into Roehampton Lane. The club is on the R.

50. St. JOHN'S WOOD

50:1
"Lina Aysgarth's Home" L
Hamilton Terrace, NW8

Renowned as a haven for artists, authors, musicians and philosophers, this peaceful North London enclave was Lina Aysgarth's temporary home in Francis Iles' *Before the Fact* (whence *Suspicion*). In a plotline omitted from the film, Lina decides to leave her suspicion-inducing husband when she learns that he has slept with half the county and sired an illegitimate child to boot. (Only one?) At the beginning of Chapter 9, Lina has taken up residence with her sister Joyce, who lives in Hamilton Terrace, a terribly posh avenue lined with both terraced houses and imposing villas. While staying here, Lina dates a smashing young writer named Ronald Kirby, who desperately wants to marry her. After two months here in Hamilton Terrace (during which time she and Ronald dine at **Café Monico**), Lina is surprised to discover a chastened Johnnie on her doorstep. Against her better judgment, she rejects Ronald for Johnnie, with whom she is still tragically smitten. Feeling "that she was leaving nothing of herself in London," Lina returns to Dorset with Johnnie, where her husband and Beaky soon take up their real estate scheme, as in the film.

Station: Maida Vale (BA) Exit R into Elgin Avenue/Albercom Place; Hamilton Terrace is the third street ahead.

Ask Mr. Memory 46: A ridiculously easy one: What is Johnnie's nickname for Lina?

51. SHEPHERD'S BUSH

51:1
***ex* Lime Grove (Shepherd's Bush) Studios F**
Lime Grove, W12

Opened in 1915, the Gaumont–British Picture Corporation's Lime Grove facility was among the most important British film studios of the 1930s. Rebuilt at a cost of £500,000 (over £28,000,000 today) in 1932, the studio complex boasted five sound stages, three private theatres, dressing rooms for 600 artists and a restaurant designed to accommodate them all. Alfred Hitchcock first came to work here in 1933, when he was contracted to shoot the independent production *Waltzes from Vienna* for producer Tom Arnold. Hitchcock had recently completed a five-year stint for BIP head John Maxwell at **Elstree Studios** and was at a decidedly loose end. During the *Waltzes* shoot (about which he apparently complained bitterly), Hitchcock was approached by Gaumont-British production head Michael Balcon, with whom he had worked at **Islington** some years before. Balcon represented a stark contrast to the conservative, parochial Maxwell: He encouraged innovation and experimentation; abjured adapting stage plays; and, at the direction of studio bosses Isidore and Mark Ostrer, sought to deliver films with an international, specifically, an American appeal. Hitchcock had truly found—or, rather,

Site of Gaumont–British Picture Corp. Lime Grove Studios

re-found—a soul mate and duly signed a five-picture contract with Gaumont-British. Ironically, his first project for Balcon, *The Man Who Knew Too Much*, was based on a treatment he and Charles Bennett (*Blackmail*) had devised at Elstree, but which Maxwell had rejected. Hitchcock, in turn, paid Maxwell £250 (today, about $25,000) for the rights to the story and resold them to Balcon for £500. Ostensibly inspired by Sapper's *Bulldog Drummond* series, the film owes rather more to John Buchan's *The Thirty-nine Steps* and *The Three Hostages*, not to mention a title pinched from a G.K. Chesterton story (see Appendix I for details). Regardless of its origins, the film was a critical success and restored Hitchcock's standing after the failures of his most recent Elstree pictures. (The film would have been a commercial success, as well, if Gaumont chairman—and old Hitchcock antagonist—C.M. Woolf hadn't resorted to an early form of "creative accounting" to sabotage it.) Hitchcock's next film, *The 39 Steps*, was explicitly derived from the Buchan novel of the same name (with the number rendered differently), although again Hitch and Bennett took a number of liberties with their source, primarily in the addition of a romance between protagonist Richard Hannay (here, tellingly, a Canadian, in contrast to Buchan's Scottish-born South African hero) and Pamela, a young woman apparently employed on the staff of a politician. In casting these roles, Hitchcock was taking no chances with his picture's fortunes in America: both Robert Donat and Madeleine Carroll had made films on the other side of the Atlantic and their appearance in *39 Steps* (along with high-class production, writing and direction) ensured its financial success. Indeed, so important was the American market (and so difficult was it to penetrate) that Hitchcock employed American actors in his next two pictures: Robert Young in *Secret Agent* (which again featured Carroll) and Sylvia Sidney in *Sabotage*. The "mistake" here, though, was the more serious approach to the material—characters expressed doubts about the correct course of action and, most significantly, innocent people died. Neither picture received the critical or commercial response of the previous pair. So, for his next film, *Young and Innocent*, Hitchcock resolved to keep things light and apart from the lack of any spy stuff, the film would evoke nothing so much as *The 39 Steps*, with a slightly younger—and less worldly—hero and heroine.

Unfortunately, Gaumont-British, like many other film companies of the time, had overextended itself in an effort to crank out the requisite number of pictures mandated by the Cinematograph Films Act of 1927—the source of the so-called "quota quickies." Thus, right in the midst of *Young and Innocent*, Isidore Ostrer decided to close Lime Grove and split the company's remaining productions between Islington and the massive new **Pinewood Studios** in Buckinghamshire. Without missing a beat, Hitchcock resumed work at Pinewood and there created two of his more famous sequences: the heroes' car falling into a pit and the extended crane shot across a crowded ballroom to the face of the twitchy villain. The **BBC** purchased Lime Grove in November 1949 as a "temporary" base for their television arm (they would in fact remain here for over 40 years), commencing production the following June. In fact, it was from the BBC's Studio D (the old Stage 6 of Hitchcock's day) that Frederick Knott's play *Dial M for Murder* debuted—as a live television broadcast—on Sunday March 23, 1952. (This was three months before the play's stage debut at the Westminster Theatre and over a year before Hitchcock filmed his adaptation.) Thirty-six-year-old Welsh actor Emrys Jones played Tony, the only member of the television cast to continue on in the stage version and the only major actor associated with the part whose age was actually right! (Knott describes Tony as being in his early 30s, which makes sense from the professional tennis angle. Ray Milland, Hitchcock's otherwise splendid choice, was 46 during filming. And Maurice Evans, who played the part on Broadway, was 51—old enough to be Tony's father!) Sadly, in 1991, Hitchcock's—and Knott's—old home was demolished and subsequently replaced with apartments.

Station: Shepherd's Bush (HC [not CE]) Exit R into the Uxbridge Road and then cross to Lime Grove. The studio was toward the bottom, where the apartment blocks now stand. For another BBC television location, see **Alexandra Palace**.

The MacGuffin: Among the musical selections used in that March 23 broadcast of *Dial M for Murder* was none other than Miklos Rosza's theme for *Spellbound*.

**51:2
Wood Lane F
W12**

According to biographer John Russell Taylor, Alfred Hitchcock devised a particularly elaborate—and expensive—way to impress American distributors (and audiences) with the production values of *Sabotage*: the construction of a full-scale working tram line here in Wood Lane, near the Lime Grove Studios (see above). The tram line was in fact constructed in the Northolt field where Hitchcock built the rest of the Verlocs' neighborhood (as well as the portion of Lower Regent Street where Stevie's bus explodes). The shots of Verloc crossing a street and boarding a bus for the **London Zoo** *do* appear to have been shot in a real street, but not Wood Lane. If anything, the shops suggest Goldhawk Road, an even shorter walk from the studio.

Station: Shepherd's Bush (HC [not CE]) Exit L into the Uxbridge Road and then turn L into Wood Lane; to see Goldhawk Road, backtrack to the intersection and continue along Shepherd's Bush Green and take the first R.

**51:3
ex White City (L)
Wood Lane, W12**

Built in 1908 for the Franco-British Exhibition, White City also hosted the fourth Olympics later that same year. In 1927 the first greyhound races were held at the stadium, an association White City maintained until the 1980s. According to the play *Dial M for Murder*, it was to the dog races at White City that Tony Wendice followed Swann on Thursdays and Saturdays (Harringay, in North London, was the preferred venue on Mondays). In the film, Tony also explains that he followed Swann to the dog races on Mondays and Thursdays but he omits the names of the tracks. In fact, author Frederick Knott omitted the names for the American version of the play, upon which the screenplay is based, presumably because the references would have been lost on an American audience. In any case, since the play reads like a dialogue script of the film, it's probably a safe bet that the film characters went to White City as well. Sadly, you and I can no longer bet on the dogs at White City—the BBC demolished the stadium in 1985 and erected a new radio headquarters in its place.

Station: White City (CE) Exit for White City.

**51:4
HM Prison Wormwood Scrubs C F L
Du Cane Road, W12**

Built appropriately enough by prison labor between 1874 and 1890, Britain's largest prison is the life-sentence center for the south of England—just the place you'd expect to find a convicted murderer like Richard Ian Blaney. Hitchcock shows us the foreboding Victorian Gothic exterior of the prison twice in *Frenzy*, once upon Blaney's arrival and again upon his departure to **St. Mary Abbott's Hospital** in an ambulance. And

Wormwood Scrubs

according to associate producer Bill Hill, these shots were not assigned to the second unit: Hitchcock insisted upon supervising them himself, which he did on September 15, 1971. (Ironically, as Hill notes, this was the only one of *Frenzy's* London locations that Hitchcock did not have to visit and approve *prior* to shooting.) A small portion of the prison interior was constructed at **Pinewood Studios**, for the scene where an escorted Blaney throws himself down the stairs. The master shot, showing the prison steps, cells and ceiling, was accomplished with the aid of one of Albert Whitlock's masterful matte paintings. Jon Finch actually took the fall, on September 27, 1971, landing on a large pile of cardboard boxes and mattresses. The following day (during which Finch complained of slight neck pain), Hitchcock set up two cameras to cover Finch's stunt double throwing himself down the stairs: "A" camera recorded the fall in a long shot; "B" camera recorded the fall in a closer panning movement. Then, for a medium close shot, Finch *started* to throw himself down the stairs, but stopped short. In the finished film, then, we see Finch's *start*, followed by the double's fall in the long shot; neither Finch's fall of the 27th nor the panning shot of the following day were used.

Wormwood Scrubs was also to be the setting for the opening of *The Short Night*, the last film project upon which the director worked before his death (see Appendix III). Based upon two books inspired by the real-life escape of Soviet mole George Blake (who received a 42-year sentence at the **Old Bailey** in 1961, the longest ever handed down in a British court), *The Short Night* was to have opened with a recreation of the prisoner's daring 1966 escape from the Scrubs, aided by a confederate waiting outside the prison wall. In the Kirkbride novel *The Short Night*, published in 1968, the Blake character escapes from Wandsworth Prison, SW18, with the help of the KGB. In *The Springing of George Blake*, published in 1970, Irishman Sean Bourke details how he in fact sprang Blake on his own, with no help from the Russians. Blake, who spied for the Soviets while working for **MI6**, and Bourke, convicted of sending a bomb to a policeman, had become fast friends during their years here at the Scrubs.

Blaney throws himself down the prison steps in *Frenzy*.

Convinced that Blake had received an unduly harsh sentence (and anxious to get back at the police), Bourke agreed to organize an escape after he himself got out of prison. With the help of friends, and using his own savings, Bourke bought a 1955 Humber Hawk, rented a small flat near the prison, and arranged for a two-way radio and other equipment necessary for the break-out to be smuggled into Blake. The two men communicated surreptitiously throughout 1966, eventually settling upon October 22 for the escape. A few minutes past six in the evening, Bourke parked the car in Artillery Road opposite the side entrance to Hammersmith Hospital. It was raining steadily and already dark. He radioed Blake to make his move. Blake responded immediately, instructing a confederate to knock out an iron bar from one of the upper windows. He then slipped through the window, down onto a roof and thence into the prison yard, where he radioed Bourke. After several agonizing minutes (people kept coming and going in Artillery Road), Bourke threw a homemade rope ladder over the wall, Blake ran across the yard, climbed up and over and thudded to the ground outside, injuring his head and breaking his wrist in the process. The two sped off to the safe house in Highlever Road (see entry 47:1), where the story continues....Hitchcock's adaptation would have replicated this highly atmospheric and suspenseful gambit, with Bourke, now called Brennan (the character does not appear in Kirkbride's novel), sitting in the Humber Hawk in Artillery Road, his radio concealed by a bouquet of chrysanthemums (Bourke's were pink), waiting for the signal to throw the ladder over the wall to Blake, now called Brand. (Typically, Hitchcock insisted upon the strictest accuracy in terms of the car, the flowers and the rope ladder.) Production designer Bob Boyle recalled that, while he actually visited Wormwood Scrubs, no filming would have been permitted there. "On a Hitchcock film, you researched it all, and then you stood back and created what was needed, bearing in mind what was actually there [on location]." Establishing shots, as well as rear-projection footage of the escapee's ride from Artillery Road (a small lane between the prison and Hammersmith Hospital) along Du Cane Road to

Highlever Road, were initially planned for the second unit, as were other sequences set in **Hyde Park** and **Gavin Brand's Flat**. However, as preproduction continued—and Hitchcock's health declined—it was decided that such shots could as well be filmed in California with matte paintings to "fill in" the London background.

Station: East Acton (CE) Go R out of the station into Erconwald Street, then L into Fitzneal Street and L again into Du Cane Road. The prison is ahead on the L, its entrance clearly recognizable from *Frenzy*. Artillery Road is farther along on the L, while Hammersmith Hospital, to which Blaney is theoretically taken (but see entry 10:2) is just beyond this.

51:5
"Dr. J.L. Baker's Office" F
165 Goldhawk Road, W12

This was the address given and shown (albeit on a Hollywood soundstage) as that of Rebecca's London doctor in Hitchcock's adaptation of the Daphne du Maurier classic. In fact, No. 165 was then, and remains, a petrol station. In the novel, the doctor's consulting rooms were located in Bloomsbury, near the **British Museum**, while his home (where the cancer revelation scene takes place) was near Barnet, then a north London suburb, today a borough of Greater London (also the home of John Rutland & Co. in the novel *Marnie*). Hitchcock's production notes indicate that at one point his intention had been to follow du Maurier and locate the doctor at 127 Aronright Road, a "typical suburban house" in Barnet. In the event, he opted for a more "depressing part of London"—Shepherd's Bush—with "squal[id] surroundings" and a "dingy but efficient" consulting room. Or as Favel bluntly derides the doctor's digs, "a dump"! Hitchcock also appears to have trained his cameras on the Goldhawk Road near Lime Grove (just down from the **Lime Grove Studios**) for the shot of Verloc crossing from the cinema to catch a bus to the **Zoo** in *Sabotage*.

Station: Goldhawk Road (HC) Exit L into Goldhawk Road and carry on to Brackenbury Road (by foot or bus—it's a bit of a hike); the petrol station is ahead on the L, with "typical" houses just beyond.

52. SPITALFIELDS

52:1

ex **Salvation Army Hostel C F**
Middlesex House
116 Middlesex Street, E1

Opened in a former shoe warehouse in 1906, the Salvation Army's Middlesex Street Hostel could accommodate over 400 down-on-their-luck gentlemen along its seven large floors. In his 1966 novel *Goodbye Piccadilly, Farewell Leicester Square*, Arthur La Bern sends a down-on-his-luck Dick Blamey [*sic*] here for shelter and a night's sleep after his final dinner with Brenda, as does Hitchcock in the film adaptation

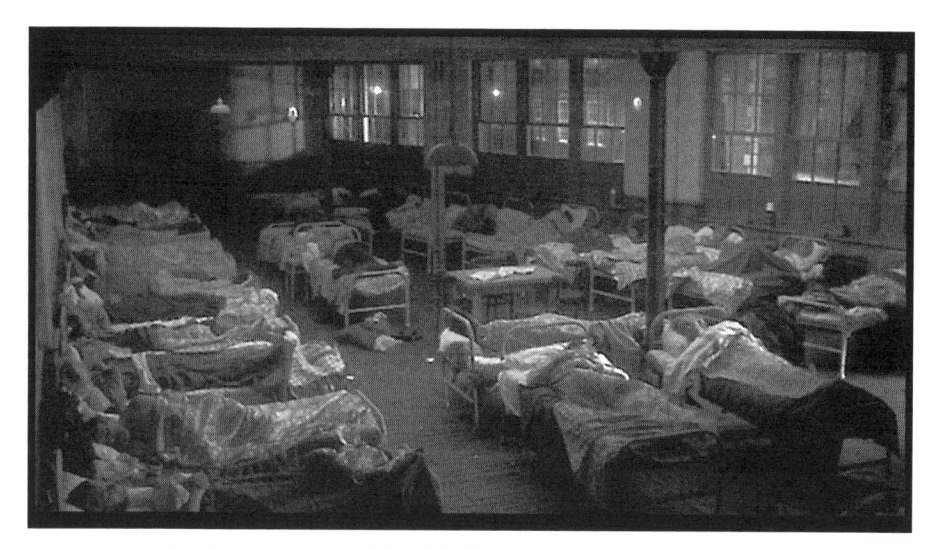

The Salvation Army Hostel in *Frenzy* was actually a studio set.

Frenzy. Actually, Hitchcock sent Dick Blaney (as he is renamed in the film) to a set at **Pinewood Studios**. However, the shooting script does specify Middlesex Street and the art department did do research at the hostel in order to ensure verisimilitude. According to set decorator Simon Wakefield, the crew also acquired ("for a donation, of course") a number of the hostel's blankets, whose distinctive "Salvation Army" logo Hitchcock would display in the finished film. Sadly, the hostel was gutted by fire in 1983, sold off in 1987 and subsequently demolished. The present building, actually rather similar in appearance to its predecessor, is used for offices.

Station: Liverpool Street (CE; CI; HC; ME) Exit L through the arcade then go R into Liverpool Street and L into Bishopsgate. Cross to Middlesex Street, ahead on the R. Middlesex House was just down from the top of the street, on the L.

53. STAMFORD HILL

53:1
ex **St. Ignatius College H**
St. Ann's Road
Stamford Hill, N15

From late 1907 until 1909, Alfred Hitchcock attended school at Howrah House Secondary School, Poplar, run by the Sisters of the Faithful Companions of Jesus. (See **Alfred Hitchcock's Childhood Home** for more on this.) In October 1910, Alfred's father enrolled him at **St. Ignatius College**, a prestigious, Jesuit-run boys' preparatory school, where the 11-year-old would be known as Pupil Number 343. Hitchcock's education here was the typically strict Roman Catholic one for which the Jesuits are famous—harsh to some, merely conservative to others. Hitchcock emphasized the conservative angle to Peter Bogdanovich: "The Jesuits taught me organization, control, and, to some degree, analysis. Their education is very strict and orderliness is one of the things that came out of that, I suppose, although my orderliness is spasmodic." However, in a 1973 filmed interview, the director evoked a harsher image of the college, elaborating slowly and methodically upon its method of punishing little boys: "The form master would say, 'Go for three.' Well, going for three was a sentence…as though it were spoken by a judge. And the sentence would then be carried out by…a special priest in a special room…with the help of a rather sort of old-fashioned strop for sharpening razor blades..Then you'd go into this room and the priest would enter your name in a book and then grab the hand that was to be punished and then lay this thing in. Never more than three [strokes] on one hand because the hand became numb and there was no good putting four on the hand because the fourth one—you'd never feel it."

St. Ignatius

Things were not all bleak at the school, though, for it was here that Hitchcock first delighted in the works of Defoe, Dickens, Shakespeare, Scott and other staples of English literature. Hitchcock left St. Ignatius in July 1913, after which he would take classes at the London County Council School of Engineering and Navigation, Poplar, and at **Goldsmiths College**, but would receive no further formal education. St. Ignatius has since relocated to Turkey Street, Enfield, North London.

Station: Seven Sisters (VI; NR) Exit R into the High Road and continue to St. Ann's Road, on the R. The school was behind St. Ignatius Church, which faces into the High Road. Young Alfred also visited the church itself on occasion, although he regularly attended mass at **St. Francis**, Stratford.

53:2
"Number Seventeen **House"** F
17 Anderson Road
Amhurst Park, N16

According to the telegram sent to Rose Ackroyd's father, the title house of *Number Seventeen* is located in Anderson Road, Amhurst Park. Anderson Road appears to have been a cinematic invention (the exteriors were filmed in the studio) but Amhurst Park definitely exists. It is located in the traditionally orthodox Jewish enclave of Stamford Hill (very near Hitchcock's old school, **St. Ignatius**), and does, indeed, pass over a railway line, specifically the Great Eastern Section of the London & North Eastern Railway. Contrarily, the film makes it clear that the setting is *another* section of the LNER, which also began at **Liverpool Street Station**, but which carried on to Harwich, while the actual railway exteriors were filmed on the Northern Section of the LNER, at **Copenhagen Tunnel** and beyond.

Station: Seven Sisters (VI) This is the closest tube stop, about a half mile N of Amhurst Road and the Stamford Hill train station.

54. STEPNEY

54:1
Site of the *Siege of Sidney Street* C (F)
100 Sidney Street, E1

On January 3, 1911, the Metropolitan Police and a small group of foreign anarchists engaged in one of the most famous gun battles in English history. Known as the "Battle of Stepney" and, later, as the "Siege of Sidney Street," the dramatic event captured both the city's and the nation's attention, not to mention that of an 11-year-old schoolboy who would eventually become Britain's greatest filmmaker. Indeed, in later years, Alfred Hitchcock would refer to "Sidney Street" on many occasions, citing it not merely as the inspiration for the climax to *The Man Who Knew Too Much* (34) but as the actual *subject* of the scene. (Note, for example, in *Hitch on Hitch* [p 190]: "I had a good deal of trouble putting Sidney Street in *The Man Who Knew Too Much*.") The background

Site of the Siege of Sidney Street

A REFERENCE GUIDE TO LOCATIONS

to the siege is somewhat complicated, involving a group of Latvian revolutionaries-cum-refugees who agitated for the overthrow of the Russian czar. Led by a chap known as "Peter the Painter" (possibly Peter Piaktow), they financed their activities through armed robbery. On January 23, 1909, two of the Latvians had robbed a car delivering wages to Schnurrman's rubber works in Tottenham High Road. The police gave chase and the ensuing gunfight left two people dead (a police constable and a 10-year-old boy) and 21 others injured. Now, on December 16, 1910, nearly two years after the "Tottenham Outrage," the gang was attempting to tunnel into a Houndsditch jewelry store from the neighboring building. A neighbor alerted the police to the strange noises and a very one-sided battle quickly erupted. The first fatality, an unarmed police sergeant, was shot as he tried to enter the building (just as Hitchcock would show in the film); four more policemen were subsequently shot, two of them fatally. The gang members escaped, although not without a casualty of their own: while pumping countless rounds into one of the policemen, chief gunman Jacob Peters inadvertently shot one of his own comrades, who ultimately died of his wounds. Needless to say, the brutal murders of the policemen both stunned and outraged the British public. Through the aid of informants, the **Metropolitan Police**, working in concert with the City of London police, were able to round up all but two of the Latvians, Fritz Svaars and "Joseph," whom they finally traced to the flat of a Mrs. Betsy Gershon, 100 Sidney Street. (In a detail replicated in the film, the gunmen removed Mrs. Gershon's skirt and shoes to prevent her from leaving the building.) Preparing for the worst, some 200 Met and City policemen (the number eventually grew to more than a thousand), now armed with revolvers, shotguns and rifles, cordoned off the area around the building, evacuated neighbors and attempted to hold back a crowd that would swell into the tens of thousands. The first shots were fired—by the anarchists—just after daybreak and the battle, now begun in earnest, would continue throughout the morning. Armed with rapid-fire Mausers, the Latvians boasted a seemingly inexhaustible supply of ammunition and, perhaps most importantly, the determination to see the battle through to the end. A call was made to the **War Office** for military reinforcements from the Tower of London and this, in turn, led to the involvement of the Home Secretary. He was none other than Winston Churchill and he was determined to see the Siege of Sidney Street for himself. Although later castigated for his "on the scene" involvement, Churchill's presence may have facilitated the end of the siege: volunteer marksmen from the Tower's Scots Guards had fired so many rounds into the upper floors of the building that it actually caught fire; Churchill forbade the intervention of the fire brigade in order to let the building burn and drive the two men out. In the event, the two men remained inside and were burned to a crisp—a grisly end to a grisly chapter in the history of the Metropolitan Police.

Hitchcock, of course, chose to conflate the events of December 16 and January 3, eliminate the fire and end the battle with his sharp-shooting heroine taking out the last of the bad guys. Still, for all the changes, the British Board of Film Censors strenuously objected to his recreation of the famous siege. Working hand in glove with the **Home Office** in 1931, the BBFC had created an extensive list of "political subjects" that could not be depicted in any way, shape or form. One of its forbidden themes was "convey[ing] a false impression of the police," which meant that London's (generally) unarmed constabulary could not be shown carrying guns or having easy recourse to guns for the climactic shoot-out. In fact, as Hitchcock recounted to Peter Bogdanov-

Frank Vosper (left), Peter Lorre and Cicely Oates wage a controversial gun battle in the 1934 *The Man Who Knew Too Much*.

ich some three decades later, the Board's representative insisted that the only way he would permit the shoot-out was if the director "had the police go to a local gunsmith and take out mixed guns and show that they're not familiar with the weapons." The gentleman was apparently unaware that in 1911, constables in outer divisions, including both Stepney and Wapping, the locale for the film climax, *could* carry revolvers on the night beat—with permission from the Superintendent. Whether or not Hitchcock knew this is uncertain, but he stuck to his guns, so to speak. He simply inserted a line (delivered to the government official who shows up at the scene) about obtaining the artillery from a nearby gunsmith and then proceeded to show a truck delivering the weapons to the police. Of course, this may explain why Hitchcock always referred to the climax of the film as "Sidney Street" itself, rather than an incident merely *inspired* by the famous battle. As long as he was recreating history, what could the Board of Censors legitimately censor?

As a postscript, one should perhaps note that the eight surviving members of the gang (apart, of course, from the elusive "Peter the Painter") were subsequently acquitted, the case being one of the most famous "botched" prosecutions in English history. The Crown had wrongly focused on George Gardstein, the anarchist accidentally killed by his own comrades, as the policemen's killer, when in fact the more likely suspect was Jacob Peters. In the end, Peters walked out of the courtroom a free man, eventually returning to Russia where he became deputy chief of the secret police and one of the new Soviet Union's most fearsome executioners. He was shot on Stalin's orders in 1938.

Station: Whitechapel (DI; EL; HC) Follow Whitechapel Road E to Sidney Street, where you will turn R. The house was on the E side of the street, between Lindley Street and Stepney Way.

Geo Barbor on Cable Street

54:2
"Geo Barbor, Dentist" F
426 Cable Street, E1

Here, intrepid travelers, just north of Wapping proper, is the actual address of the devious dentist Bob and Clive visit in *The Man Who Knew Too Much* (34)—at least according to the shooting script. There, in scene 170, "EXT. DENTIST'S. NIGHT," we dissolve from the one-word title "Wapping" to a sign that indicates the precise location of the sinister East London locale. The scene was, of course, shot on a set at **Lime Grove Studios**, with a sign that bore no trace of a street address. Why Hitchcock dropped the specific reference is uncertain—it can't have been to avoid libeling a particular part of London, since Wapping itself is clearly mentioned in the film. In any case, Cable Street—named for the ship's cables once manufactured here—is much tamer today, though I was still advised, by an elderly, life-long resident, to watch my step!

Station: Shadwell (EL; DLR) Exit L out of the station, go L again into Cable Street and brace yourself for a bit of a hike. The location would have been just past Glamis Road, to the R, a site rather nicely located across from a church.

Ask Mr. Memory 47: On what ship does Bob tell the dentist he has just arrived?

55. STRATFORD

55:1
St. Francis of Assisi H
Grove Crescent Road, E15

Alfred Hitchcock attended this, his mother's parish church, as a boy, rather than any of the Roman Catholic churches closer to their home in the Leytonstone High Road (see 43:1). It was here, according to biographer Donald Spoto, that Hitchcock the future "actor" first discovered his love of the "ceremonial" and of being part of the show.

Station: Stratford (CE; JU; DL; NR) Exit into Great Eastern Road and follow this to the L, past Angel Lane to Grove Crescent, where you will turn L. The church is ahead to the R.

56. UPPER SYDENHAM

56:1
"Miss Fergusson's Home" L
Sydenham Hill, SE26

According to the play *Banquo's Chair*, "Old Miss Fergusson" lived in "a large but rather decayed house on Sydenham Hill," Upper Sydenham, an affluent residential enclave until it fell into something of a decline toward the close of the 19th century. Here, on the first anniversary of Miss Fergusson's murder, retired police chief Sir William Brent plans to stage the shock appearance of the dead woman's "ghost" (really a well-made-up London actress) in order to induce a confession from the woman's nephew—and suspected killer—John Bedford. (The conceit—"one of the oldest tricks"—derives from Shakespeare's *Macbeth*, in which the title character nearly incriminates himself when the ghost of the murdered Banquo appears at a banquet and assumes Macbeth's chair.) In this charade, Brent will be aided by Harold Gandy, a well-known crime novelist, and Robert Stone, of no known occupation. In Hitchcock's adaptation, Stone is now a Shakespearean actor (playing in—what else?—*Macbeth*) and Gandy has been replaced by the amiable but rather lowbrow Major Cooke-Finch (see the **Tivoli** and **Eton** for more on the major). In addition, the locale has been changed from Upper Sydenham to the more sinister-sounding "Blackheath, near London," some four miles or so to the northeast (see **R Division** for a Blackheath area locale).

Station: Brixton (VI); Transfer to NR and exit at Sydenham Hill Station for College Road. Follow this to Fountain Drive (which veers off to the L) and continue to Crystal Palace Park Road, where you will turn L. Look for Sydenham Hill just ahead to the L.

Ask Mr. Memory 48: In what year is the television adaptation set?

Croydon Airport ca. 1959
57. WADDON

57:1
ex **Croydon Airport H (F)**
Purley Way, CR0

Opened in 1915 to defend London from German air attacks, Croydon became the official "London Customs Air Port" on March 29, 1920. It was expanded and improved in the 1920s, became a "gateway to the Empire" in the 1930s and remained London's principal civilian airport until 1946, when it was superseded by **Heathrow**. It closed in 1959 and was replaced by an industrial estate. In *Suspicion*, Johnnie tells the police that after dining with the late Beaky Thwaite at **The Savoy**, he saw him off at Croydon Airport. Also, as reported in *Hitch*, Hitchcock occasionally held script conferences "on the roof of Croydon Airport" ca. 1936.

Station: Victoria (CI; DI; VI; NR)
Transfer to National Rail for Epsom and exit at Waddon. Go L in Purley Way and continue toward Imperial Way on the R; Airport House, the old terminal building, still stands in Purley Way and the old Airport Hotel lives on as a Forte Posthouse.

58. WHITECHAPEL

58:1
Mann, Crossman & Paulin F
333-335 Whitechapel Road, E1

This gigantic brewery, whose building and sign are still extant, appears briefly in the sequence showing a delirious Roddy's return to London near the conclusion of *Downhill*.

Mann, Crossman & Paulin

Station: Stepney Green (DI; HC) Exit L into Whitechapel Road and look for the building ahead on the L.

58:2
Site of Jack the Ripper's First Victim C
Durward Street (formerly Buck's Row), E1

The world's most notorious serial killer began his work here in the early morning hours of August 31, 1888. Mary Ann Nichols, also known as Polly, was found with her throat cut and her abdomen horribly mutilated. (Two other East End women had recently been murdered in similar circumstances, leading some writers to describe Nichols as the second or third Ripper victim.) Over the next few months, four more women, all occasional prostitutes, were killed in this area by the same hand, the last, Mary Kelly, undergoing such grotesque mutilation that one young policeman on the scene described it as "a sight which I shall never forget to my dying day." (The policeman, Walter Dew, would later apprehend the infamous Dr. Crippen [see entry 37:2].) Letters were sent from the purported killer and the Whitechapel Murderer earned his famous "Ripper" sobriquet, but police then and now discounted the letters' authenticity. And just as suddenly as he started—the killer stopped. Suspects were questioned (one, a local boot finisher known as "Leather Apron," having to be saved by the police from an angry mob), but no one was charged with the sensational crimes. The mystery of the identity of Jack the Ripper—and no matter what one may read, his identity is still a mystery—continues to fascinate crime buffs around the world. One who turned her fascination to profit was author Marie Belloc Lowndes, penning the most famous fictional account of the Ripper and his crimes. According to her diary, Belloc Lowndes wrote the short story "The Lodger" after hearing "a man telling a woman at a dinner party that his mother had had a butler and a cook who married and kept lodgers. They were convinced that Jack the Ripper had spent a night under their roof." She later expanded the story into a novel (published in 1913), one whose theme of "religious fanaticism charged with sexual repression" (Coville and Lucanio) influenced countless writers and researchers to come. Two years later, Horace Vachell adapted the novel for the stage and, in its four-month run at the **Haymarket Theatre**, *The Lodger*, now called, *Who Is He?* attracted the attention of future filmmaker Alfred Hitchcock. Hitchcock would, of course, film the novel in 1926, famously changing the ending (his lodger is apparently not the killer and must be saved, like "Leather Apron," from an angry mob) for the benefit of censors and leading man Ivor Novello's career. Serial killers

Durward Street, site of the first Ripper murder

would fascinate Hitchcock all of his life, influencing or inspiring incidents in everything from *Shadow of a Doubt* to *Psycho*. (For more of Hitchcock's killers, see entries 36:1, 37:2, 42:1.) And, of course, Hitchcock could work in the Ripper himself from time to time, as in the *Frenzy* opening, when a **Thames**-side gawker corrects his companion, who compares the Necktie killer to you know who. "Not on your life. He used to carve 'em up. Sent a bird's kidney to Scotland Yard once…or was it a bit of her liver?" For the record, it was a kidney and as Ripper expert Philip Sugden explains, that particularly grisly bit of communication may indeed have come from Jack the Ripper.

Station: Whitechapel (DI; EL; HC) Exit for Durward Street. The body was found on the sidewalk, near the small wall about halfway down on the R, as one faces E toward Brady Street.

The MacGuffin: According to the shooting script for *The 39 Steps*, the opening "East End" music hall sequence was to have included two more questions for Mr. Memory. One was, "Who killed Cock Robin?" (interesting, given the appearance of the Disney cartoon in *Sabotage*) and the other, "Who was Jack the Ripper?"

59. WIMBLEDON

59:1
All England Lawn Tennis and Croquet Club   L   (F)
Church Road
Wimbledon, SW19

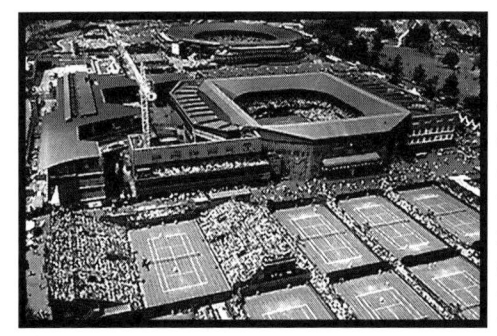

The All England Club is, of course, home to the world-famous Wimbledon open lawn tennis championships, which are held here each June. The championships began in 1877 and today the two-week event draws nearly a half million spectators to Church Road itself and hundreds of millions more through television coverage. In *Rebecca*, Mrs. Van Hopper questions the amount of time her young companion has been spending on her tennis, exclaiming that with "the number of lessons you've had you ought to be ready for Wimbledon!" And if you'd been around in the early 1950s, you may well have seen a fellow who looked a lot like Ray Milland playing tennis here at Wimbledon. Or so Milland's character, Tony Wendice, tells Swann in *Dial M for Murder* (both the film and the play). The fact that Milland was then 46 years old causes us to question the veracity of that statement, but then again he's so charming, we'll suspend our disbelief and swallow his story, net, ball and racket.

Station: Wimbledon Park (DI) From the station go L in Arthur Road then R into Church Road. **Museum Hours:** Tue-Sat 10:30 am-5 pm; Sun 11 am-5 pm; closed Fri, Sat, Sun in June before the Championships.

60. WOOD GREEN

60:1
Alexandra Palace L
Alexandra Palace Way, N22

In the play *Dial M for Murder*, Max Halliday (Mark in the film) worked as a writer for BBC Television before taking a year-long gig in America for 10 times the pay. Thus, at the beginning of the play, Max is coming *home* to England, whereas in the American version of the play, as well as the film, the American Max/Mark has sailed to England for what is apparently just a visit. (That Halliday is still around at the end of the story, months after the attempted murder, is thus a non-issue in the British version of the play, but something of a curiosity in the American version and in the film. Where did he stay, what did he do for a living, did his publisher foot the bill?) In any case, the British Max would have likely worked here at the famous "Ally Pally," a massive late Victorian exhibition hall, twice nearly destroyed by fire (once in 1873, shortly after it opened, and again in 1980). The **BBC** leased the eastern half of the building in 1935 and from here transmitted the world's first high-definition television broadcast on November 2, 1936. (The site was chosen because it was on a hill, some 300 feet above sea level. The transmitter tower itself added another 300 feet.) Television broadcasting ceased at 12:10 p.m. on September 1, 1939, the outbreak of war being imminent, and the BBC TV signal providing a possible means for German aircraft to home in on London. Broadcasting resumed—with the same, interrupted Disney cartoon (*Mickey's Gala Premiere*)—on June 7, 1946. For the next several years, the BBC broadcast a number of theatrical plays—*live*—from Ally Pally, many directed by Irish stage and film director Fred O'Donovan. O'Donovan pioneered the famous "one-camera" technique here at the Ally Pally (in contrast to the three or four cameras that were normally used for recording a production), a technique similar to that Hitchcock himself would later adapt for *Rope* and *Under Capricorn*. (Oddly enough, Hitchcock actually knew O'Donovan and cast him in a bit part in *Young and Innocent*.) Alexandra Palace remained in operation until 1956, by which time the new **Lime Grove** facilities in Shepherd's Bush had superceded it.

Hitchcock on the set of Dial M for Murder

Station: Wood Green (PI) Follow the signs for Alexandra Park. A massive fire destroyed much of the building in 1980; it has since been rebuilt along its original lines.

The MacGuffin: So how do we know that Max would have worked here? Well, The play *Dial M for Murder* debuted as a *live* television broadcast on March 23, 1952. The action commences on a Friday evening in September, presumably of the previous year.

Max left the country one year ago, i.e., in September of 1950. At that time, the BBC had just opened a new television facility in Hitchcock's old studio, **Lime Grove**, from which, indeed, the play was first transmitted. Max may well have spent a few weeks at Lime Grove, but the bulk of his TV work would have been at the Palace.

OUTSIDE LONDON

61. BERKSHIRE

61:1
Eton College (*formally* **Royal College of Our Lady at Eton by Windsor**) **(F)**
Eton
Windsor

SE cen. England, 23 mi. W of London (across the **Thames** from Windsor)

Founded by King Henry VI in 1440, Eton College is the most prestigious public (i.e., private) school in England. In "Banquo's Chair," we learn that both Major Cooke-Finch and young John Bedford were at Eton, the latter some 30 years after the former. Still, the younger Etonian recalls that "they were still talking about that catch you made against Harrow when you fell in somebody's veal and ham pie." Harrow School, northwest of London, is perhaps the second most prestigious boys' school in England and the traditional rival of Eton.

Eton

61:2
The King's Head (F)
149 Lower Cippenham Lane
Cippenham
Slough (near Windsor)

S England, 23 mi. W of London (M4 to Bath Road East, then R into Elmshott La and L into Lower Cippenham La)

As Tony and Mark prepare to depart for their Saturday evening "stag" party in *Dial M for Murder*, Margot suggests that tomorrow the three of them should drive down to Windsor and have lunch at the King's Head. Mark asks if it's right in Windsor, to which Margot quite accurately replies that it's just outside. In the British version of the play, the invitation is simply to drive down to Henley for lunch (Henley is also on the **Thames**, but farther upriver), with no particular place mentioned. Frederick Knott changed the locale to Windsor for the American version, adding the name of the restaurant for the screenplay.

**61:3
Newbury Racecourse (F) L
Newbury**

S England, 53 mi. WSW of London

One of England's premier racecourses, Newbury is today best known for the Hennesy Cognac Gold Cup steeplechase held each December. According to both *Suspicion* and the source novel *Before the Fact*, Beaky Thwaite ran into Johnnie at the Newbury Races just last week. This was news—and unwelcome news at that—to Johnnie's new bride, Lina, who had assumed that her husband had been hard at work as an estate manager. Little does she know…yet. It was also to Newbury that Mark Rutland invited Marnie in Chapter 5 of Winston Graham's novel. Marnie accepts the invitation for the following Saturday—knowing full well that by then, she will have robbed Rutland's and taken it on the lam! For the pair's previous race outing, see **Newmarket Rowley Racecourse**.

Ask Mr. Memory 49: Speaking of races, what's the name of the horse that Blaney cannot afford to back in *Frenzy*?

62. BUCKINGHAMSHIRE

**62:1
Pinewood Studios F
Pinewood Road
Iver Heath**

SE England, 20 mi. W of London

Doubles as: Aunt Mary's House and the Grand Hotel in *Young and Innocent*; County Hall, Brenda Blaney's Club, Hyde Park, Hammersmith Hospital and the Covent Garden Piazza in *Frenzy*

The largest and most famous film studio in Britain was founded in 1936 by Charles Boot, C.M. Woolf and the legendary J. Arthur Rank. The "heart" of the studio complex is the Mansion, a.k.a. Heatherden Hall, an elegant Victorian home previously used as a country club. Alfred

Pinewood Studios: A stage doubles as "Grand Hotel" in *Young and Innocent*.

Pinewood Studios Mansion doubles as "Aunt Mary's House" in *Young and Innocent*.

Hitchcock was among the first directors to use the impressive new facility, transferring the production of *Young and Innocent* from **Lime Grove** to **Pinewood** in March 1937. Apart from soundstage interiors, Hitchcock also used the exterior of the mansion itself to double as Aunt Mary's house (where Robert chats with Erica's uncle before joining the party inside) and the outside of A Stage to double as the back of the Grand Hotel (where the drummer takes a rather shaky smoke). Thirty-four years later, Hitchcock came back to Pinewood to shoot *Frenzy*, a darkly humorous homage to his London roots. He was, according to associate producer Bill Hill, greeted by one and all as a returning hero. (One aspect of his return that Hitchcock may not have found as pleasant: the barrage of letters from actors and other colleagues seeking jobs. Among those politely beseeching the Master were John Williams, John Loder, Hume Cronyn and Richard [*The Godfather*] Castellano!) Much of *Frenzy* would be shot on location, principally in **Covent Garden**, but most of the interiors—and a few exteriors—would be filmed at Pinewood. In addition to using production designer Syd Cain's realistic interior sets (including the famous corridor and steps leading to **Bob Rusk's Flat (1)**, most of them built on Stages B and D), the director also used the Mansion's Green Room for the interior of **Brenda Blaney's Club**, a room that Cain and art director Bob Laing would press into Her Majesty's Secret Service the following year for the Bond film *Live and Let Die* (it is the villain's Caribbean office). For the club scene, Cain's art department supplied 12 duplicate brandy glasses for repeat takes of Blaney smashing the glass (in the end, Hitchcock filmed only two). Interestingly, the foyer just off the Green Room, from which Brenda and Dick prepare to exit the "club," actually leads to the entrance shown in *Young and Innocent*. For the opening sequence set at **County Hall**, Hitchcock restaged the onlookers' dialogue scenes ("or was it her liver?") alongside the studio's Paddock (exterior) tank, and the recovery of the dead woman's body inside the tank itself. The scene in which Blaney tries to convince Babs of his innocence was filmed here in the studio gardens on September 13, 1971 (the long shots were filmed in **Hyde Park**), while Blaney's walk down the hospital corridor was filmed in the south corridor of D Stage (the exteriors were filmed at **St. Mary Abbots Hospital**, Kensington). The high-angle shot of Bob Rusk—actually a double for actor Barry Foster—wheeling Babs' body from his flat (see 6:7) to the **Central Market Building** in Covent Garden was done on the backlot as a "glass shot," with a portion of the building recreated to match the actual location. The sequence in which Babs' body falls off the back of the potato truck was shot just outside the studio, in Pinewood Road, about three-quarters of the way down from the main gate to the "Five Points" roundabout. Cain recalled that the October evening they filmed the body in the road was "bloody cold" and while he, Hitchcock and the rest of the crew were warmly bundled up, Anna Massey's double, Jenni Lefre, was, of course shivering in the nude. In the end, the sequence was recreated on D Stage, this time with Barbara Wendy, who also doubled for Anna Massey in the **Coburg** bathroom scene and later "played" Babs' body in the potato sack. The sequence in which the motorists alert the driver that he is spilling his load was shot a little farther down from the studio, between Five Points and Slough (see the next entry).

Double Century Public House

62:2
Double Century Public House (*now* The Green Man) and Environs F
Uxbridge Road
George Green

SE England, 20 mi. W of London

Doubles as: M1, en route to Lincolnshire

It was here, on the A412, outside the Double Century Pub, that Alfred Hitchcock shot exterior footage of the potato truck sequence in *Frenzy*. Filming took place during the first and second weeks of October 1971 and included shots of potato sacks falling off the back of the truck, the passing car blowing its horn and flashing its lights, the driver pulling off the road and walking around to the back of the truck (all of which appear before the truck stop sequence), as well as the police car pulling out into the road after the truck passes them. The pub itself served as the unit's base during the shoot. See **Pinewood Studios** and **Wally's New Café** for more on this sequence.

63. CAMBRIDGESHIRE

63:1
University of Cambridge L (F) H C
Cambridge

E England, 50 mi. NNE of London

Founded in 1209 and every bit as prestigious as the slightly older Oxford, the University of Cambridge has produced countless numbers of outstanding men and women, both good—and bad. Among the former we should have to mention both Michael Redgrave and the character he portrays in *The Lady Vanishes*. The disclosure that Gilbert is a Cambridge man comes at a critical moment behind enemy lines, when one of the foreign villains reveals that he—like Charters—went to Oxford. Gilbert very rightly conks the man on the head! In the short story "The Crystal Trench," Stella calls on a Professor Kersley here at Cambridge and learns the exact date and time at which her late husband will emerge from the title locale. (Hitchcock includes this scene in the TV adaptation, but does not indicate where the meeting takes place.) Among those Cambridge alumni of a more dubious repute we must mention both Tony Wendice and C.A. Swann (a.k.a. Lesgate, Adams, Wilson, etc.), the would-be killers in *Dial M for Murder*. Interestingly, Tony claims that he went up to Cambridge during Swann's last year, while in reality, Ray Milland, who played Tony, was actually nine years older than Anthony Dawson, who played Swann. (In the British version of the play, Tony says that he came to "Bennet's House" during Swann's last term, 15 years ago. Playwright—and Cambridge alumnus—Frederick Knott apparently didn't feel the need to mention the university itself, at least until he revised the play for its American run. In *that* version, the two men are, indeed, Cambridge alumni.) Yet another Cambridge graduate of ill repute pops up in the screenplay for *No Bail for the Judge*, the comic thriller Hitchcock planned to shoot with Audrey Hepburn in 1959. There, in a scene set in **Hyde Park**, Elizabeth Proud (Hepburn's character) asks Sir Edward Devlin if he went to Oxford; the charming murderer informs her that after Harrow, he went to Cambridge. Devlin then forces himself on Elizabeth, daughter of the wrongly accused title character, in a scene that Miss Hepburn apparently found objectionable (see Appendix III). We should perhaps also take note of the so-called "Cambridge Five," that upper crust coterie of Soviet spies—Guy Burgess, Donald Maclean, Kim Philby, Anthony Blunt and John Cairncross—recruited here by the Russians in the 1930s. (Hitchcock actually claimed that the original idea for *Torn Curtain* came from wondering about the effect of Maclean's 1951 defection on the man's wife and family.) Hitchcock himself came to Cambridge in the spring of 1966 to deliver a lecture to the university's Film Society, noting (in an eerie foreshadowing of virtual reality technology) that audiences of the future might buy a ticket, undergo mass hypnotism, then play whatever character in the film they'd like to be!

Ask Mr. Memory 50: According to the film, how long has it been since Tony and Swann were at Cambridge together?

63:2
Milton Hall (L) P
Fitzwilliam Estate
Peterborough

E England, 50 mi. NNE of London

Daphne du Maurier visited this rambling 18th-century mansion as a child, later fusing it with **Menabilly**, on the Cornish coast, to yield the house—the character—of Manderley in the novel *Rebecca*. Among the details that impressed the 10-year-old child were Milton's vast entrance hall and its imposing housekeeper, "a severe and rather frightening person" called Miss Parker. During preproduction of the screen adaptation in 1939, Alfred Hitchcock dispatched a second-unit crew to a number of English estates, including Milton, but apparently neither he nor producer David Selznick were impressed with the results. The cinematic Manderley was thus created entirely on Hollywood soundstages, comprising both full-size sets and two different miniatures.

64. CORNWALL

64:1
Menabilly Estate (L) P
Near Fowey

SW England, 215 mi. WSW of London, 1 mi. W of Fowey

In the autumn of 1928, budding novelist Daphne du Maurier (daughter of Hitchcock's actor friend Sir Gerald du Maurier [see **Wyndham's Theatre**]) discovered the inspiration for what would prove to be her most celebrated novel, *Rebecca*, published in 1938 by Victor Gollancz. It was a large, ivy-covered house on Gribbin Head, just across

Menabilly

the River Fowey (pronounced "Foy") from her family's home in Bodinnick. "Bathed in a strange mystery," she would later write, it seemed "a house of secrets" that "has no wish to be disturbed." Its name, as she soon learned, was Menabilly and it had been built by the titled Rashleigh family in the early 17th century. Now it stood empty and abandoned, unloved by its present owner, or so she imagined. "Grey, still, silent…Menabilly would sleep on, like the sleeping beauty of the fairy-tale, until someone should come to wake her." That someone, of course, was du Maurier, who visited Menabilly many times over the next 15 years, at first secretly, then with the permission of the owners. Finally, in December 1943, she obtained a lease on the house of her dreams, where she would live happily for the next 26 years. In the meantime, of course, the author had combined elements of the mysterious Menabilly with details of **Milton Hall**, a large, somber house of her acquaintance in Cambridgeshire, to create the literary "Manderley." With its remote Cornish setting and grounds (from Menabilly) and its vast entrance hall and foreboding housekeeper (from Milton), Manderley haunts *Rebecca* from the famous first sentence ("Last night I dreamt I went to Manderley again.") to the last flickering image of the house in flames, the latter being more fully and terrifyingly developed in the Hitchcock-Selznick film adaptation. (In spite of the changes, du Maurier described the film as "terrific," claiming that she was "quite pleased" with it.)

The Menabilly estate also inspired another of du Maurier's tales, the 1952 short story "The Birds." One day, while walking from the house to Menabilly Barton Farm, the author noticed a farmer working in the field and above him…a large flock of seagulls circling and diving. What if, for some reason, the birds attacked him? What if, indeed. Hitchcock, of course, transformed the story of the simple Cornish farmer and his wife into that of two American sophisticates trapped in a California farmhouse. Du Maurier, whose love of Cornwall was legendary, did *not* approve of the transformation. In 1965, Daphne's beloved husband of 23 years, Lieutenant-General Sir Frederick Browning, died at the age of 68. The author was devastated, of course, but drew strength from her surroundings at Menabilly. Within four years' time, however, these, too, would be taken from her, as the owner of the estate, Philip Rashleigh, decided to move into Menabilly himself. Daphne was forced to relocate to Kilmarth, the Menabilly dower house, where she would die at the age of 81 in 1989. The Rashleigh family have continued to refuse all requests to open the house to du Maurier's—and perhaps Hitchcock's—adoring public, so the closest you can come to "Manderley" is to stay at one of the bed and breakfasts (Tregaminion Farm or Menabilly Barton) within the estate itself. Or, from the port town of Fowey (rechristened "Kerrith" in the novel and film), you can hike west along the South West Coast Path, which passes through the coastal portion of the Menabilly estate. Be sure to continue on to the sandy beach of Polridmouth—this is the cove commemorated as the scene of Rebecca's death in the novel. Meanwhile, the du Mauriers' Bodinnick home is presently owned by Daphne's son, Christian "Kits" Browning, and is now open to the public.

Today's Jamaica Inn commemorates the life of Daphne du Maurier.

64:2
Jamaica Inn (L)
Bolventor
Launceston

SW England, 240 mi. WSW of London, halfway between Bodmin and Launceston (pronounced "Lanson"), just off of the A30 at Bolventnor

Located in the middle of "desolate, sinister" Bodmin Moor, Jamaica Inn was the setting for Daphne du Maurier's famous 1936 novel of the same name. This somber, slate-hung coaching house was built in the mid-18th century and originally called the New Inn; it was given its present name in honor of a member of the local Rodd family, who was a colonial official in Jamaica. And just as du Maurier would describe in her novel (and as Hitchcock would depict in the film), Jamaica Inn attracted all kinds of colorful rogues (i.e., smugglers), who needed a temporary place to store the goods they had run into England through Polperro (on the south coast), Boscastle (on the north coast) and other remote Cornish landing points. (These goods, including tobacco, tea, brandy and silk, were heavily taxed if legally brought in through British ports, hence the incentive to smuggle them into the country.) At the suggestion of a friend, du Maurier actually visited Jamaica Inn in 1930, where she quickly realized, in her own words, "Oh, there's a story here!" And a very compelling story it turned out to be, filled with the kind of Gothic suspense and terror at which du Maurier excelled. Hers were no mere smugglers, but rather *wreckers*, who deliberately lured ships onto the rocks, then killed their crews. And this grisly fact, as well as her uncle's involvement in the gang, is something that Mary, her

Charles Laughton, Maureen O'Hara and Marie Ney in *Jamaica Inn*

young heroine, comes to discover over the course of many suspenseful chapters, not the minute she arrives at the inn, as in the film. It's unfortunate that Hitchcock, presumably at the insistence of actor Charles Laughton and his partner Erich Pommer, the film's producer, chose to recreate *Jamaica Inn* as a sort of pirate-era spy story, with Laughton hogging center stage throughout, leaving nominal heroine Maureen O'Hara little to do besides walk around in wet underwear. The film might easily have rounded off the director's English period as well as *Rebecca* began his American period. (Laughton and O'Hara would, of course, fare much better in *The Hunchback of Notre Dame* [1939], a Hollywood production they made for director William Dieterle immediately after *Jamaica Inn*.) In any case, you can visit the Daphne du Maurier Smugglers at Jamaica Inn, to give the full title, and see for yourself the desolate setting that gripped the author's imagination "almost as much as **Menabilly**." The inn has six en suite rooms, each named after a character in the novel, as well as a memorial room dedicated to Dame Daphne, who died in 1989. This room contains, among other memorabilia, the author's Sheraton writing desk, on top of which sits her typewriter, telephone, ashtray and a package of Du Maurier cigarettes, named after her famous father (see entry 20:12). In nearby Altarnum you will find the Cathedral of the Moor, home to the villainous Reverend Davey in the novel, as well as Penhallow Manor, a former rectory, now a luxury country house hotel,

65. CUMBRIA

65:1
Rydal Water F
Rydal
Lake District

NW England, 250 mi. NW of London, off the A593

The opening shot of *The Paradine Case* "Cumberland" sequence begins here, on a hill between Ambleside and Rydal, looking across the A591 to Rydal Water and Grasmere Lake and the Cumbrian Mountains in the distance. Precisely where in Cumberland—now Cumbria—Sir Anthony Keane is supposed to be is never indicated, apart from his ultimate (and fictional) destination, Hindley Hall. In the novel, Keane journeys to coastal Cumberland, south of Whitehaven. In the film, he is literally all over the map, for which see the following entries, arranged in the order the locations appear in the film.

65:2
Coniston Station F
Coniston
Lake District

NW England, 215 mi. NW of London, off the A593

This is the first of the scenic Lake District railway stations shown in the "Cumberland" section of *The Paradine Case* (see **Braithwaite Station**, below, for the second).

Hitchcock himself had selected the location and his instructions to the second-unit cameraman were explicit: He wanted a long, day shot under a tree branch that panned with the train left to right until the train came to a stop—which is exactly what he got. He would then cut to footage taken at Braithwaite Station (some 50 miles to the north) for Keane's actual arrival. For the conclusion of the sequence, when Keane leaves Cumberland, Hitchcock still wanted the tree branch, but this time it was to be an "early evening" long shot with "a complete change of quality." Apparently the second unit wasn't able to get precisely what the director wanted, for the train's departure is simply a reversal of the earlier shot (note that the tree is now on the right of the screen).

65:3
Braithwaite Station F
Braithwaite
Lake District

NW England, 260 mi. NW of London, off the A66, 4 mi. W of Keswick

This is the *second* of the picturesque Lake District railway stations shown in the "Cumberland" section of *The Paradine Case*. (See **Coniston Station**, above, for the first.) Hitchcock and unit manager Fred Ahern discovered both stations on a visit here in May 1946. A second unit crew later filmed the location footage, with a double for actor Gregory Peck actually entering the booking hall. Peck himself is shown exiting a Hollywood mock-up of the booking hall, with a suspicious-looking gentleman carrying a cello behind him. The train itself is on the Penrith-Workington branch of the London-Glasgow "West Coast" main line. It is traveling west to east, i.e., *toward* London and not away from it, as the story actually requires.

Braithwaite Station in 1966. Today a private home is there.

65:4
The Drunken Duck Inn F
Barngates
Ambleside
Lake District

NW England, 245 mi. NW of London, off the B5286, 3 mi. S of Ambleside

Doubles as: The Station Hotel in *The Paradine Case*

Situated "at a crossroads in the middle of nothing but magnificent scenery" (to quote their on-line ad), this 400-year-old inn and restaurant hosted the distinguished London barrister Anthony Keane in *The Paradine Case*. Traveling to the Paradines' country home (see **Langdale Chase**) to investigate valet André Latour, Keane arrives at the **Braithwaite Station**, then walks the short distance to the "Station Hotel." In fact, the Drunken Duck is some 16 miles away as the crow flies! Another surprise, if you choose to visit:The nine en suite rooms are bright and modern, with all the modern conveniences, not a bit like the Spartan accommodation afforded Keane.

For detailed directions to the inn, see http://www.drunkenduckinn.co.uk/finding-us.htm

65:5
Yew Tree Farm F
Barngates
Coniston
Lake District

NW England, 246 mi. NW of London, off the A593

Yew Tree Farm

This 16th-century farmhouse (once owned by Beatrix Potter) provides the backdrop for the beginning of Anthony Keane's buggy ride to "Hindley Hall" in *The Paradine Case*. Keane, here played by Gregory Peck's stand-in, leaves the **Drunken Duck Inn**, some five miles to the north, then passes the farm here in Coniston before continuing on past the church (which I have been unable to identify) and the **Grange Bridge** at Grange. A picturesque journey to be sure, but certainly a circuitous one. The self-catering cottage here rents from £18 per person.

65:6
Grange Bridge F
Grange-in-Borrowdale
Keswick
Lake District

NW England, 255 mi. NW of London, off the B5289 at Grange

Beloved of artists and photographers, this picturesque stone bridge, spanning the River Derwent, marks the last landmark on Anthony Keane's buggy ride to "Hindley Hall" (see next entry) in *The Paradine Case*. Hitchcock had originally specified the equally photogenic Ashness Bridge, in Keswick. The reason for the switch is not clear from production documents.

65:7
Langdale Chase Hotel F
Windermere
Lake District

NW England, 244 mi. NW of London, on the A591 between Windermere and Ambleside

Doubles as: Hindley Hall in *The Paradine Case*

Begun as a private home in 1890, Langdale Chase has operated as a hotel since 1930. The Elizabethan-styled mansion, built in Cumbria's famous Brathay Blue Slate, features a magnificent landscaped garden, incomparable interiors (oak staircase, paneled walls, mosaic floors) and a large frontage onto Lake Windermere. Hitchcock discovered the hotel on a May 1946 location hunt for *The Paradine Case*, going on to incorporate a shot of the building's entrance, as well as a shot of the lake—as Gregory Peck's POV—in the finished film. Interiors were faithfully recreated in Hollywood, through a combination of studio sets and matte paintings. The 30-room Langdale Chase is open April through October, with packages ranging from £60-£95 per day.

The Langdale Chase Hotel doubled as Hindley Hall in *The Paradine Case*

Ask Mr. Memory 51: Which Hitchcock villain is said to esteem Lake Windermere as his favorite?

66. DEVON

66:1
HM Prison Dartmoor L (F)
Princetown

SW England, 185 mi. WSW of London

Built during the Napoleonic Wars to house French POWs, Dartmoor Prison is located in the middle of the bleakest of Devon's upland moors. Indeed, its setting is so bleak, so isolated that it is widely regarded as the most forbidding prison in Britain. Thus, in the American (but not the British) version of the play *Dial M for Murder*, Tony Wendice chides Swann that earning a thousand pounds (for killing Margot) and going on a long holiday with Mrs. Van Dorn "would be preferable to 10 years' detention in Dartmoor (for the murder of Miss Wallace)." Hitchcock deleted this particular reference to the prison, but, interestingly, inserted another, by way of the old blowhard's boring story at Tony's stag party.

Langley Court as seen in *Easy Virtue*

67. HAMPSHIRE

67:1
Langley Court F P
Liss

S England, 46 mi. SW of London

Doubles as: Moat House, Peveril, in *Easy Virtue*

This picturesque country house began as a relatively simple hunting lodge during the reign of Elzabeth I. In the 19th century it was expanded to its present configuration, the additions—in the same local stone—perfectly matching the original structure. In the 1920s, Langley House, as it was then called, came into the hands of Col. William Eagleson Gordon VC, a hero of the South African War and former ADC to King George V. It was Col. Gordon who changed the name to Langley Court, who hosted weekend visits from the Prince of Wales (the future Edward VIII) and who subsequently loaned the house to Alfred Hitchcock for the filming of *Easy Virtue*. Actors Isabel Jeans, Ian Hunter, Robin Irvine, et al. filmed exteriors here in the spring of 1927, with the interiors being shot later at **Islington Studios**. In those days, the estate covered hundreds of acres and required 17 indoor servants and 17 gardeners and gamekeepers. Today, the estate occupies 42 acres and its charming owners, Mr. and Mrs. James Loh, have divided the house into four separate accommodations for various branches of their family.

Note: While the address is Liss, Hampshire, the estate actually lies across the county line in West Sussex.

67:2
ex Army Aviation Centre (*now* BBC) L
Middle Wallop

S England, 74 mi. WSW of London, off the A343 between Andover and Salisbury

It was here at the Army's former Aviation Centre that Shoebridge and his wife collected their ransoms in the novel *The Rainbird Pattern*, whence *Family Plot*. As in the film, the wife (and, once, Shoebridge himself) then has the authorities fly her by helicopter to the site where the kidnap victim will be returned. In the film, the spot is an unidentified golf course; in the novel, there are three sites: Crowborough Beacon Golf Club, East Sussex; Tiverton Golf Club, Devon; and the New Forest, Hampshire—all of them real locations. The Aviation Centre is now home to the Museum of Army Flying and a prestigious international air show staged by the Army Air Corps here every two years.

67:3
Southampton Port F
Southampton

S England, 76 mi. SW of London

Hitchcock came here in the spring of 1928 to film shipboard exteriors for his comedy-drama *Champagne*, featuring popular comic actress Betty Balfour as the spoiled daughter of an American millionaire. (Though perhaps hard to imagine now, especially given her performance in *Champagne*, Balfour was a true superstar of British silent cinema, popularly known as "the English Mary Pickford.") The ship in question was the RMS *Aquitania*, which the Cunard company had launched on

Hitchcock filmed exterior shipboard scenes for the silent film *Champagne* at the Southampton Port.

May 30, 1914. As the largest, most luxurious passenger liner then afloat, the *Aquitania* quickly earned the sobriquet "the Ship Beautiful." *Champagne* contains several shots of the ship's exterior (during Betty's dramatic arrival by plane), as well as a plug for both the ship and the Cunard Line (during the scene in which she gazes into the window of the Bureau de Change). Indeed, much of the film takes place aboard ship (or, at least, studio recreations), a mode of transportation to which the director would return again and again. (Cf. everything from *The Pleasure Garden* to *Torn Curtain*, the possibilities for Hitchcockian romance, drama and intrigue being as great—if not more so—than in his other favored mode of transportation: the passenger train.) As for the majestic *Aquitania*, she was converted for military use in WWI (and, again, in WWII), operated on the famous Southampton-Cherbourg (France)-New York route (depicted in the film) and doubled as a cruise ship from 1932 onward. Sadly, she made her last run in 1949 (ferrying emigrants to Canada on behalf of the Canadian government) and was broken up in Scotland in 1950.

68. HERTFORDSHIRE

68:1
Elstree Studios (*former* BIP/ABPC/EMI Studios) F
Shenley Road
Borehamwood

SE England, 12 mi. NNW of London

Alfred Hitchcock made more films at Elstree Studios—15—than at any other studio in the U.K. *or* America. These include his last silent films, his first sound films and even one of his 1950s "American" films.[9] Hitchcock had been working at **Islington Studios** in London when he was approached by John Maxwell, the head of British International Pictures (BIP). Maxwell, a solicitor-turned-film distributor and exhibitor, had just opened BIP Studios, popularly known as Elstree Studios, one of several studios in the area—actually, Borehamwood, not Elstree—to be so dubbed at one time or another. Maxwell was determined to make BIP a successful, international concern, following the model of the American studio system, in which a single company, say, Paramount, would not only produce films, but also distribute them to their own theatre circuits. To achieve this kind of "vertical integration," Maxwell needed talented people both in front of and behind the camera, and for that he was willing to pay big. In fact, at £13,000 a year (over a million dollars in today's money), Hitchcock's three-year, 12-picture contract made him the highest-paid director in Britain. (Money was then rolling into producers' hands from eager financiers in the City, the catalyst being the Cinematograph Films Act of 1927, which mandated that a gradually increasing percentage of films shown in Britain be of British origin.) Under Maxwell's BIP banner, Hitchcock now solidified his relationship with pioneering production designer Wilfred Arnold, who had designed *The Lodger* at Islington in 1926. For *The Ring,* an original Hitchcock screenplay, *The Farmer's Wife, The Manxman, Blackmail, Rich and Strange* and *Number Seventeen,* all shot here at Elstree, Arnold followed the approach of the earlier film, creating simple, uncluttered sets that literally stood in stark contrast to the overdressed sets then in fashion. He believed that through the imaginative use of lighting and camera set-ups, the few props that were used on his sets could be exploited for dramatic purposes, like the champagne glasses in *The Ring* or the paintings in *The Lodger*. *Blackmail*, of course, was Britain's first talking picture (see **Regal Cinema** for more on the film's status as such), Maxwell having determined to beat the other studios to the punch, even to the point of hiring sound engineers from the **BBC** to supervise the studio's new recording equipment. Hitchcock readily took to the new medium, notwithstanding the fact that his camera—at least for those first few talkies—was now confined to a soundproof box so that the recording equipment would not pick up its noise. (Author Charles Barr has painstakingly compared the silent and sound versions of *Blackmail*, noting the greater fluidity of camera movement in the former.) Unfortunately, Hitchcock's later BIP films, *Rich and Strange* and *Number Seventeen* failed to score and for his final picture, the director turned producer to supervise *Lord Camber's Ladies*, which starred his old friend Gerald du Maurier and was directed by *Blackmail* dialogue writer Benn Levy. Since Maxwell was interested neither in innovation nor the American market—and Hitchcock most assuredly was interested in both—the two men parted company in 1932. Hitchcock moved back to London, where he reunited with

Michael Balcon for the famous "Thirties Thrillers" at **Lime Grove Studios**. Following these, the director made one-shot stops at **Pinewood Studios** (*Young and Innocent*) and Islington (*The Lady Vanishes*) before returning to Maxwell's rechristened ABPC (Associated British Picture Corporation) Studios in 1938 to shoot Charles Laughton in *Jamaica Inn*. During the War, ABPC was requisitioned for use as a Royal Army Ordinance Corps depot, John Maxwell died, and his family subsequently sold the studio to Hollywood giant Warner Bros., for whom Hitchcock would soon direct a number of films. Indeed, one of those films, *Stage Fright*, would actually be shot at ABPC, whose stages Warners had just spent a fortune remodeling. (*Under Capricorn*, which Hitchcock filmed immediately prior to *Stage Fright*, was based at the nearby **MGM British Studios**, ABPC being unavailable due to the refurbishment.) This was to be Hitchcock's last, true British production until *Frenzy*, some 20 years later, which he made at Pinewood. Meanwhile, ABPC was acquired by the British entertainment conglomerate EMI (Electrical and Musical Industries) in 1969, briefly merged with MGM in the early 1970s, then with Thorn, another giant electrical concern, in the late '70s. During this time, the studio—under various names (EMI, EMI-MGM, Thorn-EMI)—hosted many high-profile productions, including *Murder on the Orient Express,* the initial *Star Wars* trilogy, the Indiana Jones trilogy, *The Shining, Never Say Never Again* and even Monty Python's *The Meaning of Life*. Hard times followed in the 1980s and the studio eventually fell into the hands of the Brent Walker Entertainment Group, which sold half the property to a supermarket chain, demolishing the bulk of the old soundstages in the process. Plans to do likewise with the remainder of the site were challenged by local citizen activists and the Hertsmere Borough Council, which bought the studio in 1996 and has since erected two new soundstages. The Council has also erected plaques honoring some of Elstree's giants—including Charles Laughton and Alfred Hitchcock—in Shenley Road, along the walk from the train station to the studio.

To visit the historic locale, take the Tube to the **King's Cross St. Pancras (CI; HC; ME; NO; PI; VI; NR; Thameslink)** station; follow the signs to Thames Link, which you will take to **Elstree & Borehamwood**. Walk out of the station (toward the Gate Studios sign), veer L, then turn R into Shenley Road. The studio is ahead, past all the shops, on the R. The two small brick buildings to the right of the entrance are all that remain of the original BIP Studios; the soundstages where Hitchcock worked were located on what is now the supermarket's parking lot.

68:2
ex **MGM–British Studios F**
Elstree Way
Borehamwood

SE England, 12 mi. NNW of London

Located just up the road and across the street from the more famous **Elstree Studios**, MGM's British outpost was founded as Amalgamated Studios in 1937. MGM acquired the studio after the Second World War and determined to recreate it as a British version of their Culver City, California facility. This it largely did, hosting mega-stars like Elizabeth Taylor, Clark Gable and Spencer Tracy and legendary productions like

Kubrick's *2001: A Space Odyssey*. Less famously, perhaps, the studio also hosted Alfred Hitchcock's first post-War British film, *Under Capricorn*, which he produced with his **Transatlantic Pictures** partner Sidney Bernstein. Exteriors for the film—set in 19th-century Australia—were initially planned for the MGM backlot here in Borehamwood, but, owing to the inclement weather, were finally staged on the Hollywood backlot of Warner Bros., the company distributing the film. In fact, Hitchcock's next picture, *Stage Fright*, would be made for Warners at their newly refurbished **Elstree Studios**, just down Shenley Road. MGM itself would eventually merge its British production facilities with that very studio (as EMI-MGM Elstree Studios [see the previous entry]), closing the MGM British Studios in 1970. Its stylish Art Deco buildings were demolished in the late 1980s and the site now houses the Sainsbury Distribution Depot. The backlot—which *almost* made it into *Under Capricorn*—is now a housing estate.

68:3

ex **Welwyn Studios Ltd. (*now* Polycell) F**
Broadwater Road
Welwyn Garden City

S England, 20 mi. N of London

Founded by British Instructional Films (Proprietors) in 1928, this small studio was acquired by **Elstree** owner John Maxwell two years later. During the 1930s, Welwyn turned out mostly "Quota Quickies," low-budget films made to satisfy the Cinematograph Films Act of 1927, which mandated that at least 20 percent of films exhibited in Britain be British films. When Elstree itself was requisitioned for the war effort in 1939, Maxwell transferred his base here to Welwyn. Hitchcock first came to Welwyn in 1935 to shoot portions of the **London Palladium** sequence for *The 39 Steps*. He returned nine years later on behalf of the **Ministry of Information** to direct the two short propaganda films *Bon Voyage* and *Aventure Malgache*

(i.e., "Malagasy Adventure"). Shot in French in January-February 1944, both films featured the so-called "Molière Players," a group of exiled French actors then living in London. The plan seems to have been to exhibit these films clandestinely in occupied France in order to boost morale and pave the way for the eventual Allied liberation. In the event, neither film appears to have been screened,[10] Hitchcock's moral ambiguity and emphasis on French collaborators being a little too far removed from what the propagandists ordered. Welwyn also boasts a number of other relevant connections: *Thirty-nine Steps* author John Buchan served on the board of British Instructional Films (Proprietors) here in the late 1920s; Hitchcock actors Ann Todd, Margaret Lockwood, Maureen O'Hara, Basil Radford, Leslie Banks, Nova Pilbeam, Michael Wilding and James Mason all made films here in the 1930s and '40s; and mystery writer Josephine Tey (*A Shilling for Candles*, whence the film *Young and Innocent*) saw her novel *The Franchise Affair* shot here as the studio's last production, in 1950. Associated British Picture Corporation, owner of Elstree Studios, sold the studio to the Ardath Tobacco company in 1951. Polycell—makers of DIY products—took over in 1960 and have since extended the buildings. The original studio roof, however, can still be seen from the street, at 30 Broadwater Road.

68:4
ex **Wally's New Café F**
North Western Avenue
Watford

S England, 16 mi. NW of London, on the A41, just south of the M1 intersection

Here, just below Hartspring Lane, was the all-night pull-in where *Frenzy* killer Bob Rusk alit from the potato truck, popped into the public toilet, borrowed the clothes brush and sealed his fate. Sadly, the home of the humble food beloved of Chief Inspector Oxford has been long since demolished and replaced with a supermarket.

68:5
Ashridge Estate F
Berkhamsted

S England, 30 mi. NW of London, off the B4506, just N of Berkhamsted

On Sunday March 27, 1927, Alfred Hitchcock came here to shoot the rugby matches that begin and end *Downhill*. **Oxford University** kindly supplied enough undergrads to field two full teams, a fact dutifully reported in *Kinematograph* and other trade publications of the day. Ashridge is a magnificent estate which originated as a monastery in the 13th century. Henry VIII acquired

Ashridge Estate

the buildings after the Dissolution of the Monasteries (1536); his daughter Elizabeth I sold them in 1575. Most of the present structure was built by architect James Wyatt and his family in the early 19th century. It is considered one of the foremost examples of the so-called Gothic Revival style. The estate now houses a business management college and international conference center. The grounds are open year-round.

The *Downhill* rugby matches were filmed at Ashridge.

The MacGuffin: According to the novel *Marnie* (Chapter 4), Mark Rutland lives in a "smart-looking" house on the edge of a golf course in Little Gaddesden. That would put the businessman-cum-amateur psychiatrist right next to the famous Ashridge Golf Club, lying literally in the shadow of the Ashridge Park estate. The literary house is "not big" (though it does have tall chimneys) and appears to be altogether more intimate than its cinematic counterpart. The exterior of the latter was constructed on the Universal Studios backlot (and enhanced with matte paintings); it was located just up the street from the *Leave it to Beaver* house, which Hitchcock had used as Jackie Chester's home in the *Alfred Hitchcock Presents* episode "Bang! You're Dead."

69. KENT

69:1
Site of "The Thirty-nine Steps" L P
St. Cuby
Cliff Promenade
Broadstairs

SE England, 68 mi. E of London

Chapter 10 of *The Thirty-nine Steps* finds hero Richard Hannay in "Bradgate," Kent, where he determines to locate a house used by enemy spies, one with "thirty-nine steps" from the top of the cliff down to the beach. Hannay eventually discovers the house, called Trafalgar Lodge, from which the enemies intend to make their escape to the Continent. (They have "stolen" Allied defense plans through the ingenious device of having one of their members disguise himself as the British 1st Sea Lord and then memorizing classified documents.) Author John Buchan actually stayed here in Broadstairs (once called Bradgate) in the summer of 1914 and while recovering from illness, began writing what was to become his most famous novel (which, of course, Hitchcock would adapt some 20 years later). The villa he occupied, St. Cuby, overlooked a tunneled staircase that led from the cliff's edge down to the beach. That Buchan had in mind this particular set of steps, at this particular villa, is all but certain given the details he provides in the novel. He did, however, make one important change from fact to fiction: he halved the number of steps from 78 to 39. (Fair's fair: he *doubled* the number of cliff-side staircases from three to six.) He may have been thinking of a set of 39 wooden steps leading down from Ravenscraig Castle, in his childhood hometown of Pathhead, Fife, to the beach below (though these steps were erected long after Buchan lived and played there). Then again, the devout Calvinist may have drawn inspiration from the Old Testament, whose 39 books, notes Buchan scholar David Daniel, constitute the "39 steps to the revelation of God in Christ" (quoted in Kestner). In any case, Buchan's original oaken staircase has since been replaced with a stone structure containing more than 100 steps. According to one of the author's biographers, the carpenter who built the present staircase salvaged some of the wood from the original steps and made three sets of bookends out of it. One set he kept for himself, another he sent to Buchan and the third he sent to Alfred Hitchcock.

The steps that inspired *The Thirty-nine steps*.

Ask Mr. Memory 52: In the film the enemy spy ring is called "The 39 Steps." What is the organization's name in the novel?

69:2
Port of Dover F
Dover

SE England, 68 mi. SE of London

The shooting script for *Rich and Strange* indicates that Fred and Em depart from Britain's historic port at the start of their monumental journey. The film also depicts the bustle of Dover, though the shots—representing Fred's POV—appear to be library footage, rather than first unit material shot (or authorized) by Hitchcock himself. Dover was heavily damaged during WWII and has since undergone extensive rebuilding. Still, its majestic setting beneath the famous White Cliffs make it one of the most attractive tourist spots in the country.

70. OXFORDSHIRE

70:1
University of Oxford (F) L
Oxford

Cen. England, 52 mi. WNW of London

England's oldest university (founded in the 12th century) and, with **Cambridge**, its most famous and prestigious, pops up on a number of occasions in Hitchcock's Britain. The uniformed officer who boards the train near the end of *The Lady Vanishes* went to Oxford, as did the mustachioed half of Charters and Caldicott (you should know which one that is). The pair are well on the way to striking up a proper old Oxonian entente cordiale when Gilbert coshes the officer on the head. Gilbert, you see, went to Cambridge. In the novel *Rebecca*, we learn that Maxim's brother-in-law, Giles, was at Oxford and that Giles and Beatrice's son, Roger, will go up next term. In the play *Rope*, murder victim Ronald Kentley is—or was—an Oxford undergraduate, as are his killers. In the film, *David* Kentley was a Harvard man, although apparently the killers were not. It is also to Oxford that the play's killers intend to journey with David's body, vs. the film's journey to Brandon's mother's farm in Connecticut. Oxford, both the town and the university, plays its biggest role in Edmund Crispin 1940s novels *The Case of the Gilded Fly* and *The Moving Toyshop*. From these, Hitchcock appropriated, respectively, the climaxes for *Stage Fright* (unofficially, but apparently, since he had obtained copies of all Crispin's novels from the publisher) and *Strangers on a Train* (officially, but without credit in the film). (Another Crispin "borrowing" may appear in *Torn Curtain*. See Appendix I for details.) The former novel, a "classic" whodunit in

Oxford University

the Christie mold, climaxes at the fictitious Oxford Repertory Theatre, where amateur detective (and Professor of English Language and Literature) Gervase Fen and others witness the murderer's untimely demise as he is crushed beneath the falling safety curtain. (*Stage Fright*'s theatrical milieu may also come from Crispin, since there is nothing like it in the official source novel, Selwyn Jepson's *Man Running*.) The latter novel, as much a comic chase thriller as a whodunit, climaxes with the murderer and the hero—Fen again—having a final showdown aboard an out-of-control merry-go-round, with two other characters trying to reach the controls by crawling beneath the spinning platform (see **Botley Fair**). Otherwise, there is little overlap between *Strangers* and *Toyshop*, which sees the detective and a number of comical colleagues trying to unravel a devilishly clever plot in which an old woman is murdered for her inheritance and the proceedings disguised through the amazing title locale. From the reel to the real world, you might also like to know that Leslie Banks, star of *The Man Who Knew Too Much* (34) and *Jamaica Inn*, also went to Oxford.

70:2
ex **Site of the Botley Fair L**
Botley (near Oxford)

Cen. England, 52 mi. WNW of London

Here, in this small Oxford suburb, author Edmund Crispin set the climax of his 1946 mystrie *The Moving Toyshop*. That climax—set aboard an out-of-control merry-go-round—was borrowed for the grand finale of *Strangers on a Train*, a film otherwise based on Patricia Highsmith's 1950 novel of the same title. Hitchcock, as Richard Valley described in *Scarlet Street* magazine, had appropriated an ending from Crispin once before: that of the fatal falling curtain in *Stage Fright*, from the 1944 mystery *The Case of the Gilded Fly*. On that occasion, it was apparently without pay or permission. This time, it was with both. In the novel, the murderer (I won't give him or her away) flees to the small fun park near **Oxford**, where s/he hopes to elude amateur detective Gervase Fen and a motley assortment of others. The murderer takes refuge on a "roundabout" (i.e., a merry-go-round), a shot is fired, the operator collapses and the climax plays out much as in the film, with someone—actually, two people—crawling beneath the spinning platform in a near-suicidal attempt to reach the controls....

71. SUFFOLK

71:1
Newmarket Rowley Racecourse L
Newmarket

E England, 56 mi. NNE of London

The headquarters of British horseracing since 1622, the affluent little town of Newmarket actually boasts more horses (2,500) than people (1,700). It was here, during the autumn sport, that Marnie dazzled Mark with her ability to pick a winning horse in Chapter 5 of Winston Graham's novel. As in the film adaptation, Marnie also hints at an unpleasant childhood while attending the races. She does not ask to visit the paddock, though, and the scene in which she is mistaken for "Peggy Nicholson" actually occurs earlier in the chapter, at the Double Six roadhouse near Aylesbury, Bucks. Coincidentally (?), near the end of the High Street stands the Rutland Arms Hotel, a Newmarket fixture for over 300 years.

Ask Mr. Memory 53: What is the name of the horse Marnie sees in the paddock?

72. SURREY

72:1
Epsom Downs Racecourse (F)
Epsom and Ewell

S England, 16 mi. SW of London

Epsom Downs is the site of the world-famous Derby, an annual horse race named after Edward Stanley, 12th Earl of Derby. (All other "derbies," including the famous one in Kentucky, are named after the British original.) The race is run on the first Wednesday in June, known as "Derby Day," a sort of national holiday uniting racing fans of all classes, from the Queen on down. Alfred Hitchcock, who often attended Derby Day as a child, originally planned to shoot the climax of his film *No Bail for the Judge* (see Appendix III) here on Derby Day 1959. Letters between Hitchcock's production staff and Epsom officials were exchanged in March and April of that year, with the result that Box 53 of the Grandstand's Gallery Tier was booked for £130. Production documents indicate that as of May 14 Hitchcock still intended to shoot here on Derby Day, although the Samuel Taylor shooting script of April 15 includes no scenes set at Epsom. (There is, however, a reference to the event/racecourse toward the end of the story.) Art director Henry Bumstead cleared up the discrepancy: The original climax, as devised by Ernest Lehman, was to have had the bad guys being chased out onto the track and then trampled to death by the horses. "A terrific 'Hitchcock' ending," Bumstead enthused, over 40 years later. The Taylor script settled on a tamer climax set in a Mayfair home (see entry 15:4). The reason for Hitchcock's apparent vacillation—Epsom or no Epsom—may have had to do with his decision to shoot the bulk of the film in Hollywood—a decision that nearly exasperated Bumstead. "I was so busy measuring *all* of England—so that we could shoot this at home—I never worked so hard in my life! I really was in a panic because I was going to have build all this stuff back home and he hadn't really settled on anything. I could have done it—but it would have been a big job." So was any of the real Epsom Downs going to show up onscreen? "Oh, he may have done a few shots there, but he wanted to show the studio [Paramount] that we could 'do England at home.'" So Bumstead took dozens of reference photos, made all his measurements of the course and "was ready to go" by June 1959, when he learned that the production had been canceled due to the withdrawal of star Audrey Hepburn.

72:2
Alfred Hitchcock's Country Home H P
Winter's Grace
Stroud Lane
Shamley Green

S England, 28 mi. SW of London, off the Guildford Road (B2128)

In 1927, Alfred Hitchcock became the highest-paid director in Britain, courtesy of his three-year contract with John Maxwell's British International Pictures (see **Elstree Studios**). The following year, he and Alma spent £2,500 (a little under $200,000 in today's money) on the home of their dreams, Winter's Grace, a country complement to their London flat in Cromwell Road (see 22:1). Hitch and Alma, then pregnant with their daughter Patricia, set about the task of renovating the house and gardens, a task that, typically, seemed to take forever. When all was finished, the Hitchcocks could retreat to the country for relaxing weekends away from work and the studio, entertaining friends and family, including Elsie Randolph (*Rich and Strange, Frenzy*) and Cyril Ritchard (*Blackmail*), and Hitchcock's mother, Emma, and brother, William. On more than one occasion the professional filmmaker turned amateur to record the weekend festivities on home movies. These films show a truly relaxed, spirited, fun-loving Hitchcock, romping with his guests (and pets), delighting in his Surrey surroundings. Hitchcock eventually acquired a smaller house adjacent to the property, in which he installed his aging mother during the War. He sold Winter's Grace itself in February 1939, the month before he, Alma, and 10-year-old Patricia set sail for America. Emma Hitchcock died on September 26, 1942, and William committed suicide three months later. The property is still extant in private hands.

Hitchcock and Alma working on the set of *The Mountain Eagle* (1925)

Goodwood Racecourse in 1931
73. WEST SUSSEX

73:1
Goodwood Racecourse (L) (F)
Chichester

S England, 52 mi. SW of London

Popularly known as "Glorious Goodwood," this beautiful Sussex Downs racecourse hosts one of the most fashionable sporting and social events of the season, the so-called "Goodwood Week" each July/August. During the 1938 event, Goodwood also hosted the charming ne'er-do-well Johnnie Aysgarth, or so he tells his young bride, Lina, in *Suspicion*. In order to account for the expensive presents he lavishes on Lina, their maid and his best friend Beaky, Johnnie claims to have won £2,000 at the Goodwood Cup (over $100,000 in today's money). However, as we later learn, Johnnie has actually embezzled the money from his cousin—and employer—Captain George Melbeck. (For more of Mr. Aysgarth's racing activities, see **Newbury Racecourse**.) The track is also mentioned in Chapter 4 of *A Shilling for Candles*, whence *Young and Innocent*. There, the genial Chief Constable Burgoyne tries to relax Robert Tisdall while the latter is being questioned in connection with Christine Clay's death. He knows he mustn't shake hands—not with a man suspected of murder. So, he settles for idle chit chat. "Fine morning!" he offers. "Bad for racing, of course....You a racing man? Going to Goodwood?" Tisdall doesn't answer, though, as we later learn, he is, indeed, a racing man. In fact, as with his cinematic counterpart, Tisdall is soon wilting under **Scotland Yard** questioning. Fortunately for him, the chief constable's daughter is on hand to revive him. And, as in the film, Erica handily recalls her Girl Guide training, right down to the brandy—a staple in Hitchcock's films.

MR. MEMORY ANSWERS

1. 322
2. "A week or two before…before he died."
3. "English intellectuals," like Drayton
4. *New York Globe*
5. 50
6. A. Clarke, Baker and Confectioner
7. Mrs. Humphries, as shown in an insert shot of the note she wrote to Mr. Crewe—a shot found in the silent version but not the sound. The note also contains a blooper—Tracy's surname is spelled "Tracey."
8. Pat Hitchcock
9. *Frenzy*—Dick Blaney; references to the paper, usually in signs, occur in other films, as well, e.g., *Blackmail*.
10. Victoria
11. Forsythe's brother-in-law
12. "Beulah, peel me a grape." Mae West immortalized the line in the 1933 film *I'm No Angel*. Film historian Alexander Walker (in *Sex in the Movies*) described it as "the most imperious (and celebrated) instruction ever given to a domestic servant."
13. The Cape, California, Jaffa
14. Brandy, as do characters in nearly every Hitchcock film
15. Marnie's
16. "One-round" Jack, according to the intertitle; One Round Jack on the sign in the film
17. Michael Wilding and Marlene Dietrich during the production of *Stage Fright*
18. Just over £90,000, the equivalent of £1.5 million in today's currency!
19. Fisher, also the name of Herbert Marshall's character in *Foreign Correspondent*
20. A one-pound note, which the milkman refuses but then keeps!
21. *Blackmail*; the scene, of Alice at Scotland Yard, was the first completed for the talking version.
22. *Torn Curtain*—Michael picks up his ticket to Berlin from the Cook's located inside the Hotel D'Angleterre.
23. Twenty-year-old Charles Laughton, whose family sent him here in 1919 to learn the hotel business. They themselves ran a successful hotel, the Pavillion, in Scarborough.
24. In Piccadilly
25. "An attack of influenza"
26. The Bulldog
27. D (for "Devilish"?)
28. That it was "the centre of the world"
29. Edgar Wallace, who is estimated to have written over 170 thrillers from 1906 until his death in 1932
30. Julie Andrews, at the age of 12
31. Nova Pilbeam

32. *The Woman Alone*
33. Ten years; two years
34. £1.3.0, i.e., one pound, three shillings, or about $100 in today's money!
35. Light his cigarette
36. "Well, I've just died for it."
37. "Never climb a fence when you can sit on it."
38. Inspector Walls, as shown in Alice's message to him at the end of the film; the part is played by two actors, in both versions of the film: Sam Livesy and Harvey Braban.
39. Politicians aren't usually called upon to…do away with their guests.
40. Eight years
41. A lion
42. *Torn Curtain*, in the Hotel D'Angleterre
43. Swann, just before he moved to Carlyle Court, i.e., Carlyle Mansions
44. *Rich and Strange*
45. *Into Thin Air*, a title used for an early episode of *Alfred Hitchcock Presents*
46. Monkeyface
47. *The Saxon*, to which the dentist replies, "She's not due until tomorrow." Bob, in turn, says he actually got off at Tilbury, then took the train.
48. 1903
49. Coming Up—owned by "Mrs. S. Cain"—the wife of production designer Syd Cain!
50. 20 years
51. According to Chadwyck in *Jamaica Inn*, this was Sir Humphrey's favorite lake during his visit to the Lake District.
52. The Black Stone. Interestingly, Buchan had originally planned to call the book itself *The Black Stone*, after the enemy conspiracy. This would have paralleled Hitchcock's eventual decision to make "The 39 Steps" not an actual staircase but rather the enemy organization itself.
53. Telepathy, the name of the novel's winning horse.

Scoring:

48-53: Mr. Memory has plenty to worry about with you on the scene. You could truly be *The Man* (or *Woman*) *Who Knew Too Much*.

40-47: You still have "One More Mile To Go," but if Mr. Memory ever needs an understudy….

33-39: For now, you're a little too *Young and Innocent* to join "The 39 Steps."

32 and under: You're definitely *The Wrong Man* (or *Woman*) for this job!

BIBLIOGRAPHY

REFERENCE BOOKS/PERIODICALS
Hitchcock and British Cinema

Auiler, Dan. *Hitchcock's Notebooks An Authorized and Illustrated Look Inside the Creative Mind of Alfred Hitchcock*. New York: Spike, 1999.

Auiler, Dan. *Vertigo: The Making of a Hitchcock Classic*. New York: St. Martin's Press, 1998.

Barr, Charles. *English Hitchcock*. Moffat, Scotland: Cameron & Hollis, 1999.

Bergman, Paul, and Michael Asimov. *Reel Justice: The Courtroom Goes to the Movies*. Kansas City: Andrews and McMeel, 1996.

Bogdanovich, Peter. *Who the Devil Made It*. New York: Alfred A. Knopf, 1997.

Brown, Geoff. "'Sister of the Stage': British Film and British Theatre." *All Our Yesterdays: 90 Years of British Cinema*. London: BFI, 1986.

Carrick, Edward. *Art and Design in the British Film*. New York: Arno Press and *The New York Times*, 1972.

DeRosa. *Writing with Hitchcock: The Collaboration of Alfred Hitchcock and John Michael Hayes*. New York and London: Faber and Faber, 2001.

"Film-making in a Tube." *Daily Mail*. 28 Feb. 1927.

Freeman, David. *The Last Days of Alfred Hitchcock*. Woodstock, New York: The Overlook Press, 1984.

French, Philip. "Alfred Hitchcock: the English Film-maker as Englishman and Exile." *Sight and Sound* 54 (1985): 116-122.

Gottlieb, Sidney, ed. *Hitchcock on Hitchcock: Selected Writings and Interviews*. Berkeley and Los Angeles: University of California Press, 1995.

- - -. *Alfred Hitchcock Interviews*. Jackson: University Press of Mississippi, 2003.

Hitchcock, Alfred. Interview with François Truffaut. August 1962. Audiotape. Margaret Herrick Library, Los Angeles, Alfred Hitchcock Collection.

- - -. "Search for the Sun." *New York Times* 7 Feb. 1937.

- - -. "A Talk with Hitchcock." *Telescope*. By Fletcher Markle. CBC Television. 1964.

Huntley, John. *Railways in the Cinema*. London: Ian Allan, 1969.

Jensen, Paul M. *Hitchcock Becomes "Hitchcock": The British Years*. Baltimore, Maryland: Midnight Marquee Press, 2000.

Kuhns, J. L. "Hitchcock's *The Mountain Eagle*." *Hitchcock Annual* 1998-99 (1998): 31-108.

Leff, Leonard J. *Hitchcock and Selznick: The Rich and Strange Collaboration of Alfred Hitchcock and David O. Selznick in Hollywood*. New York: Weidenfeld and Nicholson, 1987.

Lejeune, C.A. "Cinema Cameos." *The Sketch*. July 10, 1940.

Low, Rachael. *Film Making in 1930s Britain: The History of the British Film 1929-1939*. London: George Allen & Unwin, 1985.

Margolies, Albert. "A Good Time Was Had by All in Bloomsbury." *New York Times* Aug. 14, 1949.

Martin, Pete. "Pete Martin Calls on Hitchcock." *The Saturday Evening Post* July 27, 1958: 32-37; 71-73.

McFarlane, Brian. "A Literary Cinema? British films and British novels." *All Our Yesterdays: 90 Years of British Cinema*. Ed. Charles Barr. London: British Film Institute, 1986. 120-142.

McGilligan, Patrick. *Alfred Hitchcock: A Life in Darkness and Light*. New York: ReganBooks, 2003.

Mogg, Ken. *The Alfred Hitchcock Story*. Dallas: Taylor Publishing Company, 1999.

Montagu, Ivor. *Film World: A Guide to Cinema*. Harmondsworth, Middlesex, England: Pelican Books, 1964.

Montagu, Ivor. "Working with Hitchcock." *Sight and Sound* 49 (1980): 189-193.

Park, James. *British Cinema: The Lights that Failed*. London: B.T. Batsford, 1990.

Perry, George. *The Great British Picture Show*. Rev. ed. Boston: Little, Brown and Company, 1985.

Quinlan, David. *British Sound Films: The Studio Years 1928-1959*. London: Batsford, 1984.

Rohmer, Eric, and Claude Chabrol. *Hitchcock: The First Forty-Four Films*. Trans. Stanley Hochman. New York: Frederick Ungar Publishing, 1979

Ryall, Tom. *Alfred Hitchcock & the British Cinema*. Urbana and Chicago: University of Illinois Press, 1986.

Ryall, Tom. *Blackmail*. London: British Film Institute, 1993.

Samson, Jen. "The Film Society, 1925-1939." *All Our Yesterdays: 90 Years of British Cinema*. Ed. Charles Barr. London: British Film Institute, 1986. 306-313.

Samuels, Charles Thomas. *Encountering Directors*. New York: Capricorn Books, 1972.
Sennett, Robert S. *Setting the Scene: The Great Hollywood Art Directors*. New York: Harry N. Abrams.
Spoto, Donald. *The Art of Alfred Hitchcock*. Garden City, New York: Doubleday & Company, 1976.
Spoto, Donald. *The Dark Side of Genius: The Life of Alfred Hitchcock*. New York: Ballantine Books, 1983.
Sussex, Elizabeth. "The Fate of F3080." *Sight and Sound* 53 (1984): 92-97.
Taylor, John Russell. *Hitch: The Life and Times of Alfred Hitchcock*. London: Faber & Faber, 1978.
Threadgall, Derek. *Shepperton Studios: An Independent View*. London: BFI, 1994.
Truffaut, François. *Hitchcock*. Rev. ed. New York: Simon and Schuster, 1985.
"Tube Film-making." *Evening News*. February 28, 1927
Valley, Richard. "The Trouble with Hitchcock: *Stage Fright* and *Strangers on a Train* Investigated!".*Scarlet Street* 21 (1996): 61-65.
Villien, Bruno. *Hitchcock*. Paris: Editions Colona, 1982.
Walker, Alexander. *Hollywood U.K.: The British Film Industry in the Sixties*. New York: Stein & Day, 1974.
Warren, Patricia. *British Film Studios: An Illustrated History*. London: BT Batsford, 1995.
Yacowar, Maurice. *Hitchcock's British Films*. Hamden, Connecticut: Archon Books, 1977.

London/England

Adams, Will, and Tricia Adams. *London: A Nostalgic Look at the Capital Since 1945*. London: Past and Present Publishing, 1997.
Adcock, St. John. ed. *Wonderful London*. 3 vols. London: The Fleetway House, 1926 [?].
Allison, Ronald, and Sarah Riddell, eds. *The Royal Encyclopedia*. London: Macmillan Press, 1991.
Babington, Anthony. *A House in Bow Street: Crime and the Magistracy London 1740-1881*. London: MacDonald & Co Ltd., 1969.
Bergan, Ronald. *The Great Theatres of London: An Illustrated Companion*. San Francisco: Chronicle Books, 1988.
Berkeley, Roy. *A Spy's London*. London: Leo Cooper, 1994.
Cameron, Robert, and Alistair Cooke. *Above London*. San Francisco: Cameron and Company, 1980.
Campbell, Una. *Robes of the Realm: 300 Years of Ceremonial Dress*. London: Michael O'Mara Books, 1989.
Chapman, Pauline. *Madame Tussaud's Chamber of Horrors: Two hundred Years of Crime*. London: Constable, 1984.
Coville, Gary, and Patrick Lucanio. *Jack the Ripper: His Life and Crimes in Popular Entertainment*. Jefferson, North Carolina: McFarland, 1999.
Dane, Clemence [Winifred Ashton]. *London has a Garden*. London: Michael Joseph, 1964.
Duncan, Andrew. *Secret London*. London: New Holland, 1998.
- - -. *Walking London*. 2nd ed. Chicago: Passport Books, 1999.
Duncan, Fiona, Leonie Glass, and Caroline Sharpe. *London Up Close, District by District, Street by Street*. Lincolnwood, Illinois: Passport Books, 1992.
Eyles, Allen. *Great British Cinemas*. Burgess Hill, West Sussex: Cinema Theatre Association, 1996.
Fido, Martin, and Keith Skinner. *The Official Encyclopedia of Scotland Yard*. London: Virgin Books, 1999.
Giblin, Gary. *James Bond's London*. Jersey City, New Jersey: Daleon, 2001.
Green, Benny. *The Streets of London*. London: Pavilion Books, 1983.
Harwood, Elain, and Andrew Saint. *London*. London: HMSO, 1991.
Hartnoll, Phyllis, and Peter Found. *The Concise Oxford Companion to the Theatre*. 2nd ed. Oxford and New York: Oxford University Press, 1993.
Hendershott, Barbara Sloan, and Alzina Stone Dale. *Mystery Reader's Walking Guide London*. 2nd ed.
Howard, Diana. *London Theatres and Music Halls 1850-1950*. London: The Library Association, 1970.
Howe, Sir Ronald. *The Story of Scotland Yard*. London: Arthur Barker Ltd., 1965.
James, Ewart. *NTC's Dictionary of the United Kingdom*. Lincolnwood, Illinois: NTC Publishing Group, 1996.
Jeffers, H. Paul. *Bloody Business: An Anecdotal History of Scotland Yard*. New York: Barnes & Noble, 1999.
Jones, Edward, and Christopher Woodward. *A Guide to the Architecture of London*. 2nd ed. London: Phoenix Illustrated, 1992.
Kennedy, Carol. *Mayfair: A Social History*. London: Hutchinson, 1986.

Lejeune, Anthony, and Malcolm Lewis. *The Gentlemen's Clubs of London.* London: Bracken Books, 1984.
Levine, Dan, and Richard Jones. *Frommer's Walking Tours: London.* New York: Prentice Hall Travel, 1993.
Lloyd's. *Some Unusual Risks.* London: Lloyd's, 1998.
Lord Lichfield, ed. *Courvoisier's Book of the Best.* London: Ebury Press, 1986.
Mander, Raymond, and Joe Mitchenson. *The Theatres of London.* 3rd ed. London: New English Library, 1975.
Menen, Aubrey. *London.* Amsterdam: Time-Life International, 1976.
Michelin. *Michelin Green Guide to London.* London: Michelin Tyre, 1998.
Montgomery-Massingberd, Hugh and David Watkin. *The London Ritz: A Social and Architectural History.* 2nd ed. London: Aurum Press, 1989.
O'Donnell, Bernard. *The Old Bailey and its Trials.* New York: The Macmillan Company, 1951.
Richardson, John. *Covent Garden.* New Barnet, Herts.: Historical Publications, 1979.
Room, Adrian. *An A to Z of British Life.* Oxford: Oxford University Press, 1990.
Saunders, Ann. "Forbes House, Halkin Street, SW I." *London Topographical Record* 27 (1995): 281-290.
- - -. *The Art and Architecture of London: An Illustrated Guide.* Oxford: Phaidon Press Ltd.., 1984.
Schreuders, Pet, Mark Lewisohn, and Adam Smith. *The Beatles' London: The Ultimate Guide to over 400 Beatles Sites in and around London.* New York: St. Martin's Press, 1994.
Sherwood, Shirley. *Venice Simplon Orient-Express.* 4th ed. Osceola, Wisconsin: Motorbooks International, 1996.
Sugden, Philip. *The Complete History of Jack the Ripper.* London: Robinson Publishing, 1998.
Turner, Christopher. *London Step by Step.* New York: St. Martin's Press, 1985.
Wearing, J. P. *The London Stage 1920-1929: A Calendar of Plays and Players.* 2 vols. Metuchen, New Jersey and London: The Scarecrow Press, 1984.
Wearing, J. P. *The London Stage 1930-1939: A Calendar of Plays and Players.* 2 vols. Metuchen, New Jersey and London: The Scarecrow Press, 1990.
Weinreb, Ben, and Christopher Hibbert, eds. *The London Encyclopaedia.* 2nd ed. London: Macmillan, 1995.
West, Nigel, ed. *The Faber Book of Espionage.* London: Faber and Faber, 1993.
Whitehead, David. *London Then and Now.* London: Dalton Watson, 1969.
Wilkes, John. *The London Police in the Nineteenth Century.* Minneapolis: Lerner Publications Company, 1984.
Wurman, Richard Saul. *Access London.* 6th ed. New York: Access Press, 1998.
Yapp, Nick. *London: The Secrets and the Splendour.* Cologne: Könemann, 1999.

Other Biographies/Autobiographies and Miscellaneous

Andrew, Christopher and Vasili Mitrokhin. *The Sword and the Shield: The Mitrokhin Archive and the Secret History of the KGB.* New York: Basic Books, 1999.
Bach, Steven. *Marlene Dietrich: Life and Legend.* New York, William Morrow, 1992.
Balcon, Michael. *A Lifetime in Films.* London: Hutchinson, 1969.
Behlmer, Rudy. Ed. *Memo from David O. Selznick.* 1972. New York: The Modern Library, 2000.
Blake, George. *No Other Choice: An Autobiography.* London: Jonathan Cape, 1990.
Higham, Charles. *Charles Laughton: An Intimate Biography.* Garden City, New York: Doubleday & Company, Inc., 1976.
Cotton, Joseph. *Vanity Will Get You Somewhere: An Autobiography.* New York: Avon Books, 1987.
Cullen, Tom. *The Mild Murderer: The True Story of the Dr. Crippen Case.* Boston: Houghton Miflin Company, 1977.
Du Maurier, Daphne. *Gerald.* London: Victor Gollancz, 1934.
- - -. *Growing Pains.* London: Victor Gollancz, 1977.
- - -. *Myself When Young: The Shaping of a Writer.* New York: Doubleday & Company, Inc., 1977.
Frewin, Leslie. *Dietrich.* New York: Stein and Day, 1967.
French, Sean. *Patrick Hamilton.* London: Faber and Faber, 1993.
Gielgud, John. *Early Stages: 1921-1936.* New York: Taplinger Publishing Company, 1976.
Harding, James. *Gerald du Maurier: The Last Actor-Manager.* London: Hodder & Stoughton, 1989.
Higham, Charles. *Charles Laughton: An Intimate Biography.* Garden City, New York: Doubleday & Company, Inc., 1976.
Hotchner, A.E. *Doris Day: Her Own Story.* New York: William Morrow and Company, Inc., 1976.
Lownie, Andrew. *John Buchan: the Presbyterian Cavalier.* London: Constable, 1995.

Moorehead, Caroline. *Sidney Bernstein: A Biography*. London: Jonathan Cape, 1984.
Noble, Peter. *Ivor Novello: Man of the Theatre*. London: The Falcon Press, 1951.
Shallcross, Martyn. *The Private World of Daphne du Maurier*. New York: St. Martin's Press, 1991.
Smith, Janet Adam. *John Buchan*. London: Rupert Hart-Davis, 1965.
Todd, Richard. *Caught in the Act: The Story of My Life*. London: Hutchinson, 1986.
Wilding, Michael. *The Wilding Way: The Story of My Life*. New York: St. Martin's Press, 1982.

Literary References
Bluestone, George. *Novels into Film*. Baltimore: The Johns Hopkins Press, 1957.
Greene, Graham. *Collected Essays*. London: Bodley Head, 1969.
Kestner, Joseph A. *The Edwardian Detective, 1901-1915*. Aldershot, Hampshire and Brookfield, Vermont: Ashgate Publishing, 2000.
Ousby, Ian. *Guilty Parties: A Mystery Lover's Companion*. New York: Thames and Hudson, 1997.
Treadwell, Lawrence P., Jr. *The Bulldog Drummond Encyclopedia*. Jefferson, NC: McFarland & Company, 2001.

LITERARY SOURCES
Armstrong, Anthony [George Anthony Armstrong Willis]. "The Case of Mr. Pelham." *Esquire* November 1940: 36+.
Beeding, Francis [John Leslie Palmer and Hilary Aidan St. George Saunders]. *The House of Dr. Edwardes*. New York: Little, Brown & Co., 1928.
Bennett, Charles. *Blackmail: A Play in Three Acts*. London: Rich and Cowan, 1934.
Bloch, Robert. *Psycho*. 1959. London: Bloomsbury Publishing, 1997.
Bourke, Sean. *The Springing of George Blake*. New York: The Viking Press, 1970.
Buchan, John. *The Thirty-nine Steps*. 1915. Ware, Hertfordshire: Wordsworth Editions, 1993.
- - -. *Greenmantle*. 1916. Ware, Hertfordshire: Wordsworth Editions, 1994.
- - -. *Mr Standfast*. 1919. Ware, Hertfordshire: Wordsworth Editions, 1994.
- - -. *The Three Hostages*. 1924. Ware, Hertfordshire: Wordsworth Editions, 1995.
Caine, [Sir Thomas Henry] Hall. *The Manxman*. London: William Heinemann, 1894.
Canning, Victor. *The Rainbird Pattern*. New York: William Morrow & Company, Inc., 1973.
Cecil [Leon], Henry. *No Bail for the Judge*. New York: Harper and Brothers, 1952.
- - -. *Independent Witness*. 1963. London: House of Stratus, 2000.
Chesterton, G.K. *The Man Who Knew Too Much*. New York and London: Harper & Brothers Publishers, 1922.
Collier, John. "Back for Christmas." 1951. *Fancies and Goodnights*. Alexandria, Virginia: Time-Life Books, 1965.
- - -. "Wet Saturday." 1951. *Fancies and Goodnights*. Alexandria, Virginia: Time-Life Books, 1965.
Collins, Dale. *Rich and Strange: A Novel*. London: George G. Harrap & Co., 1930.
Conrad, Joseph. *The Secret Agent: A Simple Tale*. 1907. New York: Penguin Books, 1996.
Coward, Noël. *Easy Virtue*. 1926. *Collected Plays: One*. London: Methuen, 1999. 245-358.
Crispin, Edmund [(Robert) Bruce Montgomery]. *The Case of the Gilded Fly*. London: Gollancz, 1944.
- - -. *Holy Disorders*. London: Gollancz, 1945.
- - -. *The Moving Toyshop*. London: Gollancz, 1946.
- - -. *Love Lies Bleeding*. London: Gollancz, 1948.
- - -. *Buried for Pleasure*. London: Gollancz, 1949.
Croft-Cooke, Rupert. *Banquo's Chair: A Play in One Act*. London: H.F.W. Deane & Sons, 1930.
Dahl, Roald. "Dip in the Pool." 1952. *The Best of Roald Dahl*. New York: Vintage Books, 1990.
- - -. "Lamb to the Slaughter." 1953. *The Best of Roald Dahl*. New York: Vintage Books, 1990.
- - -. "Mrs. Bixby and the Colonel's Coat." 1959. *The Best of Roald Dahl*. New York: Vintage Books, 1990.
- - -. "Poison." 1950. *Someone Like You*. New York: Dell, 1965.
Dane, Clemence [Winifred Ashton] and Helen Simpson. *Enter Sir John*. New York: Cosmopolitan Book Corporation, 1928.
- - -. *Re-enter Sir John*. New York: Farrar and Rinehart, 1932.
Dodge, David. *To Catch a Thief*. New York: Random House, 1952.
Du Maurier, Daphne. *Jamaica Inn*. London: Victor Gollancz, 1936.
- - -. *Rebecca*. London: Victor Gollancz, 1938.
- - -. "The Birds." *The Apple Tree and other Stories*. London: Victor Gollancz, 1952.

Farjeon, J[oseph] Jefferson. *Number Seventeen: A Play in Three Acts*. London: "Stage" Play Publishing Bureau, 1927.
Foote, John Taintor. "The Song of the Dragon." *The Saturday Evening Post*. 12 Nov. 1921: 3+ and 19 Nov. 1921: 18+.
Galsworthy, John. *The Skin Game*. 1920. *Five Plays*. London and New York: Methuen, 1984. 161-222.
Graham, Winston. *Marnie*. 1961. New York: Fawcett World Library, [1964?].
Hamilton, Patrick. *Rope*. London: Constable and Company, 1929.
Hichens, Robert. *The Paradine Case*. Garden City, New York: Doubleday, Doran and Company, 1933.
Hornung, E[rnest] W[illiam]. "To Catch a Thief." 1901. *The Collected Raffles Stories*. Oxford and New York: Oxford University Press, 1996.
Iles, Francis [Anthony Berkeley Cox]. *Before the Fact*. Thetford, Great Britain: Lowe & Brydone Printers Ltd., 1932.
- - -. *Malice Aforethought*. 1931. New York: Perennial Library, 1980.
Jepson, Selwyn. *Man Running* [U.S.: *Outrun the Constable*]. London: Macdonald & Co., 1948.
Kirkbride, Ronald. *The Short Night*. London: Arthur Barker, 1968.
Knott, Frederick. *Dial "M" for Murder*. New York: Random House, 1953.
- - -. *Dial M For Murder*. 1953. London: Samuel French, 1982.
La Bern, Arthur. *Goodbye Piccadilly, Farewell Leicester Square*. 1966. New York: Paperback Library, 1971.
Lowndes, Marie Belloc. *The Lodger*. 1913. Oxford and New York: Oxford University Press, 1996.
Mason, A.E.W. "The Crystal Trench." *The Four Corners of the World*. London, New York and Toronto: Hodder and Stoughton, 1917.
Maugham, William Somerset. *Ashenden, or the British Agent*. 1928. London: Mandarin Paperbacks, 1991.
O'Casey, Sean [John Casey]. *Juno and the Paycock*. 1925. *Three Plays*. New York: St. Martin's Press, 1957.
Phillpotts, Eden. *The Farmer's Wife*. London: Samuel French, 1926.
Phillpotts, Eden. *Widecombe Fair*. 1913. London: Anthony Mott Ltd., 1983.
Sandys, Oliver [Marguerite Florence Barclay]. *The Pleasure Garden*. London: Hurst & Blackett [1923].
Sapper [Herman Cyril McNeile]. *Bulldog Drummond*. 1920. London: House of Stratus, 2001.
- - -.*The Black Gang*. 1922. London: House of Stratus, 2001.
- - -.*The Third Round*. 1924. London: House of Stratus, 2001.
- - -.*The Final Count*. 1926. London: House of Stratus, 2001.
- - -.*The Female of the Species*. 1928. London: House of Stratus, 2001.
- - -.*Temple Tower*. 1929. London: House of Stratus, 2001.
- - -.*The Return of Bulldog Drummond*. 1931. London: House of Stratus, 2001.
- - -.*Knock-Out*. 1933. London: House of Stratus, 2001.
Shaffer, Anthony. "Larger than Life." *The Mammoth Book of Movie Detectives & Screen Crimes*. Ed. Peter Haining. New York: Carroll & Graf Publishers, Inc., 1988. 339-346.
Sheean, Vincent. *Personal History*. Garden City, New York: Doubleday, Doran and Co., Inc.: 1935.
- - -. *Not Peace but a Sword*. Garden City, New York: Doubleday, Doran and Co., Inc.: 1939.
Simpson, Helen. *Under Capricorn*. London and Toronto: William Heinemann, 1937.
Story, Jack Trevor. *The Trouble with Harry*. London and New York: T.V. Boardman & Co., 1949.
Tey, Josephine [Elizabeth Mackintosh]. *A Shilling for Candles*. 1936. London: Pan Books, 1964.
Wheatley, Dennis. *The Forbidden Territory*. 1933. London: Arrow Books, 1956.
White, Ethel Lina. *The Wheel Spins*. 1936. New York: Zebra Books, 1987.
Williams, Arthur [Peter Barry Way]. "Being a Murderer Myself." 1948. *Alfred Hitchcock Presents: 12 Stories They Won't Let Me Do on TV*. Ed. Alfred Hitchcock. New York: Dell Publishing Co., 1957. 9-24.

INTERNET

http://www.flyingscotsman.com/fsr/index.html
http://www.dumaurier.org/index.html
http://www.saga.co.uk/publishing/jul99/daphne_du.html
http://www.filmunlimited.com/Guardian_NFT/interview/0,4479,74591,00.html
http://www.peakrock.com/batterseabusiness/bps/bpshist.htm
http://mikes.railhistory.railfan.net/r003.html
http://www.met.police.uk/police/mps/mps/history/time4c.htm
http://www.fireworld.org.uk/Misc/Saved21/page10.html

http://ourworld.compuserve.com/homepages/Rob_Jerrard/City2.htm
http://www.pbs.org/wgbh/pages/frontline/camp/
http://www.crimelibrary.com/serial/christie/
http://www.classicthemes.com/50sTVThemes/themePages/alfredHitchcock.html#Theme
http://www.apts.org.uk/cave.htm
http://users.whsmithnet.co.uk/rob.rothwell/films.htm

INTERVIEWS

Boyle, Robert. Telephone interviews. November 27, 2000; September 8, 2001.
Bumstead, Henry. Telephone interview. March 4, 2001.
Cain, Syd. Telephone interview. August 13, 2000.
Erickson, Doc. Telephone interview. February 27, 2001.
Guest, Val. Telephone interview. April 29, 2002.
Hill, Bill. Telephone interview. September 27, 2000.
O'Connell, Patricia. Telephone interview. July 2, 2001.
Laing, Bob. Telephone interview. September 27, 2000.
Neame, Ronald. Telephone interview. November 26, 2000.
Tester, Desmond. Telephone interview. October 11, 2000.

APPENDIX I:
ENGLISH LITERARY SOURCES

Over the span of some 50 years, Alfred Hitchcock directed only a handful of original screenplays, including his own effort, *The Ring*. The remainder of his theatrical films and television plays were adapted from existing works. These include novels, theatrical plays, short stories, radio plays, magazine articles and personal memoirs, the majority of them English. Below I have listed, in chronological order, the 36 films and 10 television episodes adapted by Hitchcock and his script collaborators, in whole or in part, from English literary sources, beginning with *The Pleasure Garden* in 1925, and continuing through *Family Plot* in 1976. (*Foreign Correspondent*, although based on an American book, is included because of its English setting.) I have also provided both a commentary and a rating to suggest the fidelity with which the literary works were adapted. In so doing, I acknowledge that in transposition, certain changes are inevitable (compression, conflation, simplification,[11] accession to censorship, conversion of narrative summary to dialogue, etc.); that the two media—one verbal, one visual—possess unique, often mutually antagonistic, conventions, points of view, and techniques (e.g., the limitations of cinematic metaphor vs. literary metaphor); and that for any given novel or film there may be multiple readings or responses. Yet, for all this, I still believe that it is possible to quantify, however roughly, the degree to which a film diverges from its source: to count, à la Bluestone, the number of deletions, additions and alterations from book to film. Having done this, one can then assess whether the adaptation expresses primarily the original author's vision, the filmmaker's vision, or an amalgam of the two. Of the film *Rebecca*, for example, one may reasonably claim that it remains faithful to its source novel and thus reflects (or "paraphrases") the vision of author Daphne du Maurier, while of *Jamaica Inn* one must conclude that it bears only a superficial resemblance to the novel (also, ironically, by du Maurier) and thus constitutes a new vision.

Screenwriting credits are as they appear in the films themselves, with the exception that colons and commas have been added for clarity and the form "Screen Play" has been conventionalized to "screenplay."

The titles of books and plays are italicized, e.g., *The Short Night*; the titles of short stories and articles are enclosed in quotation marks, e.g., "The Birds." A lowercase "p" indicates the first performance of a play.

Throughout, "Hitchcock" is to be understood as shorthand for "Hitchcock and his screen collaborators."

The following abbreviations are used for the fidelity rating:

C = Conservative, an adaptation faithful in structure, themes, incidents, details, locales and characterization to the original, e.g., *Rebecca* and *Dial M for Murder*
M = Moderate, an adaptation betraying one or more notable deviations from the source, but overall reasonably faithful to the original author's vision, e.g., *Murder!* and *The Trouble with Harry*
L = Liberal, an adaptation departing from its source in a number of important areas, as much Hitchcock's work as that of the original author, e.g., *The Lodger* and *Marnie*
R = Radical, an adaptation retaining few details or themes from the source, clearly more Hitchcock's vision than that of the original author, e.g., *Jamaica Inn* and *Foreign Correspondent*

THE PLEASURE GARDEN, adapted by Eliot Stannard
Source: *The Pleasure Garden* (1923) by Oliver Sandys [Marguerite Florence Barclay]
Comments: L: While retaining much of the basic structure of the novel, including the contrast between the Pleasure Garden theatre and the real "pleasure garden" in the jungle, Hitchcock eliminates Gaynor/Patsy's racism and shifts the focus onto her and away from Jerrie/Jill.

THE LODGER: A STORY OF THE LONDON FOG, scenario: Eliot Stannard
Source: *The Lodger* (1913) by Marie Belloc Lowndes
Comments: L: Although structurally similar, the film shifts the emphasis away from Mrs. Bunting, her critique of a male-dominated society, and the nature of her responsibility in shielding the Lodger from the police, to the romance between Daisy and the title character, who, unlike his literary counterpart, is actually innocent of The Avenger killings. A further "masculinization" occurs with regard to the fate of the murderer—in Hitchcock's version, he is ultimately apprehended by the police; in Mrs. Belloc Lowndes', he escapes, thus calling into question the effectiveness of the (all-male) police force. The novel's depiction of the inner workings of Scotland Yard, while missing from this film, seems to have inspired a similar scene in the film *Blackmail*. The ongoing discussions between Joe Chandler and crime buff Bunting foreshadow

those between Joe Newton and Herbie Hawkins in *Shadow of a Doubt*. Note that Mrs. Belloc Lowndes initially published *The Lodger* as a short story in 1911. This version lacks the detective figure and sees the murderer drowned at the end.

DOWNHILL, scenario: Eliot Stannard
Source: *Down Hill* (p 1926) by David L'Estrange [pseudonym of Ivor Novello and Constance Collier]
Comments: The play was unavailable for review.

EASY VIRTUE, scenario: Eliot Stannard
Source: *Easy Virtue* (p 1926) by Noël Coward
Comments: M: The film replicates much of the play line for line, but profitably adds extended dramatizations of both Larita's painful divorce case and her Mediterranean romance with John Whittaker (events merely alluded to in the original); it also transforms Larita herself into a weaker, more fragile character than the strong, independent heroine of the play.

THE FARMER'S WIFE, adapted for the screen by Eliot Stannard
Source: *The Farmer's Wife* (p 1916) by Eden Phillpotts, based on his novel *Widecombe Fair* (1913)
Comments: M: The film is quite faithful to the play in terms of structure, dialogue and characters, with the usual "opening up" of the action through several countryside exteriors. The major changes, which concentrate the story's focus onto Sweetland and heighten our sense of his loss and loneliness, are: the depiction of the first wife's death at the beginning of the film (an event only referred to in the play); the wedding—and early departure—of his daughter Sibley (whose romance with Dick Coaker constitutes one of the play's subplots); and the complete elimination of the other daughter, Petronell, and her subplot (of initially refusing, but eventually agreeing, to marry George Smerdon). Hitchcock also deprives Churdles Ash, the comic handyman, of his socialist politics and some of his racier lines, replacing them with sight gags and other bits of physical comedy.

THE MANXMAN, scenario by Eliot Stannard
Source: *The Manxman* (1894) by [Sir Thomas Henry] Hall Caine
Comments: L: Hitchcock's adaptation greatly simplifies and compresses the 500-plus-page novel, eliminating nearly all the background for the central characters and reducing the secondary characters (those that it retains) to "walk-ons." Most of the scenes in the film do have counterparts in the novel, but Hitchcock significantly alters a number of them, including Philip's climactic revelation that he (not his friend Pete) is the baby's father. In the novel he does this voluntarily, before the court over which he presides; here, the baby's grandfather publicly denounces Philip, prompting him to confess. All in all, the film represents a somewhat darker, more cynical view of life than that of the ultimately reassuring novel.

BLACKMAIL, adapted by Alfred Hitchcock; (sound version only) dialogue by Benn Levy
Source: *Blackmail* (p 1928) by Charles Bennett
Comments: L: Hitchcock opens up the play through the addition of the introductory arrest sequence and the climactic chase to and through the British Museum; shifts the focus away from the policeman's love-vs.-duty dilemma (which Charles Bennett later adapted for *Sabotage*) and onto Alice; and, most significantly, eliminates the original's cop-out revelation that the artist actually died from a heart attack and not Alice's knife.

MURDER!, adapted by Alfred Hitchcock and Walter Mycroft; scenario by Alma Reville
Source: *Enter Sir John* (1928) by Clemence Dane [Winifred Ashton] and Helen Simpson
Comments: M: Remaining quite close to its source, the film does make Sir John an actual juror in the Baring case (in the novel he is simply an interested observer) and largely eliminates his narcissism (perhaps in deference to the director's friend—and the model for the character—Sir Gerald du Maurier). More significantly, Hitchcock replaces the novel's climactic car chase and Fane's ultimate escape with the murderer's suicide in a circus. Fane is also now a drag performer (as is another, minor, character), but, importantly, he is still half-caste—i.e., mixed race—and still in love with the heroine. That he is frequently described as "homosexual" seems to derive from the fact that he appears in drag and acts in a rather "effeminate" manner. (Even Hitchcock joined the bandwagon, referring to the character as a "half-caste homosexual" in a 1972 interview with Charles Thomas Samuels.) Yet, Fane's motive for murdering Mrs. Druce remains as in the novel: to keep her from revealing his secret *to the woman he loved*. This fact alone, notwithstanding any other "clues" or "codes" regarding the character's sexuality, precludes the use of the homosexual label.

A REFERENCE GUIDE TO LOCATIONS

Note that Hitchcock simultaneously shot a German-language version of the film called *Mary*, which utilized a translated and slightly altered version of the original screenplay.

THE SKIN GAME, adapted by Alfred Hitchcock; scenario by Alma Reville
Source: *The Skin Game* (p 1920) by John Galsworthy
Comments: M: A fairly close adaptation, the film differs primarily in its slight softening of the characters (notably Hornblower, Jill and, to a lesser extent, Mr. Hillcrist) and in aligning the star-crossed lovers—Jill Hillcrist and Rolfe Hornblower—more firmly behind their respective families.

RICH AND STRANGE, adapted by Alfred Hitchcock; scenario by Alma Reville, Val Valentine
Source: *Rich and Strange* (1930) by Dale Collins
Comments: M: Though paralleling the structure of the original, Hitchcock's version devotes more time to the characters' London life and, significantly, denies them the unambiguous happy ending of the novel.

NUMBER SEVENTEEN, scenario: Alma Reville, Alfred Hitchcock, Rodney Ackland
Number Seventeen (p 1925) by J[oseph] Jefferson Farjeon, who adapted the play as a novel in 1926
Comments: M: The film is fairly close to its source, the major change being the shift of emphasis from Ben and his shenanigans to the detective, Barton, and his investigation, and, of course, the "opening up" of the action to include the climactic train chase. The film, as Barr points out, is the first of Hitchcock's to include a "MacGuffin"—the stolen necklace—which came straight from Farjeon's play.

WALTZES FROM VIENNA, scenario: Guy Bolton, Alma Reville
Source: *Waltzes from Vienna* (p 1931) by Hassard Short, Caswell Garth and Desmond Carter, based on the German play *Walzer aus Wien* by A[lfred] M[aria] Willner, Heinz Reichert and Ernst Marischka
Comments: R: According to Yacowar (1977), the film differs radically from its source, adding "almost everything of character in the film," including "the gradual composition of the 'Blue Danube Waltz'" and the "archetypal" happy ending.

THE MAN WHO KNEW TOO MUCH, by Charles Bennett and D[ominic] B[evan] Wyndham Lewis; scenario: Edwin Greenwood and A[rthur] R. Rawlinson; additional dialogue: Emlyn Williams
Source: *Bulldog Drummond* (1920), et al., by Sapper [Herman Cyril McNeile]
Comments: R: Inspired by the notion of Hugh and Phyllis Drummond's child being kidnapped (a screen story Hitchcock and Bennett had concocted at another studio), *TMWKTM* incorporates a number of incidents from the works of both Sapper and John Buchan, not to mention a title presumably pinched from a G.K. Chesterton collection. (The title character of the latter, an amateur detective and former MP, "knows too much" about the dark side of English politics and so in some cases, for the greater good, actually has to allow the guilty parties to go unpunished. Edgar Wallace's 1919 thriller *The Man Who Knew*, which includes the discovery of a dead child in Bloomsbury, may also have been an inspiration.) From Buchan's *The Thirty-nine Steps* comes the idea of preventing a foreign assassination in London, as well as the general notion of "adventure in familiar surroundings happening to unadventurous men"; and from his *The Three Hostages* come the mysterious written clues that lead to the villains' lair; a married Hannay and his wife, Mary, trying to rescue three young hostages; the villains' use of hypnotism; Mary actually saving the youngest hostage—a stand-in for their own son, Peter; and perhaps even the ominous dentist's office (Chapter 8). From *Bulldog Drummond* itself comes the troika of smooth villain, over-the-top killer and young female companion; assorted kidnappings and torture; bypassing the police for fear of jeopardizing a loved one's life; and a rooftop standoff with a professional killer. There is even a hint of the title (two years before Chesterton used it) when the bad girl tells Drummond: "You know too much [to live]." (Sapper presumably liked the phrase—it pops up several times in the immediate follow-up, *The Black Gang*, as well as a number of other adventures.) Incidents from this 1920 potboiler (such as the hero calling attention to himself in a public setting to avoid being killed by the baddies; a kidnap victim being tortured and drugged to induce cooperation with the baddies and a duplicate sent out in his place) also turn up in *Foreign Correspondent*, *Saboteur* and *North By Northwest*. The 1934 film further recalls the follow-up novel, *The Black Gang*, in which the newly married Drummonds take on a foreign criminal conspiracy operating in England, are kidnapped for their trouble and attend a do at the Royal Albert Hall.

THE 39 STEPS, adaptation: Charles Bennett; continuity: Alma Reville; dialogue: Ian Hay
Source: *The Thirty-nine Steps* (1915) by John Buchan
Comments: L: The adaptation roughly follows Buchan's outline and retains a number of details (the milkman

disguise and political speech, for example), but eliminates many scenes and characters, adds many others and introduces the romance angle, which has no precedent in the original and, indeed, becomes the film's *raison d'être*. In this, the film more closely resembles Buchan's *Mr. Standfast*, in which Hannay works with a beautiful woman (his future wife, Mary). Moreover, the shadowy villain of *The Thirty-nine Steps* makes a splashy return in *Standfast*, where his description as a man with 50 personalities, who could make himself look like anyone, more clearly foreshadows the Professor Jordan of the film. Incidents from *The Thirty-nine Steps* (1), as well as the sequels *Greenmantle* (2), *Mr. Standfast* (3) and *The Three Hostages* (4), were also adapted for: *The Man Who Knew Too Much* (34) (political assassination in London [1]; a married couple and their friend visiting a seedy portion of London to look for a kidnapped child and the villain's use of hypnosis [4]); *Foreign Correspondent* (foreign enemy masquerading as an elegant establishment figure [4]); *Saboteur* (Barry being caught at a remote outpost and suddenly pretending to be part of the villain's organization [3]; Barry's escape from the villains' house [1]; the hero trying—and failing—to prevent the villain from plunging to his death at the end of the story [4]); *Notorious* (a suave, attractive foreign villain devoted to his powerful and ruthless mother [4]; use of the hero's love interest as bait for the villain, who also loves her [3]); and *North By Northwest* (use of the hero's love interest as bait for the villain, who also loves her [3]; a scene in a forest in which the hero pleads with the heroine not to go off with the villain [3]).

SECRET AGENT, from the play by Campbell Dixon; screenplay: Charles Bennett; dialogue: Ian Hay; continuity: Alma Reville; additional dialogue: Jesse Lasky, Jr.
Source: *Ashenden, or The British Agent* (1928) by William Somerset Maugham
Comments: R: The film is an extremely loose reworking of Maugham's leisurely paced novel, which the author based upon his own, often tedious, work for British Intelligence during WWI. Hitchcock claimed that *Secret Agent* was based upon the chapters "The Hairless Mexican" and "The Traitor," with the romance angle supposedly lifted from Campbell Dixon's 1933 play *Ashenden* (for which there is no record of its ever having been performed or published). In fact, the film borrows incidents from several chapters, not just those two, although the end result is still decidedly more Hitchcock than Maugham, notwithstanding the elaboration of the novel's somewhat vague disenchantment with espionage. The idea of a German agent stirring up Middle Easterners to turn the tide in Germany's favor has a precedent in Buchan's *Greenmantle* (see above).

SABOTAGE, screenplay: Charles Bennett; dialogue: Ian Hay, Helen Simpson; continuity: Alma Reville; additional dialogue: E.V.H. Emmett
Source: *The Secret Agent* (1907) by Joseph Conrad
Comments: L: Though certainly one of Hitchcock's more somber films, *Sabotage* is still far lighter than Conrad's dark, brooding, thoroughly depressing novel, which was inspired by an actual attempt to blow up the Royal Observatory at Greenwich. Stevie has been transformed from a mildly retarded adult into a young boy, the anarchists' role has been diminished, Mrs. Verloc's mother eliminated and a romance with a police figure added. Conrad, by contrast, has the heroine romanced by one of the anarchists, who abandons her, prompting her, in turn, to commit suicide. Hitchcock also introduces a degree of ambiguity in the death of Verloc himself (did she stab him or did he impale himself?); in the novel, there is no doubt, as Mrs. Verloc stands above her husband's recumbent figure and plunges the knife into his heart. Hitchcock's more traditional approach to the material also ensures that all the principal characters—even Verloc—have their good points, in stark contrast to Conrad's pitiful lot of losers and degenerates. Incidentally, some writers (e.g., Barr) refer to the cinematic Mrs. Verloc, who has no first name in the film itself, as "Winnie," presumably after her literary counterpart. However, in the shooting script, the character does have a first name, Sylvia, presumably in homage to the actress playing the part.

YOUNG AND INNOCENT, screenplay: Charles Bennett, Edwin Greenwood, Anthony Armstrong; dialogue: Gerald Savory; continuity: Alma Reville
Source: *A Shilling for Candles* (1936) by Josephine Tey [Elizabeth Mackintosh]
Comments: R: The film does borrow a number of characters and incidents from the novel (Christine Clay's drowning, the missing overcoat, Tisdall's flight, Erica's comical car and her efforts on Tisdall's behalf), but otherwise transforms a standard whodunit with Scotland Yard Inspector Alan Grant as protagonist into a rather breezy romance à la *The 39 Steps*. Even the murderer is different.

THE LADY VANISHES, screenplay: Sidney Gilliatt [*sic*, for Gilliat] and Frank Launder; continuity: Alma Reville
Source: *The Wheel Spins* (1936) by Ethel Lina White
Comments: L: For much of the train journey, the film follows the novel fairly closely. There are, however, a

number of dramatic changes: a new, far more comic opening at the hotel (which introduces the incomparable Charters and Caldicott, presumably inspired by the novel's "teddibly" proper Flood-Porter sisters, who refuse to get involved in anything that might delay their return to England and their beloved little dog); a far more dramatic ending (the gun battle); a heightening of the novel's romance between playgirl Iris Carr (who is not engaged and has no family) and engineer Max Hare (Gilbert the folk musicologist in the film); and a change in the motive for abducting Miss Froy. In the novel she is a simple governess who can implicate her powerful former employer in the murder of his political enemy, although, significantly, at one point, Max does suggest that she might have been a spy, trying to take secret information back to England!

JAMAICA INN, screenplay by Sidney Gilliat and Joan Harrison; dialogue: Sidney Gilliat; continuity: Alma Reville; additional dialogue: J[ohn] B[oynton] Priestly
Source: *Jamaica Inn* (1936) by Daphne du Maurier
Comments: R: Apart from the title, the setting and a few names and events, the film bears little resemblance to the novel; the focus is shifted from a young woman gradually discovering the evil that surrounds her at the title locale to the machinations of an over-the-top squire-cum-criminal mastermind, played by Charles Laughton (not coincidentally, the film's co-producer). Jem, the romantic character with whom Mary becomes smitten, is transformed from Joss's (less) criminal brother into a police figure, à la *Blackmail* and *Sabotage*, but, oddly, the romance is given shorter shrift in the film than the novel.

REBECCA, screenplay by Robert E. Sherwood and Joan Harrison; adaptation by Philip MacDonald and Michael Hogan
Source: *Rebecca* (1938) by Daphne du Maurier
Comments: C: This is clearly the most conservative of Hitchcock's novel adaptations, with only two significant changes from the original. First, in accordance with censorship demands (and audience sensibilities of the day), Maxim has no longer shot the adulterous title character, although, apparently, he had intended to do so. (The infamous Hays Office insisted that a murderer could never go free.) Instead, he explains, Rebecca tripped and fell and thereby induced her own fatal injury. (Of course, given the implausibility of Maxim's description of the incident—that he was close enough to strike her yet she somehow managed to continue toward him, trip, fall, strike her head and die—can we be sure that he isn't covering up his own misdeeds?) In any case, this is not the catastrophe that Selznick seemed to think (see Behlmer, p 305). The real impact of the scene in the boathouse comes from the revelation that Maxim hated Rebecca, that he wished her dead, not that he actually killed her. Second, after the boathouse revelations, the film shifts its focus from the second Mrs. de Winter's continuing struggle with "Rebecca," to the more melodramatically routine question of whether or not Maxim will get off. Thus, in contrast to the novel, the film's Mrs. de Winter does not accompany her husband to London to visit Rebecca's doctor. While this change permits a brief suspenseful moment at the end (when Maxim worries that his bride may be trapped in the fire), it also contributes greatly to our "disconnect" from the heroine whose plight so greatly dominates the entirety of the novel and the bulk of the film.

FOREIGN CORRESPONDENT, screenplay by Charles Bennett and Joan Harrison; dialogue by James Hilton and Robert Benchley
Source: *Personal History* (1935) by Vincent Sheean
Comments: R: The film adapts more from the book, a journalist's memoir, than is usually acknowledged, including: a naïve young American journalist becoming a "foreign correspondent"; his reaction to older, more cynical colleagues; attending an important European conference, whose goal is to set up a lasting peace on the Continent; falling in love with an idealistic young woman devoted to a political cause; and meeting false advocates of peace who really want war. A number of elements also appear to have been adapted from the canons of both Sapper and Buchan (see *The Man Who Knew Too Much* and *The 39 Steps*, above), including, e.g., the bad guys' use of a remote windmill (Sapper's *Temple Tower*) and an international peace organization being infiltrated and run by criminals bent on war (Sapper's *Bulldog Drummond at Bay*). Hitchcock historian Ken Mogg has also noted elements common to both the film and Erskine Childers' classic 1903 espionage novel, *The Riddle of the Sands*, including the relationship between the daughter and her traitorous father, as well as the father's watery death. Interestingly, Sheean describes a London bus journey in his 1939 follow-up volume, *Not Peace but a Sword*, that includes the exact route taken by Jones and Van Meer from the Carlton to the Savoy. See also *The Man Who Knew Too Much* (56).

SUSPICION, screenplay by Samson Raphaelson, Joan Harrison and Alma Reville
Source: *Before the Fact* (1932) by Francis Iles [Anthony Berkeley Cox]
Comments: L: It's all there in the novel: the charming rogue, the spinster heroine, the silly ass friend, the

aborted trip to church, the gambling, the embezzlement, the chairs, the lavish gifts, the brandy, the local crime novelist, the suspenseful car ride—even the glass of milk. But Iles' Aysgarth—in contrast to Hitchcock's—is a real rotter: He's slept with half the women in the county and sired an illegitimate child; he's apparently induced the deaths of both General McLaidlaw and Beaky; and, finally, as the novel ends, he seems to have induced Lina's death as well. (In all this, as Ken Mogg has pointed out, Aysgarth recalls the real-life English scoundrel and convicted serial killer, Dr. William Palmer [1824-56].) Still, much of the evidence against the literary Johnnie appears circumstantial, depending largely on Lina's interpretation of events and on her state of mind. In its focus on Lina's suspicions, the novel is thus far closer to Hitchcock's version than is usually acknowledged.

SPELLBOUND, screenplay by Ben Hecht; adaptation by Angus MacPhail
Source: *The House of Dr. Edwardes* (1927) by Francis Beeding [John Leslie Palmer and Hilary Aidan St. George Saunders]
Comments: R: Palmer and St. George Saunders' claustrophobic tale of an English madman who takes over an Alpine asylum (shades of Poe's "The System of Dr. Tarr and Professor Feather") and converts his fellow patients to devil worship receives a massive overhaul at the hands of Hitchcock and the perennially psychoanalyzed David Selznick. Freud, who receives relatively short shrift in the novel, is elevated to center stage in *Spellbound*, which apart from a few character names, the idea of switched identities and an asylum setting, represents an original screenplay. Here, as in the later *Paradine Case*, Selznick clearly violated his own dictum to Hitchcock that readers of a book "will not forgive substitutions" (for more on which, see the Introduction).

NOTORIOUS, screenplay by Ben Hecht
Source: *Mr. Standfast* (1919) by John Buchan (in part)
Comments: Although officially based on John Taintor Foote's 1921 story "The Song of the Dragon," *Notorious* has, as author Ken Mogg (*The Alfred Hitchcock Story*) notes, a notable parallel with Buchan's 1919 Richard Hannay adventure: the idea of a young woman with whom the hero is in love entrapping a German agent who, in turn, has asked her to marry him. The conceit is repeated in *North By Northwest* (see below).

THE PARADINE CASE, adaptation by Alma Reville; screenplay by David O. Selznick
Source: *The Paradine Case* (1933) by Robert Hichens
Comments: L: The film is essentially a watered down, "CliffsNotes" version of Hichens' 525-page novel. Among the deletions: all but two of the novel's numerous social scenes (at private dinner parties, theatres, art galleries and clubs), where the complex relationships among the characters are defined and developed; nearly all of Judge Horfield's sadism, debauchery and corruptness (the literary character is a callous, cadaverous misogynist who suggests no one so much as Mr. Burns of *The Simpsons*); the important role of his conscience-stricken wife; the intense hatred of Horfield for the flamboyant Keane, and their cat and mouse game before and during the trial. The film also dilutes Keane's obsession with the cold, enigmatic Scandinavian [*sic*] beauty who is his client, as well as his betrayal of Gay. Most dramatically, it shifts our attention away from Keane himself (whose fall constitutes the novel's focus) and onto Mrs. Paradine (notably during the opening scenes of arrest, charging and incarceration, which are not so depicted in the novel). Finally, the film has Mrs. Paradine actually confess to her husband's murder after the revelation that her lover has committed suicide. In the novel, neither incident occurs (although the jury does find her guilty) and Horfield is subsequently shot (but not killed) outside the Old Bailey, presumably by his long-suffering wife.

ROPE, adaptation by Hume Cronyn; screenplay by Arthur Laurents
Source: *Rope* (p 1929; retitled *Rope's End* for its 1929 U.S. run) by Patrick Hamilton
Comments: M: Although repudiated by Hamilton, the play retains the story, incidents, characters and motives of the play, differing primarily in dialogue and setting. Note: The play was first presented on March 3, 1929 at the Strand Theatre in London; its West End debut occurred on April 25 at the Ambassadors' Theatre. When the play was brought to America later that year, its title was changed to *Rope's End*. This has led some writers, e.g., Leff (p 268) and the compilers of the *Rope* DVD documentary, to mistake *Rope's End* as the play's proper title.

UNDER CAPRICORN, adaptation by Hume Cronyn; screenplay by James Bridie [Osborne Henry Mavor], from the play by John Colton and Margaret Linden
Source: *Under Capricorn* (1938) by Helen Simpson
Comments: R: The film follows the first third or so of the novel fairly closely, but dramatically diverges during the party scene and from there on represents a whole new story. In the novel, for example, Adare

goes off in a vain quest for gold and ends up engaged to a local woman with whom he plans to settle down in Sydney. There is, consequently, no shooting, no threat to Sam's liberty, no need for Hattie's sacrifice and no noble deed on Adare's part to save both Sam and Hattie.

STAGE FRIGHT, screenplay by Whitfield Cook; adaptation by Alma Reville
Sources: *Man Running* (1948) by Selwyn Jepson, published in the U.S. as *Outrun the Constable* and, in a slightly abridged form, as *Man Running* in the August 9-Sept. 13, 1947 issues of *Collier's* magazine; also the climax of *The Curse of the Gilded Fly* (1944) by Edmund Crispin
Comments: R: A number of the novel's scenes and ideas find their way into the film, including Charlotte's "confession" in Jonathan's mews flat and Eve posing as Charlotte's maid/dresser and later setting Charlotte up to incriminate herself on a hidden microphone. Otherwise, the changes outnumber the similarities. In the novel, no one is presently involved with the theatre, although Charlotte *was* an actress before her marriage, and Jepson takes great pains to show us how theatrical everything is. Eve has no prior relationship with Jonathan (whom she fortuitously bumps into in the street); has criminal worries of her own (she has helped her smuggler father steal a supposed Rembrandt); develops no romantic relationship with Ordinary Smith; has no mother that we know of; cozies up to the real killer, Freddy, who is identified as such early on; and organizes a climactic "sting" at her Suffolk home (the Commodore's sheep farm) where she shoots Freddy—twice! Finally, Jepson's heroine seems like a slightly older Nancy Drew, while Hitchcock's Eve is played by 35-year-old actress Jane Wyman. The film's climax—Jonathan's death on stage—was apparently lifted without credit from Crispin's theatrical murder mystery *The Curse of the Gilded Fly*, as Richard Valley first suggested in a *Scarlet Street* article. The theatrical setting of both this novel and another Crispin mystery, 1947's *Swan Song*, may have also influenced the screenplay. The shift from a "how-catch-em" to a more traditional "whodunit" further suggests the Crispin influence, since Jepson's murderer is revealed quite early in the story. The sequence at the theatrical garden party, though based on a real-life function quite familiar to Hitchcock, recalls events in Crispin's 1948 mystery *Love Lies Bleeding*, in which detective hero Gervase Fen attends a Speech Day garden party (where it threatens to rain, but does not), arranges with an acquaintance to stage a theatrical trap to expose the murderer, and meets an exuberant young woman—a *plump* young woman—who becomes an unabashed admirer. (See also *Strangers on a Train* and *Torn Curtain*, below.)

STRANGERS ON A TRAIN, screenplay by Raymond Chandler and Czenzi Ormonde; adaptation by Whitfield Cook
Source: *The Moving Toyshop* (1946) by Edmund Crispin [Robert Bruce Montgomery] (ending only)
Comments: M: Though officially adapted from Patricia Highsmith's 1950 novel *Strangers on a Train*, Hitchcock's film incorporates the fairground/merry-go-round climax of Edmund Crispin's 1946 novel. Warner Bros. paid Crispin for the right to use this sequence, but provided no onscreen credit.

DIAL M FOR MURDER, screenplay by Frederick Knott
Source: *Dial M for Murder* (p 1952) by Frederick Knott
Comments: C: Knott wrote two slightly different versions of the play: the British original and an American adaptation. In the latter, certain British words and expressions have been changed ("interval" becomes "intermission," for example), Sheila is now Margot, and the boyfriend, Max, is now an American. The film accords more closely with the Americanized version and the result is the most faithful of all Hitchcock's adaptations, the play reading like a virtual dialogue script of the film.

REAR WINDOW, screenplay by John Michael Hayes
Source: "Through a Window" (1894) by H[erbert] G[eorge] Wells
Comments: Cornell Woolrich's story "Rear Window" (and, in turn, Hitchcock's screen adaptation) bears more than a passing resemblance to Wells' 1894 story. In the latter, an Englishman named Bailey is confined to his house with both legs in casts. His only diversion is to sit beside his rear window and view the comings and goings of people boating up and down the Thames. Amused at first, he is eventually quite terrified when a murderous Malay (!) makes his way up the bank and onto Bailey's balcony. The invalid throws medicine bottles at the murderer in a vain attempt to forestall the inevitable. Bailey and his servant, Mrs. Green, are saved in the nick of time when one of the pursuing neighbors shoots the Malay. Author Ken Mogg is the first Hitchcock scholar (that I know of) to have written of the Wells story as a possible inspiration for Woolrich, Hitchcock, or both. Mogg has also called attention to Josephine Tey's (see *Young and Innocent*, above) novel *The Daughter of Time* (1951) as another possible influence.

TO CATCH A THIEF, screenplay by John Michael Hayes
Source: "To Catch a Thief" (1901) by E[rnest] W[illiam] Hornung
Comments: As with the film *Rear Window*, this Hitchcock adaptation has an official source, David Dodge's 1952 novel *To Catch a Thief*, but also, apparently, an unofficial source. Hornung's 1901 story not only bears the same title as the later work, but the plot outline—debonair gentleman jewel thief tracks and catches a copycat thief—is identical. Further, both works climax with a thief-to-thief rooftop confrontation. The hero of Hornung's story was, of course, the infamous A.J. Raffles, a London-based "cracksman" whose exploits among the upper echelons of London society thrilled audiences on both sides of the Atlantic during the early years of the 20th Century. Whether Dodge and/or Hitchcock specifically knew of "To Catch a Thief" itself is not recorded, but there seems little doubt that, consciously or unconsciously, the character of John Robie was modeled at least in part on Raffles.

THE TROUBLE WITH HARRY, screenplay by John Michael Hayes
Source: *The Trouble with Harry* (1950) by Jack Trevor Story
Comments: M: The film just misses being a conservative adaptation, deleting the antics of two adulterous couples, changing the circumstances of Arnie's conception and adding the threat posed by nosy Deputy Sheriff Calvin Wiggs, a character who does not appear in the novel (but whose predecessors date back to at least *The Lodger*). In the book, the doctor appears as a butterfly collector; in the film, he more closely resembles a character who pops up in Edmund Crispin's Gervase Fen series: an Oxford professor who "perambulate[s] the streets engrossed in a book," seemingly oblivious to his surroundings. (For more on Crispin's influence, see the entries in this Appendix on *Stage Fright*, *Strangers on a Train* and *Torn Curtain*.) Otherwise, the film follows Jack Trevor Story scene for scene and often line for line.

THE CASE OF MR. PELHAM, teleplay by Francis Cockrell
Source: "The Case of Mr. Pelham" (1940) by Anthony Armstrong [George Anthony Armstrong Willis]
Comments: C: The story has been transposed from London to New York, but otherwise remains quite faithful to the original, right down to the altered signature, loud tie and utter lack of "rational" explanation at the end! Note that original author Anthony Armstrong collaborated on the screenplay for *Young and Innocent* (see above).

BACK FOR CHRISTMAS, teleplay by Francis Cockrell
Source: "Back for Christmas" (1939) by John Collier
Comments: M: Hitchcock pads out Collier's short, Crippenesque tale with additional scenes at the beginning and end and also excises references to both the mistress and the dismemberment, the latter presumably to assuage the folks at Standards and Practices.

THE MAN WHO KNEW TOO MUCH, screenplay by John Michael Hayes, based on a story by Charles Bennett and D.B. Wyndham-Lewis [*sic*]
Source: See the entry for the 1934 film
Comments: R: See above. The Moroccan scenes contain a number of elements common to journalist Vincent Sheean's 1935 memoir, *Personal History*, whence *Foreign Correspondent*. These include: bus travel through the Moroccan countryside; reference to the consequences of removing an Arab woman's veil; dining on the floor in traditional style; intrigue in an urban marketplace; and white Westerners passing as Arabs. The ultimate source for the story, as noted above, was apparently Sapper's Bulldog Drummond cannon, in which, interestingly, the name Drayton may be found on at least two occasions—once of a house, once of a place (but never of a person).

WET SATURDAY, teleplay by Marian Cockrell
Source: "Wet Saturday" (1938) by John Collier
Comments: C: Apart from a bit of padding at the end, Hitchcock renders an extremely faithful adaptation of the Collier story, aided immensely by two of his film stalwarts: John Williams and Sir Cedric Hardwicke.

LAMB TO THE SLAUGHTER, teleplay by Roald Dahl
Source: "Lamb to the Slaughter" (1953) by Roald Dahl
Comments: C: This delightful tale—with a premise suggested to Dahl by James Bond creator Ian Fleming—is faithfully replicated with but a few minor alterations (e.g., adding a dinner party that must be cancelled, compressing the scene at the grocer's). Note: While the original story is apparently set in the U.S. (Mary knows

all the men in the *precinct*, an American term, not a British one, in this context), Dahl's use of terms such as *garden* and *spanner* (instead of *yard* and *wrench*) clearly remind us of his—and the story's—British roots.

DIP IN THE POOL, teleplay by Robert C. Dennis
Source: "Dip in the Pool" (1952) by Roald Dahl
Comments: M: The essence of the story is faithfully captured, though Hitchcock pads out Dahl's slight tale with scenes between Botibol and his unsympathetic wife (the latter is only mentioned in the story) and between Botibol and the sympathetic Renshaw, another character who does not appear in the story (although his wife does).

POISON, teleplay by Casey Robinson
Source: "Poison" (1950) by Roald Dahl
Comments: L: Most of the dialogue and details—e.g., the doctor's careful injection of the serum and gassing of the snake—are faithfully replicated in the adaptation. However, Hitchcock reimagines the story as a contest between two romantic and business rivals (none of which appears in the original) and climaxes things with an actual—and ironic—snakebite. In Dahl, there is no snake—or at least we are never shown one—and the Indian doctor's suggestion that it may have been a dream, prompts Harry to hurl a string of racial epithets at the man who tried to save him. Dahl was, in fact, accused of being a racist on the basis of this and other stories, but Harry's insults only serve to make him look like an ungrateful ass, while the doctor comes off as a true hero. Note: For some reason, Hitchcock switched the setting from India to Malaya, which had in fact gained independence as part of Malaysia in 1957, the year before the teleplay was filmed.

BANQUO'S CHAIR, teleplay by Francis Cockrell
Source: *Banquo's Chair* (p 1930) by Rupert Croft-Cooke
Comments: M: Hitchcock makes a number of small changes, adds a bit of depth to the characters, tones down Bedford's histrionics, produces the real actress (she sends a telegram in the original) and generally improves a rather shallow and obvious playlet. Note: The story was filmed in 1945 as *The Fatal Witness*.

NORTH BY NORTHWEST, screenplay by Ernest Lehman
Source: *Mr. Standfast* (1919) by John Buchan
Comments: Lehman's original screenplay reworks a number of elements from earlier Hitchcock classics, including *The 39 Steps*, *Foreign Correspondent*, *Saboteur* and *Notorious*. In the last, a young woman with whom the hero is in love is asked to entrap a charming German agent who, in turn, has asked her to marry him. This derives both from an American short story (see above) and from Buchan's novel, the third in his Richard Hannay series. In *North By Northwest* the parallel with Buchan's Hannay is even closer in Thornhill's protestations to Eve's superiors about using her as bait to entrap the enemy agent. As Hannay tells his superior, "It's such a…such a degrading business," nicely foreshadowing Thornhill's "If you think I'm going to let you go through with this dirty business…" 40 years later. The difference is in the way the two men handle the heroine's decision after the forest scene common to both works: Hannay, at the height of hostilities during World War I, assents to his beloved's patriotic call to duty. Thornhill, contemptuous of the Cold War and those who wage it, does not.

THE CRYSTAL TRENCH, teleplay by Stirling Silliphant
Source: "The Crystal Trench" (1917) by A[lfred] E[dward] W[oodley] Mason
Comments: C: Hitchcock makes a few minor changes (dramatizing Stella's meeting with the professor and Rank's revelations, for example), but otherwise closely follows the original. Interestingly, the story's hook—that someone trapped in a glacier would emerge at a precisely forecasted date and time several decades later—is also invoked in the work of another Hitchcock source author—Sapper's 1924 Bulldog Drummond adventure, *The Third Round*.

MRS. BIXBY AND THE COLONEL'S COAT, teleplay by Halsted Welles
Source: "Mrs. Bixby and the Colonel's Coat" (1959) by Roald Dahl
Comments: M: Hitchcock eliminates the literary wife's extreme bitterness toward her husband and showcases Mrs. Bixby's visit to the colonel, but otherwise delivers the story à la Dahl, with the closing shots precisely, deliciously capturing the last sentence of the story.

I SAW THE WHOLE THING, teleplay by Henry Slesar
Source: *Independent Witness* (radio play, 1958; novelized under the same title in 1963) by Henry Cecil [Leon]

Comments: L: The gist of Judge Henry Cecil Leon's play is there, including the delicious twist at the end. En route to the dénouement, though, Hitchcock takes some rather serious liberties with the original, including having the injured cyclist die; introducing a witness who actually saw the car stop; and having Michael Barnes (here a crime novelist, in Cecil's story an MP) actually defend himself against the charge of involuntary manslaughter.

THE BIRDS, screenplay by Evan Hunter [né Salvatore Lombino]
Source: "The Birds" (1952) by Daphne du Maurier
Comments: R: Apart from the notion of birds attacking humans, the film represents a complete transformation of the original story, which is centered upon a Cornish farm worker and his family and evokes the siege mentality of England during the then-recent war. Details that do survive the adaptation include boarding up the house, birds entering a child's bedroom, discovering a farmer's body in his house and the "order" represented by cups and saucers.

MARNIE, screenplay by Jay Presson Allen
Source: *Marnie* (1961) by Winston Graham
Comments: L: Although structurally similar to the novel, the film alters a number of important details, including the reason for Marnie's illness, her mother's past (prostitution *and* infanticide) and her mother's fate (she dies in the novel, thus precluding a reconciliation), not to mention a transposition of setting from England to the eastern U.S. (although through the casting and settings there remains something of an English "feel"). The film also eliminates the subplots involving business and romantic rivalries at Rutland's, replaces Mark's mother with his father, and adds all those dramatic red flashes. (What happens when Marnie comes to a red light?) Other important elements—the thunderstorm and crash of the tree, the honeymoon "rape" and suicide attempt, Strutt's "reunion" with Marnie, Forio's agonizing death—remain intact.

TORN CURTAIN, screenplay by Brian Moore
Source: *Holy Disorders* (1945) by Edmund Crispin
Comments: Hitchcock is known to have read the mystery novels of Edmund Crispin in the late 1940s and to have borrowed the climaxes from at least two of them (see *Stage Fright* and *Strangers on a Train*, above). Here, Gromek's death is foreshadowed by an incident in the 1945 novel *Holy Disorders*. Crispin's bad guys—British traitors in league with the Nazis—have attempted to kill one of the good guys and fail. They cannot risk shooting him as the fellow's associates might hear the gunshot. Instead, they drag the wounded, bleeding victim across the floor to a gas heater, remove the hose, force it into his mouth, tape it in place and then leave him to die. The idea of German sympathizers gassing this and another character would have presumably resonated quite strongly with Hitchcock given his then-recent experience supervising the editing of *Memory of the Camps*. In *Torn Curtain*, of course, the roles have been reversed: The good guys are gassing the bad guy, though the context of German-oriented intrigue remains.

FRENZY, screenplay by Anthony Shaffer
Source: *Goodbye Piccadilly, Farewell Leicester Square* (1966) by Arthur La Bern
Comments: L: The film differs primarily in its overall lighter tone, accomplished through a number of comic exchanges, notably those involving Chief Inspector Oxford's wife (a character absent from the novel), Brenda's clients, the hotel employees and punters in the pub. The Thames-side discovery of a body at the beginning of the film derives not from La Bern but from Hitchcock's own adaptation of *The Lodger*. La Bern's disparagement of modern London and his esteem for the WWII-era generation have been completely jettisoned. The lengthy trial sequence of the novel, during which Johnny and Hetty *do* stand by their friend, has been *greatly* compressed. The pairing of Oxford with Sergeant Spearman (a character original to the film) recalls a similarly complementary Scotland Yard team in Shaffer's 1953 short story "Larger than Life." It should also be noted that Rusk's line "You're my type of woman" and Babs' less graphic demise (compared to Brenda's) both originated in the novel and not with Shaffer, as the latter seemed to imply in the documentary included on Universal's *Frenzy* DVD.

FAMILY PLOT, screenplay by Ernest Lehman
Source: *The Rainbird Pattern* (1972) by Victor Canning
Comments: L: The film retains the basic plot of mediums, missing heirs, kidnappings and coincidences, but, oddly, "dumbs down" the crime caper aspects of the story. For instance, instead of a van to haul the kidnap victims away, the film characters use an ordinary car; instead of uncut diamonds, relatively easy to dispose of, they ask for cut gems; instead of an isolated country house in which to secrete their guests, they opt for

a home in the middle of San Francisco. Hitchcock also eliminates the motif of dreams and ambitions being just out of reach and ultimately frustrated for *all* the major characters. In the film, the bad guys lose and the good guys win; not so in the original. Indeed, the ending of the novel is so trenchant that three of the four major protagonists are killed off (and the fourth will likely soon join them), as is Miss Rainbird, who is also revealed to be a murderer herself! Her death is, in fact, accomplished by a character missing from the film, Shoebridge's ambitious teenage son, Martin, who, as the sole surviving Rainbird heir, coolly plans to carry on his family's evil legacy—the Rainbird pattern of murder and revenge.

APPENDIX II:
The Schüfftan Process

Alfred Hitchcock relied upon a number of special effects techniques during his long directorial career, from simple mechanical effects (blank-firing guns) to the elaborate traveling matte shots of *The Birds*. One that he used several times in his early films was the Schüfftan Process, named after German cinematographer and special effects designer Eugen Schüfftan, who employed the technique most notably in Fritz Lang's *Metropolis*. British rights to the process, which could obviate the need for expensive set construction or location filming, were obtained by the predecessor of the BIP studio, not long before Hitchcock went to work there in 1927. To achieve the effect, part of the reflective coating of a mirror is scraped away and the mirror in turn is set at a 45-degree angle to the movie camera. The camera shoots through the transparent portion of the glass, recording live action, while the remaining mirrored surface reflects a painting, photograph, or model of the background. In this way, two disparate images—actors in one portion of the stage, an artificial background in another—are combined in camera. Hitchcock explained the process in detail to Peter Bogdanovich (1963), noting that in the case of the British Museum sequence in *Blackmail*, there were nine separate photos of museum interiors, each of which was developed as a transparency and then backlit to create a more luminous image than that of an ordinary, front-lit photograph. Thus, when Tracy first enters the foyer of the museum, actor Donald Calthrop is standing on small, sparsely decorated set at Elstree; the surrounding décor (cases, exhibits, lights and so on) is actually a *reflection* of a backlit, photographic transparency of the real foyer. Similarly, when Tracy passes a man looking into an Egyptian display case, the extra was in fact looking at nothing whatever! In the case of *Blackmail*, Hitchcock employed Schüfftan shots because of the difficulty in lighting the museum interiors. For *The Man Who Knew Too Much*, he simply could not afford to fill the Royal Albert Hall with extras and shoot on location (as he was, in fact, able to do for the remake). Instead, he simply took photographs of the empty hall and then had an Italian artist paint in the audience. He then went back to the hall, set up the Schüfftan equipment in exactly the same spots as the photographs had been taken and filmed live performers in motion—with a decidedly static background. Hitchcock also employed Schüfftan shots in *The Ring* (for the Albert Hall sequences), in *The 39 Steps* (for at least one Palladium shot), and *Sabotage* (for the shot of the power station interior).

APPENDIX III:
HITCHCOCK'S UNREALIZED FILMS

Alfred Hitchcock envisioned, planned and even began a number of film projects that were never destined to see the light of a film projector. Among the most famous of these are *No Bail for the Judge* and *The Short Night*, and both are relevant to this book. The former was to be based upon a 1952 novel written by former County Court Judge Henry Cecil (Leon) (see "I Saw the Whole Thing" in Appendix I); the latter upon two books: Sean Bourke's nonfiction account of *The Springing of George Blake* and Ronald Kirkbride's novel *The Short Night*. Both Cecil's book and Bourke's are set in London. Hitchcock's plans for the former would have involved an English shoot, commencing in the summer of 1959. Preproduction was in fact well under way by June of that year: the script was finished, locations had been scouted and cast and crew were being selected. John Williams, best known for *Dial M for Murder* and *To Catch a Thief*, had committed to the part of Sir Edwin Proud, a distinguished British judge who is accused—wrongly, as it turns out—of murdering a prostitute named Flossie. Audrey Hepburn had agreed to play Sir Edwin's strong-willed daughter Elizabeth, a barrister in her own right, determined to prove her father's innocence. The other principal role, to be played by Laurence Harvey, was that of a Raffles-type burglar named Anthony Low, who, when caught in the act by Elizabeth, agrees to help her uncover the real murderer. With Elizabeth's backing, Low sets himself up in a Mayfair flat and hires retired military officers to chat up local prostitutes in the hope of turning up leads. Unfortunately, the flat is raided, Elizabeth herself is mistaken for a prostitute and they all end up in Bow Street Court, where Low successfully—and comically—defends himself against charges of receiving money from prostitutes. Eventually the pair discovers that the real killer was the dead woman's pimp, a wealthy young baronet who feared exposure for himself and his mother, who is herself the brains of the illicit organization. Hitchcock abandoned the project when Hepburn pulled out, her discomfort with the part of a woman who disguises herself as a prostitute and is ultimately raped by a murderer having apparently overcome her desire to work with the legendary director. (Then-recent changes in British law concerning streetwalkers may have also influenced Hitchcock's decision to abort.) Both the novel and the screenplay (by *Vertigo* scriptwriter Samuel Taylor) are quite good and it is a shame that the film never came to fruition. The saving grace, of course, is that Hitchcock turned immediately to a new project, a little thriller called *Psycho*.

The Short Night was inspired by the escapades of George Blake, an MI6 officer who spied for the Soviet KGB from ca. 1951 until April 1961, when he was arrested for violating Britain's Official Secrets Act. Blake was tried at the Old Bailey the following month and sentenced to 42 years' imprisonment, the longest determinate sentence ever handed down by a British court for peacetime espionage. On the night of October 22, 1966, Blake escaped from Wormwood Scrubs prison with the help of friend and former inmate Sean Bourke, a convicted IRA terrorist. Two other accomplices (and former inmates), Pat Pottle and Michael Randle, then shifted Blake from one London bedsit to another for the next several weeks. Finally, with the help of a third man, the conspirators secreted Blake in a van, which Randle and his wife, Anne, then drove from London to Berlin. From there, Blake was taken to Moscow, where he remains, unashamed and unrepentant, to this day. Hitchcock intended to replicate Blake's elaborate escape, as detailed in the Bourke book, after which his film would take up the plot of Kirkbride's novel, in which American agent Joe Bailey trails a Blake-like character named Brand to Finland and ends up falling in love with the traitor's wife. *The Short Night* would thus have marked yet another film that Hitchcock shot, at least in part, in the city of his birth. Art director Robert Boyle and unit manager Hilton Green conducted London recces in the spring of 1978, researching possible locations for Brand's Earl's Court flat, nearby shops, a safe house in Highlever Road and set-ups at familiar locales such as Heathrow Airport and Hyde Park, which Bailey would visit during his search for Brand. The director originally intended to shoot the film on location, in both London and Finland, but as his health—and that of Alma's—declined, he decided to confine London location work to a second unit, with the Finnish scenes (which included the dramatic night of the title) to be staged in Minnesota. Production was officially shut down in May 1979; Alfred Hitchcock died on April 29, 1980.

NOTES

[1] All Hitchcock quotes from Truffaut's famous interviews are taken from the actual recordings, rather than the book *Hitchcock*. In the book itself, which represents Truffaut's English translation of a French translation of Hitchcock's actual words, the above quote is rendered: "...if I like the basic idea, I just forget all about the book and start to create cinema."

[2] Trade shows were special advance screenings staged by distributors (in this case, Wardour Films) to interest potential exhibitors. The film opened to the general public on July 29 at the Capitol, Haymarket, where it ran for eight weeks.

[3] I asked Pat Hitchcock if she could confirm her mother's presence in this sequence. She said that while she was unaware of this specific appearance, it could well have been her mother. "In those days, in the crowd scenes, they did use anybody who was on the set." Indeed, this is how Hitchcock himself began the tradition of his own cameos, appearing in this very montage sequence, talking on the phone in the newsroom.

[4] I am indebted to Ann Saunders' *The Art and Architecture of London* (Phaidon Press, 1984) for this amusing contrast of opinions.

[5] The others, according to post-WWI opinion, were: Buckingham Palace, the White House, the Bank of England, the Federal Reserve Bank, and the Vatican.

[6] The quote is taken from the book *Hitchcock*.

[7] *The Trial of Norman Thorne, the Crowborough Chicken Farm Murderer*, edited by Helena Normanton and published by Geoffrey Bles in 1929.

[8] This account of Hitchcock's childhood homes reflects both independent research and consultation with biographer Patrick McGilligan. It *appears* to contradict Donald Spoto's account of Hitchcock having had childhood homes in both Poplar and Stepney (districts on either side of Limehouse). However, if Spoto had the two Salmon Lane addresses in mind (he does not specify) then the accounts may jibe.

[9] The total also includes *Elstree Calling*, to which Hitchcock contributed comedy sketches; *Lord Camber's Ladies*, which he produced but did not direct; and *An Elastic Affair*, the 1930 short which has since been lost (see the **London Palladium** for more on the film).

[10] See, for example, Bret Wood. "Foreign Correspondence: The Rediscovered War Films of Alfred Hitchcock." *Film Comment* 29, July 1993: 54-8.

[11] These techniques are, of course, employed when converting a *novel* to film. The opposite techniques—expansion, division, complication—may be employed when transferring a *short story* to the screen. In adapting *Rear Window*, for example, Hitchcock split Jeff's man, Sam, into two characters, Stella and Lisa, and expanded the male friendship of the story into the heterosexual romance of the film.

LOCATION LIST and ENTRY NUMBERS

Locations are listed alphabetically by entry title as these appear in the text, thus: **Alfred Hitchcock's Birthplace** and not **Hitchcock, Alfred, Birthplace of**. The two-part numbers following the entry titles refer to the entries themselves, not to the pages. Thus, under **Berkeley Square**, the number 15:8 indicates the eighth entry in the 15th section (Mayfair) of the book.

A.F. Chatman Bird Shop 40:1
Adelphi Theatre 23:3
Admiralty 25:5
Adolf Verloc's Shop 20:20
Air Ministry 8:5
Alexandra Palace 60:1
Alfred Hitchcock's Birthplace 43:1
Alfred Hitchcock's Childhood Home 44:1
Alfred Hitchcock's Country Home 72:2
Alfred Hitchcock's Home 22:1
All England Lawn Tennis and Croquet Club 59:1
Ambrose Chapel 1:5
Ambrose Chappell 29:1
American Club 15:19
Army Aviation Centre 67:2
Arsenal Football Club 35:1
Ashenden's Home 15:12
Ashridge Estate 68:5
Battersea Power Station 26:1
BBC (British Broadcasting Corporation) 14:7
Berkeley Square 15:8
Bijou Cinema 28:1
Blackfriars Bridge 5:6
Blackmail Chase Routes 17:10
Blaney Bureau 20:18
Bob Rusk's Flat (1) 6:7
Bob Rusk's Flat (2) 6:10
Bond Street 15:2
Bow Street Magistrates' Court/Police Station 6:1
Braithwaite Station 65:3
Brenda Blaney's Club 15:22
Brenda Blaney's Home 22:4
British Broadcasting Corporation (BBC) 14:7
British Museum 3:4
Brixton, HM Prison 27:1
Brompton Oratory (Oratory of St. Philip Neri) 11:2
Buckingham Palace 17:11
Bunting Home 14:3
C.A. Swann's Flat 4:8
Café Monico 20:5
Café Royal 20:6
Carlton Hotel 17:9
Caxton Hall 25:14
Central Criminal Court (The Old Bailey) 5:5
Central Market Building 6:5
Chapel Market 40:2
Charing Cross Station 23:1
Charlotte Inwood's Home (1) 15:13

Charlotte Inwood's Home (2) 22:6
Chelsea Old Town Hall 4:4
Chelsea Police Station 4:2
Chief Inspector Oxford's Flat 26:2
Claridge's 15:4
Cleopatra's Needle 23:6
Coburg Hotel 1:1
Coliseum Theatre (London Coliseum) 23:2
Colonial Office 25:17
Coniston Station 65:2
Connaught, The 15:7
Copenhagen Tunnel 45:1
County Hall 12:1
Crewe's Studio 4:7
Croydon Airport 57:1
Dartmoor, HM Prison 66:1
Dorchester, The 15:15
Double Century Public House 62:2
Dr. Hawley Crippen's Home 37:2
Dr. J.L. Baker's Office 51:5
Drummond (and Lawrence?) Home 15:5
Ede & Ravenscroft Ltd. 8:4
Edgar Brodie's Home 15:9
Edward Gerrard & Sons 29:2
Elsie Cameron's Home 42:1
Elstree Studios 68:1
Embankment (Victoria Embankment) 25:11
Epsom Downs Racecourse 72:1
Eros Statue 20:4
Eton College 61:1
Euston Station 18:3
Evening Standard 5:7
Florence Webster's Home 22:5
Flower Market Building 6:8
Forbes House 2:2
Foreign (& Commonwealth) Office 25:6
Fortnum & Mason Ltd. 17:5
Frenzy Telephone Booth Site 20:17
G. White Newsagents 4:5
Gaiety Theatre 23:7
Gavin Brand's Flat 30:1
Gavin Brand's Safe House 47:1
Gaynor Brand's Flat 12:4
Geo Barbor, Dentist 54:2
George Joseph Smith's Home 36:1
Gielgud Theatre 20:10
Gill Home 34:1
Globe, The 6:3
Goodwood Racecourse 73:1
Gordon Square 3:2

Grange Bridge 65:6
Grosvenor Square 15:6
Harley Street 14:9
Harrods 11:1
Harry Worp's Home 31:1
Haymarket Theatre (Theatre Royal) 17:7
Henley Telegraph Works Co., Ltd 5:1
Her Majesty's Theatre 17:8
Holborn Stadium 8:2
Holloway, HM Prison 37:1
Home Office 25:7
Home of the Foreign Secretary 25:21
Horfield Home 1:3
Horse Guards 25:4
Houses of Parliament 25:9
Hyde Park 9:1
Hyde Park Corner 9:2
Islington/Gainsborough Studios 39:1
Ivy, The 6:11
Jamaica Inn 64:2
John Christie's Home 48:1
John Galsworthy's Home 10:1
John S. King 27:2
Johnnie Aysgarth's Flat 15:21
Jonathan Cooper's Flat 2:3
Keane Home 14:6
King's Cross Station 18:2
Kingsway 8:1
L'Étoile 7:1
Lady Devlin's Home 15:14
Lake, Pelham & Co. 5:9
Langdale Chase Hotel 65:7
Langley Court 67:1
Le Caprice 17:2
Leadenhall Market
Leicester Square 20:11
Lime Grove (Shepherd's Bush) Studios 51:1
Lina Aysgarth's Home 50:1
Lincoln's Inn 8:3
Liverpool Street Station 5:12
Lloyd's of London 5:10
Lodger's Plan of the Avenger Murders, The 16:1
London (Heathrow) Airport 38:1
London Bridge 5:8
London Chief Post Office 5:4
London Coliseum (Coliseum Theatre) 23:2
London Hilton on Park Lane 15:17
London Hippodrome 20:14
London Palladium 20:19
London Zoo 14:1
Lyons Corner House 20:9
Madame Tussaud's Wax Museum 14:8
Maida Vale Police Station 13:3
Maida Vale Underground Station 13:1
Maison Rouge 7:2
Mann, Crossman & Paulin 58:1
Markham Home 41:1
May Fair (Intercontinental) Hotel 15:20

Menabilly Estate 64:1
Metropolitan Police Forensic Science Laboratory 8:6
Metropolitan Police Service, The, *ex* HQ of 25:8
Metropolitan Police Service 25:16
MGM-British Studios 68:2
MI6 25:22
Milton Hall 63:2
Miss Fergusson's Home 56:1
Mr. Pelham's Home 13:4
National Gallery, The 25:2
Nell of Old Drury, The 6:9
New Gallery Cinema 20:8
Newbury Racecourse 61:3
Newmarket Rowley Racecourse 71:1
New Scotland Yard (Metropolitan Police Service) 25:16
Number Seventeen House 54:1
Odeon Cinema 20:12
Old Bailey, The (Central Criminal Court) 5:5
Olympia 33:2
Oratory of St. Philip Neri (Brompton Oratory) 11:2
Ordinary Smith's Flat 4:3
Oxford Street 14:11
Paradine Home 2:1
Park Crescent 14:4
Park Lane House 15:16
Paxton's Head, The 11:3
Pentonville, HM Prison 45:2
Peter Hewitt's Studio 4:6
Piccadilly Circus 20:3
Piccadilly Circus Underground Station 20:1
Pinewood Studios 62:1
Port of Dover 69:2
R Division, Metropolitan Police, et al. 32:2
RADA (Royal Academy of Dramatic Art) 3:3
Regal Cinema 9:3
Regent's Park 14:2
Richard Hannay's Flat 14:5
Ritz, London, The 17:1
River Thames, The 25:12
Robert Tisdall's Home 11:4
Roddy Berwick's Flat 16:2
Roehampton Club 49:1
Royal Academy of Dramatic Art (RADA) 3:3
Royal Air Force Club 15:18
Royal Albert Hall 22:2
Royal Court Theatre 4:1
Royal Courts of Justice, The 23:9
Royal Festival Hall 21:1
Royal Horticultural Society Hall 25:19
Royal Observatory Greenwich 32:1
Royal Opera House 6:2
Russell Street 6:4
Russian Embassy 2:4
Rydal Water 65:1
Salvation Army Hostel 52:1

Savoy, The 23:5
Scala Theatre 7:3
Scotland Yard (*ex* HQ of the Metropolitan Police Service) 25:8
Selfridges 14:12
Shepherd Market 15:10
Shepherd's Tavern 15:11
Simpson's-in-the-Strand 23:4
Sir Alfred Hitchcock Hotel 43:2
Sir Edwin Proud's Home 1:4
Sir Simon Flaquer's Home 1:2
Site of Jack the Ripper's First Victim 58:2
Site of the Botley Fair 70:2
Site of the *Siege of Sidney Street* 54:1
Site of The Thirty-nine Steps 69:1
Southampton Port 67:3
St. Bartholomew's Hospital 19:1
St. Clement Danes 23:8
St. Francis of Assisi 55:1
St. George's Hanover Square 15:1
St. Giles Circus 20:16
St. Ignatius College 53:1
St. James, Piccadilly 17:6
St. James's Park 25:15
St. James's Theatre 17:4
St. Margaret's Church, Westminster Abbey 25:13
St. Martin's Theatre 20:15
St. Mary Abbotts Hospital 10:2
St. Pancras Station 18:1
St. Paul, Covent Garden 6:6
St. Paul's Cathedral 5:3
St. Saviour's Church Hall 27:3
Stephen Fisher's Home 25:18
Stevie's Final Journey 20:2
Strand Palace Hotel 23:10
Thames (River Thames) 25:12
The Drunken Duck Inn 65:4
The King's Head 61:2
Theatre Royal (Haymarket Theatre) 17:7
Thorney Court 22:3
Tivoli Music Hall 23:11
Tower Bridge 5:2
Trafalgar Square 25:1
Transatlantic Pictures, HQ of 20:7
University of Cambridge 63:1
University of London 3:1
University of Oxford 70:1
Victoria Embankment 25:11
Victoria Station 24:1
Wally's New Café 68:4
War Office, The, HQ of 25:3
Waterloo Station 12:2
Waterloo Underground Station 12:3
Welwyn Studios Ltd 68:3
Wendice Home 13:2

West End Central Police Station 15:3
Westminster Bridge 25:10
Westminster Cathedral 25:20
White City 51:3
White's 17:3
Wigmore Street 14:10
Winter's Grace (Alfred Hitchcock's Country Home) 72:2
Wood Lane 51:2
Wormwood Scrubs, HM Prison 51:4
Wyndham's Theatre 20:13

INDEX
Note that the two-part numbers indicate the entry, not the page.

Films and Television Episodes (numbers in boldface indicate filming locations)

39 Steps, The 3:4, 8:5, **14:4**, 14:5, 14:7, 14:8, **18:2**, **20:3**, **20:5**, 20:8, **20:19**, 37:2, 51:1, 68:3, 69:1
Arthur 37:2, 42:1
Aventure Malgache 3:1, **5:3**, 15:4, 68:3
Back for Christmas 37:2
Bang! You're Dead 68:5
Banquo's Chair 5:11, 23:11, 25:8, 32:2, 56:1, 61:1
Birds, The 14:7, 20:12, 25:7, 64:1
Blackmail **3:4**, 4:2, 4:4, 4:5, 4:6, 4:7, **8:1**, 9:3, **12:1**, **17:7**, **17:9**, 17:10, **20:3**, **20:5**, 20:8, **20:9**, 20:10, **25:1**, **25:2**, **25:8**, **25:9**, **25:11**, **25:12**, 36:1, 68:1
Bon Voyage 3:1, **5:3**, 15:4, 68:3
Case of Mr. Pelham, The 5:9, 13:4, 14:9, 20:14, 23:4
Champagne 20:14, **67:3**
Crystal Trench, The 15:2, 63:1
Dial M for Murder 4:8, 5:5, 9:2, 11:3, 13:2, 13:3, 14:7, 16:2, 17:11, 22:2, 23:1, 24:1, 25:7, 25:8, 26:1, 27:2, 51:1, 51:3, 59:1, 60:1, 61:2, 63:1, 66:1
Downhill **5:8**, **13:1**, 15:2, 15:14, 16:2, **20:3**, 20:14, 39:1, **58:1**, **68:5**
Easy Virtue 17:5, 20:14, 23:9, 39:1, **49:1**, **67:1**
Elastic Affair, An 20:19
Elstree Calling 6:2
Family Plot 25:11, 25:15, 67:2
Farmer's Wife, The 4:1, 20:13, 68:1
Foreign Correspondent 3:2, 5:3, 7:1, 7:2, **12:2**, 14:7, 14:10, 15:19, **17:9**, **17:10**, 17:11, **23:5**, **25:1**, 25:4, 25:6, 25:8, **25:9**, **25:10**, 25:15, **25:18**, **25:20**, 37:2; 49:1
Four O'Clock 20:16
Frenzy **1:1**, **5:2**, **5:5**, 5:12, 6:1, **6:2**, **6:3**, **6:4**, **6:5**, **6:6**, **6:7**, **6:8**, **6:9**, 6:10, 8:6, **9:1**, **10:2**, **12:1**, **14:11**, 15:4, 15:8, 15:10, 15:13, 15:15, **15:17**, 15:18, **15:22**, 17:6, **20:11**, **20:12**, 20:17,

20:18, 22:4, 23:1, 23:5, 23:10, 24:1, **25:1**, 25:8, **25:9**, **25:12**, **25:16**, **26:2**, 36:1, 37:2, 45:2, 48:1, **51:4**, 52:1, 58:2, **62:1**, **62:2**, 68:4
I Confess 20:7
I Saw the Whole Thing 5:5
Jamaica Inn 5:10, 7:1, 15:20, 17:3, 17:4, 25:7, 64:2, 68:1
Juno and the Paycock 9:3, 20:7
Lady Vanishes, The 15:1, 15:15, 20:3, 22:1, **24:1**, 25:6, 25:22, 39:1, 63:1, 70:1
Lifeboat 20:10, 20:13
Lodger, The 5:4, **5:7**, 9:3, 12:1, 14:3, 14:7, 14:8, 15:16, 16:1, 17:7, 20:3, 20:5, 20:14, 23:1, 23:7, 25:8, **25:9**, **25:10**, **25:11**, **25:12**, 25:13, 25:15, 39:1, 48:1, 58:2, 68:1
Man Who Knew Too Much, The (34) **5:2**, 15:5, **20:3**, **20:5**, 20:10, 25:6, 25:8, **25:12**, 25:14, 25:22, 51:1, 54:1, 54:2
Man Who Knew Too Much, The (56) 1:5, **2:2**, 3:2, 15:4, 15:7, 15:16, 20:3, 20:19, **21:1**, **22:2**, **22:3**, 23:5, 25:6, 25:22, 27:3, 29:1, **29:2**, **38:1**
Manxman, The 9:3, 68:1
Marnie 14:2, 14:11, 17:4, 17:7, 21:1, 25:19, 68:5, 71:1
Memory of the Camps 3:1, 15:4, 20:8
Mountain Eagle, The 20:14, 39:1
Mr. and Mrs. Smith 1:1, 6:7
Murder! 3:3, 8:1, 14:7, **15:8**, 17:1, 17:8, 20:3, 20:10, 20:13, 23:5, 25:7, 33:1, 37:1, 41:1
No Bail for the Judge (unproduced) 1:4, 5:5, 6:1, 6:2, 9:1, 15:2, 15:4, 15:10, 15:14, 23:9, 27:1, 72:1, Appendix III
North By Northwest 15:8, 25:5, 25:22
Notorious 25:22
Number Seventeen 23;1, 37:2, **45:1**, 53:2, 68:1
Paradine Case, The **1:2**, 1:3, **2:1**, **5:3**, **5:5**, **6:1**, **8:3**, 8:4, **14:6**, 15:2, 15:8, 17:7, **20:15**, 23:3, 23:5, **23:6**, 25:1, 25:8, **25:11**, **25:12**, **37:1**, **65:1**, **65:2**, **65:3**, **65:4**, **65:5**, **65:6**, **65:7**
Pleasure Garden, The 12:4, 14:7, 15:2, 20:5, 23:7, 39:1, 67:3
Psycho 6:7, 58:2
Rear Window 37:2, 48:1
Rebecca 11:1, 12:2, 15:2, 17:1, 20:10, 20:16, 22:2, 33:1, 51:5, 59:1, 63:2, 64:1, 64:2
Rich and Strange 6:2, 8:5, 9:1, **12:3**, 14:7, **20:3**, 24:1, 27:1, 68:1, **69:2**
Ring, The 4:1, 8:2, **22:2**, 68:1
Rope 4:1, 5:5, 6:7, 15:6, 17:7, 20:7, 20:8, 23:2, 60:1, 70:1
Sabotage 2:4, **5:6**, 10:1, **12:1**, 12:2, **14:1**, **14:11**, **14:12**, 17:10, 20:1, **20:2**, **20:3**, **20:4**, 20:9, **20:16**, 20:20, 23:4, **23:8**, **23:9**, **25:1**, 25:7, **25:8**, **25:9**, 25:12, **26:1**, 28:1, 32:1, 35:1, 40:1, **40:2**, 51:1, **51:2**, 51:5, 58:2
Saboteur 15:8, 17:4, 20:19, 25:22

Secret Agent 5:2, **5:3**, 15:9, 1512, 23:4, **25:3**, **25:9**, 25:22, 37:1, 51:1
Shadow of a Doubt 5:2, 6:7, 22:7, 36:1, 58:2
Short Night, The (unproduced) 5:4, 5:10, 9:1, 25:6, 25:22, 30:1, 38:1, 47:1, 51:4, Appendix III
Skin Game, The 6:7, 10:1, 17:7, 20:15, 22:1, 25:9, 43:1
Spellbound 8:4, 15:1, 19:1, 20:8, 25:8, 37:2, 51:1
Stage Fright **2:3**, **3:3**, 4:2, 4:3, **5:3**, 5:5, 5:12, 7:3, 9:2, 11:1, 14:8, 14:11, 15:3, **15:11**, **15:12**, **15:13**, **15:14**, 17:2, 20:1, 20:3, 22:5, 22:6, 23:5, **25:1**, **25:2**, 25:3, 25:8, 25:18, **34:1**, 37:1, 37:2, 43:1, 45:2, 49:1, 68:1, 68:2, 70:1, 70:2
Strangers on a Train 20:7, 70:2
Suspicion 4:1, 6:11, 12:2, 15:21, 20:5, 20:6, 23:5, 25:2, 37:1, 43:1, 50:1, 57:1, 61:3, 73:1
To Catch a Thief 5:10, 15:21, 17:4, 20:12
Topaz 15:4, 22:2, 25:22
Torn Curtain 25:22, 63:1, 67:3, 70:1
Trouble with Harry, The 15:2, 25:12, 31:1
Under Capricorn 17:7, 20:7, 23:5, 60:1, 68:1, 68:2
Vertigo 17:10, 22:2, 25:17, 37:2
Waltzes from Vienna 20:12, 51:1
Wrong Man, The 12:3, 20:8, 25:17, 47:1
Young and Innocent 11:4, 23:7, **25:1**, 33:2, 39:1, 51:1, **62:1**, 68:1, 68:3; 73:1

I would like to end with a quotation from English novelist Graham Greene's essay "The Last Buchan." The subject is, of course, the author of *The Thirty-nine Steps*, but the words could as well apply to Buchan's most successful cinematic interpreter:

[He] prepared us in his thrillers better than he knew for the death that may come to any of us...by the railings of the Park or the doorway of the mews. For certainly we can all see now "how thin is the protection of civilization."

About the author: Gary Giblin is the author of *James Bond's London: A Reference Guide to Locations* and the editor of Bond and Hitchcock production designer Syd Cain's memoirs *Not Forgetting James Bond*. He co-created and edits the webzine *Secret Intelligence* and contributes to *The MacGuffin*, the Hitchcock scholars' website. He lives with his wife, Lisa, and their two cats in Indiana.

Author Gary Giblin and wife Lisa

**If you enjoyed this book,
call or write for a free catalog
Midnight
Marquee Press
9721 Britinay Lane
Baltimore, MD 21234**

**410-665-1198
www.midmar.com**

17112492R00181

Printed in Great Britain
by Amazon